OUT of the SHADOWS

Querido Profesor Massey
with great warmth
and affection
you are my inspiration

Patricia
March 2006

OUT of the SHADOWS

POLITICAL ACTION AND THE INFORMAL ECONOMY IN LATIN AMERICA

Edited by Patricia Fernández-Kelly and Jon Shefner

The Pennsylvania State University Press
University Park, Pennsylvania

Publication of this book has been aided by a grant from
the Center for Migration and Development, Sociology
Department, Princeton University.

Library of Congress Cataloging-in-Publication Data

Out of the shadows : political action and the informal economy
in Latin America / edited by Patricia Fernández-Kelly and Jon
Shefner.
    p.   cm.
Includes bibliographical references and index.
ISBN 0-271-02750-9 (cloth : alk. paper)
ISBN 0-271-02751-7 (pbk. : alk. paper)
1. Informal sector (Economics)—Latin America.
2. Small business—Latin America.
3. Latin America—Economic conditions—1982– .
4. Civil society–Latin America.
I. Fernández-Kelly, Patricia.
II. Shefner, Jon, 1958– .

HD2346.L38088 2006
330—dc22
2005037090

Contents

ACKNOWLEDGMENTS   vii

Introduction   1
Patricia Fernández-Kelly

1   The Informal Economy in the Shadow of the State   23
    Miguel Angel Centeno and Alejandro Portes

2   Risk and Regulation in Informal and Illegal Markets   49
    John C. Cross and Sergio Peña

3   Neoliberalism, Markets, and Informal Grassroots Economies   81
    José Itzigsohn

4   Vanishing Assets: Cumulative Disadvantages Among the
    Urban Poor   97
    Mercedes González de la Rocha

5   Female Household Headship, Privation, and Power:
    Challenging the "Feminization of Poverty" Thesis   125
    Sylvia Chant

6   Protest in Contemporary Argentina: A Contentious
    Repertoire in the Making   165
    Javier Auyero

7   The Even More Difficult Transition from
    Clientelism to Citizenship: Lessons from Brazil   195
    Robert Gay

8   Informal Politics in the Mexican Democratic
    Transition: The Case of the People's Urban Movement   219
    Juan Manuel Ramírez Sáiz

9   "Do You Think Democracy Is a Magical Thing?"
    From Basic Needs to Democratization in Informal Politics   241
    Jon Shefner

LIST OF CONTRIBUTORS   269
INDEX   273

Acknowledgments

The editors would like to thank many people and organizations that have been indispensable in bringing this project to completion. First, we thank the Center for Migration and Development at Princeton University, and its Director, Alejandro Portes, for sponsoring the conference that gave birth to this book. Additional Princeton University sponsors of the conference included the Center of International Studies, Council on Regional Studies, the Department of Sociology, the Program in Latin American Studies, the Program in African Studies, and the Woodrow Wilson School for International and Public Affairs. Second, we greatly appreciate the hard work of the authors, who brought their important work through several iterations, and finally to this volume. We also appreciate the participation of other scholars who participated in the conference in varying ways, including Rina Agarwala, Joan Anderson, Marion Carter, Sara Curran, Thomas Espenshade, Carmen Elísa Florez, Jeremy Grest, Judith Adler Hellman, Jeffrey Herbst, Frances Lund, Kinuthia Macharia, Amparo Menéndez-Carrión, Julia Paley, Bryan Roberts, Caroline Skinner, Mario Luis Small, Julie Stewart, and Marta Tienda. In bringing this manuscript to fuition, Sandy Thatcher, Cherene Holland, and Andrew Lewis at Penn State Press provided great aid and enthusiasm. We also deeply appreciate the hard work and excellent suggestions of the Penn State Press reviewers.

Introduction

Patricia Fernández-Kelly

A few years ago, at an international conference held in a plush European setting, a well-known scholar advanced the notion that the informal economy is by definition apolitical—because unregulated workers ignore or violate state regulations, they try to keep a low profile, thus refraining from overt complaint, dispute, or negotiation. The chapters in this volume make clear that nothing could be further from the facts. The relationship between informal workers, employers, and public officials is more complex than logic can at first surmise.[1]

The chapters that follow provide an integrated account of the political ramifications of a phenomenon first theorized more than three decades ago. Since the 1970s, informality in both advanced and less developed countries has received sustained attention (Tokman 1982; Capecchi 1991). Methodologies have been devised to measure its size and output in places as disparate as Buenos Aires, Miami, and Bologna (Portes, Castells, and Denton 1991). Controversy has raged about the effects, beneficial as well as harmful, of economic informality (de Soto 1989; Fortuna and Prates 1991). All along, however, political dimensions have been insinuated, not investigated, suggested but not explained. This book redresses that omission.

Introduced by Keith Hart in 1970, the term "informality" was first used to designate the transactions of petty entrepreneurs in Ghana, which were typically outside official control. Informality thus encompassed economic behaviors that were not inherently illegal but occurred outside the purview of the state; it also constituted a field where economic actors—employers as well as workers—circumvented government legislation.

A lively debate soon grew about the origins and persistence of the informal economy in Latin America. Some saw it as a vestige of precapitalist social formations and the legacy of roughly three centuries of colonial domination. By the 1980s a new literature argued the opposite—informality was part and parcel of capitalist growth when (a) industry is unable to generate adequate demand for the available supply of labor, and (b) governments are incapable or unwilling to enact legislation to protect workers, discipline employers, and extract taxes from either. Informality was thus conceptualized as an effect of modernization and the byproduct of distorted or insufficient industrialization. The rapid growth of one or two cities in tandem with agricultural mechanization led to rapid rates of rural-urban migration, starting in the nineteenth century. Not able to survive in the countryside and lured by the promise of opportunity in cities, people had arrived searching for jobs in the private sector but ended up performing informal work in homes, assembly plants, or streets. Rather than a residue from the past, economic informality was understood to be an aspect of Latin America's evolving present.

As important as unraveling the origin of economic informality was accounting for its internal dynamics and effects. The relationship between capital and labor took center stage (Bonacich and Light 1991). Interpretations about the repercussions of unregulated work fell into two main camps. Groups like the International Labor Organization (ILO) and Regional Program for Education in Latin America and the Caribbean (PREALC) envisioned informality as a low-cost way to create jobs through small business formation and self-employment (Economic Commission for Latin America and the Caribbean 2000). The Peruvian Hernando de Soto took a similar but extreme position in his influential book, *The Other Path* (1989), in which he represents the "mercantile" state as a monstrous impediment to business acumen. In his view even a humble street vender would have incalculable potential for entrepreneurship were it not for the intrusions of a state bent on thwarting individual freedom. Just as Hart had done years earlier, de Soto maintained that the informal economy had been ignored as a motor of development. According to him, multiple restrictions and bureaucratic time lags suffocate independence and self-reliance.

Marxist and neo-Marxist writings, by contrast, argued that "entrepreneurs" in the informal sector were really "disguised workers" being exploited through indirect channels (Bonacich and Light 1991). In this perspective, the divide between self-definition (small business owner or self-employed worker) and actual circumstance (proletarian) leads to a fragmentation of class consciousness and an incapacity for political expression. Popular awareness of common interests is impeded when people must eke out livings without the protection of government or trade unions. Informal workers have an impact similar to that of scabs and strikebreakers, whose actions weaken collective solidarity and political mobilization.

In the final analysis, both Marxist and non-Marxist interpretations, including de Soto's oddly libertarian scheme, fall analytically short. Missing are cogent explorations of the role of the state and popular activism in the *maintenance* of economic informality. That limitation seems all the more surprising in hindsight because it is the state embodied in multiple practices, agencies, departments, and divisions that creates the conditions for the expansion or contraction of the informal economy. Without formal laws defining the relationship between employers and workers, the informal economy cannot exist. Put differently, formality breeds informality. Furthermore, underground transactions are facilitated by factors such as

1   The passage of legislation and legislative amends at various governmental levels in response to constituencies in different positions of political and economic strength;
2   The uneven enforcement capabilities of state dependencies; and
3   The actions of agencies with specific and sometimes contradictory mandates.

Elsewhere I have described the garment industry in Southern California as a pertinent example of how those three forces shape the experience of informal workers (Fernández-Kelly and García 1991). As this volume further shows, it is through the interactions between public officials and unregulated actors that the informal economy evolves, taking different shapes and acquiring varying contents over time.

The spatial dimensions of economic informality are also worth considering. Unregulated dealings often occur on avenues, plazas, sidewalks, and even buses over which government agencies have jurisdiction. It is possible to conceptualize street vending, for example, as the result of negotiations between popular groups and government personnel over the use of public ambits. How and under what conditions do such compromises happen? What are the proximate and cumulative consequences of those accommodations? To what extent do informal workers and entrepreneurs represent new economic and political interests? These are the questions broached by this book.

Situating Regulatory Control

Chapter 1, by Miguel Angel Centeno and Alejandro Portes, and Chapter 2, by John C. Cross and Sergio Peña, improve our understanding of nuances in the relationship between government structures and informal actors. This is in contrast to earlier studies, which emphasized the adversarial relationship between the state—envisioned as the organ responsible for the emission and implementation of legislative restrictions—and informal workers and entrepreneurs attempting to circumvent control. As the lead authors in this volume show, that dichotomy proved to be, at best, a simplification.

Centeno and Portes and Cross and Peña build on a rich tradition of inquiry about the relationship between unregulated workers and the state. Since the 1980s, a voluminous literature focused on advanced and less developed countries pointing to variations and regularities in the interactions between formal and informal sectors. Researchers documented, for example, how people move intermittently between the two domains, responding to need and opportunity (Fortuna and Prates 1991). They also showed how small businesses resort to unauthorized productive arrangements during times of financial crisis and how law-abiding firms occasionally engage the services of home workers to supplement production during periods of increasing demand (Benería and Roldán 1987). In other words, a mounting body of evidence made clear that a porous membrane, not a rigid boundary, separates the formal and informal sectors.

Research made obvious as well the extent to which subcontracting arrangements link formal and informal activities (Tokman 1982). Early interpretations characterized the two domains as separate, responding to different stimuli, and bearing distinct internal logics. The new evidence established that, in many cases, informality grows with and depends on urbanization and industrial expansion, two markers of modernization. Unregulated economic activity was thus proven to be not a relic from the past, as authors like Bela Balassa and colleagues (1986) or Alex Inkeles and David Smith (1974) had intimated, but a byproduct of advanced forms of production. For example, comparatively high rates of prosperity in Latin America during the 1970s paralleled the extension of the informal sector partly because of the burgeoning demand for goods and services, many of them produced outside the limits of government regulation (Fernández-Kelly and García 1991).

Nevertheless, the ties between the formal and informal sectors proved to be contingent, not inevitable. Starting in the 1980s several forces decoupled the two economic realms. Crushing national debts and austerity measures imposed by international monetary organizations throughout Latin America arrested the fragile progress of the previous decade. For the first time, even the informal sector failed to grow, as an increasing number of people retrenched into subsistence activities outside labor markets, whether regulated or not. Even more recently, the diffusion of neoliberal policies exacerbated levels of immiseration throughout the hemisphere, leading to rising predation and the reappearance of nearly extinct behaviors like barter in, of all places, Buenos Aires, a city once known as the Paris of South America (Frasce 2002).

A main contribution of the two first chapters in this volume is the elucidation of how economic behaviors intersect with regulatory structures. According to Centeno and Portes, it is not only the state's ability to pass laws but also its capacity to enforce them that determines the shape and size of the informal economy. Their distinction of *frustrated*, *welfare*, and *liberal* states finds complement in Cross and Peña's use of the terms *informal*, *illegal*, and *mafia* to identify types of economic transactions among unregulated workers and entrepreneurs. The intersections in this model produce multiple outcomes. In some cases, informalization supplements state regulation; in others, it opposes it. At first blush the informal economy may seem uniform but, as the studies in this volume reveal, it is internally heterogeneous.

Table 1 summarizes the interactions between public functionaries and unregulated actors. Informality under the aegis of a benevolent state led to complementarity, not opposition, in the case of Emilia-Romagna aptly examined by Vittorio Capecchi (1991, 1997). Aided by members of the Italian Communist party—less interested in ideological purity than in opening channels for production and accumulation—formerly unionized Fiat workers became entrepreneurs. Government facilitated that conversion by modifying existing legislation. Proletarian spirit transmogrified into business shrewdness. The result was a network of small firms dependent on mutual trust and oriented toward flexible specialization. Although later studies suggested the impracticability of its transference to other, less adaptable settings, Emilia-Romagna became a celebrated, illustration of state versatility and worker imagination.

By comparison a strong governing apparatus with ample regulatory capacity but limited ability or will for enforcement delivers what Cross and Peña call a *mafia* state. In that scenario informal actors not only fill the demand for illegal goods and services but also assume state-like functions. A case in point is the almost wholesale absorption of the Colombian structure of governance by powerful drug cartels in the 1980s (Fortuna and Prates 1991; Blanes Jiménez 1991).

Table 1   State formations and unregulated transactions

Unregulated transactions[a]	State formations[b] Frustrated	State formations[b] Welfare	State formations[b] Liberal
Informal	Street vending in Mexico[c]	Emilia-Romagna[d]	Shuttle trading in the Caribbean[e]
Illegal	Bolivian coca production[f]	Small-scale prostitution[g]	Uranium cartels[h]
Mafia	Colombia 1980s[i]	Immigrant smuggling[j]	Drug traffic in American cities[k]

[a]Cross and Peña (this volume)
[b]Centeno and Portes (this volume)
[c]Cross 1998
[d]Capecchi 1997
[e]Freeman 2000
[f]Blanes Jiménez 1991
[g]Weitzer 1999
[h]Spar 1994
[i]Fortuna and Prates 1991
[j]Massey 2002
[k]Fernández-Kelly 2003

Drug trafficking under the watch of a state unable or unwilling to control it is a related instance sketched by the same authors. Throughout the first half of the twentieth century, American cities experienced the steady arrival of black migrants from the South. Demographic change led to drops in urban investment and "white flight." Market activity in inner-city neighborhoods stagnated, and by the 1970s, ghettos became permanent enclosures. The agents of a massive state—social workers, program managers, public service providers, and police officers, among others—rapidly occupied the spaces left empty by capital defection. State omnipresence thus became a distinctive feature in U.S. cities. Paradoxically, the absence of political clout at the grassroots level enabled predatory entrepreneurs to flood poor neighborhoods with dangerous drugs, like crack cocaine, that would have been unmarketable in better-protected residential areas (Fernández-Kelly 2003).

As government programs multiplied to make up for feeble market activity in urban ghettos, youngsters, especially young men, organized and competed for the control of public spaces where they could hustle drugs and guns. Their confrontations and "drive-by shootings"—sometimes portrayed by the media as racially specific phenomena—echoed the behaviors of Italian and Irish gangsters during the Prohibition era. Shared by the two cases was the emergence of alternative mechanisms for the production and distribution of illegal commodities and the articulation of hierarchical arrangements that replicated some of the functions of the state.

The contestation of rights over the use of public space is also a central theme in John Cross's *Informal Politics: A Study of Street Venders in Mexico City* (1998), the book that most closely antedates and inspires the present volume. On the basis of ethnographic and historical research Cross showed how, in the 1960s and subsequently, local authorities combined harsh repression and negotiation to quell the informal occupation of walkways and parks in Mexico City. Street peddlers responded by seeking protection from politicians in exchange for votes. Nevertheless, the forging of patron-client relationships—a common practice in Mexico—was only part of the story. Overwhelmed by individual applications for permits to sell goods al fresco, and eager to rid themselves of continuous demands, government officials offered to negotiate with street merchants but only if they formed trade organizations. The result was not, as they expected, the elimination of perambulatory commerce but the multiplication of street vender associations—an unintended effect of the less than visible interaction between state representatives and informal economic agents. In this case, city officials acted as catalysts for the political mobilization of unregulated merchants. Jeremy Grest documents equivalent phenomena in Durban, South Africa (Grest 2001).

A dramatic illustration of the relationship between economic actors and what Centeno and Portes call the liberal state is not found in studies of the informal economy but in the emerging literature on transnational communities (Portes 1997). Growing economic integration on a world scale, cheaper and faster transportation, and sophisticated communications technologies paralleled the diffusion of neoliberal economic policies in the 1990s. Those, in turn, led to the partial informalization of national bodies of government or, put differently, to a dismantling of regulatory controls and welfare provisions. Globalization is therefore more than an economic trend aimed at maximizing capital gains through the transfer of production from advanced to less developed countries— it is also a political strategy that atomizes and weakens labor forces in various locations (Evans 1995). Partly for that reason, the age of global integration has coincided with unionization declines in advanced countries and a dearth of effective mobilization in export production zones located in Asia, Eastern Europe, Latin America, and the Caribbean. The opposite of what Karl Marx predicted has occurred—growing similarity in the experience of workers around the world has not led to alliances and unified militancy.

Nevertheless, as the research on transnational communities shows, this does not mean that workers have remained passive vis-à-vis the impact of neoliberal policies. A new class of people whose members travel regularly across borders to earn a living is using the same routes opened by international capital in its search for more productive and compliant workforces. For individual workers and entrepreneurs, international travel offers greater opportunities to circumvent the restrictions imposed by weakened national states. As José Itzigsohn shows in Chapter 3, globalization is creating new locations within which informal workers and entrepreneurs increase their command over resources. Remittances, for example, have become a major source of revenue for towns and villages in Costa Rica and the Dominican Republic—a sort of foreign aid program implemented by people from those countries who work in the United States. Although most transnational entrepreneurs are men, the channels of travel and trade associated with economic integration are also creating new opportunities for women, as research by Hatice Deniz Yenal (2000) and Carla Freeman (2000) has shown.

It is not uncommon in this brave new world for individuals to see their hometowns in less developed nations as sources of personal and collective identity while envisioning countries of destination mostly as fields of economic opportunity. The political implications of this development are momentous. As some have begun to observe, the ripping apart of *identity* and *place* is likely to have a profound effect on the very meaning of citizenship, a major dimension of political praxis (Sassen 1996).

Finally, the chapters by Centeno and Portes and Cross and Peña raise issues of significance to the new economic sociology. While early studies of the informal economy focused mostly on the extent to which workers and entrepreneurs escape state regulation, the present volume shifts emphasis to norms of trust and mutuality that social actors must deploy to maximize advantage and reduce risks. Interdependence and rules of reciprocity bring order and consistency to human interactions. It is not that the informal economy lacks regulation but that the sources and means of control are situated *within* it and not in the official structure of government. Bypassing the dictates of the law alters economic terms. The hazards stemming from informal transactions can increase costs, making it vital to distribute the risk among the members of social networks marked by what Alejandro Portes and Julia Sensenbrenner (1993) call *bounded solidarity*.

That generalization applies not just to marginal commerce in general but also and especially to trafficking in illegal products or services such as drugs and prostitution. It is in those confines that the phrase "honor among thieves" acquires its most powerful meaning.

Finally, José Itzigsohn's comparative study of families in Costa Rica and the Dominican Republic echoes the findings of the two previous chapters while moving analysis into an international plane. As standards of living fall for many throughout Latin America and the Caribbean, workers seek new avenues to survive through migration and the deployment of *transnational* economic strategies. Immigrant workers in the United States, for example, put into motion vast financial flows that energize their home economies. Remittances are already the second source of foreign exchange in the Dominican Republic, surpassed only by tourism. Even more significant from this book's perspective, migrants—and in some cases the children of migrants—increasingly participate in the political life of their ancestral countries. They stride borders bypassing government regulations and altering conventional notions of social assimilation at both ends of the geographical span (Portes 1997). Whether as undocumented migrants in some American city or as traders crossing borders back and forth on a regular basis, Latin American workers are operating within and broadening the reach of the informal economy.

The Household as a Political Category

While the first three chapters take stock of past research and conceptualize afresh the relationship between political action and the informal economy, Chapter 4, by Mercedes González de la Rocha, and Chapter 5, by Sylvia Chant, assume equivalent tasks with respect to domestic units. Households have attracted lively inquiry and debate in the social sciences, but no matter how they are defined, there is agreement that they connect various levels of economic action. It is within households that labor providers are nurtured, disciplined, and placed into circulation (Fernández-Kelly 1994; Chant 1999). Cost-benefit calculations involving age, sex, level of education, experience, and ability lead individuals into different market niches, some formal, others informal. Yet there is more to households than their reproductive functions.

Starting in the 1970s, a suggestive literature influenced by feminist thinking interrogated the relationship between private and public domains and exposed a paradoxical convention: goods produced and services provided in domestic spaces are generally understood to be outside the price system and therefore to have no explicit economic value. Household chores, mostly the responsibility of women, are performed in the name of duty, instinct, or sentiment—not as part of market exchanges. Such emphasis on biological and emotive determinants naturalizes what are, in fact, economic transactions subject to price classifi-cation and market effects of supply and demand when occurring in the public domain (Hartmann 1976). A meal may be a symbol of hospitality in the home but it is a commodity when purchased in a restaurant. Feminist critics convincingly argued that denuding domestic work of its economic significance affects the balance of power between men and women, putting the latter at a major disadvantage (Edholm 1977; Deere and Léon de Leal 1990; Kessler-Harris 1975).

In the years that followed, the separation between private and public life and the relationship between productive and reproductive processes were viewed from the perspective of gender inequality (Benería and Sen 1986). As a result, power and resource differentials between men and women received the most attention. The chapters by Chant, González de la Rocha, and Itzigsohn underscore different but equally significant political dimensions. To the extent that it is constructed as a private space outside state regulation, the household presents in extreme modalities some of the characteristics of the informal econ-omy. Furthermore, it is not possible to understand changes in the unregulated sector without appraising equivalent transformations in the domestic sphere.

González de la Rocha vividly documents the transition from what she calls the *resources of poverty* to *the poverty of resources* resulting from the application of neoliberal policies over the last two decades. Her point is that during the 1970s and 1980s informal workers throughout Latin America deployed creative strategies to maximize access to income and meet survival needs, often through the domestic production of goods and services sold in public markets. The street vendors that Cross examined in their dealings with local authorities were sons and daughters, husbands and wives, relatives and friends, putting together plastic trinkets, preparing food, or sewing garments in quarters they inhabited as members of families. In those cases the limits of personal and public action blurred as individuals confronted the challenges of daily existence. I noted earlier that during periods of economic growth the informal and formal sectors expand harmoniously partly as a result of subcon-tracting connections. Subcontracting aims at diversifying production while at the same time lowering costs. It is often within the confines of the household that those two objectives can be met most effectively.

Even in the 1980s, when external debt and cuts in public spending threw countries like Mexico into deep recession, households were able to satisfy basic needs by pushing wives and even children into the labor force (Chant 1991). Contrary to plausible expectations that crisis would result in family atomization—unemployed men deserting families they could not support;

women fleeing violence and poverty—the opposite occurred. González de la Rocha (1990) and Chant (1991) documented the increase in the average number of household members as a response to economic decline. Instructive reasons were behind that counterintuitive finding—when able to, families shared their quarters with displaced relatives or enlisted young female kin to take charge of domestic obligations while older women worked long hours outside the home.

By the 1990s even those strategies were insufficient to maintain minimum standards of living. As economic growth stagnated and then reversed, informality gave way to even more elemental transactions: scavenging, a panoply of rapacious acts, some of them terrifying, the bartering of services and goods, or the use of promissory coupons to mark economic exchanges. The dismantling of public welfare legislation, itself the fragile legacy of an earlier stage of development is thus muting to some extent the differentiation between domestic and public spheres. Older household studies emphasized the politics of gender. The chapters in this volume expose an equally important phenomenon: the extent to which the overlap between domestic and informal economic activities reflects accentuating political vulnerability for a large number of Latin American families.

Figure 1 conceptualizes two moments in the relationship between three economic fields. The first example could be Mexico during the 1970s when import substitution industrialization programs were still in effect and economic growth was comparatively vibrant. In that instance the overlap between domestic and informal activities was significant but many products assembled in homes found buyers in the formal or informal sectors. Those two domains, in turn, were often linked through subcontracting arrangements represented by the arrows in the figure.

In the second example—perhaps Argentina in the year 2002—the interaction among the three sectors has been rearticulated. In response to shrinking formal demand of goods and services, subcontracting wanes and potential workers retrench into domestic spaces, directing their energy to subsistence production and mobilization. The proliferation of communal kitchens and the use of grassroots associations to provide public services are examples of that shift. It is as if, under the impact of neoliberal reform, the private ambit extended outward, beyond conventional boundaries, in order to address survival needs formerly satisfied by the welfare state or the Keynesian market. González de la Rocha's analysis gives pause and raises anew questions about the relationship between economic efficiency and social rights (see also MacLeod 2001 and Sassen 1996). To say that the personal is political, echoing the feminist

Figure 1   Relating Three Economic Domains: Two Variations

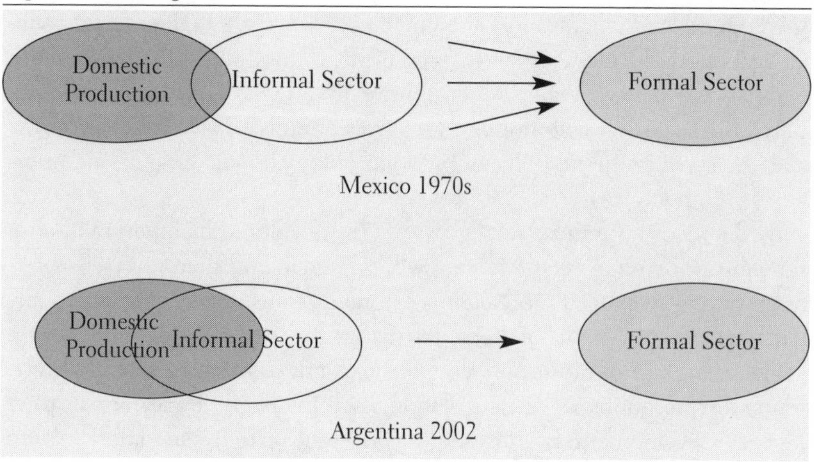

slogan of the 1970s, acquires a new significance in the early twenty-first century when economic change is leading to a tighter articulation of and greater overlap between the domestic and public sectors.

In that bleak picture, some auspicious news is available. According to Chant, the feminization of the labor force that has paralleled globalization both in central and peripheral countries does not perforce entail a further weakening of women's power or limit their access to resources. Studies published mainly in the United States associate rising numbers of female-headed households with sharp poverty levels. Chant offers persuasive evidence that such generalizations may be overstated. In places like Mexico the poorest households are not, by and large, those led by single women but those in which men are the heads. That is because escalating levels of male unemployment coupled with cultural conventions that sanction women's dependence and domesticity can exacerbate economic penury. It is at this level that gender politics backfire, creating even larger risks for both men and women.

Chant's research also shows that, in order to reinforce their masculine role, men are likely to use even modest earnings in conspicuous displays like gambling, purchasing sexual services, or drinking with friends. Women, on the other hand, exhibit a higher propensity to invest in children, even at the expense of their own well-being. Female-headed households derive substantial benefits from replacing husbands' earnings with those of grown children. In such cases the average income may be lower than that in situations where both husband and wife earn wages, but women's higher level of control over funds makes up for that limitation. In other words, the contributions of employed sons and daughters to mothers in charge of domestic services can turn female-headed households into versatile mechanisms that widen advantages where resources are in short supply.

Public Mobilization

Neoliberal economic policies may have expanded the overlap between households and markets but the demarcation between private and public spaces has not faded away. The last four chapters in this book—by Javier Auyero, Robert Gay, Juan Manuel Ramírez Sáiz, and Jon Shefner—explore the open expressions of political dissatisfaction in the global age. They thus connect our studies of the informal economy with the existing literature on social movements (Escobar and Alvarez 1992; Avritzer 2002).

In Chapter 6, Javier Auyero writes eloquently about the innovative strategies conceived and implemented by disgruntled workers in Argentina. He approaches collective unrest from the theoretical perspective first formulated by Charles Tilly (1995), thus emphasizing the cultural *repertoires* used by social actors as they try to attract attention to their plight. Auyero's is a response to an earlier, more simplistic perspective that envisioned mass protest mostly as a reaction to "grievances." In that view, the buildup of collective resentment—over low wages, inadequate working conditions, insufficient services, and government violence—inevitably leads to explosions. Two limitations mar that seemingly plausible framework: first, it equates complex social phenomena with simple laboratory events—just as gases can detonate in a heated flask, rising collective stress is said to cause public mobilization. The evidence does not confirm that generalization. Second, the focus on grievances does not explain cases in which vast resentment is not followed by violent eruptions or those in which minor complaints lead to major outbursts.

Auyero does not underestimate grievances as factors leading to popular unrest, but rather emphasizes shared traditions, communicative exchanges, and institutional expectations, that is, *cultural repertoires*. Collective strife takes place everywhere but how groups express their discontent varies markedly from context to context. In Argentina the harsh conditions resulting from the extension of neoliberal policies have had a three-fold effect: first, they have contributed to the emergence of fluid groups that, although adversarial, do not generally resort to violence. Second, they have facilitated a reshuffling of class alliances in which *el pueblo*, "the people," now encompasses not only members of the rural and urban proletariat but also a larger segment of the middle class—educators, managerial workers, and government employees. Finally, the dismantling of Argentina's welfare state has made it less likely for workers to see capitalists as the group responsible for their predicament—it is government that civil society now sees as a betrayer of the common interest. The tearing apart of what little was left of the Peronist legacy has led a people internally diverse in terms of class but united by shared political concerns to occupy streets and block intersections to galvanize public attention.

Even today, Argentina is far from being the most impoverished country in the hemisphere. In that nation public disturbances are not caused by economic privation alone but by the disjuncture between the collective memory of past promises and the collective experience of the inability of government to deliver on those promises. In John Cross's Mexico City, venders occupy streets not only to survive economically but also to apply political pressure on local authorities. Argentina offers a parallel case in which formal and informal workers take over public spaces as a way to leverage the state. It is the delicate balance between economic intention and political calculus that varies in the two cases.

In Chapter 7 Robert Gay complements Auyero's analysis by focusing on the gradual transition between clientelism and citizenship in Brazil. In conventional interpretations, political machines are activated and maintained through a complex system of reciprocity meant to garner the support of constituencies often formed by informal and marginal workers. Given the large imbalance between the material, human, and ideological resources available to politicians and those at the disposal of popular groups, the assumption has been that patron-client relationships are vertical and top-heavy. Gay paints a more complex image by describing how grassroots leaders play politicians against one another in order to maximize their own access to public services. Gay's account connects brilliantly with the typology by Centeno and Portes showing the limitations of the frustrated state. Latin American politicians are less powerful than sometimes imagined. Force and suppression are not viable means to secure popular compliance in the long run, and the assets needed to buy votes are not always available. This opens up opportunities for informal transactions that local populations use to advance their goals. By restoring agency to both political machines and constituencies, Gay makes a signal contribution. The dwellers of Brazilian *favelas* may still be dependent on employers and public officials, but now we can appreciate their enhanced capacity to manipulate benefactors. Gay's study of the new clientelism uncovers grassroots diplomacy.

As leaders of popular organizations improve their negotiating positions, their motives and objectives can change. Beyond the satisfaction of material needs they may seek firmer inclusion in the larger society. Gay hypothesizes that in Brazil, as in other parts of Latin America, the trend has been from a defense of *particularistic* interests to the *universalistic* pursuit of citizen rights. Juan Manuel Ramírez Sáiz reveals the unexpected consequences of that process in his compelling description of the rise and fall of Mexico's Movimiento Urbano Popular (MUP). The case study is of interest here because it exposes the conditions under which political means are converted into economic ends. Among affluent groups, observes the author, the acquisition of real estate is mostly an economic operation guided by market forces, just as orthodox economists would have it. By contrast, for populations without adequate employment and therefore the means to purchase homes, access to shelter depends primarily on political activism. At the peak of their success MUP leaders used mass mobilization to secure homes for nearly a million workers—a remarkable accomplishment by any standard.

In its early stages, the MUP's dazzling success depended on its autonomy vis-à-vis government officials. Although not completely immune to patron-client dealings, the movement maintained its independence for almost twenty years. That, in turn, increased its credibility and following. In the 1980s, however, the MUP fell prey to the influence of partisan politics. Ramírez Sáiz shows how, in their effort to control and mobilize resources, MUP leaders forged alliances with candidates of various political stripes. This not only produced divisions within the movement, but also put the brakes on action. To the extent that grassroots organizers had to adjust their behavior to the requirements of party bureaucracies, they were less able to meet collective needs or even maintain the detachment that had contributed to their earlier success.

The chapter by Ramírez Sáiz is in good measure the telling of a paradox: in the early stages of their development, popular movements are fueled by the expectation that collective action will bring about a better allocation of essential resources. Yet success can have a paralyzing effect. As popular leaders become part of institutional bodies, their capacity for mobilization diminishes. Put differently, the lack of bureaucratic structure gives popular movements flexibility but not necessarily ways to satisfy basic needs. Bureaucratic mechanisms, on the other hand, facilitate access to resources but hinder the capacity for the equitable distribution of limited goods. That problem, concludes Ramírez Sáiz, lingers unsolved.

In the closing chapter, Jon Shefner approaches the continuum between narrow economic ends and the broad pursuit of citizen rights from a somewhat different angle. Through his remarkable study of a marginal *colonia* in Guadalajara, Mexico, he brings into full view the paradoxes of democratic improvements amid declining material assets. Deviating from typical practice, the neighborhoods that Shefner investigated were not populated by squatters first tolerated and then sanctioned by the authorities. Instead, government representatives made those residential alternatives available as part of a populist agenda that also included plans for greater political participation and the more efficient provision of services. As in the case of Brazil described by Gay, this forged a host of patron-client relationships, but that was only the beginning. In subsequent years, government failed to heed its pledges. Evidence of this, notes Shefner, was a manhole in a central street, originally envisioned as the beginning of a public water project, which to the dismay of local residents remained exposed and untouched for more than a decade.

Working people in Latin America are familiar with disappointment. In countries where national states are limited by insufficient resources and bureaucratic sclerosis, local communities have learned to rely on their own strengths. In the case reviewed by Shefner, however, mobilization diminished despite generalized frustration among the dwellers of the humble Guadalajara *colonia*. Why? Because, replies the author, neoliberal policies may have weakened even the capacity of local communities for self-reliance. Furthermore, a multitude of nongovernmental organizations now populating the Latin American landscape may have inadvertently encouraged passivity. In earlier decades, under the rhetorical mantle of nationalism and class warfare, local residents often took an adversarial stance vis-à-vis governments and employers. More recently, NGOs have become patrons of last resort for vulnerable groups. As in the case of American inner cities, where people often use welfare agencies as one of several resource venues, the poor in Latin America increasingly depend on international philanthropy to maximize access to limited goods. The result is quiescence.

Paradoxically, narratives muting socioeconomic *inequality* and emphasizing *democratic participation* have accompanied the shift in the locus of patronage. Freedom of expression, broader involvement in the electoral process, and fairer representation in government are laudable ends. Yet as Shefner astutely shows, the very meaning of democratic participation is subverted in contexts characterized by what González de la Rocha calls earlier in this volume the *poverty of resources.*

Figure 2   The Progression from Particularistic to Universalistic Political Practices in Latin America

	Welfare State	
	Keynesian Markets	
	<u>Citizenship</u>	
Particularistic		
Universalistic		
$\longrightarrow$		
1900		1980
Frustrated State		
Underdeveloped Markets		
<u>Clientelism</u>		
		Neo-Liberal State
		Free Markets
		<u>Polyarchy</u>
		<u>New Clientelism</u>

Figure 2 summarizes the central ideas in Shefner's argument. In agreement with Auyero, Gay, and Ramírez Sáiz, he points to a progression from particularistic to universalistic political practices. Old forms of patronage gradually give way to movements oriented toward electoral participation and voters' rights. The goal is for popular groups to achieve full membership in the larger society. Yet genuine citizenship requires coordination between market activity and state regulation as it occurred in many European—and some Latin American—countries earlier in the twentieth century. By contrast, in settings affected by the extension of neoliberal policies, the movement away from early modes of patronage has not brought about full citizenship but new types of clientelism, some of them involving nongovernmental organizations.

With these insights Shefner brings our book's argument full circle. His analysis also echoes concerns advanced by authors not represented in this volume. William Robinson's prescient analysis of *polyarchy* as the language and *modus operandi* of the most advanced capitalist sectors comes to mind (Carroll and Carson 2003; Robinson 1996). In their pursuit of profit and flexible conditions for production, members of that potent international class have supported the passage of free trade agreements and the obliteration of paternalistic legislation. They have done this guided by democratic ideals through the extension of individual rights and responsibilities, even as neoliberal policies erode the capacity of many workers to meet fundamental needs (Galbraith

2000, 2002). Shefner's analysis gives pause. Are the new working classes in Latin America and beyond advancing thanks to democracy's embrace or are they just waiting, strangled and dispossessed, for a new moment of resurgence? Only time will tell.

Conclusion

The chapters in this book are united by a common preoccupation: to reveal the political dimensions of informal economic action. As a whole, they form an integrated analysis whose main tenets I summarize below.

First, in agreement with earlier studies on the subject, this book provides new evidence that the informal economy is far from a vestige of earlier stages in economic development. Instead, informality is part and parcel of the processes of modernization. Its content and type of relationship with regulated production and commerce vary in consonance with changes in the material foundations of society. Contrary to early arguments, we present the informal economy as an organized entity. Its regulatory means are not to be found at any level of structured government but within the informal economy itself. To exist, informal workers must rely on norms of reciprocity and solidarity, a subject that joins this book to the field of economic sociology.

Second, the chapters in this book make it clear that informal actors are far from apolitical. Their economic survival depends routinely on transactions they make and alliances they forge with government authorities at the local, state, and federal levels. Conversely, government entities are not always in opposition to unregulated sectors. Distinctions between formal and informal politics may be useful at the analytical level, but on the ground, government officials are often pushed into arrangements that promote the continuance and even growth of the informal economy. In other words, it is the state through its regulatory and implementing capacity that partly determines the size and shape of the unregulated sector.

Third, this book makes an important contribution to our understanding of households as economic fields in close but fluid relationship with both the informal and formal sectors. Although the reproductive functions of domestic units have received attention in the past, this is one of the first attempts to systematize the relationship between unpaid labor as it occurs in domestic ambits and the informal and formal economies. Of special interest to the present moment is the greater overlap between private and public spheres as a result of the extension of neoliberal economic policies.

Finally, this book brings to light the logic of innovative forms of clientelism emerging in the age of global economic integration. Old patron-client relationships are being displaced by new arrangements. Even as national states dismantle protective legislation and working classes resort to self-provisioning, nongovernmental organizations and self-help entities become the new loci of patronage. The language and practice of democratic participation thrive in a volatile age when inequities are on the rise throughout the hemisphere.

At its most fundamental, political action is about the collective production, dispersal, and exercise of power, authority, and influence. Too frequently in the past informal workers have been portrayed as economic players without a recognition of their active participation in the push-and-pull that alters processes of negotiation, co-optation and realignment. They have been, in Eric Wolf's memorable words, a *people without history*. With this volume we hope to redress that narrow conception of a population that constitutes the majority of workers in Latin America.

NOTES

1. The chapters in this book were first presented in November 2001 at the conference "Out of the Shadows: Political Action and the Informal Economy—Latin America and Beyond." The event, sponsored by the Princeton University Center for Migration and Development, was a first attempt to investigate systematically the relationship between income-generating labor outside government regulation and various manners of political expression.

REFERENCES

Avritzer, Leonardo. 2002. *Democracy and the Public Space in Latin America*. Princeton: Princeton University Press.

Balassa, Bela, Gerardo M. Bueno, Pedro Pablo Kuczynski, and Mario H. Simonsen. 1986. *Toward Renewed Economic Growth in Latin America*. Washington, D.C.: Institute for International Economics.

Benería, Lourdes, and Marta I. Roldán. 1987. *The Crossroads of Class and Gender: Industrial Homework, Subcontracting, and Household Dynamics in Mexico City*. Chicago: University of Chicago Press.

Benería, Lourdes, and Gita Sen. 1986. "Accumulation, Reproduction, and Women's Role in Economic Development: Boserup Revisited." In *Women's Work: Development and the Division of Labor by Gender*, ed. Eleanor B. Leacock and Helen I. Safa, 141–57. South Hadley, Mass.: Bergin and Garvey.

Blanes Jiménez, José. 1989. "Cocaine, Informality, and the Urban Economy in La Paz, Bolivia." In *The Informal Economy: Studies in Advanced and Less Developed Countries*, ed. Alejandro Portes, Manuel Castells, and Lauren Benton, 135–49. Baltimore: Johns Hopkins University Press.

Bonacich, Edna, and Ivan H. Light. 1991. *Immigrant Entrepreneurs: Koreans in Los Angeles—1965–1982*. Berkeley and Los Angeles University of California Press.

Capecchi, Vittorio. 1989. "The Informal Economy and the Development of Flexible Specialization in Emilia-Romagna." In *The Informal Economy: Studies in Advanced and Less Developed Countries*, ed. Alejandro Portes, Manuel Castells and Lauren Benton, 189–215. Baltimore: Johns Hopkins University Press.

———. 1997. "In Search of Flexibility: The Bologna Metalworking Industry, 1900–1992." In *World of Possibilities: Flexibility and Mass Production in Western Industrialization*, ed. Charles F. Sabel and Jonathan Zeitlin. Cambridge: Cambridge University Press.

Carroll, William K., and Colin Carson. 2003. "The Network of Global Corporations and Elite Policy Groups: A Structure for Transnational Capitalist Class Formation?" *Global Networks* 3, no. 1:29–57.

Chant, Sylvia. 1991. *Women and Survival in Mexican Cities: Perspectives on Gender, Labour Markets and Low-income Households*. Manchester: Manchester University Press.

———. 1999. "Informal Sector Activity in the Third World City." In *Applied Geography: An Introduction to Useful Research in Physical, Environmental and Human Geography*, ed. M. Pacione, 509–27. London: Routledge.

———. 2000. "Gender, Migration and Urban Development in Costa Rica: The Case of Guanacaste." In *Gender and Migration*, ed. K. Willis and B. Yeoh, 46–63. London: Edward Elgar.

Cross, John C. 1998. *Informal Politics: Street Vendors and the State in Mexico City*. Stanford: Stanford University Press.

Deere, Carmen Diana, and Magdalena León de Leal. 1990. *Household and Class Relations: Peasants and Landlords in Northern Peru*. Berkeley and Los Angeles: University of California Press.

de Soto, Hernando. 1989. *The Other Path*. New York: Harper and Row.

Economic Commission for Latin America and the Caribbean (ECLAC). 2000. "Social Panorama of Latin America, 1999–2000." *Annual Report*. Santiago de Chile: ECLAC.

Edholm, Felicity. 1977. "Conceptualizing Women." *Critique of Anthropology* 3:101–30.

Edin, Kathryn, and Laura Lein. 1997. "Work, Welfare, and Single Mothers' Economic Survival Strategies." *American Sociological Review* 62 (April): 253–66.

Escobar, Arturo, and Sonia E. Alvarez, eds. 1992. *The Making of Social Movements in Latin America: Identity, Strategy, and Democracy*. Boulder, Colo.: Westview Press.

Evans, Peter. 1995. *Embedded Autonomy: States and Industrial Transformation*. Princeton: Princeton University Press.

Fernández-Kelly, Patricia. 1994. "Broadening the Scope: Gender and the Study of International Development." In *Comparative National Development*, ed. Douglas Kincaid and Alejandro Portes, 143–68. Chapel Hill: University of North Carolina Press.

————. 2003. "The Hero's Fight: Endurance and Survival in West Baltimore." Manuscript.

Fernández-Kelly, Patricia, and Anna M. Garcia. 1989. "Informalization at the Core: Hispanic Women, Homework, and the Advanced Capitalist State." In *The Informal Economy: Studies in Advanced and Less Developed Countries*, ed. Alejandro Portes, Manuel Castells, and Lauren Benton, 247–64. Baltimore: Johns Hopkins University Press.

Fortuna, Juan Carlos, and Suzana Prates. 1989. "Informal Sector Versus Informalized Labor Relations in Uruguay." In *The Informal Economy: Studies in Advanced and Less Developed Countries*, ed. Alejandro Portes, Manuel Castells, and Lauren Benton, 78–84. Baltimore: Johns Hopkins University Press.

Frasce, Tom. 2002. "The Sacking of Argentina." *Nation*, May 6.

Freeman, Carla. 2000. *High Tech and High Heels in the Global Economy: Women, Work, and Pink Collar Identities in the Caribbean*. Durham: Duke University Press.

Galbraith, James K. 2000. "A Perfect Crime: Global Inequality." *Daedalus* 131 (winter): 11–25.

————. 2002. "The Brazilian Swindle and the Larger International Monetary Problem." *Policy Note*, Levy Economics Institute, Bard College. Annandale-on-Hudson, New York.

González de la Rocha, Mercedes. 1990. *Private Adjustments: Household Responses to the Erosion of Work*. SEPED Conference Paper, series 6. New York: United Nations Development Program.

Grest, Jeremy. 2001. "Urban Management, Urban Citizenship, and the Informal Economy in the 'New' South Africa: A Case Study from Central Durban." Paper presented at the conference "Out of the Shadows: Political Action and the Informal Economy—Latin America and Beyond," Princeton University, November 15–17.

Hart, Keith. 1973. "Informal Income Opportunities and Urban Employment in Ghana." *Journal of Modern African Studies* 11:61–89.

Hartmann, Heidi. 1976. "Capitalism, Patriarchy and Job Segregation by Sex." In *Women and the Workplace*, ed. M. Blaxall and B. Reagan, 137–69. Chicago: University of Chicago Press.

Inkeles, Alex, and D. Smith. 1974. *Becoming Modern: Individual Change in Six Developing Countries*. Cambridge: Harvard University Press.

Kessler-Harris, Alice. 1975. "Stratifying by Sex: Understanding the History of Working Women." In *Labor Market Segmentation*, ed. Richard C. Edwards, Michael Reich, and David M. Gordon, 217–42. Lexington, Mass.: D. C. Heath.

Klein, Emilio, and Victor Tokman. 2000. "La estratificación social bajo tensión en la era de la globalización." *Revista de la CEPAL* 72 (December): 7–30.

MacLeod, Dag. 2001. "Taking the State Back Out? Privatization and the Limits of Neoliberal Reform in Mexico." Ph.D. diss., Department of Sociology, Johns Hopkins University.

Massey, Douglas, Jorge Durand, and Nolan J. Malone. 2002. *Beyond Smoke and Mirrors: Mexican Immigration in an Era of Economic Integration*. New York: Russell Sage Foundation Press.

Portes, Alejandro. 1997. "Neoliberalism and the Sociology of Development: Emerging Trends and Unanticipated Facts." *Population and Development Review* 23 (June): 229–59.

Portes, Alejandro, Manuel Castells, and Lauren A. Benton, eds. 1989. *The Informal Economy: Studies in Advanced and Less Developed Countries.* Baltimore: Johns Hopkins University Press.

Portes, Alejandro, and Julia Sensenbrenner. 1993. "Embeddedness and Immigration: Notes on the Social Determinants of Economic Action." *American Journal of Sociology* 98:1320–50.

Robinson, William I. 1996. *Promoting Polyarchy: Globalization, U.S. Intervention, and Hegemony.* Cambridge: Cambridge University Press.

Sassen, Saskia. 1996. *Losing Control? Sovereignty in an Age of Globalization.* Leonard Hastings Schoff Memorial Lectures. New York: Columbia University Press.

Spar, Debora L. 1994. *The Cooperative Edge: The Internal Politics of International Cartels.* Ithaca: Cornell University Press.

Tilly, Charles. 1995. "Contentious Repertoires in Great Britain." In *Repertoires and Cycles of Collective Action,* ed. Mark Traugott, 63–87. Durham: Duke University Press.

Tokman, Victor. 1982. "Unequal Development and the Absorption of Labour: Latin America, 1950–1980." CEPAL *Review* 17:121–33.

Weitzer, Ronald, ed. 1999. *Sex for Sale: Prostitution, Pornography, and the Sex Industry.* New York: Routledge.

Wolf, Eric R. 1997. *Europe and the People Without History.* Berkeley and Los Angeles: University of California Press.

Yenal, Hatice Deniz. 2000. "Weaving a Market: The Informal Economy and Gender in a Transnational Trade Network Between Turkey and the former Soviet Union." Ph.D. diss., State University of New York, Binghamton.

ONE

The Informal Economy in the Shadow of the State

Miguel Angel Centeno and Alejandro Portes

The Informal Economy in the Shadow of the State

Over the past two decades, students of political and economic development have emphasized the central role that a strong "Weberian" state, or alternatively, a well-networked civil society can play in promoting both democracy and sustained economic development (Evans 1995; Putnam 1993, 2000; Oxhorn 1995). For some, an autonomous state, free from corrupting influences from civil society is a prerequisite for development (Rodrik 2000; Evans and Rauch 1999). For others, a society that lacks a vibrant network of connections forged in non-state institutions appears to have little chance of developing the institutional and cultural requisites for sustainable growth. Yet what this civil society consists of and what factors can bring about its effective mobilization remain unclear (Portes and Mooney 2002).

This is particularly true in Latin America. The standard wisdom declares that the Latin American state is too strong and that civil society is too weak. Condemned to atomistic concerns and authoritarian collectivities, Latin America cannot hope to escape its cultural and institutional heritage (Véliz 1980). Yet Latin America does possess a large and growing social and economic sector that is characterized by the autonomy of its constituent parts from any sort of institutionalization. Activities conducted in this sector regularly challenge, bypass, or ignore the dictates of alleged "strong" states. Millions interact daily in this

* The authors thank Patricia Fernández-Kelly and Jon Shefner, anonymous readers, and Javier Auyero for their comments and suggestions on this chaper. Responsibility for the contents is ours.

autonomous social space that belongs neither to the public nor to the private sector, as normally defined in developed countries. It is the informal economy.

This popularly organized sector is undoubtedly one of the most important components of Latin American societies. Travelers to any part of the continent will confront it often before they leave the airport and will continue encountering it throughout their stay (Cross 1998). For many citizens (the actual majority in several countries) the informal economy is both their employer and the major source of their consumption. Currently accounting for anywhere from one-third to over half of the economically active population, the informal sector is a poignant reflection of the distortions and failures of the development process in the region and simultaneously a key actor for implementing any solution to them (Portes and Hoffman 2003).

No analysis of contemporary Latin America and no policy proscriptions for its future are complete without reference to its informal economy. While the literature on the topic is vast (Rakowski 1994; Carpio, Klein, and Novacousky 1999), policymakers continue to have a stereotyped and shallow understanding of its dynamics, treating it either as a "cushion" to economic downturns or as simple tax evasion. Such oversight hinders the generation of meaningful and effective social, political, and economic policy. Analysis of the causes and internal dynamics of the Latin American informal economy sheds light on the three most pervasive problems facing the continent: the dearth of domestic investment, the failure of state policies, and social inequality.

The rise and continuity over time of a vast informal sector is perhaps the most glaring example of the characteristics peculiar to Latin America that make adoption of European and North American policy and scholarly models inappropriate. Within the informal economy we witness the logic, potential, and limits of the free "untamed market" (Hart 1990, 158) as actually practiced on the continent. Analysis of these activities will not only produce a better understanding of the present character of Latin American societies but also contribute to a better appreciation of how universal social principles may be applied in regionally specific settings (Centeno and López-Alves 2001).

Definition

Origins of the Concept

The concept of informal economy was born in the Third World, out of a series of studies on urban labor markets in Africa.[1] Keith Hart, the economic anthropologist who coined the term, saw it as a way of giving expression to "the gap between my experience there and anything my English education had taught me before." In his view, the empirical observations about popular entrepreneurship in Accra and other African capitals were clearly at odds with received wisdom from "the western discourse on economic development" (1990, 158).

In his report to the International Labour Office (ILO), Hart postulated a dualist model of income opportunities of the urban labor force, based largely on the distinction between wage employment and self-employment. The concept of informality was applied to the self-employed. Hart emphasized the notable dynamics and diversity of these activities, which, in his view, went well beyond "shoeshine boys and sellers of matches" (1973, 68). This dynamic characterization of the informal sector was subsequently lost as the concept became institutionalized within the ILO bureaucracy, which essentially redefined informality as synonymous with poverty.

Additional characteristics derived from this modified definition included low levels of productivity and a low capacity for accumulation (Tokman 1982). In later publications of the ILO's Regional Employment Programme for Latin America (PREALC), employment in the informal sector was consistently termed "underemployment" and assumed to affect workers who could not gain entry into the modern economy (PREALC 1985; Garcia 1982; Klein and Tokman 1988). This negative characterization of the informal sector has been challenged by other students of the subject. From this alternative stance, informal activities are regarded as a sign of the popular entrepreneurial dynamism, described by Hart (1990, 158) as "people taking back in their own hands some of the economic power that centralized agents sought to deny them." The Peruvian economist Hernando de Soto reformulated Hart's original theme and gave it renewed impulse. In his book, *The Other Path* (1989), de Soto defines informality as the popular response to the rigid "mercantilist" states dominant in Peru and other Latin American countries that survive by granting the privilege of legal participation in the economy to a small elite.

Contemporary Definitions

The strong normative component attached to these competing analyses of the informal sector in the Third World is not entirely absent in the industrialized countries, but research there has attempted to arrive at a more precise and less tendentious definition. There appears to be growing consensus among researchers in the advanced world that the proper scope of the term *informal sector* encompasses "those actions of economic agents that fail to adhere to the established institutional rules or are denied their protection" (Feige 1990, 990). Or, alternatively, it includes "all income-earning activities that are not regulated by the state in social environments where similar activities are regulated" (Castells and Portes 1989, 12). This definition does not advance an a priori judgment of whether such activities are good or bad, leaving the matter to empirical investigation. In this sense, they seem heuristically superior to those used in the Third World, which anticipate from the start the conclusions to be reached.

However, even neutral definitions are hampered by the very breadth of the subject matter they try to encompass. A key distinction must be made between informal and illegal activities because each possesses distinct characteristics that sets it apart from the other. Sociologists recognize that legal and criminal, like normal or abnormal, are socially defined categories subject to change. However, illegal enterprise involves the production and commercialization of goods that are defined in a specific society as illicit, while informal enterprise deals, for the most part, with licit goods.

Manuel Castells and Alejandro Portes (1989) attempted to clarify this distinction in the diagram reproduced as Figure 1. The basic difference between formal and informal hinges not on the character of the final product, but on the manner in which it is produced or exchanged. Thus, articles of clothing, restaurant food, or computer chips—all perfectly licit goods—may have their origins in legally regulated production arrangements or in those that bypass official rules. By explicitly distinguishing these three categories—formal, informal, and illegal activities—it is possible to explore their mutual relationships systematically, a task that becomes difficult when "illegal" and "informal" are confused.

The State in the Shadow of the Informal Economy

Following Charles Tilly's (1985) conception of the state as a "protection racket," a final alternative definition of the informal economy would be transactions where the state neither provides protection nor receives a "cut." For the purposes of this chapter, the state manifests itself in three offices: the regulator, the policeman, and the tax collector. These three persons have as their responsibility the elaboration of laws, the enforcement of those laws, and the collection of payment for their enforcement. Their job is to assure

Figure 1 Types of Economic Activities and their Interrelationships (Castells and Portes 1989, 14)

I. Definitions

Processes of production and distribution	Final product	Economic type
licit	licit	formal
illicit	licit	informal
illicit	illicit	criminal

II. Relationships

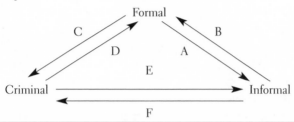

A. State interference, competition from large firms, sources of capital and technology.
B. Cheaper consumer goods and industrial inputs, flexible reserves of labor.
C. State interference and disruption, supplies of certain controlled goods.
D. Corruption, "gatekeeper's rents" for selected state officials.
E. Capital, demand for goods, new income-earning opportunities.
F. Cheaper goods, flexible reserves of labor.

the collective good by making sure that everyone lives by the rules and pay their dues. The dominant characteristic of informal enterprise is the avoidance of all contact with any of these persons, or their co-optation through bribes or other incentives (Cross 1998; Lomnitz 1988; Birbeck 1978).

Therefore, the relationship between the informal economy and the state is, by definition, one of inevitable conflict. The whole point of the state is to assert the monopoly of its authority within a territory, but the whole point of informal entrepreneurs is to avoid or to subvert that authority. As we will see, this theoretically conflictive relation devolves, in practice, into various forms of accommodation. However, for purposes of analysis, it is convenient to focus first on the essential antithesis between state power and informality.

Based on this definition, it is possible to expect a close relationship between state strength and regulatory intent and the character and scope of the informal economy. On a first approximation, it would seem that there is a linear inverse relationship between state strength and informality but, in reality, that relationship is more complex because it is affected by two additional factors:

Table 1   Types of states by regulatory capacity and regulatory intent

State regulatory capacity	State regulatory intent		
	Low	Medium	High
High	The liberal state (United States, United Kingdom)	The welfare state (France, Germany, Sweden)	The totalitarian state (former Soviet Union, North Korea, Cuba)
Low	The absent state (Somalia, Zaire)	The enclave state (Kenya, Bolivia, Angola)	The frustrated state (Argentina, Peru, Ecuador)

(a) the regulatory intent of the state, and (b) the social structure and culture of the population subject to it. In this chapter and for the sake of brevity, we focus on the first of these factors.[2]

An informal economy will develop *when and where it can.* This is true not just of underdeveloped countries but of the informal economies of richer societies as well. However, the "degrees of freedom" for this development to take place is affected both by the regulatory capacity of state agents and the scope of regulation that they are expected to enforce. The two dimensions are not necessarily related. States of the same level of enforcement capability may assume very different regulatory "loads." This gives rise to the typology presented in Table 1. First, a weak state may leave society to its own devices producing a "frontier" situation where economic exchanges are regulated exclusively by the norms and the normative enforcement capacity of society itself. In the absence of the state, there is no informal economy because there is no "formal" one. In other words, there are no legal rules to violate.

The gradual, but still restricted, application of official rules will produce an "enclave" formal economy akin to that commonly found in sub-Saharan Africa and some Latin American countries where the scope of effective state regulation seldom extends beyond the capital and a few areas producing minerals or agricultural goods for export. Most of the actual economy of these Third World countries remains self-regulated rather than informal (Makaria 1997; Pérez Sáinz 1992; Meagher 1995). On the other hand, a weak state may assign to itself a large "load" of regulatory measures over civil society. This is the situation common in Latin America and poignantly criticized by de Soto and his followers (de Soto 1989; Bromley 1994). These states may be described as "frustrated" because of the permanent contradiction between the voluminous paper regulations that they spawn and their inability to enforce them in practice. They give rise to a vast informal sector precisely because ever expanding rules force economic actors to find ways around them and because a weak and frequently corrupt state apparatus facilitates the systematic violation of these rules.

According to de Soto, these states, which he labels "mercantilist," promote permanent inequality because they restrict the protections and resources associated with formality, that is the rule of law, to an elite while forcing the majority of the population to survive outside the law and to cope with the erratic, but costly state attempts at its implementation (Bromley 1990; Portes and Schauffler 1993).

Thus an economy needs to be informal only to the extent that it *has to be*. A state that did not require any costs for entrance into the formal world by limiting the scope of regulation would, by definition, not generate an informal economy. Thus even a weak state could theoretically expand the formal economy by limiting the scope of regulation and reducing the costs of entry for the majority of the population. This was theoretically what the "reform" of the state in Latin America aimed at accomplishing during the last two decades of the last century. The results, as we will see, were quite at variance with that intent.

The relationship between the state and the informal economy is thus cyclically causal and negatively correlated. In general, the weaker the state, the greater the likelihood of an economy being able to escape its grasp. The more ambitious the scope of state regulation, the more cause for escape. The informalization of vast sectors of economic life leads, in turn, to the weakening of state institutions and the rule of law. The state responds by attempting to reestablish its authority, at least in some sectors, which, in turn, produces more avoidance mechanisms, thereby further weakening official authority. Larissa Lomnitz (1988, 54) put it succinctly: " Order creates disorder. The formal economy creates its own informality." For the best part of the last century, Latin America has found itself locked in this apparently inescapable pattern, graphically portrayed in Figure 2. This theoretical vicious circle has, of course, its limits. Weak states are not entirely impotent, and the dominant classes in these countries have a vested interest in the preservation of the rule of law and, hence, predictable contractual relations in certain spheres. This is why the reality on the ground in most Latin American countries features a limited, but diversified sphere of formal relationships—associated generally with interests and activities of the dominant classes—along with a vast informal economy where patterns and practices of avoidance of state regulation become the norm (Roberts 1995, chap. 5; Fortuna and Prates 1989).

Using Michael Mann's (1986) distinction between forms of state power, we can differentiate a despotic state that makes a lot of regulations from an

Figure 2   The process of informalization under "frustrated" states

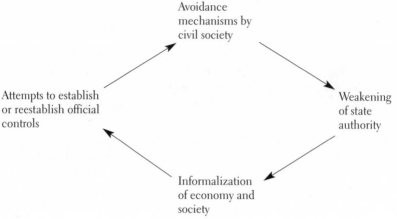

effective state that is actually able to enforce them. Informal economies arise when there is a discrepancy between these two forms of state power. Mann's distinction is useful to introduce the top row of our own typology in Table 1. When states possess extensive regulatory powers, the vicious circle portrayed in Figure 2 has no chance to materialize. Instead, other dynamics take its place. At one extreme is the "liberal" state, dear to neoclassical and public-choice theorists. In these instances, the costs of formality are presumably low because regulations are deliberately restricted. The informal economy is small because there are few rules to violate and such rules as do exist are effectively enforced.

In the intermediate situation, "welfare" states, authorities take a more proactive role toward civil society for the sake of ameliorating the inequalities produced by an entirely free market and thus producing a guaranteed economic "floor" to all. To the extent that welfare programs are administered universalistically and fairly, a large informal economy will not emerge despite the greater number of rules that could be profitably violated. This is because the citizenry itself takes a role in policing the rules, which are viewed as legitimate. Thus working "on the side" while receiving fair unemployment benefits or engaging in prohibited forms of production or marketing is met with social disapproval and likely to be denounced to the authorities rather than supported by peers and neighbors (Roberts 1989; Leonard 1998). Relationships of "complicity" between producers, consumers, and state agents characteristics of flourishing informal economies under frustrated states are absent in these instances. Germany, the Netherlands, and the Scandinavian nations approach this ideal type.

In the limiting case—where a strong state seeks to substitute itself for civil society by controlling its every aspect—a different dynamic sets in. While Stalinist totalitarianism may be overwhelmingly dominant for a while, society eventually reasserts itself, drawing on any possible grounds of solidarity to bypass state controls. The attempt by a totalitarian government to suffocate any manifestation of popular entrepreneurship ends up, over time, encouraging its proliferation. The result, evident in every case where this path has been attempted, is a bourgeoning "second economy" which contradicts and undermines at every turn that subject to official rules (Rev 1986; Stark 1989; Grossman 1989).

The circular dynamics produced by this situation and graphically portrayed in Figure 3 are not too dissimilar from those affecting "frustrated" states (Figure 2), except that the effective tool in the hands of informal entrepreneurs is not open defiance, but the withdrawal of information. Since totalitarian planning of an entire economy depends on massive amounts of information and since accurate information is not forthcoming as actors in civil society regularly conceal, cheat, and exaggerate, the formal "first" economy ends up trapped in a make-believe world of false statistics and illusory achievements. In the end stages of this process, as it happened in the defunct socialist states of Eastern Europe and is currently happening in Cuba, the "second" economy becomes the real economy of the country, effectively displacing the economy subject to official planning (Burawoy and Lukacs 1985; Stark 1989; Roque 2002). Managers and other responsible actors in the latter are often forced to rely on informal providers to meet official targets or by-pass the myriad constraints that formal regulation creates and does not resolve.

In the end, attempts by states, weak and strong, to impose themselves on civil society by implementing pervasive controls backfire, leading to self-reinforcing circles that negate the intent of the rules. In the case of weak states, such as those of Latin America, state protection and resources—including access to predictable, legal transactions—are appropriated by a minority, while the rest of the population is left to fend for itself through widespread violation of the law. In the case of totalitarian states, the occupation of every crevice of economic activity by informal enterprise and the generalized withdrawal of information from official agents lead the state-ruled economy to spiral into a fantasy world. In both cases, there is a progressive divorce between stated aims and reality, written rules and actual practice. Best conditions leading to a reduction of informality are found where limited regulation of private activity by a capable state is

Figure 3   The circular character of informalization under totalitarian states

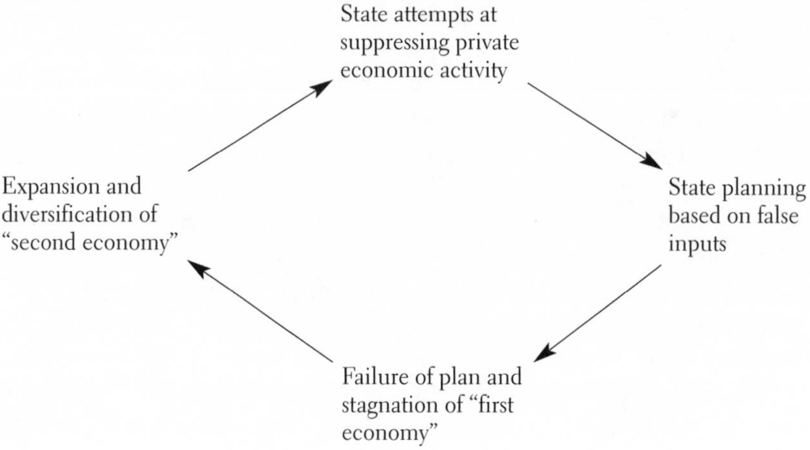

State attempts at
suppressing private
economic activity

Expansion and
diversification of
"second economy"

State planning
based on false
inputs

Failure of plan and
stagnation of "first
economy"

coupled with widespread legitimacy of existing rules among the citizenry. In these instances, society itself becomes an enforcer and guarantor of the rule of law. Weak states can not reproduce, but may seek to approach this situation through various measures. We will return to this point in the conclusion.

The Functions of Informality

From the definition of the phenomenon used in our analysis, it is clear that the elements composing the informal economy will vary across countries and over time.[3] The relationship between the state and civil society defines the character of informality, and that relationship is in constant flux. As just seen, the changing geometry of formal/informal economic activities follows the contours delineated by past history and the character of state authority. There is, therefore, no great mystery in the diversity of formal/informal interactions reported in the literature. Every concrete situation has in common the existence of economic practices that violate or bypass state regulation, but what these are varies according to the character of state-society relations. Hence, what is informal and persecuted in one setting may be perfectly legal in another, and the same activity may shift its location across the formal/informal divide over time.

The research literature on the topic also illustrates the diverse functionality of informal activities for the actors involved. While a good portion of this literature, coming from economics, views the phenomenon as tax evasion (Spiro 1997), sociological and anthropological field studies take a more nuanced view. It is obvious that informal enterprise is "functional" for those so employed in terms of providing a minimum means of survival. It is equally obvious that the formal firms that subcontract production and marketing to informal entrepreneurs or who hire workers off the books benefit from the higher flexibility and lower costs thus obtained. It is less evident, however, that the informal economy can also have positive consequences for the very actor whose existence and logic it challenges—the state.

This central paradox also adopts different forms depending on national context. In less developed countries, such as those of Latin America, informal enterprise has a double economic function. First, it employs and provides incomes to a large segment of the population that otherwise would be deprived of any means of subsistence. The "cushion" provided by a dynamic informal economy can make all the difference between relative tranquility and political instability in these nations (Meagher 1995; Cheng and Gereffi 1994; Diaz 1993). Second, the goods and services provided by informal producers lower the costs of consumption for formal workers and the costs of production and distribution for formal firms, contributing significantly to their viability (Portes and Walton 1981). Thus the low wages received by formal sector employees in Third World nations are partially compensated for by the greater acquisitive power of these wages through cheap, informally produced goods and services. In turn, large firms can compensate for costly tax and labor codes by restricting the size of their formally employed labor force and subcontracting work to informal entrepreneurs (Benería and Roldán 1987).

Through these mechanisms, the informal economy contributes to the political stability and economic viability of poorer nations. These realities help explain why informal activities have been commonly tolerated by Latin American governments in direct contradiction to their manifest law-enforcement duties. The "frustration" of these states, described previously, stems not only from their inability to enforce their own rules but also from their common dependence for survival on the very sector of economic activity that habitually violates these rules. Paradoxically, the perpetuation of weak states which overreach their limits relies on an informal economy which provides means of subsistence for a large segment of the population and subsidizes the consumption and profits of actors in the formal economy.[4]

A similar, albeit more limited situation obtains in developed economies governed by "liberal" states. A laissez-faire stance toward the economic activities of private actors is commonly accompanied, in these cases, by a system of minimum compensation for the victims of the market—the unemployed and the unemployable. These classes are thus compelled to engage in underground activities for survival, be they in the criminal or in the informal economy. Hence, the situation described by Edwina MacDonald (1994) in Cleveland's inner city, where coupling paltry unemployment and welfare benefits with off-the-books casual jobs becomes a "way of life" for the poor. The same situation has been regularly described by poverty researchers (Edin and Lein 1997; Fernández-Kelly 1995; Stack 1974; Uehara 1990). Those who criticize such practices as law-breaking and tax evasion conveniently forget that they de facto subsidize a low-cost welfare system bearing little relation to the actual costs of survival for vulnerable sectors.

The Costs of Informality

All indications point to a continuation of the retreat of the state and the continuing weakness of its enforcement capacity in most Latin American countries. No one associated with the region disputes the rising importance of informality. But despite the functions described previously, there is much less certainty about the *desirability* of a growing informal economy. Given the central role assigned to civil society in the recent literature on democratization and the evident functionality of the informal sector, it would seem as if this is one "Latin American disease" that may actually be good for the patient. The active promotion of self-regulated activities and even further retreats of the state, leaving economic life to its own devices may appear as a reasonable response to the continuing frustration of state authority.

Before advocating such a policy, the long-term costs of informality need to be recognized. There is no question that as a lubricating device—a form of massive social arbitrage—an informal economy is fine and may even be necessary. As just seen, informal activities may provide relief during downtimes in the modern economy and help subsidize both its firms and its workers through cheaper goods, services, and labor. However, this very functionality of informal activities contributes to the perpetuation of economic underdevelopment and political backwardness, "locking in place" the conditions that make these countries peripheral (Castells and Laserna 1989). The "functions" of the Latin American informal sector only exist because of the continuing ineffectiveness of its states and stagnation of its economies. This conclusion requires additional elaboration.

Given a large informal or self-regulated economy, the capacity of the state to generate the resources needed to impose its authority remains limited. Within these limits, the state has little hope of providing the kinds of public incentives needed to create the conditions for modern capitalist development, generate more "good" jobs, and hence persuade those in the informal economy to "come into" the formal sector. In Albert O. Hirschman's terms, given the attraction or inevitability of an informal "exit," the state has great difficulty building the required "loyalty" (Hirschman 1970; Roberts, Frank, and Lozano-Asencio 1999). The absence of such institutionalized assurances discourages investment in more productive and effective institutions. In the long term, the absence of these institutions perpetuates underdevelopment.

The informal economy frustrates the resolution of collective action problems or the adequate compensation for hidden costs that are normally solved by a modern state. By this we mean the kinds of costs not borne directly by the participants (be they employers or employees): long-term health, retirement, public safety, and social services. Informal activities also commonly carry "hidden" costs, such as environmental degradation or the appropriation of collective goods. Informal enterprise, from street vending to pirate production and sale of goods, frequently depends on the use of publicly provided services without contributing anything to cover their costs.

Because of the absence of resources and because of the pervasiveness of illegal activity, it is difficult for the state to sustain a credible role as universal enforcer of rules and contracts. As seen previously, the scope of such enforcement remains limited and is usually conditional by the concerns and interests of the dominant classes. This is what Guillermo O'Donnell (1993) refers to when he speaks of the *"browning of Latin America"* or the disappearance (or continued deficiency) of the rule of law. Associated problems range from the massive corruption of poorly paid policemen to the unavailability of civil courts to settle contracts. This has enormous long-term consequences. Because the policeman or the judge cannot be trusted, citizens have no way of enforcing the most basic regulations. Into the vacuum left by the state, we get not a Rousseauian paradise but a gigantic Hobbesian problem of order. Civil society in such contexts finds its own mechanisms of self-regulation, but these do not provide a basis for sustained modern development.

In Latin America, the incapacity of the state to protect the citizenry has led to the massive growth of private security services, the withdrawal of the wealthy into fortress-like gated communities, and extraordinary rates of victimization among the rest of the population (Ayres 1998; Bourguignon 1999; Portes and Hoffman 2003). In the absence of credible enforcement of rules, people take things in their own hands, be they to protect themselves by force or to engage in unorthodox criminal enterprise that victimizes others. While this Hobbesian dilemma is fairly obvious, the economic consequences of informality are less so. Some neoclassical economists and public-choice theorists propose that this "natural" economic order is an ideal to be achieved, not a problem to be solved. De Soto's initial analysis of informality runs in the same direction (de Soto 1989; Buchanan, Tollison, and Tullock 1980). Unfortunately, in the absence of institutionalized rules, the economy runs into several significant obstacles. Transaction costs become very high when there is no reliable external enforcer of universalistic rules. The weakness or near absence of a functioning judicial system makes contracts impossible. Contracts are, of course, a prerequisite for the depersonalization of economic transactions that is crucial to the development of the modern capitalist market. Transactions become limited in space and time and, outside of a limited elite sphere, much more costly as economic actors must search for their own unorthodox ways to enforce agreements.

Transactions can actually take place without an impartial regulator as long as they are "embedded" in a preexisting web of social networks or larger social structures. These allow for the trust required to engage in long-term exchange without legal guarantees (Portes and Haller 2003). This "social capital" becomes even more significant as the scale or duration of the exchange increases. For transactions involving certain goods or services, social embeddedness may represent a sufficient guarantee (Lomnitz 1988). But it is difficult to imagine a modern industrial economy functioning on this basis. The exchange of goods and services among millions of anonymous transactors is at the very core of a modern capitalist economy. It is not possible to regulate such a volume of exchange on the basis of social network and "enforceable" trust. These mechanisms may function well at the local or community levels, but not at the level of entire national economies. For the latter to develop along a modern path, a legally governed contractual system is a must (Evans and Rauch 1999; O'Donnell 1993; Centeno 1994).

When such a system does not exist, enforcement of commercial agreements may be paid through excess pricing under the assumption that a large number of exchanges will go badly. Some luxury goods and those transacted in the criminal economy, such as drugs, operate in this fashion. But even in these markets, enforcers are usually required whether they are owned or rented.

The costs of maintaining a large "bodyguard" class adds considerably to transaction costs, for they must supplant a key function assumed elsewhere by the modern state.

There is a major difference between private and public warriors, however. The latter operate under some form of law, with explicit prohibitions and known sanctions. While a measure of corruption is to be expected, there is at least a theoretical possibility that the bodyguards are under collective authority. Private equivalents, by definition, work only for those who pay them. Their loyalties are therefore personalized. In the worst-case scenario, the body-guards start working only for themselves. The recent examples of Colombia, Guatemala, and other countries where private self-defense forces hired by landowners and businessmen turned to kidnapping and plundering for their own profit offer a poignant example of the downside of this strategy (Jonas 2000; Arriagada and Godoy 2000; Economic Commission for Latin America and the Caribbean 2001).

The limitations on stability and the ability to plan in systems with such high transaction costs also inhibit the concentration of capital and its use for invest-ment. Immediate consumption is encouraged rather than systematic saving and investment. Those with much wealth have a strong incentive to protect their patrimony. Having no assurances about the future, wealth is preserved in goods of high use value (land) or historically accepted exchange value (gold or dollars). Such conservative strategies do not lend themselves to the kinds of systematic reinvestment and long-term planning required by a modern indus-trial economy (Polanyi [1944] 1957; Hirschman 1958; Evans 1979).

Finally, the perpetuation of the informal economy also insures the continua-tion of vast social inequalities. A significant part of the economically active population laboring without protection and without the possibility of collective representation may comprise a considerable comparative advantage for some industries, but it bodes ill for the possibility of reducing inequality and wide-spread poverty in these nations. In a sense, the functionality of the informal sector for the state and firms in the formal economy depends precisely on the continuing vulnerability and poverty of those laboring in underground activity. This inequality, in turn, further limits the chances for the development of an effective state because those with resources to tax have the political weight to avoid such payments. The final picture is a familiar one to students of Latin America: a small, powerful elite, a state too weak to discipline this elite and create or extract the resources necessary for sustained development, and a dispossessed mass that survives by providing low-cost goods and services to the privileged few.

Neoliberalism: The Wrong Recipe

The failure of the interventionist Latin American state and the concentrated attack on it by powerful multilateral institutions and by internal critics led to a growing consensus that a shift of course was necessary. Countries were to reverse their old policies in the direction of flexibilization, the liberalization of markets, and the privatization of state enterprises. This "Washington consensus" took the region by storm and was swiftly adopted by nations large and small throughout the continent. The character of the new policies and their social and political effects have been described at length in the literature (Diaz 1996; Centeno 1997; Klein and Tokman 2000; Portes 1997; Galbraith 2000). Here, we wish to focus on the relationship between these new policies and the typology of state strength and intent reviewed previously.

It is clear that the intention of the new policies was to transform frustrated states into liberal states. The idea was that, by copying the policies that have been allegedly successful in developed nations like the United States and the United Kingdom, Latin American countries could begin approaching the economic and conditions prevalent in these nations. By taking the state out of the economy and fostering a regime of minimal, but dependable regulation, the powerful developmental potential of free markets would be unchained, capital investment would be stimulated, and enterprises would both increase their profits and reinvest them in new technologies. The result would be sustained growth leading to higher wages and full employment. The rising economic tide "would lift all boats," including the smallest ones (Williamson 1994; Balassa et al. 1986).

The problem with these rosy scenarios is that the underlying societies are quite different from those ruled by developed liberal states. Not only are poverty, underemployment, and economic inequality far greater in Latin America, but these ills tend to be aggravated by the arrival of privatization and market liberalization. Privatization reduces public employment, which had been the backbone of Latin America's middle class and a large portion of its formal proletariat. The newly privatized firms not only shed employment but also, in the absence of strong unions and government regulators, make free use of temporary and off-the-books workers or subcontract production and sales to informal microentrepreneurs. The end result is the decline of formal protected work, a significant rise in microenterprises and informal employment, and a sustained increase in economic inequality. All of these results have been well documented by international agencies and individual researchers (Economic Commission for Latin America and the Caribbean 2000; Klein and Tokman 2000).

Nor are these short-term effects to be promptly superseded by the "tide that lifts all boats." The character of Latin American societies subjected to neoliberal adjustment prevents this from happening. Local economic elites that benefit from privatization and liberalization, a minute proportion of the population to begin with, have proven notably adept at taking their profits abroad or investing them in speculative ventures rather than productive industry. Multinational investors, on the other hand, commonly arrive in a country searching for short-term financial profits; those who have acquired state firms have proven themselves to be notably skittish at state attempts to monitor their employment practices or protect jobs (MacLeod 2001; Korzeniewicz and Smith 2000; Piore 1990).

Domestic industrial firms born during the period of import substitution and suddenly exposed to foreign competition have had a hard time surviving. The "shock treatment" of making these firms compete, without state support, with larger, more efficient foreign producers has not resulted in the elimination of alleged "rental havens," but in the elimination of national firms forced to close their doors or sell out to foreign investors (Sunkel 2001; Galbraith 2000).

Beneath all, there is the sea of poor and poorly educated people whose skills and resources are just too limited to be lifted by anything but the most powerful of economic booms. The latter has not happened and shows no signs of happening in any country of the region, forcing its population to continue scratching a living in invented self-employment or in the precarious, low-wage jobs offered by private firms.[5] The chorus of criticism against the "frustrated" Latin American state neglects the fact that, despite its many limitations and errors, it did seek to respond to the realities of the underlying society and find ways to ameliorate them. The protective policies implemented during the import substitution era did succeed in industrializing many countries of the region and, in the process, created a limited but growing formal proletariat (Roberts 1978; Tokman 1982; Quijano 1998). The question during that period centered on how to incorporate the rest of the population, as workers and consumers, into the modern economy. While in the end, protective Latin American states failed to achieve this goal, they had moved partially toward it before their demise.

The remedy to the frustrations of the old Latin American state has thus proven worse than the disease. The new policies have assumed that markets are essentially the same and yield parallel benefits everywhere without regard for the underlying societies and the characteristics and achievements of the states in need of reform. The application of these policies have certainly rebounded to the benefits of investors in the First World, who have found new profitable niches for investment—be they in plants producing goods for export to wealthy consumers or in the acquisition of state-owned and private domestic firms at fire-sale prices. The growing resistance of Latin American publics to these policies is not based on lack of understanding of their long-term goals, but on direct exposure to their actual consequences (Roberts 2002; Hoffman and Centeno 2003).

As far as the informal sector is concerned, the shift from protectionism and regulation to free markets has not led to its absorption into the modern economy, but to two unanticipated consequences: first, the weakening of labor standards and state protection produced a blurring of the line between the two sectors. When work in the formal sector becomes increasingly low-paid and insecure, it begins to approximate the conditions previously associated with the informal economy. As the state ceases to regulate, the distinction between a formal and informal economy gradually loses its meaning (Castells and Portes 1989).

Second, informal self-employment ceases to be a "cushion" against the ups-and-downs of the formal-sector labor demand to become a *desirable* alternative to it. Street vending, for instance, becomes preferable to the wages and work conditions available in "formal" privatized plants (Cross 1998). In his comparative study of the informal economy in the Caribbean region, Itzigsohn (2000) has shown how informal entrepreneurs receive higher incomes and consider their lot far more desirable than that of workers in the special exports zones that have become the trademark of the new market-oriented policies. An underlying labor surplus and lack of state protections insure that firms can pretty much do as they please in dictating the conditions for new "formal" jobs. Thus, the meaning of informality has changed markedly in the neoliberal era. In the past, it was the sector where those excluded from the modern economy found employment; in the present it has become a place for those escaping the degradation of formerly secure jobs.

Conclusion: The True Other Path

Returning to Table 1, one can say that neoliberal adjustment policies failed in Latin America because they had the wrong goal. Given the conditions of Latin

American societies, the strong welfare states of Western Europe should have been the model, not the liberal United States. This is because the conditions of marginalization and want of vast segments of the Latin American population require deliberate state intervention. Further, the feebleness of private domestic enterprise requires both a measure of protection and state support before they can compete internationally. Two of the few Latin American success stories in the global markets, the Brazilian airplane manufacturer Embraer and the Brazilian petrochemical giant Petrobras provide examples of this point (Evans 1986).[6]

It may be argued that creating a net of social safety measures while simultaneously pushing toward the development of autonomous domestic enterprise exceeds the capabilities of a weak state. It may be further argued that the failures of the frustrated Latin American states was due precisely to its attempting to assume a similar heavy load of social and economic tasks (Castells and Laserna 1989). While these points are well taken, there is reason to assert that the failure of Latin American states had less to do with their creation of basic social service systems or their support of domestic industries than with the proliferation of rules accompanied by an inefficient and corrupt enforcement apparatus. A legalistic turn of mind led governments and legislatures alike to issue decrees and laws regulating nearly everything, while worrying little about how they could be implemented. On the ground, an enforcement machinery made up of poorly trained and poorly paid officials ensured that the proliferating rules only served as additional opportunities for rent-seeking (O'Donnell 1994; Morris 1991; Adelman and Centeno 2001).

The obvious solution is less regulation coupled with a state machinery capable of implementing existing laws. A state does not become weaker because it regulates less, it is weakened by the inability to enforce its own rules. It follows, in principle, that the lesser the volume of regulation, the greater the ability of enforcers to implement it in strategic areas. This is specially the case if this reduction is accompanied by improvements in the "quality" of the enforcement apparatus. What Peter Evans (1995) dubbed a "Weberian" state bureaucracy, composed of officials selected on merit, identified with their service, and immune to bribe-taking, is a goal that has so far eluded all Latin American nations. It is also a precondition for their sustained long-term development. Deliberate efforts to instill a measure of "Weberianness" in these state machineries, through the creation of "islands of efficiency" (Evans 1989, 577) that bypass corrupt agencies thus represent a top national and regional priority.

So far these prescriptions are not too different from those stemming from the "Washington Consensus." Indeed, the quest for "flexibility," which is one of the pillars of the neoliberal program is quite compatible, in principle, with the goal of "less state/more efficient state" just described. The fundamental difference lies in the strategic orientation of this strengthened state: an impartial enforcer of contractual obligations on the one hand, an active provider of a safety net of basic services and incubator of domestic entrepreneurial initiatives on the other. Given their initial weakness, Latin American states cannot hope to match the achievements of West European welfare models. However, they can take the first steps toward emulating that goal by adopting a two-pronged strategy of taking deliberate steps toward self-reconstruction through shedding regulatory load and increasing the quality of the civil service, judiciary, and police and focusing on a viable, limited program of social protection for the poorest sectors, basic infrastructure, and support of internationally viable economic sectors.

Neoliberal adjustment applied to poor and unequal societies not only failed to lift all but the largest boats; it also deprived these societies of the few dynamic enterprises and the little economic autonomy achieved during the prior era. It is time to start anew, learning from the errors of the past, and reasserting the rights of these nations to pursue their own path toward social integration and economic development, rather than being controlled from the outside. No nation has ever been developed by external market forces. That the "magic of the markets" would accomplish this for Latin America in the late twentieth century was just an illusion.

As a sign of underdevelopment and stagnation and a pillar sustaining the status quo, the informal economy has a role to play in this revamped consensus. That role is to disappear. While informality will never entirely evaporate, a reform program that reduces the scope of state regulation reduces concomitantly the opportunities for its violation; limited and fairly applied laws weaken the legitimacy of these practices; and a policy that promotes the growth of viable national enterprises can also increase employment opportunities better than the degraded jobs of today's special export zones. There will be no better sign that Latin America is on the mend and on the path toward sustained development than when the bulk of its labor force ceases to depend on invented self-employment and on precarious and unprotected jobs for survival. In such a world, the "functions" played today by the informal economy will cease to exist.

NOTES

1. These and the following sections are adapted from Portes and Haller 2003.

2. An analysis of the relation between the character of civil society and the development of an informal sector is presented in a parallel essay (Portes and Haller 2003).

3. This section is adapted from Portes and Haller 2003.

4. The recent experience of Argentina highlights another form of such dependence, namely the reliance of authorities on informal political entrepreneurs to distribute minimum assistance to an unemployed population so as to partially co-opt it and, hence, avoid social explosions. These practices highlight again the fact that these states are not impotent, just not strong enough to implement universalistic programs and enforceable rules. This forces them to implement particularistic relief practices dependent, as in Argentina, on informal arrangements and brokers (Auyero, Chapter 6 herein).

5. Chile is often cited as an exception to this rule and as an example of the success of neoliberal adjustment policies. This is a naïve conclusion for two reasons: first, the economic policies that finally succeeded in lifting the Chilean economy out of its depressed state were neoliberal in name only and represented a pragmatic response to the repeated failure of orthodox "Chicago"-inspired neoliberalism to produce growth and generate employment. Second, the relative economic success of this pragmatic model did not alleviate preexisting economic inequalities, but actually increased them. While poverty and unemployment were reduced in Chile during the 1990s, these positive developments were accompanied by increasingly precarious employment, with unprotected and insecure jobs becoming the norm for large sectors of the Chilean working class. With the removal of state regulation, firms—domestic and foreign alike—found themselves free to fire labor at will and to put it to work under harsh and frequently unsafe conditions (Diaz 1993, 1996; Economic Commission for Latin America and the Caribbean 2000). Thus jobs created under the new set of market-oriented policies could scarcely be said to have "lifted" Chilean workers out of a condition of continuous precariousness and scarcity.

6. Both are actually state-owned companies which have proven sufficiently viable and profitable to avoid the wave of privatization. Another example is the Chilean state-owned copper company, CODELCO (Diaz 1996).

REFERENCES

Adelman, Jeremy, and Miguel A. Centeno. 2001. "Between Liberalism and Neoliberalism: Law's Dilemma in Latin America." In *Global Prescriptions*, ed. Yves Dezalay and Bryant G. Garth. Ann Arbor: University of Michigan Press.

Arriagada, Irma, and Lorena Godoy. 2000. "Prevention or Repression? The False Dilemma of Citizen Security." CEPAL *Review* 70 (April): 111–36.

Ayres, Robert L. 1998. *Crime and Violence as Development Issues in Latin America and the Caribbean*. World Bank Latin American and Caribbean Studies. Washington, D.C.: World Bank.

Balassa, Bela, Gerardo M. Bueno, Pedro Pablo Kuczynski, and Mario H. Simonsen. 1986. *Toward Renewed Economic Growth in Latin America*. Washington, D.C.: Institute for International Economics.

Benería, Lourdes, and Marta I. Roldán. 1987. *The Crossroads of Class and Gender: Homework, Subcontracting, and Household Dynamics in Mexico City*. Chicago: University of Chicago Press.

Birbeck, Chris. 1978. "Self-Employed Proletarians in an Informal Factory: The Case of Cali's Garbage Dump." *World Development* 6:1173–85.

Bourguignon, François. 1999. "Crime, Violence, and Inequitable Development." Paper prepared for the Annual Conference on Development Economics, The World Bank, Washington, D.C.

Bromley, Ray. 1990. "A New Path to Development? The Significance and Impact of Hernando de Soto's Ideas on Underdevelopment, Production, and Reproduction." *Economic Geography* 66:328–48.

———. 1994. "Informality, de Soto Style: From Concept to Policy." In *Contrapunto: The Informal Sector Debate in Latin America*, ed. C. A. Rakowski, 131–51. Albany: State University of New York Press.

Buchanan, James M., Robert D. Tollison, and Gordon Tullock. 1980. *Toward a Theory of the Rent-Seeking Society*. College Station: Texas A&M University Press.

Burawoy, Michael, and János Lukács. 1985. "Mythologies of Work: A Comparison of Firms in State Socialism and Advanced Capitalism." *American Sociological Review* 50:723–37.

Carpio, Jorge, Emilio Klein, and Irene Novacousky. 1999. *Informalidad y exclusión social*. Buenos Aires: Fondo de Cultura Económica.

Castells, Manuel, and Roberto Laserna. 1989. "The New Dependency: Technological Change and Socio-Economic Restructuring in Latin America." *Sociological Forum* 4:535–60.

Castells, Manuel, and Alejandro Portes. 1989. "World Underneath: The Origins, Dynamics, and Effects of the Informal Economy." In *The Informal Economy: Studies in Advanced and Less Developed Countries*, ed. Alejandro Portes, Manuel Castells, and Lauren Benton, 11–37. Baltimore: Johns Hopkins University Press.

Centeno, Miguel Angel. 1994. "Between Rocky Democracies and Hard Markets." *Annual Review of Sociology* 20:125–47.

———. 1997. *Democracy Within Reason*. 2nd edition. University Park: Pennsylvania State University Press.

Centeno, Miguel Angel, and Fernando López-Alves, eds. 2001. *The Other Mirror: Grand Theory Through the Lens of Latin America*. Princeton: Princeton University Press.

Cheng, Lu-lin, and Gary Gereffi. 1994. "The Informal Economy in East Asian Development." *International Journal of Urban and Regional Research* 18:194–219.

Cross, John C. 1998. *Informal Politics: Street Vendors and the State in Mexico City*. Stanford: Stanford University Press.

de Soto, Hernando. 1989. *The Other Path*. New York: Harper and Row.

Diaz, Alvaro. 1993. "Restructuring and the New Working Classes in Chile: Trends in Waged Employment, Informality, and Poverty, 1973–1990." Working Paper DP47, United Nations Research Institute for Social Development, October.

————. 1996. "¿Chile: Hacia el pos-neoliberalismo?" Paper presented at the conference "Responses of Civil Society to Neo-Liberal Adjustment," Department of Sociology, University of Texas at Austin, April.

Economic Commission for Latin America and the Caribbean (ECLAC). 2000. "Social Panorama of Latin America, 1999–2000." *Annual Report*. Santiago de Chile: ECLAC.

————. 2001. "Agenda social: Seguridad cuidadana y violencia." In *Panorama social de América Latina*, 205–40. Santiago de Chile: ECLAC.

Edin, Kathryn, and Laura Lein. 1997. "Work, Welfare, and Single Mothers' Economic Survival Strategies." *American Sociological Review* 62 (April): 253–66.

Evans, Peter. 1979. *Dependent Development: The Alliance of Multinational, State, and Local Capital in Brazil*. Princeton: Princeton University Press.

————. 1986. "Generalized Linkages in Industrial Development: A Reexamination of Basic Petrochemicals in Brazil." In *Development, Democracy, and the Art of Trespassing*, ed. A. Foxley, M. McPherson, and G. O'Donnell, 7–26. Notre Dame: University of Notre Dame Press.

————. 1989. "Predatory, Developmental, and Other Apparatuses: A Comparative Political Economy Perspective on the Third World State." *Sociological Forum* 4:561–87.

————. 1995. *Embedded Autonomy: States and Industrial Transformation*. Princeton: Princeton University Press.

Evans, Peter, and James E. Rauch. 1999. "Bureaucracy and Growth: A Cross-National Analysis of the Effects of 'Weberian' State Structures on Economic Growth." *American Sociological Review* 64:748–65.

Feige, Edgar. 1990. "Defining and Estimating Underground and Informal Economies: The New Institutional Economics Approach." *World Development* 18, no. 7.

Fernández-Kelly, Patricia. 1995. "Social and Cultural Capital in the Urban Ghetto: Implications for the Economic Sociology of Immigration." In *The Economic Sociology of Immigration: Essays in Network, Ethnicity, and Entrepreneurship*, ed. Alejandro Portes, 213–47. New York: Russell Sage Foundation.

Fortuna, Juan Carlos, and Suzana Prates. 1989. "Informal Sector Versus Informalized Labor Relations in Uruguay." In *The Informal Economy: Studies in Advanced and Less Developed Countries*, ed. Alejandro Portes, Manuel Castells, and Lauren Benton, 78–84. Baltimore: Johns Hopkins University Press.

Galbraith, James K. 2000. "A Perfect Crime: Global Inequality." *Daedalus* 131 (winter): 11–25.

Garcia, Norberto E. 1982. "Growing Labor Absorption with Persistent Unemployment." *CEPAL Review* 18:45–64.

Grossman, Gregory. 1989. "Informal Personal Incomes and Outlays of the Soviet Urban Population." In *The Informal Economy: Studies in Advanced and Less Developed Countries*, ed. Alejandro Portes, Manuel Castells, and Lauren Benton, 150–72. Baltimore: Johns Hopkins University Press.

Hart, Keith. 1973. "Informal Income Opportunities and Urban Employment in Ghana." *Journal of Modern African Studies* 11:61–89.

————. 1990. "The Idea of Economy: Six Modern Dissenters." In *Beyond the Marketplace: Rethinking Economy and Society*, ed. R. Friedland and A. F. Robertson, 137–60. New York: Aldine de Gruyter.

Hirschman, Albert O. 1958. *The Strategy of Economic Development*. New Haven: Yale University Press.

———. 1970. *Exit, Voice, and Loyalty: Responses to Decline in Firms, Organizations, and States*. Cambridge: Harvard University Press.

Hoffman, Kelly, and Miguel A. Centeno. 2003. "The Lopsided Continent: Inequality in Latin America." *Annual Review of Sociology* 29.

Itzigsohn, José. 2000. *Developing Poverty: The State, Labor Market Deregulation, and the Informal Economy in Costa Rica and the Dominican Republic*. University Park: Pennsylvania State University Press.

Jonas, Susanne. 2000. *Of Centaurs and Doves: Guatemala's Peace Process*. Boulder, Colo.: Westview Press.

Klein, Emilio, and Victor E. Tokman. 1988. "Sector informal: Una forma de utilizar el trabajo como consecuencia de la manera de producir y no viceversa." *Estudios Sociologicos* 6:205–12.

———. 2000. "La estratifcación social bajo tensión en la era de la globalización." *Revista de la CEPAL* 72 (December): 7–30.

Korzeniewicz, Roberto Patricio, and William C. Smith. 2000. "Poverty, Inequality, and Growth in Latin America: Searching for the High Road to Globalization." *Latin American Research Review* 35:7–54.

Leonard, Madeleine. 1998. *Invisible Work, Invisible Workers: The Informal Economy in Europe and the U.S.* London: Macmillan.

Lomnitz, Larissa. 1988. "Informal Exchange Networks in Formal Systems: A Theoretical Model." *American Anthropologist* 90:42–55.

MacDonald, R. 1994. "Fiddly Jobs, Undeclared Working, and the Something for Nothing Society." *Work, Employment, and Society* 8:507–30.

MacLeod, Dag. 2001. "Taking the State Back Out? Privatization and the Limits of Neoliberal Reform in Mexico." Ph.D. diss., Department of Sociology, Johns Hopkins University.

Makaria, Kinuthia. 1997. *Social and Political Dynamics of the Informal Economy in African Cities*. Lanham, Md.: University Press of America.

Mann, Michael. 1986. *The Sources of Social Power*. Vol. 1. New York: Cambridge University Press.

Meagher, Kate. 1995. "Crisis, Informalization, and the Urban Informal Sector in Sub-Saharan Africa." *Development and Change* 26 (April): 259–84.

Morris, Stephen D. 1991. *Corruption and Politics in Contemporary Mexico*. Tuscaloosa: University of Alabama Press.

O'Donnell, Guillermo. 1993. "The Browning of Latin America." *New Perspectives Quarterly* 10, no. 4.

———. 1994. "The State, Democratization, and Some Conceptual Problems." In *Latin American Political Economy in the Age of Neoliberal Reform*, ed. W. C. Smith, C. H. Acuña, and E. A. Gamarra, 157–79. New Brunswick, N.J.: Transaction Books.

Oxhorn, Philip. 1995. *Organizing Civil Society: The Popular Sectors and the Struggle for Democracy in Chile*. University Park: Pennsylvania State University Press.

Pérez Sáinz, Juan Pablo. 1992. *Informalidad urbana en América Latina: Enfoques, problemáticas e interrogantes*. Caracas: Editorial Nueva Sociedad.

Piore, Michael. 1990. "Labor Standards and Business Strategies." In *Labor Standards and Development in the Global Economy*, ed. S. Herzenberg and J. Perez-López, 35–49. Washington, D.C.: U.S. Department of Labor.

Polanyi, Karl. [1944] 1957. *The Great Transformation: The Political and Economic Origins of Our Time*. Boston: Beacon Press.

Portes, Alejandro. 1997. "Neoliberalism and the Sociology of Development: Emerging Trends and Unanticipated Facts." *Population and Development Review* 23 (June): 229–59.

Portes, Alejandro, and William Haller. 2003. "The Informal Economy." In *Handbook of Economic Sociology*, 2nd edition, ed. by Neil Smelser and Richard Swedberg. New York: Russell Sage Foundation.

Portes, Alejandro, and Kelly Hoffman. 2003. "Latin American Class Structures: Their Composition and Change During the Neoliberal Era." *Latin American Research Review* 38, no. 1.

Portes, Alejandro, and Margarita Mooney. 2002. "Social Capital and Community Development." In *The New Economic Sociology: Developments in an Emerging Field*, ed. M. F. Guillen, R. Collins, P. England, and M. Meyer, 303–29. New York: Russell Sage Foundation.

Portes, Alejandro, and Richard Schauffler. 1993. "The Informal Economy in Latin America: Definition, Measurement, and Policies." *Population and Development Review* 19, no. 1 (March): 33–60.

Portes, Alejandro, and John Walton. 1981. *Labor, Class, and the International System*. New York: Academic Press.

PREALC. 1985. *Mas alla de la crisis*. Santiago de Chile: International Labor Office.

Putnam, Robert D. 1993. *Making Democracy Work: Civic Traditions in Modern Italy*. Princeton: Princeton University Press.

———. 2000. *Bowling Alone: The Collapse and Revival of American Community*. New York: Simon & Schuster.

Quijano, Anibal. 1998. "La colonialidad del poder y la experiencia Latinoamericana." In *Pueblo, epoca y desarrollo: La sociología de América Latina*, ed. R. Briceno-Leon and H. R. Sonntag, 27–38. Caracas: Nueva Sociedad.

Rakowski, Cathy A., ed. 1994. *Contrapunto: The Informal Sector Debate in Latin America*. Albany: State University of New York Press.

Rev, Ivan. 1986. "The Advantages of Being Atomized." Working Paper, The Institute for Advanced Study, Princeton University.

Roberts, Bryan. 1978. *Cities of Peasants: The Political Economy of Urbanization in the Third World*. London: Edward Arnold.

———. 1989. "The Other Working Class: Uncommitted Labor in Britain, Spain, and Mexico." In *Cross-National Research in Sociology*, ed. M. L. Kohn, 352–72. Newbury Park, Calif.: Sage Publications.

———. 1995. *The Making of Citizens: Cities of Peasants Revisited*. London: Arnold.

Roberts, Bryan, Reanne Frank, and Fernando Lozano-Asencio. 1999. "Transnational Migrant Communities and Mexican Migration to the United States." *Ethnic and Racial Studies* 22 (March): 238–66.

Roberts, Kenneth. 2002. "Social Inequalities Without Class Cleavages in Latin America's Neoliberal Era." *Studies in Comparative International Development* 36 (winter): 3–33.

Rodrik, Dani. 2000. "Institutions for High-Quality Growth: What They Are and How to Acquire Them." *Studies in Comparative International Development* 35 (fall): 3–31.

Roque, Martha Beatriz. 2002. "Economia informal en Cuba." Report Commissioned by the Center for Migration and Development, Princeton University, May.

Spiro, Peter S. 1997. "Taxes, Deficits, and the Underground Economy." In *The Underground Economy: Global Evidence of Its Size and Impact*, ed. O. Lippert and M. Walker, 37–52. Vancouver: The Fraser Institute.

Stack, Carol. 1974. *All Our Kin*. New York: Harper and Row.

Stark, David. 1989. "Bending the Bars of the Iron Cage: Bureaucratization and Informalization in Capitalism and Socialism." *Sociological Forum* 4 (December): 637–64.

Sunkel, Osvaldo. 2001. "The Unbearable Lightness of Neoliberalism." Paper presented at the Conference on Latin American Sociology, University of Florida, Gainesville, April.

Tilly, Charles. 1985. "War Making and State Making as Organized Crime." In *Bringing the State Back In*, ed. Peter Evans, Dietrich Rueschemeyer, and Theda Skocpol. New York: Cambridge University Press.

Tokman, Victor. 1982. "Unequal Development and the Absorption of Labour: Latin America, 1950–1980." *CEPAL Review* 17:121–33.

Uehara, Edwina. 1990. "Dual Exchange Theory, Social Networks, and Informal Social Support." *American Journal of Sociology* 96:521–57.

Véliz, Claudio. 1980. *The Centralist Tradition of Latin America*. Princeton: Princeton University Press.

Williamson, John. 1994. *The Political Economy of Policy Reform*. Washington, D.C.: Institute for International Economics.

TWO

RISK AND REGULATION IN INFORMAL AND ILLEGAL MARKETS

John C. Cross and Sergio Peña

Sociology takes for granted that all human interaction is socially regulated, but this assumption may appear so obvious that it is easy to overlook, even in our analysis of regulatory systems. When scholars argue that the informal and illegal sectors are "unregulated," what they actually should say is that they are regulated informally or illegally. In this chapter, we discuss the implications of such a statement by comparing the regulatory systems of street vendors in Mexico City and crack dealers in New York City within the context of institutional economics.

Regulatory systems are primarily a way of socially managing the risks that individuals expose themselves to when they become involved in transactions with other individuals. Risk management involves reducing uncertainty to the point that liabilities can be calculated based upon the probability that transaction partners will act in predictable ways assuming common cultural values and norms. Historically, most human interaction has been on a personal, face-to-face level with impersonal interactions being important for only a small percentage of the population such as rulers and merchants. As a result,

* Support for part of this chapter was provided by the Behavioral Sciences Training in Drug Abuse Research program sponsored by the Medical and Health Research Association of New York City (MHRA) and the National Development Research Institutes (NDRI) with funding from the National Institute of Drug Abuse (5T32 DA07233-09). Points of view, opinions, and conclusions in this paper do not necessarily represent the official position of the United States government, MHRA, NDRI, University of Texas, or any other supporting institution.

most people have operated almost exclusively within informal systems of regulations managed by the community, clan, or family.

In industrial and postindustrial societies, however, the impersonal has become the dominant mode of human interaction. Virtually everyone depends for the bulk of their survival needs on people they will never meet or know, who appear to them simply as remote market forces or legal systems. One of the modern state's most important tasks is the regulation of such impersonal interactions, a role that has grown in importance as social relations become more distant as a result of the expansion of interaction beyond self-regulating social groups as a byproduct of the mass quality of production and consumption. On the macroeconomic level economists such as Adam Smith and Keynes advocated government action that would help growth or stability in the marketplace. On the microlevel, a host of competing pressure groups have promoted regulations concerning business practices, enforcing professional ethics, protecting consumer concerns, and safeguarding the rights of workers. Those measures have then been implemented by a public sector bending to popular pressure, but also following internal interests that benefit from government's enlargement and its ability to intervene in the economy.

Nevertheless, the state's regulatory role of risk management is not politically or socially neutral. Instead, it tends to overcompensate elites in the marketplace by creating and protecting privileged market spaces that allow rent extraction. It does so in tandem with several other "formal" systems of regulation that have developed alongside it in the marketplace. Typically, but not always, aligned with the state are the internal regulatory practices that have emerged with the advent of large businesses and mega-corporations with their own internal bureaucracies. In a similar fashion, although for different motives, the rise of labor unions has also had an important regulatory impact on the market through their demands for wage and work security standardization. These three forces operate together to create what is taken for granted today as the "natural" dominant market system, which we will refer to as the "formal/legal market."

Theoretically, we can define this marketplace as an arena of state-approved production and distribution practices justified according to a set of social welfare criteria such as consumer and worker safety and broader market stability, but also placing great emphasis on reducing the risks related to capital investment decisions. In practice, the types of activities that are considered appropriate and the level of enforcement against "inappropriate" activity is a constant function of interest groups involved in defining this sector: "authorized" businesses, labor organizations, state bureaucrats, consumer groups, and so on.[1] As such, of course, the dominant regulatory system can be seen as a form of dominant "infra-politics" (Scott 1990) that masks its distribution role under a guise of political neutrality.

However, the groups that participate in this infra-politics are hardly evenly matched. While political analysts often focus on the unequal conflict between "capital" and "labor" as categories of interests competing over the definition of the formal regulatory system, these categories are far from exhaustive. Particularly in the Third World, but even in the First, large numbers of people are excluded from this struggle and rely primarily upon avoiding or subverting the dominant regulatory system. These people are sometimes referred to as the "underground" or "black" market, terms that suggest a set of negative definitions, of things that go on behind closed doors, hidden away from the light of day, illegal, unregulated, and out of control. Seen in this context, these activities were typically seen as a "problem" tainted by the criminality of tax evasion (e.g., Simon and Witte 1982) and, from a developmentalist perspective, the equally criminal act of inefficiency (Bairoch 1973; Jones 1968).

The concept of *informal sector* attempts to differentiate between clearly illegal activity that takes place in the "underground" market (drug selling, the fencing of stolen articles, and so on) from activity that is arguably legal in nature, but carried on without deferring to the state-regulatory system (Portes, Castells, and Benton 1989; de Soto 1989), such as unlicensed taxis and street vendors. This separation into "illegal" and "informal" markets is not without its own problems—a subject that we discuss later—but it allowed for the formulation of much more specific questions about the nature of regulation and enforcement. First, it opened the possibility that "informal" activities may have a positive social effect, thus permitting analysts and public policy advocates to see them with a more benign eye. The informal sector could be seen as a terrain formed by legitimate activities made illegal only because the participants cannot afford the costs of regulation. The differentiation between "illegal" and "informal" also led to a renewed interest in the functionality of the official regulatory system per se, and whether it was doing its job adequately given the needs of a particular society, especially the needs of the poor who are excluded from formal systems both as entrepreneurs and as workers.

While there has been some research about structures of regulation in both the illegal and informal sectors (Bromley 1978; Cross 1998b; Dorn, Oette, and White 1998; Reuter 1985), these have rarely been compared to see how they oppose or supplement the regulatory role of the state. In other words, if the dominant (formal) regulatory system represents the dominant infra-politics, how do the infra-politics of alternative (subordinate) regulatory systems interact with it and each other? Are they *competing* forms of regulation that help to resist the dominant paradigm, or are they supplementary forms of regulation that help to resolve contradictions or blind spots within the dominant regulatory system? These important questions are completely overlooked by the dominant Western paradigm, which focuses only on "state" and "market" forces in the economy. Paradoxically, while the dominant neoliberal ideology in Latin America would seem to favor deregulation, in fact it implies a simple shift in regulations from social concerns to purely technocratic and profit-centered priorities and is just as opposed to the alternative regulatory systems used by the informal sector.

We will use two examples to ground our discussion of the informal and illegal sectors: the case of street vendors in Mexico City and crack dealers in New York. While these groups may seem worlds apart, they are both engaged in similar activities under conditions of regulatory and legal uncertainty that require each to create what de Soto (2000) refers to as an "extralegal" regulatory mechanism to enforce a shadow system of property rights and risk management. In both cases, their activities are considered illegal, but it is far more problematic politically for the Mexican state to take effective action against street vending than it is for the U.S. state to take action against crack dealers. Nevertheless, neither activity was actually prevented by state action, although they created very different regulatory systems as a reaction to state antagonism.

The next section presents four regulatory models that were identified through a literature review of different fields such as institutional economics, economic sociology, urban planning, and so on and that provide the theoretical framework to analyze alternative (extralegal) regulatory systems. Then, we use the theoretical framework to analyze systematically the regulatory systems in the informal and illegal sectors represented by our two cases.

Regulation and Organizational Models

The concept of market failures (in the form of asymmetric information, public goods, monopolies, and externalities) is the main argument used by mainstream economists to justify state regulation of market activities (Levy 1995). This is particularly necessary to manage the risk faced by large-scale enterprises that cannot use face-to-face regulatory means. However, the state is hardly monolithic or omnipresent, even in the First World. The concept of a "frustrated state" which is unable to enforce its own mandates certainly applies to Latin America and even the United States where drug trafficking is concerned.

Where the state is unable to fully enforce its regulatory system, alternative forms of regulation emerge that some authors refer to as extralegal (de Soto 1989). Furthermore, these alternative forms of regulation may provide new opportunities for those who, because of their lack of economic and social capital, are relatively disadvantaged within the formal economy.

The literature of economic sociology and institutional economics is valuable in analyzing these alternative forms since it points to social variables such as friendship, family, and other types of social ties (Ben-Porath 1980; Coleman 1988) that play an important role in market activities. Markets are seen as embedded in broader social relationships rather than separate from society (Granovetter 1985). Finally, institutional economics focuses on the role of institutions and (criminal or social) organizations in market activities (Williamson 1981).

We will describe four main types of regulatory models: (1) the laissez-faire model, (2) the government regulatory model (both drawn from mainstream economics), (3) the social-institutional model, and (4) the mafia regulatory model (both drawn from institutional economics and economic sociology).

The Laissez-Faire Model

In the pure laissez-faire model the assumption is that normal social regulation is sufficient to manage behavior in the marketplace. Market forces regulate the interaction of economic agents who decide to enter or leave transactions on the basis of rational assessments of their self-interest. Each agent seeks to maximize his or her resources by agreeing to trade when conditions appear advantageous and closing up shop when they are not, creating a social balance between the average cost of providing goods and services and the price of those items on the market. Different actors have different positions relative to the market, however. Some may be forced into exchanges because they lack essential resources, such as Marx's proletariat, and thus may trade even at a disadvantage. Others benefit from the control of key resources such as prime locations or key assets that allow them to trade consistently at an advantage. This differential appears in the concept of *rent:* an advantage or disadvantage derived from one's position in the market, whether this be geographic, social (status), resource based, or even psychological.

For example, absent an outside system of regulations, and following their rational self-interest, street vendors will compete for places where they can get the highest rents.[2] V. N. Jagganathan's (1987) peanut sellers and William

Alonso's beach competition case (1975) are examples of the laissez-faire model. Jagganathan (1987, 71–74) concludes that territorial control and the appropriation of locational rents would be determined by the ability to defend the territory, which is a function of the optimum benefits (profits) which can be extracted from the site. The equilibrium territory would be where marginal (optimal) revenue of the location is equal to the marginal costs of defending the location. The rent is thus equivalent to the cost of maintaining effective control over the space or concept defended.

Where revenues are scarce—such as in poor neighborhoods where little economic activity takes place, these costs are low or even nonexistent. In effect, anyone can set up a stall at any time, and normal social relationships are adequate to regulate the economic behavior. But where revenues are large, such as in highly traveled areas with many potential consumers, or lucrative products such as illegal drugs, competition for space will become intense, driving up the defense costs. In effect, heightened competition will surpass the capacity of the normal social regulatory system to restrain conflict. Without any other regulatory system, such high costs may create incentives for violence, with the use of force substituting for the distribution of marginal utilities: there is value to fight over. Taken to an extreme, the result is social chaos, a Hobbesian war of all against all.

Of course, even in apparently chaotic markets some regulation exists in the form of informal agreements between actors based on preexisting or even ad hoc social conventions. Nevertheless, this solution is typically limited to situations in which all the relevant actors can come to a face-to-face social understanding. As markets become more impersonal and more lucrative, however, more actors threaten to invade the scene and small-scale social regulation becomes untenable. According to Jagganathan (1987), the social chaos that results from the laissez-faire approach can be avoided by developing a new "technology" or an agent that would control the use and allocation of urban space. The regulatory agents could be government, mafias, or social institutions that the group itself develops to self-regulate.

The Government Regulatory Model

The modern bureaucratic state evolved along with the growth of an increasingly impersonal market system in which universal values (currency) allow exchanges to take place among multiple value systems without regard to persons or social relations. This process required the intervention of a higher power that stood above everyday social life: the state. As Weber argues, without the modern state, modern industrial society would be impossible.

The Coase theorem—which states that in the absence of transaction costs, resources would be allocated to the highest and best use—explains why government regulation is needed (Holcombe 1996). Transaction costs refer to the charges of exchanging goods, which can be divided into direct outlays (time and effort) and indirect losses, or transaction risks, such as the possibility that one of the agents in the exchange may fail to fulfill his or her end of the bargain, or that intervention from another party may disrupt the transaction. These two elements have an inverse relationship: all risks can be hypothetically reduced to near zero by taking the additional time and effort to trade goods directly (bartering), collecting full information about the market, and so on, but in practice this would doom almost all but the most local attempts at exchange. The only way to expand transactions is to create systems of trust backed up by social norms, which will work as long as exchanges take place within preexisting social networks. In order for trust to grow beyond the interpersonal sphere, the exchanging agents must be able to appeal to a more powerful agent to enforce contracts. Thus, the development of the market and the development of the state go hand in hand in most theories of social development.

In this model, the government is the agent that regulates the use and allocation of social utilities. As economists frequently observe, government becomes the "remedy" for market failures (Levy 1995, 82–91). In essence, the role of the state in this model is to prevent overt conflict in the marketplace by protecting a defined set of social utilities from which rents can be extracted. This has a series of important effects for the state and the marketplace: (1) regulatory norms and limits on allowed activities control transaction costs, but also raise the threshold of independent economic activity, making it difficult for small and microbusinesses to compete in the marketplace; (2) the lack of competition effectively creates a higher value for the rents that remain; and (3) the state can extract a portion of those rents in the form of taxes to fund its own activities.

A secondary effect of this function is that greater inequality is inserted into the marketplace as regulations and their attendant costs are used to manage risks. Because transaction risks arise under circumstances of lack of trust, they are highest for large economic enterprises operating in impersonal markets.[3] At the same time, they are difficult to predict, thus increasing capital risk factors. In other words, all other factors being equal, transaction risks are more problematic for larger, capital-intensive enterprises. Regulatory costs, on the other hand, can be predicted, making assessments about capital investments easier and more manageable by larger firms. Lawyers and accountants can reduce the unit costs of compliance, while large labor plants allow greater flexibility in complying with regulatory requirements.[4] Large firms and elites also have an edge in being able to affect the way such regulations are written to reflect their needs over those of smaller firms (as well as obtaining legal exemptions when necessary, such as tax credits given to large investors).[5] Furthermore, regulatory costs are often regressive in nature: they often have high initial threshold levels, meaning that there is a declining marginal cost for each added unit of regulated economic activity carried out by a specific firm.

Smaller, low-capital and labor intensive firms, however, find that this shift from transaction risks to regulatory costs creates a competitive disadvantage relative to larger firms. Because of their small size, which allows them to operate on a face-to-face level, they often operate through preexisting social networks. This gives them greater flexibility—they are better equipped than large firms are to manage transaction risks. On the other hand, the rise of regulatory costs puts them at a disadvantage relative to larger firms. It is more difficult for them to hire specialized staff to deal with technical aspects of regulatory systems, and labor management requirements (such as insurance, safety, and so on) are more costly to fulfill. In effect, overregulation may occur, since most of their needs are already met by preexisting social regulatory systems, and they do not necessarily compete in the impersonal market spaces that state regulation is designed to ameliorate.[6]

Normal social regulation works well for small, local economic transactions, but is exorbitantly expensive for large enterprises. Government regulation levels out these transaction costs and thus reverses the relative advantage of small over large enterprises. The end result is that state regulatory systems create an advantage for larger, more capital-intensive enterprises and tend to squeeze smaller, more labor-intensive enterprises out of the formal marketplace. Because the state acts to exclude other economic activities, these "costs of formality" (de Soto 1989; Cross 1998b) effectively create a protected market and thus a form of rents for those firms that are able to meet requirements: they are effectively protected from competition from smaller, less capital-intensive enterprises.[7]

Hypothetically, any economic practice can be regulated, and there are many examples of activities that we often think of as informal, such as street vending, which are heavily regulated in some areas. For instance, street vendors in Washington (Spalther-Roth 1988) and El Paso (Staudt 1996) or vendors that sell at fairs and festivals get their permits directly from local government.

Even at this level, however, the general rule applies: government regulation implies direct and indirect regulatory costs, which therefore limits the number of vendors who can afford a legal permit. Other vendors may be excluded from this system because they cannot meet the basic conditions for entrance into the market. The effect is often that the few vendors who survive are allowed to charge higher prices, effectively benefiting from the "rents" provided by state protection.[8]

The effective level of these rents rests on the ability of the state to enforce the regulatory system. The government control model is optimized when the state is able to effectively enforce its regulatory measures throughout the market, since all firms are then forced to pay those costs. Nevertheless, under conditions of "low state-integration" (Cross 1998b) a combination of factors—confusing and contradictory requirements, competition between agencies for resources, lack of information, corruption among state agents, and so on—allow some individuals to escape all or some of the regulations. In this case, some economic actors, and particularly the smallest, could operate outside the regulatory system by staying hidden or by bribing low-level government officials to overlook noncompliance.[9] As a result, a laissez-faire model may reappear on the fringes or even in the middle of the "formal" regulatory system, which again returns from regulatory costs to transaction costs.[10] With notable exceptions that often involve recent immigrant groups, the United States has historically had a relatively effective regulatory system, which limits the size of the informal sector. Mexico, much like many other Latin American nations, faces many more difficulties enforcing regulations. Not only is corruption a hindrance, but also the political needs of state actors often lead them to rely on the informal sector for political support.

Total state regulation and pure market anarchy are not the only options available, however. As many scholars studying the informal and illegal markets have noted, extralegal systems of regulation may exist, which have been described by some as "semi-formality" (de Soto 1989; Cross 1998b), in particular the social-institutional regulatory model and the mafia regulatory control model.

The Social-Institutional Regulatory Model

The social-institutional regulatory model describes the situation of informal commerce in many developing countries. According to E. M. Smith (1988), there are four main reasons why the state may be absent from these informal market activities: (1) they may be seen as part of a lifestyle; (2) they may seem too trivial to be tracked or regulated; (3) they may be important but ignored because of the monitoring costs; and (4) they may provide the state some political capital. In other words, the costs of regulating these sectors cannot be justified given other needs for state resources and the high cost of and lack of benefits from policing this sector.

The economic sociology literature offers a great deal of insight into how social relations influence market activities that are particularly relevant to the informal sector (see Ben-Porath 1980, Granovetter 1985, Coleman 1988, de Soto 1989, Portes and Sensenbrenner 1993, and Portes 1994). These authors agree that social factors play an important role in the way economic activities and markets organize; market transactions are "embedded" (Granovetter 1985) in social relations.

According to Ragui Assaad (1993), there are four principal paradigms put forward for the study of informal or social institutions: transaction costs, agency theory, property rights, and collective action. These paradigms are not necessarily mutually exclusive and together can provide a useful theoretical framework for understanding the process of informal regulation.

O. E. Williamson (1981) argues that "transaction cost economizing" is crucial for studying and understanding organizations. Specifically, organization is seen as the least-cost solution to problems of uncertainty in the business environment. Avner Ben-Ner, J. M. Montias, and Egon Neuberger (1993) point out that organizations deal with problems of opportunism derived from the lack of information. Drawing their ideas from agency theory, they note that organizations are set up in such a way that minimizes technical-administrative and principal and agent problems. The property rights approach focuses on "the role of institutions in guiding decision making within the economy by specifying and assigning property rights" (Assaad 1993, 928). Furthermore, Jagganathan (1987) observes that *usufruct rights* are the only property entitlements that matter and that the role of informal institutions is to administer "social usufruct rights." The main feature in this type of right is that it does not receive legal recognition and therefore cannot be legally traded or used as collateral.[11] The collective action approach focuses on the role of institutions in overcoming the type of problem known as "free riding" so that people can be excluded from the benefits of the group if they do not pay their share or comply with the group's norms. This approach maintains that people are better off if they cooperate.

In summary, social institutions or organizations become mechanisms to minimize transaction costs, resolve problems between agent and principal, and solve free rider problems by forcing people to team up to defend themselves.

Examples of these informal institutions or forms of organization by street vendors are found in Peru (de Soto 1989), Colombia (Bromley 1978; Nelson 1992), Ecuador (Teltscher 1992 and 1994), Mexico (Cross 1998a; Peña 1999b), and Nigeria (Smith and Lutrell 1994). These authors show that in the absence of effective and efficient government regulation vendors develop their own institutions to regulate themselves to avoid social chaos.

Using the definition suggested by de Soto and developed by Manuel Castells and Alejandro Portes (1989), we can regard informal activities as legal activities conducted outside the regulatory control of the state. They avoid regulatory outlays but then become affected by additional transaction costs, including the risks of evading regulatory enforcement. De Soto (1989) describes these as the "costs of formality" and the "costs of informality" respectively. As an example consider the problems faced by a street vendor who must stay hidden from official view to avoid regulatory enforcement, which limits her potential market to times and places where she is unlikely to attract attention, but must sell aggressively to make a living, which is likely to draw attention to her actions. The dilemma is a balance between "evasion" costs and "punishment" costs (Cross 1998b). Any truly laissez-faire approach can only follow evasion techniques, limiting the potential market. To go beyond that level, vendors form organizations in order to resist state enforcement techniques by working together to either suborn low-level officials or press for an informal arrangement with mid-level state officials. However, this process assumes that the activity in question can claim some social legitimacy in order to justify the process of negotiation between state actors and social organizations. Where that legitimacy is lacking, such as in the case of activity that is considered clearly criminal, open negotiation becomes impossible and social organizations provide no advantage.

The Mafia Regulatory Model

The mafia regulatory model is another form of organization or model that arises in a region or market segment characterized as having a "power vacuum that the state is unable to fill" (Skaperdas and Syropoulos 1995, 63). Moreover, Annelise Anderson (1995) identifies three "conditions" under which Mafiosi develop: (1) the "abdication of power" by the state, (2) "excessive bureaucratic power," and (3) "the potential of illegal markets" (Anderson 1995, 35). In addition, Herschel Grossman (1995) points out that criminal organizations become "alternative providers of public services" particularly as "alternative enforcers of property rights" (Grossman 1995, 144). In other words, where the state is unable to enforce rent-seeking privileges, mafias may emerge that carry out this function.

Earlier we discussed a number of reasons why the state may fail to adequately regulate a sector of the economy. A mafia-style organization emerges in advanced societies most commonly when the state tries to repress specific activities by making them illegal, in which case regulation shifts to a policing function by virtue of which the state attempts to regulate the supply and demand of the proscribed products by increasing transaction costs. In this model, street vendors or illegal drug mafias perform similar functions to the social-institutional model; they regulate competition and protect participants from state action in exchange for part of the rent vendors obtain from the territory that the mafia-style organization controls. The methods used, however, may differ.

Regulation, Informality, and Illegality

The analysis by Castells and Portes (1989) of the dimensions of the informal sector is useful for understanding these issues in more depth and identifying some key differences between the social-institutional organization model and the mafia model, which policymakers often confuse. The authors identify three dimensions in the economy—formal, informal, and criminal. In the formal sector, legal products are produced following the state regulatory system; in the informal sector, legal products are produced outside the state regulatory system; and in the criminal sector illegal products are produced outside the regulatory system. In practice, of course, it is difficult to distinguish between legal ends and regulatory means. Products seen as illegal, such as marijuana or cocaine, are in fact legal when they are produced and distributed in accordance with strict regulatory guidelines. Thus, illegal drug sales could be seen as a market that provides a legal good in unregulated circumstances, making it not a different category of offense but simply a more serious offense than selling carrots without a license. Similarly, videocassette or DVD sales may seem innocuous but may violate intellectual property rights legislation, and cellular phones may seem completely legal, unless they are smuggled into the country or stolen from a warehouse. Similarly, failing to follow regulatory practices may be illegal in itself. Is the failure to pay taxes (used by many as a benchmark of informality) simply the avoidance of regulatory norms, or is it a crime that taints the perpetrator? What about the possibility of criminal negligence in small-scale workshops leading to injury and even the death of employees? Thus, the delineation of product types is not as clear-cut as initially suggested, and therefore the boundary between illegal and informal activities exists as a series of gradations, much like the distinction between the formal and informal sectors.

The main differentiation is the relationship between economic activity and state enforcement. Activities against which proscription rules are strictly and consistently enforced can only exist in opposition to the state. Regulation in those cases must occur in the face of state antagonism, and thus must make up for the inability to appeal to the state on any level to reduce transaction costs that arise between economic actors. The state's role as the enforcer of norms and contracts through its "monopoly of the legitimate use or threat of force" (to use Weber's classic formula) must be replaced by another organization that can use violence or the threat of violence to impose agreements: a form of mafia. The criminal organization will "regulate" illegal products such as drugs or money laundering.

On the other hand, activities that can claim some legitimacy, such as street vendors under certain circumstances, can still appeal to the state for some regulatory guidance, but will simply supplement this role by forming organizations to regulate markets where legal products are sold. That is, products associated with criminal organizations are outlawed and socially unacceptable, whereas activities associated with street vending are seen as legal and socially acceptable. Table 1 shows the four types of regulation.

Thus, the fundamental difference between "informal" and "illegal" markets is not based on the activity per se, but on claims of legitimacy and the resulting ability to negotiate a level of coexistence between legal (state) and extralegal forms of regulation.

Street Vendors in Mexico City

Street vending in Mexico City bears some relationship with street vending in many other Third World cities, but also some differences.[12] We present them here as one way economic actors operating outside the formal regulatory system can create alternative systems of regulation. Although city officials have declared them illegal on a number of occasions, street vendors in Mexico City appear to be remarkably successful in creating alternative systems. We have argued elsewhere that their effectiveness can be partly attributed to the corporatist structure of the Institutional Revolutionary Party (PRI), which

Table 1 Regulatory models and organizational forms

Model	Situational dynamics	Organizational form	Types of costs	Motives	Outcome
Laissez-faire	Ind. and family firms Local market Low competition	Face-to-face social conventions	Low regulatory costs, but growth increases transaction risks	Individual rationality	Social chaos as market grows
Formal/state regulatory	Large firms Regional or global market High competition	Public sector regulation of market norms	High regulatory costs; low transaction risks	Political benefits (taxes, legitimacy)	Stable market with high overhead favoring large-scale businesses
Informal/ social-institutional	Ind. & family firms Local market High competition Legitimate activity	Member-based associations in negotiation with state	Medium regulatory costs; medium transaction risks	Collective interests	Relatively stable market with low overhead favoring small-scale businesses
Illegal/mafia	Medium-size firms Local, regional or global market High competition Illegitimate activity	Control of market by use of violence in conflict with state	High regulatory costs; high transaction costs	Rent-seeking	Market unstable because of disruption and violence

needed popular organizations such as street vendor unions to maintain their control over the state for over sixty years (Cross 1998a). In addition, street vendors in Mexico have been able to appeal to a constitutional right to work and to conduct trade embedded in the 1917 constitution. But the rise of similar organizations has also been documented in other cases, from the United States (Spalther-Ross 1988) to Asia, Africa, and Latin America (de Soto 1989).

Even within Mexico City there is a broad diversity of vendors who have different regulatory stances with regard to the state. We will identify five broad relational categories that account for the vast majority of vendors in the city. It should be kept in mind, however, that these relationships are dynamic and have shifted radically over time. For example, while all forms of street vending were severely repressed in the 1950s and 1960s, the populist administrations of Luis Echeverría (1970–76) and López Portillo (1976–82) tended to treat vendors with benign neglect as long as they were supportive of the PRI. After the fiscal crisis of the early 1980s and the shift to neoliberal policies, the state defined vendors as tax evaders and adopted policies that unsuccessfully attempted to control them.

1 *Independent neighborhood vendors:* In marginal neighborhoods, street vending consists of local people who may set up stalls outside their houses, local stores, or schools peddling to neighbors or clients of other establishments as they pass by. This is completely unregulated since state regulatory enforcement rarely enters into their areas.

2 *Concentrations:* In the city center, or in other prime market locations, larger street markets have formed on a daily or weekly basis built around either high pedestrian concentrations or historical marketing patterns that attract clients from around the city. Misnamed "ambulatory" vendors by the city, these are usually permanent markets in which each seller has a fixed pitch, often with metal tube stalls that can be removed if necessary. Around the historical city center there are a number of these market areas, typically offering durable goods, such as Tepito, La Merced, San Cosme, and others, that date back to the nineteenth century. Given urban renewal plans to gentrify many of these areas, these vendors have a rocky relationship with the city, with periodic but generally ineffective attempts at eliminating them (Gordon 1997).

3 *Tianguis:* Another established form of street vending is the *tianguis*, which is a street market with a core of basic goods such as fresh foods, that sets up in a specific area for only one day a week. These are often tied into a circuit, with the same core group of vendors working each

day of the week in different neighborhoods. While still operating without legal permits, these vendors have generally settled into a stable *modus operandi* with the city because they provide an important neighborhood service with a minimum of disruption.

4 *Metro vendors/Toreros:* There are a number of vendors who operate in high-transit areas but who use their mobility to avoid regulations, such as *toreros* who sell at intersections to passing cars, carry their goods with them, or display their goods on a cloth that can be rapidly picked up in the case of regulatory enforcement. Another example is vendors in the city's underground transport system (the "metro"), who go from carriage to carriage selling their goods. In the metro particularly the city has refused to grant any legitimacy to these sellers, claiming that the underground transport system is private property and thus that the vendors have no constitutional rights whatsoever in regard to it.

5 *Public Markets/Plazas:* there have been sporadic attempts by the city to formalize small-retail trade by building public markets and commercial plazas with large numbers of small stalls that are designed to relocate street vendors into specific areas off the street where they can be subjected to greater regulatory control. One such attempt took place in the historical city center in 1993–94, and resulted in the building of twenty-four plazas with approximately ten thousand stalls, although it was only partially successful in its goal of ridding the historical center of vendors (Cross 1998b).

The government has attempted to keep track of the number of *tianguis* and concentration vendors, as well as those in public markets and plazas, but their numbers fluctuate by season and according to other factors such as changes in enforcement patterns. The number of *toreros*, metro vendors, and independent neighborhood vendors can often only be guessed at. Estimates fluctuate from 250,000 to 400,000.

Laissez-faire vending, in the sense of economic participation that relies only on face-to-face interactions, has the lowest regulatory costs, but really operates in its purest sense only among independent neighborhood vendors. Where larger concentrations of vendors gather, two factors limit the laissez-faire system: the competition between vendors for space, which threatens to dissolve into social chaos, and whether they will attract government regulatory attention because of complaints from formal businesses or neighbors. Both of these represent added transaction risks from the standpoint of the individual vendor, since either confrontation with fellow merchants or a government crackdown creates the risk of market disruptions and inventory losses. On the other hand, full formalization, which is one way of dealing with these costs, represents a far greater expense than it is worth. Licenses may be too expensive, too limiting, or simply not available. Furthermore, a free rider problem emerges: if some vendors pay the costs of formalization, they may reduce some problems for the market, but they now have a competitive disadvantage with other vendors who fail to do so.

Social-institutional Organizations: One solution to this dilemma is the formation of vendor organizations that claim control of the entire market area. The organizational leadership can adjudicate vendor conflicts internally, maintain a certain level of control to limit external complaints, and also form a collective front to regulatory agents who are then confronted with a political dilemma, since an organization can mobilize the resources of the vendors to attract public attention to their concerns and appeal to political figures for support. In Mexico this process was facilitated by the corporatist nature of the PRI's control over the state, which allowed such organizations to become members of the party, giving them some access to political support. Furthermore, the corporatist structure of the state supported the idea that negotiations would be carried out with the organization rather than with individual vendors, meaning that free riders were eliminated: nonmembers would be excluded from the marketplace. Even with the decline of the PRI, a similar relationship has emerged between many vendors and the PRD, which dominates politically in Mexico City. The result is that virtually all the vendors in *tianguis* and concentrations are organized, although through a number of different organizations that compete among themselves for space, vendors, and access to political support.

In effect, these organizations became political and economic intermediaries between the state and individual vendors. As Table 2 shows, organizations were seen as most effective by members at controlling conflict that emerged between vendors and between vendors and the state. The negotiation between the state and organizations established a "quasi-formal" system of regulations that were largely enforced at the market level by the organizations themselves. The state's role was somewhat fuzzily divided between an ideal set of "norms" that purported to regulate individual conduct and a pragmatic application of ad hoc and shifting agreements between regulatory agencies and the organizations. The organizations, themselves, while nominally democratic, were more likely to be run autocratically by a leadership clique that was better able to maintain order internally and enforce a common front with regard to officials. The result gave an advantage to the more stable organizations

Table 2   The functions and effectiveness of street vendor organizations

Function	Mean	Effectiveness
Enforce respect for assigned spaces	1.77	Very effective
Negotiating with authorities	1.77	
Help with permits	2.00	
System of stall distribution	2.00	
Conflict mediation among vendors	2.07	
Enforce work schedule	2.20	
Punishment system	2.23	
Protection from authorities' extortion	2.27	
Cleaning services	2.47	
Safety of vendor and client	2.63	
Legal services	2.70	
Help when merchandise is stolen	3.10	Ineffective
Grand Mean	2.27	
S.D.	.3972	
Upper (95% C. I.)	2.51	
Lower (95% C. I.)	2.01	

SOURCE: Street vendors survey, summer 1998.
NOTE: N = 30. In the responses, "very effective" = 1, "effective" = 2, "ineffective" = 3, and "very ineffective" = 4.

over officials who were often changed every few years as positions within the state were rotated between different elites. That corruption and quid-pro-quo agreements about electoral support was a common feature of this system reflects not the evil nature of leaders and officials but rather the need to make sense of the gap between ideals and pragmatism.

State Regulation: in areas where state regulations were more heavily enforced, such a solution was not feasible. Two results could emerge in these situations. During periods of heightened state focus on street vending, city leaders emerged who were willing to dedicate large amounts of state resources to imposing a resolution to this "problem." During the 1960s Ernest P. Uruchurtu, mayor of Mexico City from 1952 to 1966, built hundreds of new markets to relocate sixty-thousand street vendors and applied a series of incentives, both positive (e.g., low rents) and negative (e.g., an active imprisonment policy) to force vendors to occupy them (Cross 1996). In 1993–94, Mayor Camacho Solis, under pressure from then president Carlos Salinas de Gortari, built twenty-four "plazas comerciales" for ten thousand vendors in the historical center (Cross 1997). Lower-level officials and vendor leaders were forced to negotiate within the context of these imposed solutions. In both cases, the imposed solutions faced substantial short-term and long-term obstacles that consumed unsustainable amounts of political and financial resources, and limited their success until a return to earlier patterns that allowed the reemergence of street vending.

Many street vendors found that they were unable to afford the added costs involved with enclosed markets (rents, lack of direct access to pedestrians, often exacerbated by poor site planning and abysmal floor plans and stall designs), and in interviews carried out with vendors shortly after the 1993–94 project, some claimed that they had been forced into poverty and others claimed to be suicidal. Other vendors found the market or plaza systems to be an advantage over the street, and thus welcomed their transition into a more secure status within the regulatory system (although a low level of regulatory enforcement was often a part of the incentives for moving into the markets).

In a small survey carried out among former street vendors working in plazas (Table 3), the trade-off between street vending and plaza vending appeared to be largely one of income versus security and stability. In addition, the limits of the social-institutional regulation were seen from the perspective of vendors who wanted to be more secure or who found that the "community solidarity" required by such organizations limited their individual initiative. For example, one vendor claimed "[street vendor] . . . organizations restrain people's success because when people want another stall, the organization believes you already have achieved success and you are not entitled to become better than the rest; therefore, they don't give you another stall. Organizations are only a channel to get a fixed and secure location in the street. Success depends on the merchant and the product."

For more ambitious vendors, the quasi-formal social-institutional system represents a disadvantage because it ultimately cannot guarantee capital inputs to the same extent that the formal system can. At the same time, organizations and their leaders benefit from the insecurity of their members: within the plazas, their role becomes reduced or switches to a purely administrative function that ultimately makes them subservient to the state. One result of the market program of the 1960s and the plaza program of the 1990s was, therefore, to weaken preexisting street vendor organizations that "bought into" the project, setting up a sometimes violent struggle for the street space left open until a new system of negotiated rights could be established.

Mafias: Street vendor organizations in Mexico City are often accused of being "mafias" by city officials and formal business leaders who see street

Table 3   The comparative advantages of street vending and formal vending (according to former street vendors)

The advantages of street vending	%	The advantages of formal vending	%
Lower operation costs	44.0	Convenience	47.0
Higher sales	28.0	Security	28.0
Higher profits	25.0	Independence from street vendor organizations	25.0
Location near customers	25.0	Better care of merchandise and larger stock	25.0
None	19.0	Stable clientele base	16.0
Better options for growth	3.1	Higher profits	9.0
More freedom	3.1	Schedule	6.0
		None	3.0

SOURCE: Survey data from former street vendors.
NOTES: $N = 32$. Percentages exceed 100 percent because of multiple responses. The question was open and the answers were coded as dummy variables.

vending as a problem, but this designation does not properly apply to most of the organizations in negotiation with the state, although they have some capacity to sanction members and violence might occur in cases where there is instability within or between organizations such as a fight between rival organizations for control of a particular area or internal competition for control of an organization. In these cases, the normal regulatory function of the organization fails to provide solutions, and often city officials have to intervene to prevent further chaos.

But in those cases in which state officials refused to officially negotiate with vendors, mafia-type solutions emerged as the only alternative form of regulation. The best example is in the city's metro system, where vending was strictly outlawed and thus any compromise was unavailable. Vending did emerge in the system, at times at a very large scale. In the early 1990s the city counted about five thousand vendors in the metro and collected criminal files on those who claimed to be leaders, in preparation for a massive clampdown on metro vending that was carried out in 1992. "They were criminals, and that's why we weren't going to deal with them," one high-level official claimed (Cross 1998b), but in fact their criminal records were largely related to their vending activities.

The vendors were forced to resort to mafia-style tactics because the lack of any negotiation with the state pushed them to operate without the ability to appeal to the state for redress. Instead, they relied on bribes to low-level officials (station guards and managers) and the threat of direct physical violence to make sure that vendors in the areas they controlled helped pay their share of these costs. In some cases, it could be argued that low-level officials created their own mafias, using their position to force vendors to pay bribes in order to avoid being arrested. This state-mafia system is also reported in the historical center, where thousands of *toreros* have reemerged after the street vendor organizations in the area agreed to move into plazas.

Even after the crackdown, some itinerant vendors have continued selling in the train carriages themselves. These sellers are largely hidden from the view of the regular metro security force tied to the stations. Nevertheless, some regulation is still needed internally to prevent informal merchants from bunching up on the trains and becoming too obvious to officials. As a result organizations have emerged. Typically, these organizations "control" a specific metro line, or a portion of a longer line by charging entry fees to prospective vendors and weekly dues. On one such line, the organization "Don Pancho" controls 120 vendors who must pay about US$30 initially and US$1 every other week. The costs of membership are modest because these positions are not very lucrative. Costs must be kept low also to prevent vendors from moving to another organization, to keep their loyalty—thus avoiding a rebellion or takeover—and to solicit their support for actions against nonmembers. Thus, mafia-type organizations may exist but they are relatively weak and not sharply distinguished in their actions from regular street vendor associations. Still, the main criteria of mafia organization—that they operate a regulatory system that contradicts state regulations and laws, is still applicable, although we will see in the next section that this is far more relevant to lucrative illegal activities such as drug sales.

In summary, street vending, where it can claim some legitimacy, oscillates between laissez-faire, social organization, and state regulation. Mafia-type organizations only emerge when the state refuses to recognize any rights for vending. In this case, the state claimed that the metro facilities were private property and thus the constitutional guarantee to work and trade did not apply. This prevented the vendors from establishing any negotiable rights within the political system. Although Mexican officials and elites often claim that all vendor associations are mafias, even the metro vendors can be seen to form mafia-style organizations in only the weakest possible sense. This is largely due to the low level of earnings available to the vendors. In addition, while negotiation with the state is not a feasible option, the enforcement risks are still rather mild, generally consisting of small fines, short periods of detention, and possible physical abuse. In the next section we will use the case of crack dealers in New York City to compare street vendor organizations with the much more violent types of mafia-style organizations that emerge when state harassment has a much stronger and more consistent bite.

Crack Sales in New York City

Illegal drug vendors face many of the same problems as informal vendors, but with higher risks because of the severe penalties and more consistent enforcement policies they face. Like informal vendors, there is a trade-off between the transaction costs involved with making contact with potential buyers and the transaction risks involved with becoming too visible to authorities, but it lacks the type of legitimacy that vendors of less destructive products can claim.[13]

Crack emerged initially in inner-city neighborhoods that had faced severe economic downturns in the 1970s (Mieczkowski 1990; Williams 1992). In those areas "cocaine and crack . . . represented new economic opportunities where legal economic activities had been lost" (Fagan 1992, 103) and large numbers of young people were, because of poor educational facilities and a collapsed formal economy, largely unemployable in the formal sector (Wilson 1997). Because of the low level of police attention to these areas in the 1970s and 1980s, it was not uncommon for drug markets to exist relatively unmolested. As a result, the most common form of organization was that of the user/dealer who worked freelance and considered himself an entrepreneur. Because of the relative openness of sales, it was easy to attract customers, and the crack market grew fast and profitably. "By 1988, crack had become the most frequently sold and most lucrative substance in the street drug market" (Johnson, Golub, and Fagan 1995, 281). Drug retail exchanges would therefore be best characterized during this period as laissez-faire markets constrained only by occasional police harassment.

By the mid-1980s crack was portrayed as a major threat to society. New resources were assigned to urban police forces, legislation requiring mandatory minimum sentences was passed, and civil forfeiture laws allowed police departments to benefit directly from the war on drugs (Jensen and Gerber 1996). The effect was heightened police attention to crack markets (Johnson and Natarajan 1995, 50), and in response crack markets moved underground in two major patterns. One was a less conspicuous continuation of street selling, with freelance dealers catering more carefully to known customers only (Jacobs 1996a, 1996b; Jacobs and Miller 1998). Another reaction was to create mafia-style organizations—either in terms of more organized street sales, or in terms of the development of crack houses, which provided enclosed locations for the peddling of crack (Mieczkowski 1992). These organizations provided jobs in low-level distribution for crack dealers who could not survive as entrepreneurs either because of lack of skills or because they had lost their capital through overuse of their own product. Those organizations also offered some protection from arrest by distributing roles and responsibilities to make it more difficult to tie crack to sales:

> The vertical organization structure makes it difficult for police to arrest "sellers" with standard buy-and-bust techniques because a variety of roles are performed by several persons: "holders" conceal bulk crack supplies on the street, "counters" or "money men" check and receive buyers' money, "hand-off men" provide the drug to buyers, "lookouts" warn of police or competitors, "muscle men" serve as guards and intimidate passersby and competitors, "lieutenants" or "crew bosses" supervise the whole street operation and collect money at regular intervals, "storekeepers" commingle drug money with legal store income, "runners" take cocaine to different buyers, "transporters" transfer larger amounts across state lines and "baby-sit" in prearranged locations. The lead "supplier" maintains separate apartments for "stashes" of drugs and money, as well as several locations for "packaging" and "selling." (Johnson, Golub, and Fagan 1990, 19)

J. M. Hagedorn (1994) and J. A. Fagan (1992, 115–16) make similar arguments about why one or the other type of market emerged at this point. Fagan noticed that in Harlem, where the crack market primarily serviced locals, less-conspicuous freelance dealers predominated. By contrast, in Washington Heights, where the crack market was still experiencing growth and furthermore serviced many middle-class users who came to the neighborhood in search of drugs, hierarchical organizations predominated. Hagedorn noted the same pattern in Milwaukee, with more profitable and expanding markets becoming organized while stable and less lucrative markets remained freelance. Thus, organization appeared to grow in markets where social network patterns were insufficient to resolve the problems caused by the increased transaction risks of impersonal market growth.

Ric Curtis and Travis Wendel (2000) suggest that as the crack markets have matured and stagnated, many of these complex organizations (which they refer to as "corporations") have become less profitable. Less well organized, "socially bonded" organizations have taken over much of the business that remains. These organizations are based more on loose family or social ties among cooperating dealers, who share the market in specific areas. While these groups still retain mafia-style elements, such as control over territory, that restrict the need to aggressively (and obviously) compete for customers, they do not need a tight structure because the market has shrunk to the point that social networks are often sufficient as a regulatory mechanism.[14]

In other words, like street vendors, crack dealers organize primarily in response to market pressures and state antagonism. However, given their lack of legitimacy, there is no benefit to the formation of social-institutional organizations that negotiate their regulatory processes with the state. Instead, when they organize, they will choose mafia-style articulations that rely on violence or the threat of violence to regulate the marketplace and reduce their enforcement risks.

Conclusion: Regulation and Risk Factors

The legal/formal regulatory system emerged with the development of a modern mass market to help businesses and individuals deal with the problem of transaction costs in an impersonal market place where face-to-face social conventions were impossible to enforce. As we have argued, this regulatory system tends to favor larger businesses and discriminate against smaller ones. As a result, the only feasible option for most individuals within this system is to be dependent on these large firms. That, in turn, has spurred the development of one of the most important aspects of the regulatory system itself: the labor code.

However, as J. C. Cross and B. D. Johnson (2000) argue, the modern mass market has not and perhaps cannot penetrate into all spheres of exchange. Both "luxury" markets and "poverty" markets may be difficult to service with mass production and distribution techniques, and high regulatory costs may make them unprofitable for formal firms. Illegal goods, of course, are also difficult to offer through the formal market. Needs remain, however, whether they are "basic" requirements for food and clothes, or the "sinful" craving for drugs. At the same time, social inequality in all its forms reproduces itself in the formal economic sphere, creating not only the working poor but a class of people largely excluded from formal employment. The needs listed above create a demand that cannot be met by the legal/formal sector and thus becomes available to this underclass, which can thus obtain income through either the informal or illegal sectors.

In Latin America millions of individuals and families make their living in the informal economy, relying on informal regulatory systems that are only grudgingly recognized by states. Instead, governments have created legal systems copied largely from advanced Western nations that have little relation to the problems faced by the bulk of their populations. For example, even as officials in Mexico negotiate with organizations representing vendors, they consistently plan as if those organizations did not exist, or in ways that attempt to minimize their power. One such policy is the current attempt in Mexico City to create an individualized regulatory system that would undercut vendor organizations by ignoring their control over territory. This often leads to violence between vendors and market disruption as the formal (state) and informal (social organization) regulatory systems clash.

Nevertheless, the vibrant informal sector provides real economic options that help to explain the relative lack of political instability in Latin America despite a number of recent economic recessions. It also provides options to the illegal economy. Those alternatives often do not exist in the United States, where state regulation may allow street vending, but only on an individual basis. That typically excludes organizations and places the costs of street vending out of the reach of most citizens because of the insistence that sellers meet the same regulatory criteria as other businesses. As a result, in the United States often the only option to the formal sector is illegal economic activity.

In either case, laissez-faire market conditions will continue as long as practical, since it is preferable to pay no regulation costs unless it is clearly beneficial to do so. Once markets become crowded, or once state regulatory pressures are applied, internal regulatory systems will emerge as a response to the resulting growth in transaction risks. In the case of the informal sector these will most likely operate in the form of social-institutional organizations that can control growing transaction costs by adjudicating between individual vendors (reducing the potential for violence and uncertainty) and presenting a collective front to officials (reducing potential enforcement costs). This process will allow individual vendors to operate with greater (but not optimal) security and will give them some freedom to conduct their dealings. At the same time, the organization imposes some regulatory costs, but not the full costs of formalization. It also has a tendency to limit individual initiative for the good of the group, so vendors who are more ambitious, and have the capital, may find it more beneficial to move up to a more regulated environment. Thus, these organizations provide a vital role for vendors between these two extremes, and while they often confront the state in terms of vendor policy, they also work alongside the state as a supplementary form of regulation that can appeal to the authorities for mediation in the case of conflicts between organizations.

By contrast, illegal drug vendors are unable to benefit from social-institutional organizations, which cannot protect them from enforcement costs. Thus, they resort to mafia-style models. Mafias can adjudicate between members of the same group and regulate the market to some extent, but they cannot protect their members from arrest. Therefore, mafia strategies focus on organizing activities to thwart enforcement, either by keeping those activities as hidden as possible or by making it more difficult to make a case against participants. Because they are unable to appeal to any state mediation, violence may be necessary as the ultimate method of settling major disputes either internally or externally, but it should be kept in mind that the goal of a mafia is to control random violence that could emerge in a highly competitive laissez-faire market. Some street vendors in situations such as Mexico's metro, where selling cannot be collectively negotiated, find themselves in a similar position as crack dealers in New York. The difference is one of degree, not kind. Thus, it is not the type of goods and services that they sell but the type and level of enforcement that they face that differentiates informal sector activities from illegal ones.

De Soto (2000) and others have argued for a single regulatory system that would bring street vendors and other informal economic actors back under state control. Our conclusion based on the study of alternative regulatory systems rejects such a simplistic conclusion. To say that the state is not the only actor regulating the economy may seem obvious, but the implications of that statement are still far too often overlooked. We have shown that inter-mediate social regulatory forms between laissez-faire and state regulation can have an important role in allowing economic activity to emerge among those excluded from the formal sector. The question is whether those organizations should be repressed or supported. Typically, the state and even nongovernmental organizations have taken a negative or at best apathetic posture toward such orga-nizations. Even when they are tolerated, they are rarely incorporated into urban planning systems in the way that we now take for granted for corporations, which are, after all, just another example of intermediate social organization based on financial capital.

Where the activities involved do need to be suppressed, and such could be argued in the case of crack dealers, understanding the regulatory role of the organizations is the key for effective state action. However, where the activities show promise of social development objectives, such as in many cases of informal economic activity, a proper understanding of the role such organizations can play may be a vital step toward helping to control the *negative* aspects of informality, such as pollution, congestion, and exploitation, while helping to accentuate the *positive*, such as the vital provision of goods, services, and jobs in underserved market segments.

Economic sociology and institutional economics, combined with an analysis of political practices, can therefore help us to understand how different regulatory systems work together, and hopefully how they could work together more effectively. Alternative regulatory systems may confront the state, as in the case of mafia-style organizations, but in social-institutional cases there is a huge potential for states to work with organizations as allies to create regulatory systems that would be more responsive to the needs of small-scale entrepreneurs. By allowing informal businesses to remain informally regulated, the state takes care of its own regulatory needs as well as doing something far more important: enabling vendors and other informal actors to have an effective voice for their own interests and practices.

NOTES

1. Fernández-Kelly and Garcia (1989), for example, discuss this "flexibility" in the definition of informality primarily from a state-centered perspective, but their conception can also encompass the role of outside interest groups.

2. The term "rent" is used to refer to the economic benefits that a person draws from any privilege that affects their market position, whether this refers to a physical location, psychological advantage, or social, political, or economic "rights."

3. Standard firm theory argues that firm size increases as a way of controlling transaction costs, since a firm can control internal transaction costs better than external ones. However, this can only happen after state regulation of the labor market, which creates the employee as a dependent of the firm with specific legal obligations toward the firm.

4. For example, large firms can more easily accommodate requirements for specialized personnel and advanced division of labor necessitated by many regulations and comply with other labor regulations, such as providing insurance.

5. Rogelio Pérez Perdomo (1992) notes that elites are "super-citizens" with respect to the state because they are often able to use loopholes and good lawyers to get around the law, and thus are able to benefit from a legal system that protects their privileges relative to the poor but which is unable to control their own activities.

6. We speak of "overregulation" in terms of internal enterprise needs. Of course, broader social concerns for worker and consumer security may call for still greater regulation, such as in the case of sweatshops and other exploitative enterprises that take advantage of the lack of regulatory controls to take advantage of workers or consumers.

7. This is an important factor, as Tokman (1978) notes that supermarkets in Chile were unable to compete with street markets in poor neighborhoods, an observation that can be applied in many other nations.

8. The benefits, at least from a middle-class and elite perspective, can be seen in terms of decreased congestion and nuisance in the streets, for which the consumer pays with higher product costs, and potential vendors pay with the loss of their potential (albeit smaller) income.

9. The state's regulatory efficiency can be seen in terms of an optimizing dynamic of its own. An efficient regulatory state may require high costs that simply cannot be paid because of other cultural, economic, political, and social factors that impinge on the state. Thus, the level of regulatory effectiveness is a balance between the costs of applying the rules and the benefits that the state derives from this exercise, much like the issue of tax collection (Kiser and Toug 1992).

10. These are the conditions in which "formal" firms complain about "disloyal competition" because the "informals" are not paying the full costs of formality. But they typically ignore the argument that the costs of formality, if applied universally, would benefit larger firms.

11. De Soto (2000) points out that the value of these rights may amount to hundreds of millions of dollars, but this capital cannot be efficiently utilized because of its lack of legal status.

12. This section is based on research carried out by both authors in Mexico City. See Cross 1996, 1997, 1998a, and 1998b; Cross and Johnson 2000; and Peña 1999a and 1999b.

13. This section is primarily based upon secondary analysis of original data and research produced in New York City by the Natural History of Crack project. This project was carried out by National Development and Research Institutes, under a grant from the National Institute of Justice.

14. A more in-depth analysis of risk management in the illegal crack market is provided in Cross and Johnson 2000.

REFERENCES

Alonso, J., et al. 1980. *Lucha urbana y acumulación de capital.* Mexico City: La Casa Chata.
Alonso, W. 1975. "Location Theory." In *Regional Policy: Readings in Theory and Policy,* ed. W. Alonso and J. Friedman, 35–63. Cambridge: MIT Press.
Anderson, A. 1995. "Organized Crime, Mafia and Governments." In *The Economics of Organized Crime,* ed. G. Fiorentini and S. Peltzman, 33–60. Cambridge: Cambridge University Press.
Assaad, R. 1993. "Formal and Informal Institutions in the Labor Market, with Applications to the Construction Sector in Egypt." *World Development* 21:925–39.
Bairoch, P. 1973. *Urban Unemployment in Developing Countries.* Geneva: ILO.

Becker, G. S. 1968. "Crime and Punishment: An Economic Approach." *Journal of Political Economy* 76, no. 2:169–217.

Belenko, S. 1993. *Crack and the Evolution of Anti-Drug Policy.* Westport, Conn.: Greenwood Press.

Belenko, S., J. A. Fagan, and Ko-Lin Chin. 1991. "Criminal Justice Responds to Crack." *Journal of Research in Crime and Delinquency* 28:55–74.

Ben-Ner, A., J. M. Montias, and E. Neuberger. 1993. "Basic Issues in Organization: A Comprehensive Perspective." *Journal of Comparative Economics* 17:207–42.

Ben-Porath, Y. 1980. "The F-Connection: Families, Friends, and Firms and the Organization of Exchange." *Population and Development Review* 6:1–30.

Bromley, R. 1978. "Organization, Regulation and Exploitation in the So-Called 'Urban Informal Sector': The Street Traders of Cali, Colombia." *World Development* 6:1161–71.

Castells, M., and A. Portes. 1989. "World Underneath: The Origins, Dynamic, and Effects of the Informal Economy." In *The Informal Economy: Studies in Advanced and Less Developed Countries*, ed. Alejandro Portes, Manuel Castells, and Lauren Benton, 11–37. Baltimore: Johns Hopkins University Press.

Caulkins, J. P. 1997. "Modeling the Domestic Distribution Network for Illicit Drugs." *Management Science* 43, no. 10:1364–71.

Caulkins, J. P., B. D. Johnson, A. Taylor, and L. Taylor. 1999. "What Drug Dealers Tell Us About Their Costs of Doing Business." *Journal of Drug Issues* 29, no. 2:323–40.

Coleman, J. S. 1988. "Social Capital in the Creation of Human Capital." *American Journal of Sociology* 94:S95–S120.

Cross, J. C. 1996. "El desalojo de los vendedores ambulantes: Paralelismos históricos en la ciudad de México." *Revista Mexicana de Sociología* 58, no. 2:95–115.

———. 1997. "Debilitando al clientelismo: La formalización del ambulantaje en la ciudad de México." *Revista Mexicana de Sociología* 59, no. 4:93–115.

———. 1998a. "Co-optation, Competition, and Resistance: State and Street Vendors in Mexico City." *Latin American Perspectives* 99:41–61.

———. 1998b. *Informal Politics: Street Vendors and the State in Mexico City.* Stanford: Stanford University Press.

Cross, J. C., and B. D. Johnson. 2000. "Expanding Dual Labor Market Theory: Crack Dealers and the Informal Sector." *International Journal of Sociology and Social Policy* 21, no. 1/2.

Curtis, Ric, and Travis Wendel. 2000. "Toward the Typology of Illegal Drug Markets." In *Illegal Drug Markets: From Research to Prevention Policy*, ed. Margai Natarajan and Mike Hough. Morsey, N.Y.: Criminal Justice Press.

de Soto, Hernando. 1989. *The Other Path.* New York: Harper & Row.

———. 2000. *The Mystery of Capital: Why Capitalism Triumphs in the West and Fails Everywhere Else.* New York: Basic Books.

Dorn, Nicholas, Lutz Oette, and Simone White. 1998. "Drugs Importation and the Bifurcation of Risk." *The British Journal of Criminology* 38, no. 4:537–60.

Fagan, Jeffrey. 1992. "Drug Selling and Illicit Income in Distressed Neighborhoods: The Economic Lives of Street-Level Drug Users and Dealers." In *Drugs, Crime,* and Social Isolation: Barriers to Urban Opportunity, ed. Adele V. Harrell and George E. Peterson. Washington, D.C.: Urban Institute Press.

Fernández-Kelly, Patricia, and Anna M. Garcia. 1989. "Informalization at the Core: Hispanic Women, Homework, and the Advanced Capitalist State." In The Informal Economy: Studies in Advanced and Less Developed Countries, ed. Alejandro Portes, Manuel Castells, and Lauren Benton. Baltimore: Johns Hopkins University Press.

Gordon, G. I. 1997. "Peddlers, Pesos and Power: The Political Economy of Street Vending in Mexico City." Ph.D. diss., University of Chicago.

Granovetter, M. 1985. "Economic Action and Social Structure: The Problem of Embeddedness." American Journal of Sociology 91:481–510.

Grossman, H. 1995. "Organized Crime and State Intervention in the Economy." In The Economics of Organized Crime, ed. G. Fiorentini and S. Peltzman, 143–60. Cambridge: Cambridge University Press.

Hagedorn, J. M. 1994. "Neighborhoods, Markets, and Gang Drug Organization." Journal of Research in Crime and Delinquency 31:264–94.

Hatsukami, Dorothy K., and Marian W. Fischmans. 1996. "Crack Cocaine and Cocaine Hydrochloride: Are the Differences Myth or Reality?" Journal of the American Medical Association 276:1580–88.

Holcombe, R. 1996. "Public Finance: Government Revenues and Expenditures in the United States Economy." St. Paul, Minn.: West Publishing.

Jacobs, B. A. 1996a. "Crack Dealer's Apprehension Avoidance Techniques: A Case of Restrictive Deterrence." Justice Quarterly 13:359–81.

———. 1996b. "Crack Dealers and Restrictive Deterrence: Identifying Narcs." Criminology 34:409–31.

Jacobs, B. A., and J. Miller 1998. "Crack Dealing, Gender, and Arrest Avoidance." Social Problems 45, no. 4:550–69.

Jagannathan, V. N. 1987. Informal Markets in Developing Countries. New York: Oxford University Press.

Jensen, E. L., and J. Gerber. 1996. "The Civil Forfeiture of Assets and the War on Drugs: Expanding Criminal Sanctions While Reducing Due Process Protections." Crime and Delinquency 42, no. 3:421–34.

Johnson, B. D., and J. Muffler. 1992. "Sociocultural Aspects of Drug Use and Abuse in the 1990s." In Substance Abuse Treatment, 2nd edition, ed. J. Lowinson, P. Ruiz, and R. Millman, 118–35. Baltimore: Williams and Wilkins.

Johnson, B. D., and M. Natarajan. 1995. "Strategies to Avoid Arrest: Crack Seller's Response to Intensified Policing." American Journal of Police 14, no. 3/4:49–69.

Johnson, B. D., A. Golub, and J. Fagan. 1995. "Careers in Crack, Drug Use, Drug Distribution, and Nondrug Criminality." Crime & Delinquency 41, no. 3:275–95.

Johnson, B. D., T. Williams, K. Dei, and H. Sanabria 1990. "Drug Abuse and the Inner City: Impact on Hard Drug Users and the Community." In Drugs and Crime, ed. Michael Tory and James Q. Wilson, 13:9–67. Chicago: University of Chicago Press.

Jones, G. W. 1968. "Underutilization of Manpower and Demographic Trends in Latin America." International Labor Review 98:451–69.

Kiser, E., and X. Toug. 1992. "Determinants of the Amount and Type of Corruption in State Fiscal Bureaucracies." *Comparative Political Studies* 25:300–331.

Levy, J. M. 1995. *Essential Microeconomics for Public Policy Analysis*. Westport, Conn.: Praeger.

Mieczkowski, T. 1990. "Crack Distribution in Detroit." *Contemporary Drug Problems* 17, no. 1:9–30.

———. 1992. "Crack Dealing on the Street: The Crew System and the Crack House." *Justice Quarterly* 9:151–63.

Nelson, N. L. 1992. "Public Order and Private Entrepreneurs: The Pocket Economy of Street Vendors in Bogota, Colombia." Ph.D. diss., University of New Mexico.

Peña, S. 1999a. "Informal Markets Organization: Street Vendors in Mexico City." Ph.D. diss., Florida State University.

———. 1999b. "Informal Markets: Street Vendors in Mexico City." *Habitat International* 23, no. 3:363–72.

Pérez Perdomo, Rogelio. 1992. "Law and Urban Explosion in Latin America." In *Rethinking the Latin American City*, ed. Richard M. Morse and Jorge Hardoy. Baltimore: Johns Hopkins University Press.

Portes, A. 1994. "The Informal Economy and Its Paradox." In *The Handbook of Economic Sociology*, ed. N. J. Smelser and S. R. Smelser, 426–47. Princeton: Princeton University Press.

Portes, Alejandro, Manuel Castells, and Lauren A. Benton, eds. 1989. *The Informal Economy: Studies in Advanced and Less Developed Countries*. Baltimore: Johns Hopkins University Press.

Portes, Alejandro, and Julia Sensenbrenner. 1993. "Embeddedness and Immigration: Notes on the Social Determinants of Economic Action." *American Journal of Sociology* 98:1320–50.

Priest, G. L. 1994. "The Ambiguous Moral Foundations of the Underground Economy." *Yale Law Journal* 103:2259–88.

Reuter, P. 1985. *The Organization of Illegal Markets*. Port Townsend, Wash.: Loompanics Unlimited.

Scott, James C. 1990. *Domination and the Arts of Resistance*. New Haven: Yale University Press.

Simon, C. P., and A. D. Witte. 1982. *Beating the System: The Underground Economy*. Boston: Auburn House.

Skaperdas, S., and C. Syropoulous. 1995. "Gangs as Primitive States." In *The Economics of Organized Crime*, ed. G. Fiorentini and S. Peltzman, 61–86. Cambridge: Cambridge University Press.

Smith, E. M. 1988. "Overview: The Informal Economy and the State." In *Traders Versus the State: Anthropological Approaches to Unofficial Economies*, ed. G. Clark, 189–99. Boulder, Colo.: Westview Press.

Smith, H.M.I., and M. E. Luttrell. 1994. "Cartels in an "Nth-Best" World: The Wholesale Foodstuff Trade in Ibadan, Nigeria." *World Development* 22:323–35.

Spalther-Roth, R. M. 1988. "The Sexual Political Economy of Street Vending in Washington, D.C." In *Traders Versus the State: Anthropological Approaches to Unofficial Economies*, ed. G. Clark, 165–87. Boulder, Colo.: Westview Press.

Staudt, K. 1996. "Struggle in Urban Space: Street Vendors in El Paso and Ciudad Juarez." *Urban Affairs Review* 31:435–54.

Teltscher, S. 1992. "Informal Trading in Quito, Ecuador: Economic Integration, Internal Diversity, and Life Chances." Ph.D. diss., University of Washington.

———. 1994. "Small Trade and the World Economy: Informal Vendors in Quito, Ecuador." *Economic Geography* 70:167–87.

Tokman, V. E. 1978. "An Exploration into the Nature of Informal-Formal Sector Relationships." *World Development* 6:1065–76.

Van Nostrand, L., and R. Tewksbury. 1999. "The Motives and Mechanics of Operating an Illegal Drug Enterprise." *Deviant Behavior* 20:57–83.

Williams, T. 1992. *Crackhouse: Notes from the End of the Line.* Reading, Mass.: Addison-Wesley.

Williamson, O. E. 1981. "The Economics of Organization: The Transaction Cost Approach. *American Journal of Sociology* 87:548–77.

Wilson, William Julius. 1997. *When Work Disappears: The World of the New Urban Poor.* New York: Vintage Books.

THREE

Neoliberalism, Markets, and Informal Grassroots Economies

José Itzigsohn

The implementation of neoliberal policies globally has led to the deterioration of the working and living conditions of large sectors of the population and to the declining ability of the state to respond to social demands. Under these conditions, the self-help activities of the poor acquire increasing importance for subsistence and social mobility. The reduction of wage-earning opportunities among the poor, however, may negatively affect the possibilities to develop self-help activities. As Mercedes González de la Rocha suggests in this volume, increasing poverty lessens the capacity of the poor to maintain networks of social exchange. According to her, the survival of the poor under import substitution industrialization was best understood through the "resources of poverty" model. Under neoliberalism the poor confront a situation marked by the "poverty of resources" (González de la Rocha 2001).

This chapter focuses on a particular paradox surrounding this new development. Market-based policies have created socioeconomic contexts in which the informal economy is central to subsistence and social mobility. In such circumstances, cooperation among grassroots economic actors acquires vital significance—it is necessary for grassroots economic activities to run smoothly or thrive in settings characterized by very large power differentials between economic actors. Yet the depletion of the resources of the poor described by González de la Rocha (2001) also means that the social bases for trust and cooperation in the informal economy are severely eroded.

This chapter has three objectives: (1) to analyze the importance of trust and cooperation in grassroots economic activities; (2) to understand the social basis and limits of trust and cooperation in informal grassroots economies;

and (3) to assess the likely impact of neoliberal policies on the social basis of grassroots trust and cooperation.

Neoliberalism, Markets, and Informality

Markets are key economic coordinating mechanisms but they are not level playing fields. Existing market economies are social formations affected by power differentials. Markets have always needed legal frameworks to operate, and for that reason market economies have always depended on the action of states and the presence of state regulations. A central argument of this chapter though is that neoliberalism, for all its trumpeting of "market reform," is not about reducing state intervention for the purpose of facilitating market functioning. On the contrary, neoliberalism is about using state power to enable the unrestrained action of powerful corporate actors on a global scale.[1] Neoliberal reform in fact precludes the development of markets at the grassroots level. In that sense, neoliberal reform can be considered "anti-market."[2]

The viability of informal enterprises and local and regional economies depends to a large extent on the presence of relations of trust and mutual aid that can counterbalance the tilted playing fields created by large power differentials. Indeed, in a book that was designed to sing the praises of the individual entrepreneur, Hernando de Soto (1989) inadvertently describes the importance of cooperative arrangements and informal rules of enforcement for the success of unregulated endeavors. Research has shown that informal producers, workers, and traders usually have to operate in two different types of markets. The first are highly competitive settings, where people have very low income-generating capacity, and where profit margins are consequently very small. The second combines oligopolic and oligopsonic markets, where small producers have very little power to determine outcomes. Competing in these arenas is extremely hard, and the possibilities of success and growth rather limited.

The possibility for subsistence and perhaps success for informal grassroots market economies is predicated upon the presence of networks of cooperation that can help strengthen the position of informal actors (Capecchi 1989; Itzigsohn 2000; Portes and Itzigsohn 1997; Pérez Sáinz 1997a). Cooperation can help level the playing field and allow informal actors to compete more successfully. By creating situations marked by the "poverty of resources," neoliberal policies undermine the conditions for the emergence of trust and cooperation in grassroots economies. Therefore, neoliberal policies hamper the development of grassroots-based market economies.

The Development of the Informal Economy

In Latin America, industrialization was predicated on the idea that the mass of the rural population would be absorbed by urban formal employment. Both the United Nations Economic Commission for Latin America and the Caribbean (ECLAC) and Arthur W. Lewis (1954) provided models under which economies with large reserves of labor—such as Latin America and the Caribbean—would undergo a transition toward manufacturing and high-wage employment. Yet Latin American and Caribbean realities soon proved the limitations of these models. The process of industrialization and urbanization was accompanied by the growth of large urban informal economies. Industrialization was unable to absorb all of the labor force into formal employment, forcing people to find their livelihoods in the unregulated sector. Moreover, many of the new informal endeavors were not the result of a failure to absorb the population into formal activities, but the result of particular forms of organizing production and marketing under peripheral capitalism (Portes and Schauffler 1993; Itzigsohn 2000).[3] Informal activities were not external but internal to the process of capital accumulation in the region.

Informal economies, hence, are not new in Latin America. Nevertheless, the end of internally oriented developmentalist policies and the rise of neoliberalism changed the position of informal economies in Latin American societies. Internally oriented developmentalism was based on the goal of integrating the whole of the population to achieve standards of living equivalent to those in advanced countries. In this model, the state played a central role both in promoting and directing industrialization and in fostering integration through social policies. The integrationist goals were certainly limited by the presence of exclusionary class hierarchies and the pervasiveness of what Anibal Quijano (2000) calls the coloniality of power.[4] Yet despite its well-known limitations, developmentalism led to partial integration of Latin American societies and to rises in living standards.

The exhaustion of internally oriented developmentalism and the advent of neoliberal policies changed the Latin American socioeconomic context. The mechanism for social integration shifted under the new model from state-based social protection to the achievement of subsistence resources through the market. Those who succeed in the increasingly globalized markets are the integrated segments of the population. The state is to leave the space of economic decisions to the private sector, and to fulfill a subsidiary role on social protection, focusing its policies and efforts on measures to alleviate the situation of the most marginalized groups ("the poorest of the poor"). This change in the economic model and in the model of sociopolitical regulation also led to broad changes in the labor market.

Under internally oriented developmentalism, the protection of formal work was limited but usually effective, creating a difference between formal and informal work. Formal workers would have access to better wages and protection than informal workers would. Yet, as González de la Rocha (2001) shows, poor households included formal and informal workers and the presence of the resources provided by formal work helped to develop informal activities and the creation of "resources of poverty." Formal income provided capital for informal endeavors, and formal workers constituted a market for informal products.

Neoliberalism led to the growth of the informal economy and to the informalization of the formal economy, blurring the lines between the two domains (Itzigsohn 2000; Lozano 1998). New export-oriented industries, although protected in theory, present working conditions that are not so different from informal work.[5] For many people, the informal economy has thus become not only a shelter from unemployment but also an employment of choice (Itzigsohn 2000). This is not because informal jobs are protected, but because suddenly they are not as distinct from formal ones as they once were. Under these conditions, formal income does not provide capital for informal enterprises, and formal workers have very little capacity for consumption of informal products.

Pérez Sáinz (1998) argues that the blurring of the lines between formality and informality has reduced the utility of the latter category. He has dubbed the new situation neo-informality, arguing that under that concept we can distinguish three different scenarios based on different articulations of informal activities to the global economy. The first scenario is constituted by informal activities that are integrated in a dynamic way into the global economy, occupying special niches and developing local forms of cooperation. The second scenario entails activities articulated to the global economy through subcontracting relations. The third scenario consists of informal actors marginalized from the global economy. These scenarios are useful analytical tools to investigate the social basis and roles of cooperation in informal activities.[6] Mutual help and trust play a role in the three situations.

The next section discusses examples of the formation of trust and cooperation in each of these three types of informal activities.

It also addresses a new phenomenon of cooperation in the development of local and regional economies made possible by the emergence of immigration-based transnational collaboration. This phenomenon has not usually been included in studies of the informal economy.[7] Nevertheless, migration, informal work in the cities of the core of the world-system, and remittances have in part replaced the resources previously provided by formal work for those households with migrant members. This model of social mobility implies that social integration, to the extent that it happens, takes place in a transnational rather than a national terrain. Social integration is achieved through the effort of migrants who often risk their lives to reach the cities of the developed world and live and work under precarious conditions to be able to send money to their relatives in home countries. Transnational activities of that kind—particularly those related to the formation of businesses or the promotion of regional development—represent a new form of *grassroots economies* with enough traits shared with the informal economy to merit inclusion here (Portes, Haller, and Guarnizo 2002).

Trust and Cooperation in the Informal Economy

Cooperation and trust are central to the viability of informal endeavors in all three scenarios described by Pérez Sáinz (1997a, 1998).[8] This is clearest perhaps in the first case—one that has previously received little attention—where informality is dynamically articulated to the global economy. It is well known that some informal entrepreneurs did well, earning more than formal workers. Nevertheless, the focus on dynamic regional economies is the result of a new interest in the conglomeration of small firms as engines of local economic growth and the shift of the analytical lens from the city to the countryside. There are in fact very few documented cases of dynamic grassroots economies in Latin America, but those that exist cast light on the importance of trust and cooperation as a condition for viability.

Pérez Sáinz (1997a, 1998) has documented the case of Sarchi in Costa Rica, a town of successful craftspeople who have managed to introduce their wares in global circuits of consumption. These artisans' effectiveness depends on shared pride and daily interaction with others engaged in similar activities in the same geographical area—people confronting the same constraints and challenges. Cooperation in this case is based on norms of reciprocity, mainly in the form of assistance when starting new businesses and also in the presence of a marketing cooperative.

Another case of successful regional economic development founded on cooperation and integration into global networks of trade is that of Otavalo, Ecuador. Otavalo is not only a successful town of indigenous entrepreneurs but also one that gave rise to a diaspora of itinerant traders and musicians. Otavalo's success is based on the long-term role of middlemen in regional economies and the presence of ethnic solidarity among the members of the community (Kyle 2000). Similarly, Hubert Schmitz (1995) has described the emergence of a successful concentration of small shoemaking firms in Brazil's Sinos Valley. Again, cooperation based on ethnic solidarity—the region is home to a large community of German immigrants—was essential to its success. In that instance, internal differentiation within the region undermined ethnic ties. Nevertheless, when the competitive costs of noncooperation became clear to producers in the region, it was replaced by cooperation based on sectoral interests (Schmitz 1995).

A sustained group effort was essential for the emergence and continuation of those lively regional economies. Trust and cooperation alone are, of course, not sufficient to ensure success. Other factors, such as the type and quality of the product being produced and the characteristics of markets in which those products sell are important. Yet as the literature on industrial districts has shown, the presence of some form of solidarity is a necessary condition for the formation of informal economies of growth.

Trust and solidarity are also important in the second category of informal activities identified by Pérez Sáinz: those linked to the global economy through subcontracting networks. If in the previous scenario cooperation was related to improving production and marketing to compete globally, in the second case cooperation is required to impose discipline in the labor process and thus comply with subcontracting demands. Global subcontracting is usually associated with attempts at lowering labor costs. While that is an important goal for many companies, an equally significant consideration is to control work time and quality. This is a salient issue regarding global chains of subcontracting that reach informal firms and small firms in general. In the present economic context in Latin America, global firms can subcontract work to companies in export processing zones that combine cheap labor with strict control over the production process. Hence, informal firms are often excluded from these chains. Yet, in some cases, mechanisms of solidarity can recreate forms of labor control that allow small firms access to global subcontracting chains. This seems to be the case in San Pedro Sacatepequez, where ethnic solidarity and the knowledge that town people have about each other operate as a mechanism to guarantee discipline in the production process. In this Kakchiquel town located in the outskirts of Guatemala City, local entrepreneurs produce cloth for local and international subcontractors. The town's ability to enter subcontracting chains depended on the introduction of modern sewing machines and electricity into production. This, in turn, was a result of the mobilization and collaboration among local workers and entrepreneurs (Pérez Sáinz 1997b).

Similarly, in my own research on the informal economy in San José, Costa Rica, I found several women's cooperatives engaged in the production of clothing. In those cooperatives, groups of women pool efforts to create a viable source of livelihood. Only one of them, however, was able to get access to global subcontracts. The decisive factor in that case was that the cooperative had imposed a strict discipline in production. Workers were subjected to rigid working times and controls made possible in part because of the cooperative's decision to provide child care. It was discipline and control that allowed the group to take on large subcontracting orders.

Mutual support and regular interaction are also important within marginalized informal activities—Pérez Sáinz's third scenario. Cooperation and trust are fundamental to the success of the *grupos solidarios* loan method adopted by NGOs to provide credit to informal producers. The promotion of mutual aid is at the root of attempts on the part of NGOs to organize groups of informal entrepreneurs for production, marketing, or other community-based development programs (Itzigsohn 2000).

I observed the importance of teamwork among craftspeople in Santo Domingo, Dominican Republic. The organization of crafts production opens up some spaces for shared work. Craftspeople sometimes lent their workshops and machines to fellow artisans. For example, in cases in which particular individuals obtained orders from shops or intermediaries and did not have the necessary tools, they could borrow equipment from fellow craftsmen. In addition, craftsmen hired each other depending on the flow of demand for each particular producer. In those cases, the instability of demand and the contacts that arise from belonging to the same trade opened spaces for some forms of cooperation in production. Often, mutual assistance took place between people who came from the same town or lived in the same neighborhood. Furthermore, at the time of my research there was an association of craftsmen in Santo Domingo who attempted to promote collaboration among members to expand markets. This was seen as key to efficacy and as the only way to break the oligopsonic control of intermediaries. The organization, however, was not very successful in achieving its goals, partly because of rivalries between groups of craftsmen.

In San José I also found groups of artisans working together in attempts to open new markets for crafts either within Costa Rica or abroad. I even found cases of state support for those efforts. For example, I interviewed a group that was trying to open a store in a town with a large influx of tourists. This case shows the importance of external agents in the emergence of cooperation between informal producers. The artisans were brought together by a state agency aiming at expanding the crafts market. Although that project eventually failed, the participants were already organized and went ahead independently, creating an association and opening a craft store on one of the main tourist routes of the country.

The establishment of a national chamber of informal entrepreneurs in the tourism sector in Costa Rica provides another example. That organization was promoted by an NGO working to help microenterprises. Instead of providing loans to individuals, the NGO incorporated groups into a national organization that helped them address common concerns and support policies of benefit to their activities. That organization was still operating in the late 1990s despite internal disputes and the defection of some members. Nevertheless, some of its more ambitious plans, such as the creation of a travel agency to serve its members, had not been realized.

The last case illustrates difficulties in the organization of cooperative institutions among informal producers in the marginalized sector. Two elements complicate such attempts. One is the lack of faith in the integrity of others among people whose daily activities take place in isolation from potential collaborators. A second barrier entails the burden of managing a firm and workday. Microentrepreneurs usually do not have personnel who can take their place if they are absent, and their workday is often very long. This does not leave much time for meetings and other forms of interaction that nurture fellowship.

There is yet another form of cooperation in the development of local regional economies that has been largely ignored in studies of the informal economy but which is crucial for the livelihood of people and regions experiencing the effects of neoliberal policies. I am referring to transnational cooperative networks. It is well known that remittances are indispensable to the subsistence of people in peripheral countries (Itzigsohn 1995). It is also well known that immigrants maintain multifaceted ties with their countries of origin. New research on migration has shown the importance of immigrant associations for local development. Immigrants, as well, organize committees on the basis of town or regional membership and send money to make possible development projects in their home countries. This is a process extensively documented for nations such as El Salvador, the Dominican Republic, and Mexico (Goldring 1998; Landolt, Autler, and Baires 1999; Levitt 2001). Grassroots transnational cooperative initiatives are not free of conflict. Immigrants and nonimmigrants do not always agree on priorities and on ways to carry out projects. Yet the success of certain regions is increasingly tied to the emergence and institutionalization of transnational ties.

The Social Bases and Limits of Trust and Cooperation

Trust and cooperation do not emerge easily. They need to be embedded in institutional arrangements—social, political, and cultural—that allow people to identify and empathize with others. As Vittorio Capecchi (1989) argues, the emergence of informal economies of growth is based on the existence of previous bonds of solidarity. Cohesion and mutual aid are enhanced, first, when there are clearly defined common interests present (as in the case of crafts associations) and, second, when there is regular social interaction, such as living in the same neighborhood or being from the same region, or belonging to the same community.

One of the main sources of trust and collaboration is interaction and mutual knowledge rooted in territorial proximity. This is particularly important in the case of dynamic regional economies. People relating to each other in a common space accumulate personal knowledge that enables them to develop expectations about one another. Familiarity and predictability nurture both confidence and reciprocal exchanges. The importance of what he calls *socioterritoriality* led Pérez Sáinz to emphasize the non-urban character of regional economies of growth. Indeed, most of those successful informal or local economies are located in small towns or in the countryside. Density of interaction in towns and regions expands the flow of information necessary to exert social control and maximize certainty in social interactions.

A common geographical space is also important in the subsistence sector of the informal economy. This may consist of shared living quarters or residence in the same neighborhood.[9] That was the case with several organizations formed by small informal firms I found in San José. They had been assembled by an NGO based on their common activities and urban space. Another type of solidarity built with space in mind is found among urban migrants from the same region.[10] I witnessed its importance in the establishment of cooperative ties among craftspeople.

Cultural affinities and solidarities embedded in cultural expectations form another basis for trust and solidarity. It is also well documented that expectations of mutual help may be rooted in value systems. We witness the emergence of trust on the basis of shared indigenous identity in the case of San Pedro Sacatepequez and Otavalo. This form of solidarity is also present in the case of transnational economic action.[11]

Solidarity may also grow as a function of common social position. People facing similar obstacles tend to organize in their attempts to overcome them. This was a factor in the women's cooperative in San José that I investigated, and in other groups of local microentrepreneurs in that city. It was also a factor leading to cooperation in Brazil's Sinos Valley. Merely sharing a common social position is seldom enough to trigger shared aims. Also necessary is the presence of individuals who can articulate a vision for collective action or a frame for dealing with problems resulting from breaches of trust. Different social actors can play that part. In many urban economies of subsistence that role has been filled by developmental NGOs. In regional economies of growth, public officials often meet that function.[12]

Teamwork and mutual assistance are not new elements in studies of the informal economy. Yet, as we saw, those elements emerge only as the result of complex social processes—and despite numerous barriers to their development.[13] Hindrances are found in the three scenarios of informality described by Pérez Sáinz but also in transnational activities and networks. The first of these problems is competition. At first blush this seems obvious and redundant, since informal actors are engaged in attempts to earn a living or improve their social position and competition is an inherent component of markets. Competition, as well, is an incentive for increased productivity and innovation. Finally, it is important to remember that informal economic actors usually compete in oversaturated markets or markets where suppliers or buyers hold enormous power. At stake in the competitive struggle is the livelihood of the informal actor and her or his family.

The presence of reciprocity and solidarity does not eliminate the stratification of businesses within the community and the presence of contending interests within the region that can tear the social fabric of local grassroots economies. Pérez Sáinz argues that in Sarchi there is cutthroat price competition between many of the small informal establishments that threatens the success of the local economy. According to him, "*Sarchi has not succeeded in achieving the virtuous combination of cooperation and competition that has been central to the success of the industrial districts of the North"* (1998, 175; italics mine).

As the literature on industrial districts has shown, for regional economies of growth, the challenge is to balance cooperation and competitiveness. Institutional checks are needed that can restore amity to a community if the pressures of the market impinge upon it. Studies of industrial districts and small business conglomerates show that, in addition to mutual aid, a certain measure of regulation and support by a regional or national government is necessary for the existence of successful grassroots economies (Pyke, Becatini, and Sengenberger 1990; Capechi 1989; Schmitz 1995). Regulation and support by regional or national state institutions reinforce virtuous cycles of cooperation and competition characteristic of informal economies of growth. As Schmitz (1995) notes, an important element in the success of the shoe industry in the Sinos Valley was the partnership between the public sector and local entrepreneurs.

The national and local states in Latin America have historically been rather oblivious to this type of development. Neoliberalism, with its emphasis on the reduction of state capacity to intervene in the economy has not improved the situation. Nongovernmental organizations can sometimes replace the state, but their resources are limited and their authority and legitimacy lack universal recognition. Without legal agencies at the local or national levels to balance and regulate the competitive pressures that often rip the social fabric sustaining cooperation, dynamic grassroots economies will continue to be scattered phenomena—as indeed they have been in Latin America.

An additional social limit to cooperation is the strain on the resources of the poor. For economies of subsistence, cooperation is necessary to muster very scarce resources, coordinate the labor process efficiently, create marketing ties, and deal with oligopolic or oligopsonic markets. In my research on the informal economies of Santo Domingo and San José, informal entrepreneurs often agreed on the advantages of mutual support but immediately went on to point out the difficulties in creating frameworks for successful cooperation and the building of trust (Itzigsohn 2000). Impediments had to do with working conditions and the organization of economic activities. Isolation, long work days, economic instability and high turnover represent powerful obstacles to the development of collaborative arrangements in the informal economy. This is especially true in the exclusion scenario, which is the largest. Under such conditions people do not have time to maintain contact with others, to cultivate trusting interactions, or to take part in organizations that sustain mutually supportive efforts. Finally, people in such circumstances do not have at their disposal social institutions to mediate problems and address cases of malfeasance.

Knowledge about the strains on time and physical resources of informal actors is not new; those pressures are characteristic of informal endeavors. Yet neoliberal policies have exacerbated them, making poverty and informality even more precarious and limiting access to resources previously provided by formal work. The subsistence economic activities of the poor are increasingly characterized by a paucity of material assets to produce goods for sale (González de la Rocha 2001). Given those constraints it is remarkable that teamwork and mutual assistance organizations continue to emerge. Nevertheless, in environments affected by neoliberal policies, cooperation and trust are bound to remain isolated examples of the human capacity to endure and survive despite all obstacles.

Grassroots Economies, Neoliberalism, and Politics

I have argued that under current circumstances, trust and cooperation are central to the well-being of large numbers of people in Latin America. In the neoliberal model, with its emphasis on integration through markets, cooperation is almost necessary for decent subsistence. This is one of the paradoxes of market-oriented policies. The more the market determines the fate of people, the more social organization and coordination matter for subsistence and success.

Long ago Karl Polanyi (1957) noted the importance of social constraints for the creation of viable markets. According to him, in the absence of institutional orders to restrict and regulate their action, markets can unravel the social fabric. Despite their rhetoric neoliberal reforms are not about promoting markets but about eliminating restraints on the actions of powerful global economic actors that hamper the development of grassroots-based market economies. Neoliberalism, in fact, undermines the conditions necessary for the development of trust and cooperation in three ways: first, it reduces the assets available to the poor, thus shrinking their ability to share and exchange goods. Second, it worsens working conditions by increasing the amount of time necessary to achieve an income that will provide for household subsistence, therefore limiting the time available for social interaction and the building of trust. Third, it dismantles state institutions, thus constraining the state's ability to promote grassroots economies of growth. Cutthroat competition in markets characterized by very low demand capacities added to the lack of basic services and the precariousness of working and living conditions, severely constrain cooperation and solidarity.

The importance of mutual aid and the existence of numerous popular organizations has lead some scholars to see informal activities as an alternative economy, a popular economy that functions on the basis of solidarity and in agreement with a non-market logic (Burbach, Nuñez, and Kagarlitsky 1997; Palma 1988). In those perspectives informality represents a blueprint for an alternative social order.[14] Such hopes are exaggerated. On the one hand, although cooperation and collective action do exist—as the literature on social movements shows—they often have a temporary and specific character. The poverty of resources makes the growth of grassroots economies even harder. On the other hand, grassroots economic activities are often organized around solidarity and cooperation but *not* against the market—in every case the purpose is, in fact, market participation. As a result, informality can hardly be portrayed as an alternative to the market. If we are serious about the potential of grassroots-based economies, however, we need to think beyond neoliberalism.

Under neoliberalism, cooperation and solidarity can indeed provide a blueprint for a new model of social development and integration. If top-down models of socioeconomic integration characterized an earlier period, the demise of the entrepreneurial and social assistance state can usher in a new type of state-society relations—one based on the support and promotion of local initiatives and solidarities. In this sense, instances of successful cooperation such as the ones described in this chapter can be used as tools to rethink the social order and put forward alternatives of social integration based on grassroots projects. The experience of numerous social movements and participatory local political orders give us hope. So does the experience of regional economies, transnational development, and subsistence mutual help. Now what we need to think about is how to open and create institutional spaces and local, national, and global policy frames that will allow these experiences to gain strength and multiply.

NOTES

1. This is seen clearly in the privatization processes throughout the continent, which have dismantled protected and often inefficient state monopolies only to replace them with protected and often inefficient private monopolies.

2. Here I am following Braudel's argument that capitalism is the "anti-market." For Braudel, capitalists are powerful economic actors who operate above and disrupt the work of market economies for the purpose of obtaining profits (Arrighi 2001).

3. For discussions of the different theories used to explain the development and functioning of the informal economy, see Itzigsohn 2000 and Pérez Sáinz 1992.

4. By "coloniality of power" Quijano means the continuous presence of sociocultural hierarchies and exclusions based on colonial ethnoracial categories.

5. As Lozano (1998) points out, there are important differences in the working conditions within the new export sectors. Yet, important segments of the export sectors are de facto informalized.

6. The adoption of these three scenarios as analytical tools does not imply agreement with Pérez Sáinz's contention that informality is no longer a useful analytical category. It does, however, sidestep the discussion about what constitutes informality to focus on different forms of popular and grassroots economic activities.

7. For works that have looked at the informal economy in the context of transnational migration, see Gordon, Anderson, and Robotham 1997; Portes and Itzigsohn 1997; and Portes 1996.

8. This section provides evidence for the importance of cooperation for the success of grassroots economic activities. It is based on a reading of the existing literature. Those who want to know more details about the cases mentioned here can turn to the mentioned sources.

9. The literature on social movements and self-help organizations has emphasized the importance of the neighborhood as a basis for social action (see, for example, Friedman 1989 and Portes and Itzigsohn 1997).

10. This is something that has been emphasized in numerous writings about urban social structures in Latin America (Roberts 1995).

11. We need to be careful not to reify ethnic communities. As Kyle's (2000) excellent study of Otavalo shows, class, gender, and locality fault lines cross ethnic economies. This affects the level of resources that people participating in the ethnic economy can access.

12. Other actors that have fulfilled that role are social movements. One such example is the Landless Peasants Movement in Brazil (MST), which has both mobilized the peasant population for making political demands for land reform and for concrete projects of settlement in unused lands. I do not address this case simply because I have not studied it.

13. Moreover, the rise of cooperation does not imply the lack of malfeasance. Doing research on the informal economy one comes across numerous stories of breaches of trust.

14. It is interesting to note how people from widely different parts of the political spectrum, such as de Soto (1989), Palma (1988), and Burbach, Nuñez, and Kagarlitsky (1997) coincide in pinning their hopes for a better model of social organization in the informal economy.

REFERENCES

Arrighi, Giovanni. 2001. "Braudel, Capitalism, and the New Economic Sociology." *Review* 24, no. 1:107–23.

Burbach, Roger, Orlando Nuñez, and Boris Kagarlitsky. 1997. *Globalization and Its Discontents: The Rise of Postmodern Socialisms.* London: Pluto Press.

Capecchi, Vittorio. 1989. "The Informal Economy and the Development of Flexible Specialization in Emilia-Romagna." In *The Informal Economy: Studies in Advanced and Less Developed Countries,* ed. Alejandro Portes, Manuel Castells, and Lauren Benton, 189–215. Baltimore: Johns Hopkins University Press.

de Soto, Hernando. 1989. *The Other Path.* New York: Harper and Row.

Freidman, John. 1989. "The Latin American Barrio Movement as a Social Movement: Contribution to a Debate." *International Journal of Urban and Regional Research* 13, no. 3:501–10.

Goldring, Luin. 1998. "The Power of Status in Transnational Social Fields." *Comparative Urban and Community Research* 6:165–95.

González de la Rocha, Mercedes. 2001. "From the Resources of Poverty to the Poverty of Resources? The Erosion of a Survival Model." *Latin American Perspectives* 28, no. 4:72–100.

Gordon, Derek, Patricia Anderson, and Dan Robotham. 1997. "Jamaica: Urbanization During the Years of the Crisis." In *The Urban Caribbean,* ed. A. Portes, C. Dore-Cabral, and P. Landolt, 190–226. Baltimore: Johns Hopkins University Press.

Itzigsohn, José. 1995. "Migrant Remittances, Labor Markets, and Household Strategies: A Comparative Analysis of Low-Income Household Strategies in the Caribbean Basin." *Social Forces* 74, no. 2:633–55.

———. 2000. *Developing Poverty: The State, Labor Market Deregulation, and the Informal Economy in Costa Rica and the Dominican Republic.* University Park: Pennsylvania State University Press.

Kyle, David. 2000. *Transnational Peasants.* Baltimore: Johns Hopkins University Press.

Landolt, Patricia, Lilian Autler, and Sonia Baires. 1999. "From Hermano Lejano to Hermano Mayor: The Dialectics of Salvadoran Transnationalism." *Ethnic and Racial Studies* 22:290–315.

Levitt, Peggy. 2001. *The Transnational Villagers.* Berkeley and Los Angeles: University of California Press.

Lewis, Arthur W. 1954. "Economic Development with Unlimited Supplies of Labor." *Manchester School of Economics and Social Studies* 22:139–91.

Lozano, Wilfredo. 1998. "Desregulación laboral, estado y mercado en América Latina: Balances y retos sociopolíticos." *Perfiles Latinoamericanos,* no. 13:113–51.

Palma, Diego. 1988. *La informalidad, lo popular y el cambio social.* Lima: DESCO.

Pérez Sáinz, Juan Pablo. 1992. *Informalidad urbana en América Latina: Enfoques, problemáticas e interrogantes.* Caracas: Nueva Sociedad.

———. 1997a. "Entre lo global y lo local: Economías comunitarias de Centroamérica." *Sociología del Trabajo,* nueva época, no. 30 (spring): 3–19.

———. 1997b. "Guatemala: The Two Faces of the Metropolitan Area." In *The Urban Caribbean,* ed. A. Portes, C. Dore-Cabral, and P. Landolt, 124–52. Baltimore: Johns Hopkins University Press.

———. 1998. "The New Faces of Informality in Central America." *Journal of Latin American Studies* 30, no. 1 (February): 157–79.

Polanyi, Karl. [1944] 1957. *The Great Transformation*. Boston: Beacon Press.

Portes, Alejandro. 1996. "Transnational Communities: Their Emergence and Significance in the Contemporary World System." In *Latin America in the World Economy*, ed. R. P. Korzeniewicz and W. C. Smith, 151–68. Westport, Conn.: Greenwood Press.

Portes, Alejandro, William Haller, and Luis Guarnizo. 2002. "Transnational Entrepreneurs: Alternative Forms of Immigrant Adaptation." *American Sociological Review* 67, no. 2:278–98.

Portes, Alejandro, and José Itzigsohn. 1997. "Coping with Change: The Politics and Economics of Urban Poverty." In *The Urban Caribbean*, ed. A. Portes, C. Dore-Cabral, and P. Landolt, 227–52. Baltimore: Johns Hopkins University Press.

Portes, Alejandro, and Richard Schauffler. 1993. "Competing Perspectives on the Latin American Informal Sector." *Population and Development Review* 19, no. 1 (March): 33–60.

Pyke, Frank, Giacomo Becattini, and Werner Sengenberger. 1990. *Industrial Districts and Inter-Firm Co-operation in Italy*. Geneva: International Institute for Labour Studies.

Quijano, Anibal. 2000. "Coloniality of Power and Eurocentrism in Latin America." *International Sociology* 15, no. 2:215–32.

Roberts, Bryan. 1995. *The Making of Citizens: Cities of Peasants Revisited*. London: Arnold.

Schmitz, Hubert. 1995. "Small Shoemakers and Fordist Giants: Tale of a Supercluster." *World Development* 23, no. 1:9–28.

FOUR

Vanishing Assets: Cumulative Disadvantages Among the Urban Poor

Mercedes González de la Rocha

Since the 1980s, Mexico's opportunity structures have experienced changes that are deeply affecting household economies. Their vulnerability has risen as labor markets and the character and extent of state intervention have drastically reduced the possibilities to convert resources into real assets. Economic instability has ushered in a new era of uncertainty that challenges the household's capacity to face economic crises and resist the erosion of its means. In this chapter, I discuss the main components of the process that has led to the decline of household funds and the creation of cumulative disadvantages among the urban poor in Mexico.

Research on households has made key conceptual contributions to our understanding of how the urban poor survive. As rich in new data and ideas as this literature has been, gaps in knowledge persist. In particular, the recurrence of economic setbacks in the developing world since the early 1980s leads me to wonder about the usefulness of existing analytical tools for assessing current conditions. An important question concerns the limits of *survival strategies*. To what extent are the poor able to face new hardships? At what point does a survival strategy cease to be effective? Until now, we have held the idea that the poor simply work hard (or harder) in order to make ends meet. Whether, or at what point, they might face *constraints* to their reproductive capacity has not been investigated.

* The author wishes to thank Patricia Price for insights and her helpful participation in the editing of a previous version of this article published by *Latin American Perspectives* under the title "From the Resources of Poverty to the Poverty of Resources? The Erosion of a Survival Model."

Here I discuss the limits of survival strategies in light of the ongoing economic calamities faced by poor households across Latin America. I argue that the deep restructuring over the last two decades has severely undermined the capacity of poor and working-class urban households to endure. They have thus moved from a situation characterized by the availability of *resources in poverty* to one distinguished by a *poverty of resources*. In other words, the survival-strategies approach is no longer theoretically or empirically viable.

The capacity of households and individuals to achieve well-being and income levels commensurate with their needs is the result of the interaction of a group of complex social processes in which labor market opportunities and the provision of public services and benefits play an important role. The ability of the poor to act in their own behalf depends on government development strategies and social policies that either facilitate or constrain survival, social mobility, and reproduction.[1] In urban Mexico, economic conditions and labor market opportunities have deteriorated to the point where middle-class households have become significantly poorer and poor households have lost even minimal choices to earn a living.[2] The limited means to garner income in the formal sector has also eroded self-provisioning among the urban poor, that is, self-employment, petty-commodity marketing, and household production for consumption. Reciprocal exchanges among domestic units have also been negatively affected.

Although participation in the labor market is central to my analysis, shrinking economic opportunity for the poor affects other dimensions of life. The multifaceted nature of poverty entails a recognition that "the capabilities of individuals and households are deeply influenced by factors ranging from the prospects of earning a living to the social and psychological effects of deprivation and exclusion" (Moser 1996, 23). I suggest that increasing poverty erodes even the aptitude of low-income sectors to maintain networks of social exchange (see Moser 1996 for similar findings regarding the erosion of social capital). Furthermore, I suggest that, as economic uncertainty continues, a sociocultural context of *radical exclusion* is emerging in urban Mexico. A recent study of the emotional ramifications of poverty in Guadalajara shows that low-income women are increasingly experiencing emotional disorders that include a wide variety of symptoms such as headaches, distrust, loneliness, and acute anxiety (Enríquez Rosas 2002).

This chapter is based on research conducted in Guadalajara, Mexico's second-largest city, which experienced high levels of unemployment and

deteriorating living conditions in the mid-1990s. Although employment opportunities expanded after 1996, recent analyses have uncovered new setbacks on
the employment front with an increasing number of individuals earning
extremely low wages and excluded from remunerative and secure occupations
(Enríquez Rosas 2002; Román 2001). According to Georgina Rojas (2002), the
redefinition of labor demand and state involvement have increasingly exposed
households to market forces without the protection of government policies to
make up for eroding resources. The same author shows that the number of
urban poor households increased from 1993 to 2000, regardless of specific
characteristics. Low-income sectors have not recovered from the impact of
economic crises, especially the Peso Crisis of 1995. The much-heralded recovery
after 1996 has not restored household economies. My skepticism about the usefulness of an approach based on *the resources of poverty* is applicable to other
countries in the hemisphere, given radical changes resulting from the recent
application of neoliberal economic policies.

Household Research and Survival Strategies

To argue for a conceptual shift from the *resources of poverty* to the *poverty of
resources*, I draw from my own long-held interest in gender and the shifting
dynamics of household organization in urban Mexico. In designing and
implementing this research, my main concern has never been to measure
poverty but to understand how poor people conduct their lives (Nussbaum
and Sen 1993). This requires participant observation, in-depth interviewing,
and the collection of "thick" ethnographic data. During almost two decades
of research and analysis, I have used a combination of quantitative and qualitative methods to elucidate changing means of survival and reproduction
among the urban working poor. While quantitative data have allowed me to
construct profiles and gain insight into trends and patterns, qualitative information, case studies, and family histories have been especially valuable to my
thinking about household dynamics and change.

I argue that coping with poverty involves a multiplicity of resources
deployed by men, women, and children in domestic settings. Nevertheless,
household *capabilities* (in this case, combining resources and using them to
improve purchasing power and standards of living) are not static with respect
to or isolated from other social factors. Capabilities are, in fact, highly sensitive to broader economic change and themselves subject to variation.[3]

Households and Change

The household has been defined as "a locus of competing interests, rights, obligations and resources" (Moore 1994) and as a site of "cooperative conflict" (Sen 1991). It has also been portrayed as a social unit characterized by contradictory interests and unequal access to resources (González de la Rocha 1994a). However defined, households must be studied as stratified entities that allocate uneven burdens and rewards to their constituents in terms of age and gender (Benería 1992). Conflict, inequality, and differential income distribution within households have been widely examined (García and Oliveira 1994; Blumberg 1995; Chant 1996). That scrutiny reveals the changing character of domestic units as they meet historical and economic pressures (Sen 1993).

Households have also been conceptualized as a mediating mechanism between individuals and the socioeconomic structure. It is within households that crucial choices—not free of strife and negotiation—and actions vis-à-vis dynamic labor markets and changing social conditions take place (García, Muñoz, and Oliveira 1982; Benería 1992; Benería and Roldán 1987; Anderson, Bechhofer, and Gershuny 1994; González de la Rocha 1994a). Writings on Mexico emphasize internal structure, domestic cycles, and power interactions in the shaping of different household functions (García, Muñoz, and Oliveira 1982; García and Oliveira 1994; Selby, Murphy, and Lorenzen 1990; González de la Rocha 1994a; Chant 1991).

Understanding how poor families cope has been an enduring theme in the literature on socioeconomic development. Early analyses highlighted the possible breakdown or marginalization of domestic units as a result of rapid urbanization. In the 1980s, research began to focus on the drastic impact of economic crisis on household organization and economic prospects (Roberts 1995). Nevertheless, survival-strategy approaches predate crisis-focused empirical research. The concept of family strategy was first adopted as a way to move away from writings on modernization "that denied instrumental rationality to pre-industrial, early industrial and, more generally, poor people because of their lack of resources and power" (Tilly 1987). To impute agency and strategic thinking to the poor was a reaction against earlier views portraying individuals and households as puppets of forces beyond their control (e.g., Roberts 1995; Schmink 1984; Anderson 1980).

Nevertheless, survival-strategy approaches have not been immune to strong counter-criticism. Writing on gender, household dynamics, and rural industrialization in Java, Diane Lauren Wolf (1992) discusses analytical misconceptions underlying the notion of household strategy in the development literature. She argues that the poor have few if any choices and can hardly engage in long-term planning (see also Selby, Murphy, and Lorenzen 1990). Many poor families cannot advance the interests of their individual constituents or deploy actions based on consensus, solidarity, or unified action. Wolf's strongest objection is to the "analytical merging" of individuals and households, that is, treating women and other household members as fully submerged in the household. Other authors have questioned the existence of strategies, since decisions are often made by individual household members with greater power—men, for example (see, e.g., Crow 1989). In a similar light, women's labor, both paid and unremunerated, has been identified as an effective but not always visible source of income.

The Resources of Poverty

In periods of economic growth, when the number of jobs expands, household members pour into the labor market in search of subsistence. That was the case in Guadalajara and other Mexican cities between the 1940s and 1970s under the aegis of government-sponsored import substitution industrialization (Chant 1991; Benería and Roldán 1987; Selby, Murphy, and Lorenzen 1990; González de la Rocha 1994a). The economic model during that period was comprehensive. According to Agustín Escobar Latapí (1994) the Latin American order was closely articulated and capable of integrating many economic and social sectors into a single structure. In other words, the *system may have been exploitative but it was also inclusive*.[4] Aggregate demand expanded on the basis of commodity production for internal consumption. Employment opportunities grew; so did the purchasing power of middle-class families and, to a lesser extent, those in the working class. In most of Latin America, poverty experienced sensible decreases, and formal and measurable informal activities grew harmoniously through subcontracting chains (Benería and Roldán 1987).[5] Low-income households depended on a multiplicity of income sources, some provided by the market and others made possible by state policy (Kaztman 1999; González de la Rocha 1994a).

The resources-of-poverty model points to a plurality of income sources and to the organizational capacity of households to make survival possible. I developed that model on the basis of research carried out in Guadalajara immediately before the 1982 economic crisis (González de la Rocha 1994a). Although it was meant to describe and explain the coping behaviors of the urban poor in a particular Mexican city, research conducted by other scholars throughout Latin America confirmed its widespread relevance (Chant 1991; Feijoó 1991; Pastore, Zilberstajn, and Pagotto 1983; Barrig 1993). Regardless of geographical location or culture, households accounted for the reproduction of the labor force. Households managed scarcity through the labor market participation of multiple members and the pooling of their incomes. Earnings derived from wages obtained in the formal and informal sectors.

Although men were the main wage earners, women also made important contributions. Their participation in the labor market depended on the characteristics and developmental stage of their households. Extended families with several adult women were more likely to foster female participation in paid employment (Chant 1991). Women tended to be involved in waged labor in early phases of the domestic cycle while sons and daughters became important sources of income in later stages. Many young households adopted a traditional division of labor with a man acting as the principal wage earner. Nevertheless, older households had at least two members fully participating in the labor market. It was also common for young housewives to work for pay during emergency periods (caused by illness of the main provider, for example), while women living in extended households often worked on a more regular basis.

Households relied heavily on income-generating activity such as petty commodity production and petty trade. Women were especially important in that respect—almost every household included a mother, wife, or sister who baked, cooked, or sewed for sale. Men also participated in petty commodity production but in different trades, such as carpentry, bricklaying, and plumbing.

The production of goods and services for self-consumption, performed mainly by women, was also an essential source of household well-being. It included daily activities such as cooking, washing and ironing, housecleaning, mending, and home construction. Women's days were long, especially when they were also working for a wage—paid employment did not exempt them from domestic chores (Cockcroft 1998).

In addition, income and assets accruing from reciprocal exchanges between families proved to be crucial for the survival of urban working-poor households. Both men and women were involved in networking. Sociability fields, and the benefits derived from them, were distinguished by gender. The flow of goods and services within networks formed by friends, neighbors, workmates, and relatives aided low-income households to meet acceptable standards of living. Larissa Lomnitz (1977) was among the first to show that social networks are key to survival. Social networks are central to people's lives both when social exchanges are present and when they are absent. My research in Guadalajara showed that, although few in number, the poorest of poor households were socially isolated (González de la Rocha 1994a).

In the resources-of-poverty model households were not homogeneous in occupational terms, and it was common to find different types of workers within specific domestic units. Even a single worker could participate in various occupational niches not only in the course of a lifetime but also during the working day. Occupational diversification on the part of some household members was often used to compensate for the unemployment of others. This cushioned the impact of transitory crisis caused, for example, by dismissal, illness, or death.

Occupational diversification was also the inevitable result of low wages and the need to combine several incomes to ensure household survival. Households with more resources and working members to take advantage of labor market opportunities could expand their domestic budget. Occupational diversification, as well, muted class differences, since workers in the formal sector shared dwellings with street vendors and other kinds of unregulated laborers.

Implications of the Resources-of-Poverty Model

Elsewhere I have argued (González de la Rocha 1994a; González de la Rocha, Escobar, and Martínez 1990) that households are highly contradictory units characterized by the coexistence of solidarity and confrontation and, as a result, impoverishment has different effects on women and men, adults and children. Households must therefore be examined in a diachronic way with an aim at detecting processes and pinpointing evolutionary stages likely to heighten the risk of poverty. Before 1985, household survival and reproduction in Guadalajara were achieved through the pooling of resources, only some of which were secured by the main provider. Important as they were, women's contributions paralleled those of men and, except in the case of some female-headed households, there was no awareness of the feminization of household economies. Collaboration did not necessarily entail equality in the distribution of burdens and rewards or harmony in daily interactions. Extended and mature households were economically better off. Worse-off units were smaller and either younger or formed almost entirely by old people.

Women and children's lives were not easy at the time when I constructed the resources-of-poverty model. I saw many women agonize when they had to leave their small children locked up on their own while they went to work.

Youngsters were especially vulnerable to extreme poverty, and suffering was a daily experience in the lives of poor households. Often, women endured a triple burden as care providers, wage earners, and participants in neighborhood actions for the provisioning of services. Domestic chores were especially hard to carry out where the lack of water, sewers, and other services made them not only time-consuming, but also energy-depleting (Chant 1996).

Despite those difficulties, families endured, thanks largely to the availability of formal and informal employment. With various degrees of difficulty, both men and women could find jobs. Grown children in their mid-teens were also expected to work, and although early entrance into the labor market meant a halt in education, their contributions were highly valued by parents and siblings. Unemployment was very low, and I did not hear anyone saying, as people commonly do nowadays, "there are no jobs," "there is no work." In addition to formal employment, informal activities were an attractive option. Wages in that sector were not necessarily lower than those in the regulated sector (see, e.g., Escobar Latapí 1986).

Structures in Transition

Structural adjustment since the mid-1980s has deeply transformed the panorama sketched above, altering the articulation between macrolevel economic and political arrangements and microlevel household adaptations. Earlier studies made it clear that in earlier stages of development the poor were socially integrated as low-waged workers. The concept of "the working poor" was coined to call attention to the coexistence of poverty and economic participation (Horrigan and Mincy 1994; Levitan and Shapiro 1987; McFate, Smeeding, and Rainwater 1995; Escobar Latapí 1986; González de la Rocha 1994a). Research made it obvious that, given extremely low levels of remuneration, the survival of the working poor could not be guaranteed on an individual basis but the household made up for market failure (González de la Rocha 1994a; Roberts 1995). Household restructuring in the 1980s included the increased participation of household members in the labor market, especially adult women working mainly in the informal sector. That shift led also to the expansion of domestic chores and the reorganization of consumption patterns as households became extended or incorporated new members (see González de la Rocha 1988, 1991). So-called strategies of survival depended on longer or harder labor, "the poor's greatest asset" (Moser 1996). Cooperative arrangements at the neighborhood level further cushioned families against adversity and penury (Lomnitz 1977; González de la Rocha 1994a; Moser 1996).

From 1982, when Mexico's debt crisis exploded, to 1986, official and real wages declined dramatically, and the peso dropped to one-eighth of its previous dollar value. Capital flight and fiscal austerity led to uncertainty. The formal sector began to shrink, and informal jobs became one of few alternatives available to low-income groups. Between 1980 and 1987, informal employment grew by 80 percent in absolute terms (CEPAL 1992a) and rose from 24 percent to 33 percent as a proportion of the economically active population (Escobar Latapí 1996; Roberts 1995). Maquiladoras grew in number and importance as a source of foreign currency but remained marginal with respect to the percentage of the total labor force they employed

Between 1986 to 1988 deep economic restructuring took place. Wages continued to decline while inflation rose, reaching a peak of 159 percent in 1987 (Escobar Latapí 1996). State-owned enterprises were privatized, and social expenditures fell from 7.6 percent of the gross domestic product (GDP) in 1981 to 5.6 percent in 1987–88 (Cordera and González Tiburcio 1991). After Mexico signed the General Agreement on Tariffs and Trade in 1986, the opening of local markets to foreign goods dealt a serious blow to domestic firms, many of which closed down. Guadalajara, the quintessential "big city of small industry" (Arias 1985), was particularly hard hit by the new *open economy*, which brought cheaper imported shoes, clothing, and textiles to local shops and thus all but annihilated Guadalajara's main manufactures.

Under those circumstances, lowering production costs became an important means for local enterprises to endure, and both national and multinational firms cut wages to retain their competitive edge. By 1987 wages in new maquiladora plants were 60 percent lower than eight years earlier (see Carrillo 1991 and Escobar Latapí 1996). In contrast to the previous era, in which informal employment coexisted with formal jobs, informality grew even as the formal sector declined.

Inequality increased during those years. According to Fernando Cortés (1997) the richest 10 percent of the population earned 55 percent more in real terms in 1992 than in 1977, while the real income of other social groups plummeted. The middle class, especially in its lower strata, experienced substantial losses (González de la Rocha 1995b). Living standards sank to unprecedented levels in recent memory for the working class and the poor, that is, the bottom 40 percent of Mexico's population. Real wage deterioration, incipient but actual unemployment, and job insecurity further accelerated the shift toward insolvency.

Adjusting the Household

Household responses to the crisis of the 1980s entailed an intensification of the coping behaviors identified by the resources-of-poverty model. Household resources, mainly labor, proved crucial. Flexibility and adaptive capacity kept household income from falling as rapidly as individual wages. Household income in Guadalajara fell only 11 percent between 1982 and 1985, while individual wages fell by 35 percent. The household acted as a buffer protecting individual members from the impact of economic crisis.[6] That relative success did not include improved levels of well-being. In order to defend their incomes, household members had to work much harder and intensify the use of available assets, particularly the labor of women and children. This placed a heavy burden on women, who, in addition to working for pay, saw domestic chores augmented without much help from their male counterparts (González de la Rocha 1988, 1991).

Research conducted in the 1980s and early 1990s showed that households were experiencing a privatization of the economic crisis (Benería 1992; González de la Rocha 1988, 1991) by absorbing many of the functions earlier fulfilled by government and markets. Mexico was not exceptional in that regard; studies in other Latin American countries confirmed the existence of similar responses (Fortuna and Prates 1989; Hardy 1989; Ortega and Tironi 1988; Pastore, Zilberstajn, and Pagotto 1983; Schkolnik and Teitelboim 1988; González de la Rocha 1994b, 1995a).

Although nuclear households continued to be in the majority, the proportion of extended units increased. The expansion of households was achieved through the incorporation of adult members to reduce housing expenses and increase the pool of available labor. Extended households, although less numerous than nuclear households, gave shelter to a greater number of people during the years of the crisis (CEPAL 1992a). My research showed that living with parents after marriage became a common practice among young couples (González de la Rocha 1988, 1991, 1995a). The extended household became a savings mechanism and a means to protect members from hardship and insecurity.

The decreasing value of wages affected the participation of household members who were not considered primary earners. Married women with children aggressively sought paid employment. This was in contrast to earlier trends leading mostly young, educated, and single females into the labor force. Anthropological studies first revealed that shift (González de la Rocha 1988; Barrig 1993; Moser 1989), later confirmed by statistical analyses of national-based data (García and Oliveira 1994). In addition to adult women, young men—sons—also increased their participation in the labor market. This was to compensate for the decreasing capacity of adult males to act as main breadwinners. The importance of women and children as income earners grew during those years, while the contribution of male heads of household fell.[7]

Apart from increasing the number of wage earners, urban households broadened their income venues to counterbalance the fragility of their wage sources. The proportion of household income derived from wages diminished, while self-employment and self-provisioning increased (CEPAL 1991). Self-employment became more appealing as wages in the formal sector shrank. The number of women working in family businesses without a wage is difficult to measure, but some studies suggest that this category of workers grew significantly (Escobar Latapí 1996).

The weight of domestic chores also increased as households came to include more members, and many stopped buying goods and services that could be replaced by homemade equivalents like recycling used objects, repairing domestic appliances, mending old clothes, eating only home-cooked meals, and so on.

Reciprocal exchanges among households took center stage. Collaboration, mutual help, the exchange of favors, and the daily flow of goods and services among relatives, neighbors, and friends became fundamental to the preservation of households. Women's networks, in particular, became an essential adaptation providing support in child care and household chores as well as information about possible sources of income.

Household consumption patterns were transformed. Some categories, like clothing and entertainment, were severely restricted or eliminated to protect access to vital goods such as food and shelter. Nevertheless, basic consumption suffered too as real wages deteriorated and employment became scarcer. Meat purchases were reduced in favor of carbohydrates and less expensive protein provided by items such as eggs or organ meat like calf liver and heart.

The crisis had a differential impact on households of varying sizes and structures—some types were more vulnerable than others. Smaller, often nuclear households and households in the expansion stage, also small with a high dependency ratio, had a limited capacity to defend income and maintain adequate consumption patterns. A dramatic implication of this finding is that the more vulnerable households were also those with more children, whose nutrition, health, and educational levels were seriously jeopardized.

In a similar fashion, household restructuring did not weigh equally upon all household members. Accumulated evidence suggests that women endured a heavier share of the cost of economic restructuring and change (Benería 1992). Women had to work harder both as waged workers and producers of goods and services within the household. Their unpaid domestic work made it "easier for employers to pay all workers less, while . . . gender ideologies [made] women superexploitable" (Cockcroft 1998, 43).

The case of female-headed households is particularly interesting in that it shows that women's control over resources is crucial for well-being. Studies conducted in Mexico and elsewhere have shown that, contrary to a common misimpression, female-headed households are spread over all income strata and are, in fact, more frequent among the non-poor (Chant 1997; González de la Rocha 1999a; see also CEPAL 1996, for Latin America as a whole). The poorest households in Mexico tend to be headed by men as the only economic providers (Cortés and Rubalcava 1995). According to those studies, household headship, whether held by men or women, does not by itself explain greater or lesser poverty. Within vulnerable sectors, those households with a single income earner, whether male or female, tend to be poorer (Cortés and Rubalcava 1995). The combination of female and male incomes leads to better economic situations, and this combination is found in households with more than two workers. Those households that rely heavily on women's incomes tend to be better off whether they are led by females or include men as well. My research also showed that female-headed households were better equipped than male-headed households to protect patterns of adequate consumption. In fact, households headed by women showed less dramatic changes in their diets, less violence, and a more equal distribution of responsibilities (González de la Rocha 1991, 1999b; Chant 1997, 1999). Women's greater control over household income is an effective tool for protecting priority areas like food and health. These insights highlight the need for more sensitive measuring tools able to detect assets other than income.

Rethinking Survival: The Poverty of Resources

Since labor is the wealth of the poor (Moser 1996; González de la Rocha 1994a), the true impact of current economic change is to be found in the exclusion of workers even from precarious employment.[8] The severity and length of restructuring is reducing the capacity of households to respond in the typical ways. As neoliberal policies become extensive, the resources-of-poverty model loses empirical and theoretical viability. Instead, it is the poverty of resources that characterizes the present moment. The poverty of resources available to low-income families is the result of exclusion from the labor market. It signals the erosion of social and economic conditions necessary for survival and reproduction.

The collapse of social systems of support and self-help organizations is due not to any inherent incapacity of people to survive or escape from poverty but to the rapid deterioration of labor markets. The reduction or elimination of government-sponsored protections and benefits has compounded the effect of decreasing opportunities for employment. I agree with Caroline Moser (1996) that the persistent economic crisis has made the strategies and resourcefulness of the poor insufficient to offset the shrinkage of their asset base. I argue, in addition, that it is not only social capital that is being chipped away but also poor people's capacity to participate in alternative occupations and self-provisioning. The result is a perverse process of *cumulative disadvantage*.

Throughout the 1990s, export-oriented models of development gained momentum in Mexico. Non-petroleum exports increased from 17.2 percent in 1993 to 36.2 percent in 2000. This happened even as Mexico's economy became more vulnerable to the fluctuating state of economic affairs in the United States (Rojas 2002). Social inequality rose during that decade as another outcome of neoliberal reform (Cortés 2000).

The social implications of those changes have yet to be fully assessed, and much research is needed to understand them. Some indications of the profound effect of restructuring on household organization can, however, be found in recent analyses of national data and research conducted in Guadalajara. Rojas (2002) finds that economic liberalization and export-oriented production have not brought about improvement in living conditions for most households in Mexico. The opposite is a more accurate characterization: although poverty rates were higher in 1996 than in 2000, Mexicans were poorer at the turn of the twenty-first century than in 1993. While macroeconomic indicators improved after 1995, the benefits of that recovery did not reach the household level. According to a recent study of poverty in Mexico, in 2000 one in every five households (18.6 percent of total households and 24.2 percent of the overall population) did not have enough income to buy the staples necessary for survival (Comité Técnico para la Medición de la Pobreza 2002). Five out of every ten households (25.3 percent of households and 31.9 percent of the population) did not have sufficient resources to satisfy basic requirements for food, health, and education. Six out of ten households (45.9 percent of households and 53.7 percent of the population) could not meet needs for food, clothing (including shoes), housing, health, public transport, and education.

Current development policies exhibit a limited capacity to address the needs of workers with low levels of education and skill. Many firms have closed, others have reduced production, and those experiencing growth are far from accessible to most workers. Neoliberal policies benefit educated and technical workers, international markets, and high-tech production. Although still an ambiguous concept, I use the term *new unemployed* to designate displaced and potential workers facing decreased opportunities for employment (Fontes 1997). Neoliberalism goes hand in hand with restructuring of the labor process and the labor market (Escobar Latapí 1996) and, I would add, with changes in household structure and reproductive systems. That model has created a selective occupational niche for unmarried men and women with secondary educations who are not necessarily skilled but who are willing to work for low wages while at the same time excluding vast sectors whose members do not even have access to that kind of employment. Increasing poverty and new forms of exclusion are the main elements of life in Guadalajara and Mexico as a whole.

As Adolfo Figueroa, Teófilo Altamirano, and Denis Sulmont (1996) make clear, economic exclusion is defined in relation to a dominant organization that prevents the participation of certain groups or individuals in vital and desirable activities. It affects individuals who do not have the means, abilities, credentials, age, and sex to take part in the productive system. It involves increasing unemployment, especially among the young and decreasing male participation in the labor market.[9] Finally, it goes hand in hand with feminization, as more and more jobs adopt characteristics formerly associated with female employment (low wages, temporality, a paucity of benefits) and more and more men are forced into jobs once earmarked for women. These shifts are part of trends to maximize capital utility and expansion in the age of globalization (Fontes 1997). As Virginia Fontes has argued, in the context of present transformations the threat seems to be coming from within the capitalist structure, whose expansion has paralleled forced inclusions and exclusions. A result is the creation of redundant sectors formed by people permanently ousted from the labor market.

Even in a developing country like Mexico, manufacturing has lost its share of employment, except for the maquiladoras. As a result, many potential workers have turned to self-employment at an early age—they are becoming disposable in youth, not as old people. Regional differences have increased, as an employment belt grows in the Northern border area, a growth fed by the maquiladoras, while the South faces a lack of employment alternatives and increasing poverty.

According to Escobar Latapí (1996), the 1994 financial crisis signals a watershed because, for the first time since 1982, the population did not respond with a general intensification of work and informal employment. Instead, unemployment soared. While women's participation rates continued to rise, men's fell—approximately 700,000 women but only 300,000 men entered the labor force between 1993 and 1995. Unemployment among young men in main metropolitan areas reached an unprecedented 30 percent in 1995. Although employment rates grew after 1996, the share of workers in "critical" conditions has not diminished. By 2001, almost 42 percent of the occupied population was working in firms with fewer than five workers. Almost half of all workers were classified as "occupied without benefits." More than 20 percent had wages but no benefits or security (Banco de Información Económica 2002). According to Rojas (2002), the proportions of poor and non-poor households that have no access to social security increased in the 1990s with more than half of poor households and a third of the non-poor not having any type of social security by the year 2000. Unstable conditions rule labor arrangements: the absence of permanent contracts give way to insecure, low-paying, casual and temporal employment. Since *male* employment has continued to fall, Escobar suggests that the abatement of unemployment rates after 1995 may have been caused by the withdrawal of large numbers of people from job searches. In fact, male employment was lower in the first half of 2002 than during the first three months of 1996 (Banco de Información Económica). In an earlier article (Escobar and González de la Rocha 1995), I showed that informal employment and informal incomes stagnated toward the end of the Salinas de Gortari presidency in the early 1990s. Those declines were caused by the saturation of occupational niches (for example, in the maquiladoras) and by marginalization in other sectors. The opening of external trade and the influx of low-priced Asian products drastically affected Mexican labor-intensive industries, which relied most heavily on subcontracting and informal work. The flood of imports devastated Mexican firms, especially small and medium-sized manufacturing enterprises, which found the competition with commodities produced abroad a challenge too difficult to overcome.

From 1987 to 1993, the labor market participation of women rose from 33.2 to 40.0 percent in Guadalajara, from 34.5 to 38.7 percent in Mexico City, and from 26.6 to 39.1 percent in Monterrey. This increase in the presence of women in the labor market has continued. In Guadalajara, for example, the rate of women's participation during the first three months of 2002 was 45.2 percent (Banco de Información Económica, web page). This is occurring mostly in informal occupations and self-employment, and entails women with limited schooling, over thirty years old, with young children, and either married or separated.[10] By the late 1980s and early 1990s, self-employed women were working longer hours than self-employed men (Escobar Latapí 1996), and more women were working in family businesses without remuneration. More work for less income seems to be the dominant situation for many women in Mexico today.

Sustained Crisis and the Erosion of Survival

Although with great difficulty, the resources-of-poverty model operated as long as there were opportunities to work. Work brought in low wages, but households still had the option of sending members into the labor force. A good deal of household income originated in sources other than wages—reciprocal exchanges, domestic production of goods and services—but households depended primarily on the availability of jobs for monetary funds. Furthermore, they relied on wages from relatively stable work to pursue other sources of income, such as petty commodity production and small-scale trade.

Poor urban households face significantly different conditions today. The current situation, characterized by new forms of exclusion and increasing precariousness, is unfavorable to the operation of traditional household mechanisms of work intensification. Instead of talking about the resources of poverty, the present situation requires that we shift attention to the poverty of resources.

Unlike in the 1980s, poor households in the 1990s did not increase their number of wage earners. Rojas (2002) found the opposite: for sixteen urban areas throughout the country, the number of income earners per household has constantly fallen over the past decade. While households had an average of 2.5 earners in 1993, that number dropped to 2.2 in 1996 and to 2.1 in the year 2000. Although it is crucial for poor households to diversify and increase incomes, they simply could not accomplish that objective in recent times.

The general lack of employment has fundamentally disrupted household economies and organization. If labor is the most important resource available to the urban poor, then the exclusion of poor workers must have important effects on their capacity for survival and reproduction. In the past, precarious employment coexisted with formal employment and independent income sources. The current situation, by contrast, combines a lack of jobs and precarious employment for the majority. Permanent employment has become rare and available only to a diminishing number of skilled and educated workers. A new type of labor market segmentation seems to be emerging, not along the formal/informal lines, but between a privileged minority and the rest of the population, who are struggling to survive with very limited resources.

Being unemployed means, first of all, losing the regular wages associated with a job. In addition, as Jahoda (quoted in Gershuny and Miles 1985) points out, being unemployed deprives one of experiences and social links that are crucial for well-being and social identity—physical activity, social contact, collective purpose, time structure, and social status. Living outside employment structures is a disrupting and dislocating experience at both the individual and the collective levels. It affects the use of time and the quality of social relationships. Daily habits and long-term social behaviors are challenged. The inability of young people, especially men, to find work is diminishing the capacity of households to supplement the low incomes of male and female heads. Young people used to be important sources of income through the late 1980s, contributing to the expansion of household funds and making it possible for younger siblings to continue their education. The comparative advantage of certain types of households and the consolidation stage of the domestic cycle vanish when the labor capacity of young people cannot be mobilized.

One of the latest responses to employment shortages is the increasing migration of young men and women to the United States. The difficulty of obtaining and keeping jobs in Mexican cities, together with the low pay that most jobs offer, underlie decisions to emigrate and become part of transnational communities of workers (see also Safa 1998, for the case of the Dominican Republic). International migration used to be associated with limited opportunities in rural areas, it now includes growing numbers of urban men and women. In comparison with earlier, less permanent migratory patterns, the new trend of international migration is toward permanent settlement. Families staying in Mexico are losing their youngest and strongest constituents.[11] Survival in Guadalajara and other Mexican cities is even harder without the contributions of those household members and without the daily social exchange that they used to provide.

Low wages and lack of work opportunities also threaten the internal resources of urban households. The role that sons used to play tends to disappear through emigration or unemployment. Traditionally, the resources of poverty were in the hands and arms of young men and women. Current conditions have reduced adult men's capacity to act as providers and undermined prospects for the young, pushing them into transnational labor markets.

Female labor is one of the few resources still available for the survival of poor households. The declining role of men as breadwinners has occurred in a context in which women increasingly work for wages that (although very low) have become crucial for daily household maintenance (Safa 1995). Women of all kinds—young and mature, single and married, educated or unskilled, mothers and daughters—are becoming main providers, not just supplemental wage earners.

Labor exclusion also diminishes the capacity of individuals to participate in self-provisioning, self-employment, and household petty production. It is not accurate to say that people will increasingly turn to those activities in the spare time made available by unemployment (Pahl 1984; Pahl and Wallace 1985). My case studies show that men and women without regular incomes (obtained in the labor market) face enormous difficulties in self-provisioning because there is simply no money for them to invest in materials, transportation, and other necessary supplies. This calls into question the "autonomous" nature of self-provisioning and suggests a different hypothesis: self-provisioning activities and household production of goods and services for household consumption are connected to regular wages obtained in the labor market. In situations where there is at least one regular wage, individuals within households can devote time and other resources, including some money, to self-provisioning and household production. In contexts where wages are sporadic, casual, or nonexistent, individuals have very little margin for self-provisioning. Therefore, unemployment and, specifically, labor exclusion entails a lack of access to a whole range of income-generating alternatives.

More generally, we could argue that households need regular wages to tap into *other* income sources. Even benefits accruing from reciprocal exchanges depend to a certain extent on regular wages. Networks are not simply "there" for people to use when needed. Their availability depends on regular social interaction. They require, as in the case of self-provisioning activities, that some assets be invested. Individuals who have resources to deploy as part of a reciprocal relationship, for example, will also be in a position to cultivate social ties; those without assets are kept out. Many women and men whom I have interviewed recently described social isolation as a symptom of extreme poverty.

Under these circumstances, households atomize and the social fabric deteriorates even as insecurity and distrust rise, fueled by alcohol and drug consumption. Symptoms of social decline and deviance—theft, assault and battery, and other crimes—are on the rise in *colonias populares* (low-income urban settlements). Support networks, as described by Lomnitz (1977) and others several decades ago, have all but disappeared (González de la Rocha

1999c; Enríquez Rosas 2002). This bleak scenario evokes Javier Auyero's discussion of neoliberal violence in Argentina (Auyero 2000). The deleterious effects of radical economic reform are not exclusive to Mexico.

Conclusion

Labor reorganization of the type I discuss in this chapter favors a minority of workers and prevents the majority from entering occupational niches fostered and protected by export-oriented economic policies. Although export-oriented economic models have brought about the feminization of the labor force, they cannot be described as inclusive. Recent industrialization has been as much female-led as export-led (Joekes 1987, 82), and the declining participation of men in the labor market is widely recognized: That does not mean, however, that women are taking up the jobs that men used to have, nor is their position the same as male workers used to enjoy. Even Susan P. Joekes (1987), who believes that export-oriented policies favor women, acknowledges persistent and substantial gender gaps in wages and the segregation of the occupational structure in terms of sex. Women continue to be at the low-paid end of the job scale. Therefore, in a context where women are concentrated in low-skilled work offering extremely low wages and few prospects for promotion and advancement, we cannot talk about an economic development model that benefits "girls."[12] The issue here, as Joekes recognizes, is that internationalization lowers wages in many economic sectors. We should not be surprised at women's decisions to continue working even though they are aware of their unequal exchange of hard work for low returns. Women need and appreciate earning an income, to say nothing about the requirements of their households. But although paid work has its positive features, they are not enough to counter the general of exclusion and segmentation of low-income populations caused by current models of development.

More research and thinking are needed, however, to obtain a clearer picture of the differential impact of current economic conditions on men and women. I have suggested that labor exclusion is creating new gendered household patterns in which men are losing their capacity to perform their socially assigned role as providers and women are emerging as the new breadwinners despite their very low wages (Safa 1995). Whether this is giving women more authority and a bargaining edge at the household level is not known. That possibility has been discussed in Mexico since women's participation in the labor force first increased in the early 1980s but debates have not led to consensus. My impression is that economic, social, and cultural changes proceed at different paces, the first rapidly and the others slowly.

On the other hand, women are not passive victims of forces over which they have no control. They are undertaking acts of resistance in need of serious analysis. The increasing rates of divorce and separation, as outcomes of women's own decisions, and the growing numbers of "reconstituted" households based on democratic relationships suggest that women are in search of less oppressive lives. Perhaps future generations of women workers and women breadwinners will encounter more favorable circumstances to perform their duties as providers, mothers, and wives.

Households are dynamic and diverse social units that evolve and change both as a response to external forces and in accordance with their internal dynamics. Within a wide range of diversity that includes nuclear, extended, reconstituted, and female-headed households, there are structures better able to cope with external social and economic changes. Among these are female-headed households, which, despite the difficulties they face, have managed to protect their consumption patterns during economic crises. Rojas's logistic models show that in Mexican cities male-headed households consistently faced higher risks of poverty throughout the 1990s. Her study supports earlier qualitative findings (Chant 1991, 1997; González de la Rocha 1991, 1999b). Extended and consolidated (mature) households have traditionally been more successful at protecting income, since they have a larger pool of labor to draw from. Nevertheless, the current economic situation has undermined that comparative advantage as workers, especially young men, face exclusion in the labor market.

Sources of income other than wages critically depend on the capacity of households to draw monetary earnings through the employment of at least some of their members. Better-off households are those that manage to develop multiple means for income generation from diverse sources, but wages remain a critical component. In other words, petty commodity production, domestic production of goods and services for household consumption, and reciprocal exchanges through networking are not independent factors. They require an investment of time, effort (labor), and money.[13] This is not a trivial insight. People need remunerated employment to extract benefits from noneconomic activities. Income from other sources can complement but not replace wages in a capitalist society. Emphasizing survival strategies to the point of losing sight of the limits of those strategies can only lead to analytical dead ends. The emphasis on multiple income sources that was part of the resources-of-poverty model helped to create the impression that the poor would survive even without employment. This view is wrong. Past analyses did not give enough attention to wages as the motor of reproduction and could not predict the erosion of other sources of income in the absence of wages.

The occupational diversification that is part of the resources-of-poverty model once led me to argue that households contained both formal and informal workers. The current situation, marked by the scarcity of labor options for the majority, is producing a real deterioration of income and survival sources. A huge gap between the very privileged who can obtain permanent employment and those excluded from it is growing. This time households seem to be less able to cope. The "melting pot" has fewer ingredients for its stew.

There are, fortunately, many exceptions to the poverty-of-resources model. The elements of what I have called the erosion of survival mechanisms are, however, real. If employment continues to shrink and labor markets continue to be characterized by exclusion and precariousness, fewer exceptions and a more general application of the model may be expected, leading to a crisis of social reproduction for the excluded, disposable urban majorities.

NOTES

1. See Torrado 1995 for an interesting view of the relevance of social policies and development strategies to the capacity of the poor in Argentina to overcome "the intergenerational trap of poverty" through upward social mobility.

2. The absence of options is clearly an extreme situation that very few households experience. What I want to point out is that the deterioration of the labor market is increasingly narrowing households' options.

3. Sen's (1993) concept of "capabilities" is especially appropriate for referring to the alternative combinations of characters and functions that households may have at different times or under different social situations. It allows one to think about wider or narrower alternative combinations and therefore the more or less real opportunities to act and to perform certain functions.

4. I do not want to give the wrong impression of the import-substitution-industrialization model as "good." Low wages and difficult living conditions were part of it.

5. While at the beginning of the 1970s 40 percent of the Latin American population was poor, by 1980 the percentage of the poor had decreased to 35. Urban poverty also diminished, although to a lesser extent, from 26 percent of urban households in 1970 to 25 percent in 1980 (CEPAL 1991; González de la Rocha 1995a).

6. Data from other countries show the same trend. Household total income in Venezuela fell 22 percent while individual incomes fell 34 percent, and in Costa Rica it declined 14 percent compared with 22 percent of individual incomes (CEPAL 1991, 23). The Mexican data come from my own fieldwork (based on the follow-up of the households originally studied). See González de la Rocha 1988, 1991, and 1994a.

7. The contribution of male heads of households came to represent no more than 60 percent of households' incomes in most Latin American countries (CEPAL 1991).

8. Experts on labor structures argue that unemployment is not a good indicator of labor market transformations in Mexico (Brígida García, personal communication). Unemployment, however, is an ethnographic datum, a phenomenon that people describe as a new problem in their lives and an obstacle to better material conditions. It can be considered, therefore, as an indicator of people's perspectives of increasing exclusion and precariousness.

9. The new unemployed are individuals who fall into the traditional category of "not working and looking for work." For these individuals, however, extended periods of unemployment are a permanent feature of their lives. Latin American academics have often pointed out that unemployment is a luxury that Latin American populations cannot afford. Indeed, we are witnessing the creation of a social category that without the support of state agencies falls into destitution or becomes an extra burden on already impoverished households.

10. Sixty-seven of the women working on their own account in Guadalajara in 1990 had not been active in 1982, and the average schooling of these women was less than six years (Escobar Latapí 1996).

11. Remittances are an important asset for many households in Mexico, but the progressive settlement of migrants in the United States, with marriage and the later appearance of U.S.-born children, regularly reduces, at least temporarily, such remittances. See Serrano 2002 for an anthropological analysis of remittances, a phenomenon that is based on intergenerational cycles of deferred reciprocity that are frequently interrupted when the migrants create their own procreation families.

12. Contrary to Joekes's view, it is hard to argue that the export-oriented economic model has favored women's economic emancipation through their inclusion in paid work. My work and that of other researchers in Mexico has shown that earnings control is not an automatic outcome of women's labor market participation, much less a more favorable position for bargaining and making decisions within the household. Benería and Roldán (1987) found that women's earnings were subject to male control. García and Oliveira (1994) showed that households in which women were the main providers but lived with their husbands were the sites of the most evident household violence, women frequently being battered and "punished." My own findings also revealed that women's earnings could hardly be seen as a means of emancipation, since many women have to hide their paid work from husbands and their wages are so deeply committed to subsistence that they are consumed immediately and almost invisibly (González de la Rocha 1994a).

13. Pahl's research in Britain (1984) also pointed to the intimate relationship between wages obtained in the labor market and the household's capacity to undertake "do-it-yourself" activities (painting, repairs, carpentry, and so on). These activities were mainly performed by households in which there was at least one member employed. Employment of one member was found to be associated with the employment of other members of the household, while unemployment of one member was associated with unemployment of the rest and there was no possibility of devoting resources to "do-it-yourself" activities (see also Pahl and Wallace 1985).

REFERENCES

Anderson, Michael, ed. 1980. *Sociology of the Family.* Harmondsworth: Penguin.

Anderson, Michael, Frank Bechhofer, and Jonathan Gershuny. 1994. Introduction to *The Social and Political Economy of the Household,* ed. Anderson, Bechhofer, and Gershuny. New York: Oxford University Press.

Arias, Patricia, ed. 1985. *Guadalajara, la gran ciudad de la pequeña industria.* Zamora: El Colegio de Michoacán.

Auyero, Javier. 2000. "The Hyper-Shantytown: Neo-liberal Violence(s) in the Argentine Slum." *Ethnography* 1, no. 1:93–116.

Banco de Información Económica. 2003. http://www.inegi.gob.mx/.

Barrig, Maruja. 1993. *Seis familias en la crisis.* Lima: ADEC-ATC / Asociación Laboral para el Desarrollo.

Benería, Lourdes. 1992. "The Mexican Debt Crisis: Restructuring the Economy and the Household." In *Unequal Burden: Economic Crises, Persistent Poverty, and Women's Work,* ed. Lourdes Benería and Shelley Feldman. Boulder, Colo.: Westview Press.

Benería, Lourdes, and Marta I. Roldán. 1987. *The Crossroads of Class and Gender: Industrial Homework, Subcontracting, and Household Dynamics in Mexico City.* Chicago: University of Chicago Press.

Blumberg, Rae Lesser. 1995. "Introduction: Engendering Wealth and Well-being in an Era of Economic Transformation." In *EnGENDERing Wealth and Well-Being: Empowerment for Global Change,* ed. Rae Lesser Blumberg, Cathy A. Rakowski, Irene Tinker, and Michael Monteón. Boulder, Colo.: Westview Press.

Carrillo, Jorge. 1991. *Mercados de trabajo en la industria maquiladora de exportación.* Mexico City: Secretaría del Trabajo y Previsión Social / El Colegio de la Frontera Norte.

Chant, Sylvia. 1991. *Women and Survival in Mexican Cities: Perspectives on Gender, Labour Markets and Low-income Households.* Manchester: Manchester University Press.

———. 1996. *Gender, Urban Development, and Housing.* Vol. 2. United Nations Development Programme Publication Series for Habitat, no. 2. New York: United Nations Development Programme.

———. 1997. *Women-Headed Households: Diversity and Dynamics in the Developing World.* London: Macmillan.

———. 1999. "Las unidades domésticas encabezadas por mujeres en México y Costa Rica: Perspectivas populares y globales sobre el tema de las mujeres solas." In *Divergencias del modelo tradicional: Hogares de jefatura femenina en América Latina,* ed. Mercedes González de la Rocha. Mexico City: Centro de Investigaciones y Estudios Superiores en Antropología Social and Plaza y Valdés Editores.

Cockcroft, James D. 1998. "Gendered Class Analysis: Internationalizing, Feminizing, and Latinizing Labor's Struggle in the Americas." *Latin American Perspectives* 25, no. 6:42–46.

Comisión Económica para América Latina (CEPAL). 1991. *La equidad en el panorama social de América Latina durante los años ochenta.* Santiago: CEPAL.

————. 1992a. *El perfil de la pobreza en América Latina a comienzos de los años 90.* Santiago: CEPAL.

————. 1992b. *Hacia un perfil de la familia actual en Latinoamérica y el Caribe.* Santiago: CEPAL.

————. 1996. *Panorama social 1996.* http://www.eclac.cl/.

Comité Técnico para la Medición de la Pobreza. 2002. *Medición de la pobreza. Variantes metodológicas y estimación preliminar.* Mexico City: Secretaría de Desarrollo Social (SEDESOL).

Cordera, Rolando, and Enrique González Tiburcio. 1991. "Crisis and Transition in the Mexican Economy." In *Social Responses to Mexico's Economic Crisis of the 1980's,* ed. Mercedes González de la Rocha and Agustín Escobar. La Jolla: University of California at San Diego, Center for U.S.-Mexican Studies.

Cortés, Fernando. 1997. "La distribución del ingreso en México en épocas de estabilización y reforma económica." Ph.D. diss., CIESAS / Universidad de Guadalajara.

————. 2000. *La distribución del ingreso en México en épocas de estabilización y reforma económica.* Mexico City: CIESAS / Porrúa.

Cortés, Fernando, and Rosa María Rubalcava. 1995. *El ingreso de los hogares.* Vol. 7. Mexico City: Instituto Nacional de Estadística, Geografía e Informática.

Cravey, Altha J. 1997. "The Politics of Reproduction: Households in the Mexican Industrial Transition." *Economic Geography* 73, no. 2:166–86.

Crow, Graham. 1989. "The Use of the Concept of 'Strategy' in Recent Sociological Literature." *Sociology* 23, no. 1:1–24.

Enríquez Rosas, Rocío. 2002. "El crisol de la pobreza: Malestar emocional y redes de apoyo social en mujeres pobres urbanas." Ph.D. diss., Ciencias Sociales, CIESAS Occidente.

Escobar Latapí, Agustín. 1986. *Con el sudor de tu frente: Mercado de trabajo y clase obrera en Guadalajara.* Guadalajara: El Colegio de Jalisco.

————. 1994. "¿De la informalidad al vacío? Notas sobre el desuso de un concepto." *Antropológicas* 9 (January): 10–13.

————. 1996. "The Mexican Labor Market, 1976–1995." Manuscript.

Escobar, Agustín, and Mercedes González de la Rocha. 1995. "Crisis, Restructuring and Urban Poverty in Mexico." *Environment and Urbanization,* 2nd series, 7, no. 1 (April).

Feijoó, María del Carmen. 1991. *Alquimistas en la crisis. Experiencias de mujeres en el Gran Buenos Aires.* Buenos Aires: UNICEF.

Figueroa, Adolfo, Teófilo Altamirano, and Denis Sulmont. 1996. *Social Exclusion and Inequality in Peru.* Geneva: International Labour Organization (International Institute for Labour Studies / United Nations Development Programme).

Fontes, Virginia. 1997. "Capitalismo, exclusões e inclusão forçada." *Tempo* (Universidade Federal Fluminense, Departamento de Historia) 2, no. 3:34–58.

Fortuna, Juan Carlos, and Suzana Prates. 1989. "Informal Sector Versus Informalized Labor Relations in Uruguay." In *The Informal Economy: Studies in Advanced and Less Developed Countries,* ed. Alejandro Portes, Manuel Castells, and Lauren Benton. Baltimore: Johns Hopkins University Press.

García, Brígida, Humberto Muñoz, and Orlandina de Oliveira. 1982. *Hogares y trabajadores en la Ciudad de México.* Mexico City: El Colegio de México / Instituto de Investigaciones Sociales, Universidad Nacional Autónoma de México.

García, Brígida, and Orlandina de Oliveira. 1994. *Trabajo femenino y vida familiar en México*. Mexico City: El Colegio de México.

Gershuny, Jonathan, and I. D. Miles. 1985. "Towards a New Social Economics." In *New Approaches to Economic Life: Economic Restructuring, Unemployment, and the Social Division of Labour*, ed. Bryan Roberts, Ruth Finnegan, and Duncan Gallie. Manchester: Manchester University Press.

González de la Rocha, Mercedes. 1988. "Economic Crisis, Domestic Reorganisation and Women's Work in Guadalajara, Mexico." *Bulletin of Latin American Research* 7, no. 2:207–23.

———. 1991. "Family, Well-being, Food Consumption, and Survival Strategies During Mexico's Economic Crisis." In *Social Responses to Mexico's Economic Crisis of the 1980's*, ed. Mercedes González de la Rocha and Agustín Escobar Latapí. La Jolla: University of California at San Diego, Center for U.S.-Mexican Studies.

———. 1994a. *The Resources of Poverty: Women and Survival in a Mexican City*. Oxford: Blackwell.

———. 1994b. "Familia urbana y pobreza en América Latina." In *Familia y futuro*. Santiago de Chile: CEPAL.

———. 1995a. "The Urban Family and Poverty in Latin America." *Latin American Perspectives* 22, no. 2:12–32.

———. 1995b. "Social Restructuring in Two Mexican Cities: An Analysis of Domestic Groups in Guadalajara and Monterrey." *European Journal of Development Research* 7, no. 2:389–406.

———. 1998. "Exclusión laboral: Dilemas vitales y retos analíticos. Algunas reflexiones sobre el impacto del desempleo en la vida doméstica." In *A Ocupação na América Latina: Tempos mais duros*, ed. Nadya A. Castro and Claudio S. Dedecca. São Paulo: ALAST.

———. 1999a. "A manera de introducción: Cambio social, transformación de la familia y divergencias del modelo tradicional." In *Divergencias del modelo tradicional: Hogares de jefatura femenina en América Latina*, ed. Mercedes González de la Rocha, 19–36. Mexico City: Centro de Investigaciones y Estudios Superiores en Antropología Social and Plaza y Valdés Editores.

———. 1999b. "Hogares de jefatura en México: Patrones y formas de vida." In *Divergencias del modelo tradicional: Hogares de jefatura femenina en América Latina*, ed. Mercedes González de la Rocha. Mexico City: Centro de Investigaciones y Estudios Superiores en Antropología Social and Plaza y Valdés Editores.

———. 1999c. "La reciprocidad amenazada: Un costo más de la pobreza urbana." In *Hogar, pobreza y bienestar en México*, ed. Rocío Enríquez Rosas. Guadalajara: ITESO.

González de la Rocha, Mercedes, Agustín Escobar, and María de la O Martínez. 1990. "Estrategias vs. conflicto: Reflexiones para el estudio del grupo doméstico en época de crisis." In *Crisis, conflicto y sobrevivencia. Estudios sobre la sociedad urbana en México*, ed. Guillermo de la Peña, Juan Manuel Durán, Agustín Escobar, and Javier García de Alba. Guadalajara: Universidad de Guadalajara and Centro de Investigaciones y Estudios Superiores en Antropología Social.

Hardy, Clarissa. 1989. *La ciudad escindida: Los problemas nacionales y la región metropolitana*. Santiago: Sociedad Editora e Impresora Alborada.

Horrigan, Michael, and Ronald Mincy. 1994. "The Minimum Wage, Earnings and Income Inequality." In *Uneven Tides,* ed. Sheldon Danzinger and Peter Gottshalk. New York: Russell Sage Foundation.

Joekes, Susan P. 1987. *Women in the World Economy: An INSTRAW Study.* New York: Oxford University Press.

Kaztman, Rubén, ed. 1999. *Activos y estructuras de oportunidades. Estudios sobre las raíces de la vulnerabilidad social en Uruguay.* Montevideo: PNUD/CEPAL.

Levitan, Sar, and Isaac Shapiro. 1987. *Working Poor: America's Contradiction.* Baltimore: Johns Hopkins University Press.

Lomnitz, Larissa. 1977. *Networks and Marginality: Life in a Mexican Shantytown.* New York: Academic Press.

McFate, K., T. Smeeding, and L. Rainwater. 1995. "Markets and States: Poverty Trends and Transfer System Effectiveness in the 1980s." In *Poverty, Inequality and the Future of Social Policy,* ed. K. McFate, R. Lawson, and W. J. Wilson. New York: Russell Sage Foundation.

Moore, Henrietta. 1994. *A Passion for Difference: Essays in Anthropology and Gender.* Cambridge: Polity Press.

Moser, Caroline. 1989. "The Impact of Recession and Adjustment Policies at the Micro-level: Low-income Women and Their Households in Guayaquil, Ecuador." In *The Invisible Adjustment: Poor Women and the Economic Crisis,* ed. UNICEF. Santiago: UNICEF.

———. 1996. *Confronting Crisis: A Comparative Study of Household Responses to Poverty and Vulnerability in Four Poor Urban Communities.* World Bank Environmentally Sustainable Development Studies and Monographs Series, no. 8. Washington, D.C.: World Bank.

Nussbaum, Martha, and Amartya Sen. 1993. Introduction to *The Quality of Life: A Study Prepared for the World Institute for Development Economics Research (WIDER) of the United Nations University,* ed. Martha Nussbaum and Amartya Sen. New York: Clarendon Press, Oxford University Press.

Ortega, Eugenio, and Ernesto Tironi. 1988. *Pobreza en Chile.* Santiago: Centro de Estudios del Desarrollo.

Pahl, R. E. 1984. *Divisions of Labour.* Oxford: Basil Blackwell.

Pahl, R. E., and Claire Wallace. 1985. "Household Work Strategies in Economic Recession." In *Beyond Employment: Household, Gender, and Subsistence,* ed. N. Redclift and E. Mingione. Oxford: Basil Blackwell.

Pastore, José, Helio Zilberstajn, and Carmen Silvia Pagotto. 1983. *Mudança social e pobreza no Brasil: 1970–1980 (O que ocurreu com a familia brasileira?).* São Paulo: Fundação Instituto de Pesquisas Económicas / Livraria Pionera Editora.

Roberts, Bryan. 1973. *Organizing Strangers: Poor Families in Guatemala City.* Austin: University of Texas Press.

———. 1995. *The Making of Citizens: Cities of Peasants Revisited.* London: Arnold.

Rojas, Georgina. 2002. "'Cuando yo me reajusté . . .': Vulnerability to Poverty in a Context of Regional Economic Restructuring in Urban Mexico. Three Case Studies." Ph.D. diss., University of Texas, Austin.

Román, Ignacio. 2001. "Market Liberalization and Employment Restructuration in Mexico." *Development and Society* (Seoul National University), no. 2 (December): 79–107.

Safa, Helen I. 1995. *The Myth of the Male Breadwinner: Women and Industrialization in the Caribbean.* Boulder, Colo.: Westview Press.

———. 1998. "Export Manufacturing, Sustainable Development and the Feminization of Labor in the Dominican Republic." Manuscript.

Salas, Carlos. 1998. "Employment Structure in Mexico: Old Tendencies and New Trends." Paper presented at the U.S.-Mexico Discussion Group, Population Research Center, University of Texas at Austin, March 5.

Schkolnik, Mariana, and Berta Teitelboim. 1988. *Pobreza y desempleo en poblaciones. La otra cara del modelo neoliberal.* Programa Economía del Trabajo, Colección Temas Sociales 2. Santiago: Programa Economía del Trabajo.

Schmink, Marianne. 1984. "Household Economic Strategies: Review and Research Agenda." *Latin American Research Review* 19, no. 3:87–101.

Selby, Henry, Arthur Murphy, and Stephen Lorenzen. 1990. *The Mexican Urban Household: Organizing for Self-Defense.* Austin: University of Texas Press.

Sen, Amartya. 1990. "Gender and Cooperative Conflicts." In *Persistent Inequalities: Women and World Development,* ed. Irene Tinker, 123–49. New York: Oxford University Press.

———. 1993. "Capability and Well-being." In *The Quality of Life: A Study Prepared for the World Institute for Development Economics Research (WIDER) of the United Nations University,* ed. Martha Nussbaum and Amartya Sen. New York: Clarendon Press, Oxford University Press.

Serrano, Javier. 2002. "La dimensión simbólica de las remesas." Master's thesis, CIESAS Occidente, Guadalajara.

Tilly, Louise A. 1987. "Beyond Family Strategies, What?" *Historical Methods, A Journal of Quantitative and Interdisciplinary History* 20, no. 3:123–25.

Torrado, Susana. 1995. "Vivir apurado para morirse joven: Reflexiones sobre la transferencia intergeneracional de la pobreza." *Sociedad,* no. 7 (October).

Wolf, Diane Lauren. 1992. *Factory Daughters: Gender, Household Dynamics, and Rural Industrialization in Java.* Berkeley and Los Angeles: University of California Press.

FIVE

FEMALE HOUSEHOLD HEADSHIP, PRIVATION, AND POWER:
CHALLENGING THE "FEMINIZATION OF POVERTY" THESIS

Sylvia Chant

In Latin America, and most other regions of the world, the *feminization of household headship* has been so strongly embedded within discourses of the *feminization of poverty*, that female-headed households have commonly been depicted as the poorest of the poor.[1] In this chapter I argue that while women as individuals are often more vulnerable than men because of such factors as gender differentials in assets and earnings, this does not necessarily mean that households headed by women face the same fate.

Income data do not reveal a systematic association between female household headship and poverty. Furthermore, important challenges to that relationship are posed by in-depth intra-household research that reveals the importance of considering the variegated character of household composition and internal dynamics beyond a narrow focus on monetary earnings. From

* Some sections of this chapter draw heavily on a presentation I gave at a workshop on gender and poverty at the Institute of Development Studies, Sussex, in March 1997, subsequently published in a special issue of the IDS *Bulletin*, edited by Naila Kabeer (see Chant 1997b).

Thanks are due Cathy McIlwaine, Mercedes González de la Rocha, María Leiton, Jon Shefner, Patricia Fernández Kelly, and two anonymous reviewers for their advice and assistance in preparing and revising this paper. In addition, comments provided by the discussant of the first version of this paper, Carmen Elisa Florez, at the "Out of the Shadows" conference in Princeton, November 2001, are duly acknowledged. The final revisions to this chapter have also drawn from dedicated comparative research on gendered and generational dimensions of poverty made possible by a Leverhulme Trust Major Research Fellowship 2003–6 (Award no. F07004R).

the perspective of grassroots women, for example, power over the allocation of household resources may be valued as highly as, if not more than, actual earnings. Women often make trade-offs between one form of privation and another. When they manage households without men, for instance, they may have fewer material resources but experience greater personal empowerment and even security than they do in situations where male earnings do not translate regularly or substantially into disposable income for domestic use.

Stating that some benefits accrue to women from evading patriarchy in the domestic sphere does not mean that policymakers should ignore gender biases in poverty. Instead, they should recognize that poverty-generating processes among women are more complex than for men, and that gender inequality needs to be addressed within as well as beyond the boundaries of domestic units. In elaborating these arguments, I draw not only on my own fieldwork with low-income households in Mexico and Costa Rica but also from other studies of female headship in Latin America and beyond.[2]

This chapter is divided into four sections. The first raises questions about the categorical link between the feminization of poverty and female household headship on the basis of macro- and microlevel income data. The second section considers the reasons why female-headed households are routinely assumed to be disproportionately represented among the poor. The third section challenges the "poorest of the poor" stereotyping. In the concluding section I discuss the potential policy dilemmas arising from more subtle analyses that, on the one hand, improve our understanding of poverty's multidimensional character but, on the other, could be misconstrued as a justification for neglecting the survival needs of a significant and growing segment of the population.

Two Feminizations, One Link, Many Problems

The *feminization of household headship* refers to the increasing proportion of domestic units led by women. Conversely, the *feminization of poverty* refers to the increasing proportion of poor people that are female. The two terms are so frequently associated that few have dared to suggest that there may *not* be an intrinsic link between the two phenomena. That the term "feminization of poverty" purportedly originated in the United States in the late 1970s in relation to the fast-rising numbers of households formed by low-income women and their children may be one of the reasons why poverty and female headship originally became intertwined (Moghadam 1997). That the connection between poverty and female headship should have persisted over time remains something of an enigma.

The links commonly drawn between the feminization of poverty and household headship derive, first, from perceptions that households lacking male breadwinners form a disproportionate number of the poor in most societies worldwide and, second, that they are prone to experience higher degrees of poverty than male-headed units (see Moghadam 1997 and Paolisso and Gammage 1996, 23–25). Those perceptions have, in turn, spawned two other intersecting notions. The first is that women-headed households are "automatic outcomes of poverty" (Fonseca 1991, 138). They are thought most likely to arise in contexts of economic stress and privation, whether through labor migration, conjugal instability, or the inability of impoverished kin groups to assume responsibility for abandoned women and children. The second notion is that female headship itself exacerbates poverty, since women are disadvantaged with respect to employment and earnings and are unable to avail themselves of the work provisioned by wives in male-headed units.[3]

In light of this bleak array of circular interconnections, it is no surprise that statements about women-headed households as the poorest of the poor have proliferated in writings on gender, not only in developing regions, but on a global scale (see, for example, Acosta-Belén and Bose 1995, 25; Bullock 1994, 17–18; Buvinic 1995, 3; Buvinic and Gupta 1993; Kennedy 1994; Tinker 1990, 5; and UNDAW 1991). Yet serious doubts remain about the accuracy of such inferences, given lack of dependable data. Estimates of poverty in general, female poverty in particular, and female headship are notoriously unreliable (Chant 1997a; Folbre 1991; Fuwa 2000; UN 2000; Varley 1996). For example, the "persistent and increasing burden of poverty on women" became one of twelve central points in the Global Platform for Action established at the Fourth World Conference on Women in Beijing in 1995. That tenet, however, was based on an estimate that 70 percent of the world's poor are female (UNDP 1995, 4; see also DFID 2000, 13), an assessment that has been sharply contested in recent years (Marcoux 1997). As Valentine Moghadam (1997, 3) argues, "That poverty has taken on a female face (as well as a child's face) is not a controversial proposition. What may be questioned is the assertion that '70 percent of the world's poor are women'. . . or that in any given society female-headed households are poorer than male-headed households."

Many writings on the subject of female household headship and poverty do not explicitly refer to the statistical sources on which they base their claims. In addition, even if more holistic measures of poverty encompassing capabilities and subjectivities have entered academic and policy arenas, the measurement of poverty solely in terms of income and consumption prevails (Kabeer 2003). Finally, even when data on income poverty are invoked, these do not show that women-headed units are a consistently higher percentage of poor households. For example, in a comparative regional study undertaken by the World Bank, Kennedy (1994, 35–36) found that while female-headed households tended to be overrepresented among the poor in Asia and Latin America, this was less the case in Africa. In a more recent World Bank analysis Moghadam (1997, 8) observed that, except for Latin America, the presence of women-headed households among low-income groups was no greater than among populations in general. Even then, the 2001 *Social Panorama* report from the Economic Commission for Latin America concludes that female household headship does not predict an above average probability of poverty in the region (CEPAL 2001, 20). This echoes the conclusions of several national studies of Latin American and Caribbean countries such as Colombia (Wartenburg 1999), Panama (Fuwa 2000), and Guyana (Gafar 1998), which challenge the view that female household headship is "a proxy for poverty" (Gafar 1998, 609). These latest results do not necessarily imply recent changes, since a comparative review of official data on Central America from the late 1980s also found that female household headship did not display any notable relationship with poverty as measured by income or consumption (Menjívar and Trejos 1992).[4] In only two countries in the region—Nicaragua and El Salvador—did female heads feature disproportionately among the poor. Moreover, although many have assumed that resource scarcity plays an important part in the rise of female-headed households, their incidence appears to bear little relation to national levels of poverty. Whereas 40 percent of households in Panama were classified as poor in the late 1980s, only 20 percent were female-headed. In Guatemala, 83 percent of households were poor but only 12 percent were headed by women (Menjívar and Trejos 1992, 75–76 and 83–84).[5]

On a related point, growth in female headship tends to have occurred regardless of whether poverty has risen as well. In Costa Rica, for example, a modest growth in women-headed households (from 17.6 percent to 18 percent between 1980 and 1990) paralleled an increase in the number of households below the poverty line (from 22 percent to 24 percent between 1984 and 1990). Nevertheless, in the following decade trends in female household headship and levels of poverty diverged. While female household headship rose substantially—from 18 percent to 22 percent between 1990 and 1998—the proportion of households below the poverty line declined from 24 percent to 20 percent during the same period (Chant 1997a, chap. 5; Chant with Craske 2003, table 3.3).[6] For Latin America, more generally, upward trends in female household headship in *urban* areas—where their incidence is usually higher—occurred in every single country for which data exist between 1990 and 1999 (CEPAL 2001, table V3), whereas the regional proportion of poor households in urban areas fell from 35 percent to 29.8 percent, and the proportion of indigent households dropped from almost 18 percent to 14 percent during the same period (table 1.2). Irma Arriagada (1998, 91) notes that "the majority of households with a female head are not poor and are those which have increased most in recent decades." It is worth pointing out that the overall average incidence of female headship is lower in poor or developing regions than in the richer and developed North (see Varley 1996, table 2).

That female headship is not necessarily a poverty-specific phenomenon is also evident from detailed microlevel data generated by in-depth household surveys in developing and transitional economies. It is true that some micro studies indicate that women-headed households are likely to be poorer in income terms than male-headed units (see for example, González de la Rocha 1994b, 6–7, and Paolisso and Gammage 1996, 18–21). An ambitious comparative review of sixty-six studies from Latin America, Africa, and Asia by Mayra Buvinic and Geeta Rao Gupta (1993) further concludes that in about two-thirds of cases (44) women-headed households are poorer than male-headed households.[7] Nevertheless, many other studies provide contrasting evidence. For instance, Caroline Moser's (1996, 50) comparative analysis of the effects of structural adjustment in low-income neighborhoods of Guayaquil, Manila, Budapest, and Lusaka showed that in all but the last city, there was no relationship between the sex of household heads and income levels. My own research in poor urban settlements in Mexico and Costa Rica echoes those findings.

The straightforward equation of income poverty with female household headship is also challenged by cross-national studies showing that female-headed households are not confined to the poorest strata. For example, Katie Willis's research in Oaxaca City, Mexico, found more female heads in a middle-income neighborhood (41.5 percent) than in a low-income settlement (26 percent) (Willis 2000, 33). Other authors have also stressed how women-headed households are just as likely to be present among middle- and upper-income groups as among the poor (see Appleton 1996 on Uganda; Geldstein 1994 and 1997 on Argentina; González de la Rocha 1999, 31, on Mexico; Hackenberg,

Murphey, and Selby 1981, 20, on the Philippines; Kumari 1989, 31, on India; Lewis 1993, 23, on Bangladesh; Wartenburg 1999, 78, on Colombia; and Weekes-Vagliani 1992, 42, on the Côte d'Ivoire). Given that many younger lone mothers tend not to be able to afford their own accommodations and so live with kin or friends as "embedded female-headed sub-families" (Chant and McIlwaine 1995, on the Philippines; Marenco et al. 1998, on Costa Rica; Wartenburg 1999, on Colombia), it is entirely possible that pockets of poverty are just as likely, if not more in domestic units headed by men

Since the relationship between female household headship and poverty does not appear to be systematic (Chant 1997b; González de la Rocha and Grinspun 2001, 61–62), one might well ask why so much emphasis has been placed on that association. It is even *more* interesting to ask how female heads manage to escape poverty given widespread economic inequalities between men and women.

Rationales for the Poverty of Female-Headed Households

In her extensive review of the feminization of poverty, Moghadam (1997) identifies three main reasons that, *prima facie*, make women poorer than men. These are first, women's disadvantage with respect to entitlements and capabilities; second, their heavier work burdens and lower earnings; and third, constraints on upward mobility caused by cultural, legal, and labor market barriers.

With respect to earnings, for example, lone mother units are often thought to be worse off because they are likely to have fewer adult wage earners than two-parent households (see Fuwa 2000, 1535; Safa and Antrobus 1992, 54; and UNDAW 1991, 38).[8] These constraints on labor supply are, in turn, exacerbated by gender segmentation in labor markets and the inferior kinds of jobs that women obtain because of discrimination by employers, domestic demands, and so on (see Chant 1997a, 50–52, for discussion and references). Women with children, in particular, often have to resort to part-time, flexible, or home-based work in order to reconcile income-generating ventures with child care (Arriagada 1998, 91; Fuwa 2000, 1535). Partly as a result, several studies show that female heads have considerably greater involvement in informal sector occupations than their male counterparts (see Chant with Craske 2003, chap. 8). This is important, since generally speaking, the "gender gap" in earnings is greater in informal than formal employment. In Colombia, for example, the evidence suggests that women's average earnings are 86 percent of men's in the formal sector, but only 74 percent in the informal sector (Tokman 1989, 1971). In Honduras, the equivalent figures are 83 percent and 53 percent (López de Mazier 1997, 263), and for Central America, more generally, the gender earnings gap in informal employment averages 25 percent against 10 percent in formal occupations (Funkhouser 1996, 1746).

The tendency for women in general and female heads in particular to be disproportionately engaged in the informal sector shows few signs of abating. For example, Mexican women's labor force participation continued to increase in the 1990s, as it did in the region as a whole—from 39 percent in 1990 to 44.7 percent in 1998 (CEPAL 2001, V9)—but those in the informal sector rose from 38 percent to 42 percent of the national female labor force between 1991 and 1995. This could help to explain why disparities between male and female average earnings expanded between the 1980s and the 1990s (see González de la Rocha 1999, 28). That women's average wages across Latin America and the Caribbean are only 67 percent of men's (CRLP 1997, 12) is due in large part to women's greater involvement in informal economic activities (see UN 2000, 122, chart 5.13). Given the common disadvantages of unregulated work not only with respect to earnings but also in terms of fringe benefits, social security coverage, and pensions, the short- and long-term implications for female heads of household are potentially serious.

It is also important to remember that women's common disadvantages with respect to material assets such as land and property ownership may compound earning difficulties. Since informal sector businesses are often based in the home, and given landlords' and lenders' restrictions, female heads confined to rental or sharing arrangements may face sharp limits to their entrepreneurial capacity (see Chant 1996, chap. 3).

Another major reason invoked to explain the poverty of lone mother households, especially in advanced economies, is their low receipt of financial support from external parties, particularly the state or the (absent) fathers of their children (see Edwards and Duncan 1996; Hardey and Glover 1991, 94; Hobson 1994, 180; Mägde and Neusüss 1994, 1420; and Millar 1992, 15).[9] Since there are few studies that examine how state or paternal support affect poverty among female household heads in developing societies, and since I have not yet worked systematically on these issues myself, I give only a cursory idea of the situation, on the basis of case studies in Mexico and Costa Rica.[10]

My interviews with women in low-income communities in both Mexico and Costa Rica over the last fifteen to twenty years indicate that the vast majority receive little help from the state, even if Costa Rica has a long tradition of providing social welfare assistance, and in recent years has introduced specific measures to address the poverty of lone mothers. Since the mid-twentieth century, poor families in Costa Rica (including lone mothers) have technically been entitled to *pensiones familiares*, encompassing public health care; a range of pensions for disability, retirement, old age, widowhood, and so on; and benefits such as free milk for children under five. All this notwithstanding, my 1989 survey of 350 low-income households in Liberia, Cañas, and Santa Cruz in Guanacaste showed that only 37.5 percent of widows were in receipt of an old age or widow's pension, and a mere 15 percent of households (including male-headed units) received child allowances or free milk (Chant 1997a, 175).

As far as targeted support is concerned, the first program for lone mothers in Costa Rica was introduced during the regime of President José María Figueres (1994–98), under the auspices of the Programa de Formación Integral para Mujeres Jefas de Hogar en Condiciones de Pobreza (Comprehensive Training Program for Female Household Heads in Conditions of Poverty). This provided female heads with temporary stipends, or *asignaciónes familiar temporal,* for a maximum of six months, during which they would take courses in personal development (including the building of self-esteem) and receive employment-related training. The monthly value of the allotment was only about half the minimum wage (or equivalent to 1.5 times the basic basket of foodstuffs), but the aim was to help households subsist until their head was able to enter the labor force with a higher level of human capital (Chant 1997a, 151; Marenco et al. 1998, 52). A significant aspect of the initiative was that it represented the first direct financial assistance to lone mothers in the country that did not take the form of a "passive benefit." Instead, given its emphasis on "women's empowerment," and its juxtaposition with increased childcare facilities, it was developmentally (as opposed to purely welfare) oriented (see Budowksi 2000; Fauné 1997, 79; and Marenco et al. 1998). The scheme continued in a revised form under the Social Christian Unity regime of President Miguel Angel Rodríguez (1998–2002) under the title Creciendo Juntas (Growing Together). Although it was extended to all women in poverty (see IMAS 2001), an estimated half of the 15,290 beneficiaries covered during the period 1999–2001 were female heads of household.[11]

Theoretically at least, female heads in Costa Rica have also been assisted in their pursuit of training or labor force participation by an expanded number of childcare centers in *hogares comunitarios* (community homes).[12] Administered by the Social Welfare Institute (Instituto Mixto de Ayuda Social, or

IMAS), and concentrated primarily in low-income settlements, they allow women to receive training in child care and obtain a small state subvention for looking after other people's children in the same neighborhood. Lone mothers are given priority for such assignments. Individuals using their services pay what they can as a token gesture (see Sancho Montero 1995).[13]

Although Costa Rica's record on assisting female household heads compares favorably to Mexico's (where initiatives have not as yet extended much beyond policy statements about giving female heads priority in income-generating projects and eliminating barriers to their access to social interest housing [Secretaría de Gobernación 1996, 96]) actual coverage is low. Creciendo Juntas, for example, has targeted female household heads but less than 17 percent of those classified as poor benefited during the period 1999–2001. Furthermore, Costa Rica's current and previous administrations have explicitly stated that they do not wish to provide incentives for an increase in lone parenthood (Chant 2002).[14] Although Creciendo Juntas has only been in operation since 1999, and may have a more positive impact down the line, the proportion of female heads among the poor actually rose from 27.1 percent to 30 percent between 1998 and 2000 (IMAS 2001, 5; see also note 7). That social programs to date have not had an appreciable effect on pulling poor female household heads out of poverty is possibly one reason why the Costa Rican state has made increasing attempts to improve the record of paternal contributions.

Traditionally, paternal support has been inscribed in family law in both Mexico and Costa Rica, and in cases of divorce it is decreed that noncustodial parents (usually, fathers) should uphold financial obligations to children. More specifically, Article 287 of the Mexican Civil Code declares that the absent parent is liable for the upkeep of children (including subsistence and schooling costs) until they become legal adults (at the age of eighteen in the case of unmarried children) (Editorial Porrua 1992, 99). In Costa Rica, where the Family Code identifies husbands as the principal economic providers (Article 35), fathers are expected to continue paying for children following conjugal breakdown (Article 56), and in cases where men are the "guilty party," they are also bound to pay food money to their (ex-) wives (Article 57) (Vincenzi 1991, 262 and 268; see also Folbre 1994, 244). In 1995, this latter provision was extended to judicially recognized common-law unions under Article 245 of the Family Code (Badilla and Blanco 1996, 160).

Despite these legal stipulations, many fathers evade supporting their children when they leave their children's mothers. In a national study of Costa Rica, for example, it was found that only 28 percent of lone mothers received officially determined child support. Although some women reported that their ex-partners gave them money on a voluntary basis, as many as 38 percent received no assistance whatsoever (Budowski and Rosero Bixby 2003; see also Marenco et al. 1998, 9). As for my own low-income case study communities in Guanacaste, maintenance from ex-partners applies to only 20 percent of lone mothers, and the figure is lower still in Mexico.[15] One possible reason for the lack of child support in Costa Rica is the low incidence of formal marriage in Guanacaste (less than one-third of couples in my survey communities had been involved in a civil or religious wedding). In the Mexican study, most lone mothers had not been married to the fathers of their children either. Although rights for women and children in so-called consensual unions in both countries are increasingly recognized by the state, family law has traditionally been geared to married couples.[16] In this light, men may have been less fearful of recrimination if they remained single, and women in the same position may have been more reluctant to press maintenance charges.[17] Beyond this, chasing absent spouses and forcing them to pay usually requires legal intervention, which is beyond the reach of most low-income women. There has been a steady increase in the nonregistration of fathers' names on children's birth certificates, such that by 1999 nearly one in three children born in Costa Rica had a *padre desconocido* (unknown father). Nonetheless, in 2001 the Rodríguez government launched a radical new Law for Responsible Paternity that requires men who do not voluntarily register as fathers on their children's birth certificates to undergo a compulsory DNA test at the Social Security Institute. If the result is positive, they not only have to pay alimony and child support, but are liable to contribute to the costs of the pregnancy and birth, and to pay their children's food expenses for the first twelve months of life (INAMU 2001). This initiative is likely to go some way to improving the economic conditions of lone mother households and may well encourage men to prevent births. Whether it will be sufficient to substantially change long-standing patterns of paternal neglect remains another issue.

Men's reluctance to offer child maintenance following conjugal breakdown mirrors a tendency *within* marriages or unions for men not to comply with normative financial responsibilities. This is particularly pertinent to the Costa Rican study area, Guanacaste, where agriculture is dominated by the seasonally intensive production of tropical export crops such as sugar. As a result, temporary male out-migration is a typical phenomenon. Since nonmigrants and migrants alike are often employed only casually (usually on a daily basis), earnings (and remittances) may be highly sporadic or variable (see Chant 1991b).

Practical difficulties aside, there is also considerable evidence to suggest that even where men *do* earn income, they do not necessarily favor expenditures on the maintenance of their wives and children. Instead, they often devote large shares of their earnings on individual pursuits such as drinking, gambling, and extramarital affairs. Such disbursements conceivably provide a "refuge" from the pressure of repeated unemployment and economic uncertainty, as well as bolster masculine identity in situations that afford few opportunities to legitimize "manhood."[18] Further discussion of this topic requires more detailed investigation and lies beyond the scope of the present chapter.[19] Nevertheless, the main point I wish to emphasize is that for fathers to support children *after* they have left their partners would represent more of a disjuncture than a continuity. In addition, despite a widespread pattern of men fathering children with different women, they tend not to regard the children of those they are no longer emotionally involved with as having much, if anything, to do with them. This applies in particular to cases where the couple never lived together. Child support thus needs to be seen not just in terms of normative legal and social definitions according to which a "good father" honors financial obligations toward children. Employment scarcities in tandem with gendered cultural traditions give women little choice but to assume primary responsibility for offspring.

Thus, low levels of paternal maintenance help explain poverty among some lone mother households in Costa Rica, as well as in Mexico. Nevertheless, it is interesting that while some female heads express anger about men's evasion of familial responsibilities, others prefer to cope with financial hardship than pay the price that male support can bring with it. The small minority of men who *do* offer financial support following separation are usually those who wish to maintain ongoing contact with children. Yet some women not only describe this as men "buying rights" to their offspring, but to them as well. Socorro, one of my respondents in Querétaro, Mexico, for example, reported that she was effectively forced into having sex with her ex-partner in return for maintenance payments. This compromising situation became so stressful and degrading that in the end Socorro decided it would be better to cut off ties completely and to fend for the children on her own.

Aside from women who claim their pride and personal integrity will not allow them to accept money from men, some who take the decision to leave their partners do not even allow for the possibility of further communication. One Costa Rican respondent, Martilina, was so fearful about her husband's prospective reaction to her leaving, that she moved to Liberia, a town a hundred kilometers away, in the dead of the night, with her five children and

all they could carry with them. Women like Martilina forgo whatever economic assistance might be forthcoming after separation (Chant 1997a, chap. 6).
They are also prepared to sacrifice assets such as their houses and neighborhood networks in which they have usually invested a good deal of time,
effort, and resources. Yet despite the high price women often have to pay for
their independence (see also Jackson 1996 and Molyneux 2001, chap. 4),
benefits in other dimensions of their lives may outweigh the costs. Although
trade-offs may effectively be made between one form of privation and another,
therefore, and the options available to poor women are usually "bleak," not to
mention "painful" (see Kabeer 1997 and 1999), women's exercise of agency
serves to reinforce the notion that poverty is a multidimensional phenomenon:
while male incomes may be higher than women's, and thus potentially beneficial, they can also carry too many conditions to make them worthwhile.
Somewhat ironically, perhaps, women may thus forfeit male support in the
interests of reducing personal and family vulnerability. The notion of trade-offs
is discussed further as we proceed to look more closely at both perceived and
actual poverty in female-headed versus male-headed households.

Challenges to "Poorest of the Poor" Stereotyping

Despite the undoubtedly negative impacts of women's low earning capacity
and their limited receipt of external assistance through or outside the courts
and state welfare systems, a mounting body of research argues that female
headship does not automatically consign households to near-destitution.
Feminist critiques of orthodox "household economics" models have dis-
credited the idea that households are unitary entities operating on altruistic
principles and instead emphasize how they are more likely to be characterized
by competing claims, rights, power, interests, and resources. Summed up
most notably in Amartya Sen's "cooperative conflict" model (see Sen 1987b
and 1990); this perspective requires us to look *inside* households rather than
leaving them as unproblematic, undeconstructed "blank boxes" or conceptualizing them as naturalistic entities governed by benevolence, consensus, and
joint welfare imperatives (see also Baden and Milward 1995; Bradshaw 1996a;
Kabeer 1994, chap. 5; Lewis 1993; and Molyneux 2001, chap. 4).

A second set of challenges to the "poorest of the poor" argument has
emerged from writings that have called for more holistic conceptualizations
of poverty that extend beyond a narrow focus on incomes and consumption

and encompass notions of well-being, self-esteem, agency, and power (see Baden and Milward 1995, Baulch 1996, Chambers 1995, Moser et al. 1996a and 1996b, and Wratten 1995). The shift toward more multidimensional conceptualizations of poverty owes much to Amartya Sen's work on entitlements and capabilities and has stimulated investigation of not only how the poor *obtain* resources, but how they *command* them (Sen 1981, 1985, 1987a). Additional inputs to this debate have been provided by Robert Chambers's ideas of vulnerability, dependency and "poverty as process" (Chambers 1983, 1988, 1989). Chambers's work has also been significant in calling for resistance to homogenizing and narrowly based analyses of poverty. Indeed, his argument about the rural poor "scanned in misleading surveys, smoothed out in statistical averages, and molded into stereotypes" (1983, 106) has considerable resonance for debates on the poverty of female-headed households.

Writings within this genre have stressed that low incomes *per se* may not be particularly problematic if people reside in adequate shelter, have access to services and medical care, and have a healthy base of assets. Assets, as indicated earlier, are not only financial or physical in nature (labor, savings, tools, natural resources, for instance), but include "human capital" such as education and skills, and "social capital" such as kin and friendship networks and community organizations (Chambers 1995; Moser 1996; Moser and McIlwaine 1997; McIlwaine 2002; Willis 2000; Wratten 1995; see also World Bank 2000). In addition to emphasizing issues of power, perception, and participatory methodologies, there is a strong distributional emphasis in these formulations which harks back to feminist research on the household. As Mercedes González de la Rocha and Alejandro Grinspun (2001, 59–60) observe: "Analyzing vulnerability requires opening up the households so as to assess how resources are generated and used, how they are converted into assets, and how the returns from these assets are distributed among household members."

A third, and related, set of challenges to "poorest of the poor" slogan has come from resistance by a range of feminist scholars and activists to blanket generalizations about gender and households in the South. As asserted by Alison MacEwen Scott (1994, 86), the widespread tendency to exaggerate the "plight of female-headed households" can lead to many assumptions that do not hold for local realities (see also Fonseca 1991, 138, and Razavi 1999, 410). In short, the survival capacity, bargaining power, and "fall-back" position (Sen 1990) of female heads can vary greatly in different social, cultural, and economic contexts. Beyond this, meanings of poverty in the household domain are highly subjective and context-specific, with evidence from a number of quarters echoing the arguments of "new poverty" theorists in suggesting that *power over* resources may be more important than *levels of* resources in influencing people's perceived capacities to cope with hardship (see Chambers 1983, 183–84).

Bearing these points in mind, the following sections focus on more specific observations made on the basis of case study evidence from Mexico, Costa Rica, and elsewhere relevant to resisting generalization about the poverty of women-headed households.

Variations in Household Employment and Earning Strategies

While, as indicated earlier, women-headed households may be disadvantaged by gender inequalities in earnings, we cannot assume that heads of household are sole breadwinners in households, or that female heads are necessarily responsible for the upkeep of their members (Varley 1996). Indeed, among the poor in Latin America and other developing regions, a much more common pattern is for households to comprise multiple earners. On top of this, studies based in Latin America suggest that relative to household size, female-headed households may have more earners (and earnings) than their male-headed counterparts, who for various reasons (for example, pride, honor, and jealousy) fail to mobilize their full potential labor supply. In many parts of Mexico, for example, it seems that a number of men adhere to a long-standing (if increasingly unviable) practice not only of forbidding their wives to work, but daughters as well, especially in jobs outside the home (see Benería and Roldán 1987, 146; Chant 1997b; Fernández-Kelly 1983; Townsend et al. 1999, 38; and Willis 1993, 71). When this leaves households living from a single wage, the result may be not only higher dependency ratios (greater numbers of nonearners per worker) but also greater risks of destitution. Notwithstanding that female-headed households may *need* more workers (in other words, women's wages may require supplementation by the earnings of others), dependency burdens are often lower, and per capita incomes higher, in female-headed households (see Selby, Murphy, and Lorenzen 1990, 95, and Varley 1996, table 5, on Mexico; also see Kennedy 1994; Paolisso and Gammage 1996, 21; Quisumbing, Haddad, and Peña 1995; and Shanthi 1994, 23, on other contexts). In short, because female household heads tend to be more economically active than wives in male-headed units, and because they are more likely to tolerate daughters working, this helps compensate for their lower earning power. Indeed, although many female heads of household interviewed in my case study localities complained of financial difficulties, they tended to be better off than their counterparts in male-headed households in average per capita incomes (total household income divided by household size) (see Chant 1991a, 204, table 7.1, on Mexico, and Chant 1991b, 73, on Costa Rica). The average dependency ratio (dependents per earner) in female- and male-headed households is the same in Mexico, but in Costa Rica it is lower in female-headed households (at 3.2 dependents per earner) than in male (3.6) (Chant 1997a, 210).

Household Composition and Stage in the Life Course

Leading on from this, comparisons of poverty between male- and female-headed households must also take into account that household composition is highly variable, and may itself be a conscious means of enhancing livelihood capacity. Given that extended households tend to be associated with more workers, lower dependency ratios, and are able to avail themselves of more helpers in domestic tasks, child care, and non-market production, it is perhaps no surprise to find a greater incidence of extension among female-headed units (see Chant 1997a, chaps. 6 and 7). Composition is likely to interact with stage in the life course insofar as older heads are more likely to extend their membership through the marriage of sons and daughters. This means too, that female-headed households may contain male adults, who can potentially make a significant contribution to welfare, in turn underlining Claudia Fonseca's (1991) point that "female-headed" household does not equate with "male-absent" household.[20]

Stage in the life course can, in itself or in association with household composition, also exert an important influence on household well-being, and it is significant that in both the Mexican and Costa Rican case study localities, the average age of female household heads is at least five years greater than that of male household heads. "Consolidated" households at older stages of the life course are often better off than younger households in the "expansion" phase, because, among other things, they have fewer dependent children (González de la Rocha 1994b, 8). Indeed on the basis of National Household Survey data from Costa Rica, Leda Marenco and colleagues (1998, 11) observe that in households with children under twelve, the risk of poverty is

55 percent greater than in households without children of this age. Despite the common assumption that female heads of household send young children out to work, in my case study communities in Mexico and Costa Rica, female household heads were no more likely to send their school-age children out to work than their male counterparts (Chant 1997a, 230ff.).

In households at later stages of the life course, by contrast, older children often help out with a range of household responsibilities as well as making financial contributions. The latter may also come in the form of remittances from those who have moved out. In this respect, female heads seem to be more fortunate than male heads. For example, only 11 percent of male-headed households in the Mexican study communities in 1986 were sent remittances by kin (mainly sons and daughters), and this amounted to only 1.6 percent of average household income, whereas 31 percent of female household heads received remittances yielding a mean of 12.5 percent of household income (Chant 1997a, 210–11; see also Appleton 1996, on Uganda; Brydon and Legge 1996, 49 and 69, and Lloyd and Gage-Brandon 1993, 121 and 123, on Ghana; and Chant and McIlwaine 1995, on the Philippines).

The intersection of life-course differences with headship and poverty seems to find some support in work among female-headed multiperson households in Chile, which reports the average age of "non-poor" female heads as 56.9 years, compared with 51.9 years for those classified as "poor," and 46 years for those classified as "destitute" (Thomas 1995, 82, table 3.3). For women living alone, however, the situation is reversed, with the mean age of destitute lone women being marginally higher (at 63.2 years) than the non-poor (62 years) (ibid.), further highlighting the interrelated importance of composition.

Intra-Household Resource Distribution

Adding to the influence of household composition and stage in the life course in mitigating economic privation in female-headed units is the fact that earning differentials between households may be tempered by *intra-household* distributional factors (Folbre 1991, 110).

One major danger of comparing male- and female-headed households as *units*, for example, is that this can obscure poverty among women in male-headed households and thereby overemphasize the difficulties of female heads. As Hilary Graham (1987, 57) points out with reference to lone mothers in the United Kingdom, the tendency to categorize the poverty of female-headed lone-parent families separately seems to have been much more pervasive than research that has "uncovered poverty for women within marriage and argues that, again, particularly for women and children, lone parenthood can often herald an improvement in their living standards." Female household headship has been associated with poverty in part because of the visibility of this group in household income statistics (Kabeer 1996, 14). Yet as Sibongile Muthwa (1993, 8) notes (concerning South Africa): "Within the household, there is much exploitation of women by men which goes unnoticed when we use poverty measures which simply treat households as units and ignore intra-household aspects of exploitation. When we measure poverty, for example, we need measures which illuminate unequal access to resources between men and women in the household."

Many studies conducted in other parts of the world confirm that male household heads do not contribute all their wage to household needs, but retain varying proportions for discretionary personal expenditure. This may include spending on items or activities that prejudice the well-being of other household members, such as alcohol, tobacco, and extramarital affairs, which have both short- and long-term costs in respect of time off work, medicines, health visits, managing debt, and so on (see Appleton 1991; Benería and Roldán 1987, 114; Chant 1997a; Dwyer and Bruce 1988; Hoddinott and Haddad 1991; Kabeer 1994, 104; and Young 1992, 14). This is clearly serious, particularly where incomes are low and livelihoods precarious (Tasies Castro 1996). Certainly such expenditure on extra-domestic pursuits may form a critical element of masculine identities in various parts of the world, not to mention confer solace and compensate low self-esteem where men have limited access to employment, but the personally symbolic and psychological value of such actions can hardly justify the extreme costs of "secondary poverty" imposed upon women and children.

Indeed, Carolyn Baylies's (1996, 77) suggestion that "the presence of two parents in the same residence gives no guarantee of either financial or emotional support" seems to be widely applicable, with a number of studies documenting significant retention of male earnings (see Chant 2003, 23, for discussion and references). Coupled with the fact that, as discussed earlier, female-headed households often have higher incomes per capita than male-headed units helps to account for the apparently paradoxical situation whereby more money is available for common expenditure within households headed by women. In turn, greater relative disposable income in female-headed units is usually invested in items that benefit the household as a whole, such as housing, with a number of female heads reporting that they were only able to consolidate their dwellings after their husbands had died or deserted (see Chant 1997a, 227–28). As Naila Kabeer (1996, 13) points out more generally, it is entirely possible that in certain contexts women within higher-income households may have lower levels of nutritional intake than male members of lower-income households. Indeed, indicators of child nutrition, health care, and education too are often comparable, if not better, in female-headed households and show less gender inequality (see Blumberg 1995, 215ff.; Chant 1997a, chap. 8; and Engle 1995). These patterns are compounded in some instances by the fact that male heads of household may not only retain substantial amounts of their own earnings for personal use but take money from working wives as well. In Thailand, for example, Blanc-Szanton (1990, 93) observes that it is culturally acceptable for husbands to gamble and go drinking with friends after work and to demand money from their spouses (see also Chant and McIlwaine 1995, 283, on the Philippines). These findings underline Nancy Folbre's (1991, 108) argument that male heads may command a larger share of resources (because of their privileged bargaining position) than they actually bring to the household (see also Baylies 1996, 77). Accordingly, instead of resulting in economic ruin, a man's demise or departure may well enhance a household's economic prospects. In contrast to Rudi Dallos's (1995, 184) assertion in relation to advanced economies that many women are "shocked to realize the extent of their inequality and dependence when their relationships disintegrate," this is often the converse in the case study localities, not to mention other developing countries. Many women in the study communities talk about how they find it altogether easier to plan their budgets and expenditure when men are gone, even when their own earnings are low or prone to fluctuation. They also claim to feel better able to cope with hardship when they are not at the mercy of male dictate and are freer to make their own decisions.

Control over Resources, Perceptions of Poverty and Power

The foregoing brings to light the point that, aside from some of the direct material advantages accruing from female headship, there are also important ideological and psychological elements attached to the ability of women in this position to exert greater control over household labor, resources, income, and expenditure. The critical point here is that even if women *are* poorer in income terms as heads of their own households than they are as wives or partners in male-headed units, they may *feel* they are better off and, what is important, less vulnerable. This echoes the idea that "single parenthood can represent not only a different but a preferable kind of poverty for lone mothers" (Graham 1987, 59; also UNDAW 1991, 41). As Graham (1987, 58–59) sums-up with reference to the United Kingdom, whereas "the origins of women's poverty in and beyond marriage may share a common root in women's economic dependency, the experience of it can be very different. For while one is mediated directly through a man, the other is indirect though supplementary benefit, maintenance and wage packets." In other words, women's *perceptions* of poverty may well be contingent upon the power they themselves have over money and the degree to which the generation, allocation, and use of income is dictated by their spouses or used as an instrument of male control. This point is borne out by the work of González de la Rocha (1994a, 210) in Guadalajara, Mexico, where although lone-parent units usually have lower incomes (both total and per capita) than other households, she claims that the women who head them "are not under the same violent oppression and are not as powerless as female heads with partners." This further underlines the argument that "poverty" is constituted by more than income alone and is better conceived as a package of assets and entitlements within which the power to manage expenditure and to mobilize labor are vital elements (see Chambers 1983 and 1995; Fukuda-Parr 1999; Lewis 1993; Lind 1997; and Sen 1987a and 1987b). As summed up by Shahra Razavi (1999, 417): "From a gender perspective, broader concepts of poverty are more useful than a focus purely on household income levels because they allow a better grasp of the multi-dimensional aspects of gender disadvantage, such as lack of power to control important decisions that affect one's life."

While financial pressures may force some women to search for other partners following conjugal breakdown,[21] it is also significant that most female heads in the case study localities choose to remain alone rather than return to ex-partners or to form new relationships (see Chant 1997a, chap. 7; also see Bradshaw 1996a on Honduras). These decisions may be easier to make (and adhere to) where sons are able and willing to replace the support given by former spouses. Indeed, one respondent in Puerto Vallarta, Mexico, commented that once her sons had gone out to work and were contributing to household income she felt infinitely more secure than she had been when her husband (formerly the sole worker in the household), would return from drinking sprees on pay day stating "no hay para comer" [there's no money for food] (Chant 1997a, 210). Fonseca's research in Porto Alegre, Brazil, suggests that "son substitution" is more widely applicable, maintaining that while many women in Porto Alegre aspire to a happy marriage, experience "slowly eats away at these aspirations. After menopause, a single woman no longer represents a taunt to male virility; having gained a moment of respite in the battlefield of the sexes, she considers her options from a new vantage point— and, not uncommonly, her choice falls on sons rather than husbands" (Fonseca 1991, 157). Many of the single women interviewed by Fonseca claimed to live alone "not because they lacked opportunities, but by choice" (156).

Costs and Benefits of Female Household Headship

The foregoing discussion shows that contrary to conventional wisdom, female-headed households often have comparable, if not higher levels of per capita income than their male-headed counterparts. This state of affairs is largely accounted for not only by the smaller average size of female-headed households but also by their later stage in the life course, their greater tendency for extended composition, and their higher use of multiple-earning strategies. As argued by Lucy Wartenburg (1999, 95) concerning Colombia, the manner in which female-headed households organize themselves can optimize the positive elements of such arrangements and thereby contribute to neutralizing the negative effects of gender bias. Aside from the fact that multiple earning strategies help to protect households from outright destitution, they also seem to be associated with the translation of a greater and more regular amount of earnings into disposable income for household use, mainly by allowing women to sidestep the vagaries of resource contributions from male "breadwinners." Accepting too that poverty is not just a material state, but a perceptual one influenced by feelings of vulnerability, power, and control over resources, it is interesting that many female heads not only declare that they are better-off without men but sometimes forfeit material assets (a spouse's wage, a family home, and so on) in the interests of enhancing the overall or longer-term well-being of their households.

Although these findings suggest that sweeping stereotypes about the poverty of women-headed households are misplaced, I am not by any means making a counter-stereotypical proposition. Female headship is far from being a "panacea for poverty" (see Feijoó 1999, 162), when some women's individual endowments and household characteristics make them more vulnerable than others. Lone-parent households (especially those with young children) rarely "compete on an equal playing field" with their two-parent counterparts (Hewitt and Leach 1993, v), whether in terms of labor resources or access to jobs. This puts some female heads in the position of having to become "time-poor" in the interests of overcoming income deficiency and taking ultimate responsibility for both economic provisioning and reproductive work (see also Fuwa 2000, 1517, and Panda 1997). This, in turn, can greatly constrain their possibilities for rest and leisure, with major implications for personal well-being, health, the potential economic productivity of their remunerated work, and time available to spend with children. While the older average age of female-headed households and their greater tendency to be extended means that other help is often at hand, that they are no more likely to send sons and daughters into the labor force earlier than in male-headed households, and to some extent, informal employment—especially where this is part-time or domestic based—allows them some scope to combine work and home life, there is little doubt that costs as well as benefits accrue from opting for domestic arrangements that have traditionally been accorded little support from formal institutions. As such, recognizing that poverty is multicausal and multifaceted, and that, in some instances, female household headship can represent a positive and empowering survival strategy, is no justification for lack of state assistance.

Concluding Comments and Policy Implications

Over and above the fact that there is little substantive macro- or microlevel evidence to suggest that women-headed households are the "poorest of the poor," among the most important reasons for delinking women-headed households from discourses on the feminization of poverty is, first, that the association suggests that poverty is confined to this group alone, and thereby overlooks the situation of the bulk of women in general (Feijoó 1999, 156; Jackson 1996; 1997, 152; Kabeer 1996; May 2001, 50). A second reason is that it conveys an impression that the poverty of female-headed households owes more to their household characteristics (including the marital or civil status of their heads) than to broader structural processes of poverty and gender inequality. In the context of the United Kingdom, for example, the centrality of lone motherhood in debates about the country's growing "underclass" are leveled by Ann Phoenix (1996, 174) as having contributed to "a construction of lone mothers as 'feckless,' willfully responsible for the poverty that has been well-documented to be a feature of lone parenting," or as Sophie Laws (1996, 68–69) puts it: "It is argued that lone parenthood itself is the problem, not the conditions in which it occurs" (see also Roseneil and Mann 1996, 205). These lines of argument, which are noted in other contexts such as the United States (see Lewis 1989, Stacey 1997, and Waldfogel 1996), not only scapegoat women but take emphasis away from wider structures of gender inequality (Moore 1996, 74). They also imply that motherhood is only viable or acceptable in the context of marriage or under the aegis of male household headship (see Chant 1997b; Collins 1991, 159; and Hewitt and Leach 1993). Third, and related to this, persistent portrayals of the economic disadvantage of female-headed units which implicitly or otherwise place the main onus for this on their household circumstances, not only misrepresent and devalue the enormous efforts made by female heads to overcome the problems they face on account of their gender, but also contribute to a more general image of these households as deviant or "inferior" to a male-headed "norm." On the one hand, this can perpetuate the idea that male-headed households are the sole embodiment of "intact" and essentially unproblematic family arrangements (Feijoó 1999, 156). At another level, stigmatizing female heads can condemn them to greater privation, for example, by limiting their social networks, which, in many parts of the world, act as sources of job information, as arenas for the exchange of labor and finance, and as contexts for securing the prospective marriages of offspring (see for example, Lewis 1993, 34–35; Monk 1993, 10; and Winchester 1990, 82). Last, but not least, the association between female household headship and poverty tends to homogenize female-headed households as poor households and to ignore the vast number that are not poor. Summing up some of these concepts, Henrietta Moore (1996, 61) contends that "the straightforward assumption that poverty is always associated with female-headed households is dangerous, because it leaves the causes and nature of poverty unexamined and because it rests on the prior implication that children will be consistently worse-off in such households because they represent incomplete families."

While the foregoing reasons present a persuasive case for delinking female household headship and poverty, I realize that they might also be construed as grounds for resisting the idea that women-headed households need policy attention. In other words, denying that households headed by women are the "poorest of the poor" potentially deprives them of resources that could enable them to overcome some of the inequities that face women in general, and lone mothers in particular. Is this wise in a situation of diminishing public funds for social expenditure and increasing market-driven economic pressure on households, especially given that many female-headed households have struggled under the auspices of a "survival model" requiring high degrees of self-exploitation, that, at the turn of the twenty-first century, now looks to be exhausting its possibilities (see González de la Rocha 2001; also González de la Rocha, this volume)?

I think the question that arises here is not *whether* low-income female-headed households need help or not (since many do), but *how* they should be assisted. One such mode, as discussed earlier in relation to Costa Rica, and which seems to be gradually gaining ground in Latin America more generally, is that of targeting female-headed households in poverty alleviation programs. As noted by Buvinic and Gupta (1997, 259), there are limited data on the outcomes of programs which have targeted female household heads thus far. Some of the problems include the practical difficulties of identifying in a dynamic household universe and the dangers of leakage to non-poor households by using female headship as an indicator of poverty (270; see also Grosh 1994). Other problems include the construction of female-headed households as a vulnerable and residual group, and the political costs of excluding male-headed units, especially where resources are not perceived as female-specific, such as housing subsidies, food coupons, and cash transfers (Buvinic and Gupta 1997, 271). As I have argued elsewhere, directing resources to lone mothers can also alienate men still further from assuming responsibilities for their children's upkeep (Chant 2002). Another critical factor is the limited impacts that targeted schemes for female household heads are likely to have (and indeed are observed to have had), when the resources allocated to women heads are small and not especially effective in achieving stated aims, and where broader structures of gender inequality remain intact (see for example, Arriagada 1998, 97, and Badia 1999, on Chile; Budowski 2000 and Marenco et al. 1998, on Costa Rica; and Rico de Alonso and López Tellez 1998, 197, on Colombia). Indeed, it is instructive that in Cuba, where although Castro's government has resisted providing special welfare benefits to female heads, policies favoring greater gender equality in general, high levels of female labor force participation, and the availability of support services such as day care have all made it easier for women to raise children alone (see Safa 1995).

While in some respects a targeted approach at least makes visible the poverty that some female-headed households have to cope with, an appreciation of the fact that all women suffer poverty, but of differing types according to their household circumstances, could potentially go further, given the argument that it is "gender rather than family status which is key to understanding the situation of lone mothers" (Millar 1996, 113), and the observation that while "not all women are poor and not all poor people are women . . . all women suffer from discrimination" (Kabeer 1996, 20). As concluded in the study by Agnes Quisumbing, Lawrence Haddad, and Christine Peña (1995), whose analysis of ten developing countries found no systematic evidence of a relationship between female headship and poverty, gender should still be there in the formulation of models and policies because women generally have lower levels of education, resources, and social support than men. Or as argued by Moghadam in relation to the "feminization of poverty," it is "not only that poverty has a female face, but that the social relations of gender predict greater vulnerability among women" (Moghadam 1997, 41).

While policies aimed at equalizing gender gaps are now in place in varying degrees throughout Latin America, especially in domains such as employment, credit, land, housing, and political representation, considerably more could be done with respect to parenthood and other family obligations. Just as much as "efficiency grounds" for "investing in women" have often been more persuasive in getting gender initiatives off the ground than questions of rights and social justice, so too could current emphases on strengthening "social capital" (see World Bank 2000) be a means to making investments that effect positive changes in and for families, as well as for society at large. While greater public-sponsored provision of child care and family benefits could help households better navigate their way through the dilemmas of increasing burdens of work and financial pressure (see Chant 2002), much could also be achieved for women and children by policies which promote (not to mention guarantee) male participation in a portfolio of "family" activities that extends beyond the generation of income for their "dependents," to emotional support and practical care, whether as resident or nonresident spouses and fathers (ibid). This might not be as difficult as anticipated given that some partners in male-headed units willingly comply with these responsibilities already (ibid.; also Gutmann 1996, 1999), and because in women-headed households men often perform these roles in their capacities as grandfathers, uncles, brothers, and sons (see Fonseca 1991). Recalling too, that poverty is not just about incomes, but about power, self-esteem, and social legitimacy, legislation and campaigns to promote a socially inclusive stance to a broad sweep of family arrangements could make major progress toward equalizing the status and opportunities of female- and male-headed households. There is potentially much to be gained by bringing female-headed households more squarely into the formal remit of "family options" and treating them as a part of, rather than outside, normative or legally endorsed arrangements for the rearing of children. If concerted efforts were made to pursue such strategies, there could be even weaker grounds for linking the "feminization of household headship" with the "feminization of poverty," not to mention a slowing or reversal of the latter trend in cases where it applies.

NOTES

1. While there are several debates in the gender and development literature on the desirability (or otherwise) of universal definitions, the most common definition of "household" for developing societies (and that favored by international organizations such as the United Nations) emphasizes coresidence and shared consumption. In other words, a household is designated as comprising individuals who live in the same dwelling and who have common arrangements for basic domestic and reproductive activities such as cooking and eating (see Chant 1997a, 5ff., for discussion and references). In turn, a "female-headed household" is classified in most national and international data sources as a unit where an adult woman (usually with children) resides without a male partner (or, in some cases, another adult male such as a father or brother) (ibid.; also Wartenburg 1999, 77). Although there are several difficulties with these definitions, not least because headship is not a politically neutral concept (see Buvinic and Gupta 1997, 260; Feijoó 1999, 162; Folbre 1991; and Harris 1981), they suffice in the context of the present discussion, since my respondents in Mexico and Costa Rica conceive of households as shared living spaces and regard themselves as household heads only if they do not have a husband or partner in residence. While the majority of female-headed households are lone mother households (i.e., units comprising a mother and her children), the term "female household headship" encompasses many other subgroups such as grandmother-headed units, female-headed extended arrangements, and lone female households (see Chant 1991b and 1997a, chap. 1; also see Folbre 1991). It is also important to stress that a "lone mother" is not necessarily an "unmarried mother," but may be separated, divorced, or widowed (Chant 1997a, chap. 6; see also Marenco et al. 1998, 8). As of the late twentieth century, women-headed households were estimated to be in the region of 20–25 percent of households worldwide (Moghadam 1997).

2. The primary case study material used in this chapter has been gathered over varying periods of time in urban and urbanizing localities in the two countries. In Mexico, interviews were held with a cumulative total of over 400 male- and female-headed low-income households in the cities of Querétaro, León, and Puerto Vallarta in 1982–83, 1986, 1992, 1994, and 1997. In Costa Rica, a total of 350 households were interviewed in the towns of Cañas, Liberia, and Santa Cruz in the northwestern province of Guanacaste in 1989, 1992, 1994, 1996, and 1997 (see Chant 1997a, chap. 6; also see Chant 1991a and 1991b for further methodological details). Funding for the different research projects in which these interviews were conducted came from the Nuffield Foundation, the Economic and Social Research Council, and the Leverhulme Trust.

3. I am grateful to Nancy Folbre for drawing my attention to this point, which clearly applies where female-headed households consist only of mothers and children. In the case study communities, however, a substantial proportion of lone mothers head extended households containing female and male relatives, as discussed later in the chapter.

4. The specific criteria for measuring poverty vary from country to country. Broadly speaking, however, Costa Rica, El Salvador, Panama, and Guatemala rely on the "poverty line," which is based on income and defines the poor as those who are unable to afford a "basic basket" of foodstuffs. Nicaragua and Honduras, on the other hand, use a "basic needs" assessment, where poverty is equated with the nonsatisfaction of necessities that extend beyond food to include access to basic goods and services (see Menjívar and Trejos 1992, 55–56, table 7).

5. Menjívar and Trejos (1992, 83–84) argue that the low levels of female headship in Guatemala in the late 1980s can be accounted for in part by indigenous women's needs for male protection in the wake of political unrest. This at some level is at odds with El Salvador and Nicaragua, where the proportions reached 26.4 percent and 28.8 percent, and are attributed both to military conscription and to heavy death tolls as a result of armed struggle. A possible reason for the disparity is that women in Guatemala may have been absorbed into larger extended households headed by male kin during conflict. Other factors leading to high levels of female headship in countries such as Nicaragua include long-standing sociocultural patterns such as male desertion, migration, and serial polygyny, which the Sandinista government sought to counteract via changes in family law in the early 1980s (see Lancaster 1992 and Molyneux 2001, chap. 2).

6. This said, the proportion of female-headed households among the poor rose from 20.1 percent in 1986 to 27 percent in 1995 (Trejos and Montiel 1999, 10). According to Costa Rica's 2000 census, women-headed households were 22.2 percent of the total population but represented 30 percent of households in poverty (INEC 2001, table 31).

In Mexico, the other case study country, levels of female headship rose from an estimated level of 15.2 percent in 1980, to 17.3 percent in 1990, to 20.6 percent in 2000 (UNDP 1995, 63, table A2.5), against an overall rise the proportion of households below the poverty line from 32 percent to 43 percent between 1977 and 1997 (Chant with Craske 2003, table 3.3).

7. Thirty-two of the studies were conducted in Latin America, twenty in Africa, and fourteen in Asia, between the years 1979 and 1989 (see Buvinic and Gupta 1993 and 1997). The indicators of poverty used included, among others, total and per capita household income and consumption, mean income per adult equivalence, expenditure, access to services, and ownership of land or assets.

8. Although extended households may also be headed by lone mothers, much of the focus on lone mothers in the literature is confined to households that consist of mothers and children only.

9. Other "external parties" include nonresident children and nonresident kin. These, however, are rarely cited as contributing to the poverty of lone mothers, but are more usually identified as bolstering the income of female-headed households, as discussed later in the chapter.

10. A notable exception is the work of Iman Bibars (2001) in Egypt on the impacts on female heads of household of "the gendered ideology of the welfare state and its bureaucracy" (5).

11. Thanks are due to María Leiton from the Instituto Mixto de Ayuda Social (IMAS), the implementing body, for providing this information

12. The *hogares comunitarios* system dates back to President Calderón's administration but remained extremely limited until Figueres took office in 1994 (Chant 1997a, 51).

13. Some day care in Costa Rica has also been provided as part of the CEN-CINAI program (Centros Infantiles de Nutrición y Atención Integral), which is oriented toward children under seven at high nutritional and psychosocial risk. Admission to the program is based on the calculation of points attributed to different risk factors, such as mothers being out of work (10 points), mothers under the age of eighteen (20 points), mothers with no more than primary education (10 points), presence of "social pathology" in the family (15 points), and other elements, such as insecure employment and informal housing (5 points each). Within this framework, single motherhood is attributed a high risk value of 15 points, although this has by no means guaranteed their children's eligibility to date (see Grosh 1994, 89–91).

14. A common current in policy discourses on lone mothers is the idea that state welfare provides perverse incentives for increased numbers, thereby contributing to a growing "underclass" of citizens reliant on government handouts (see Buvinic and Gupta 1997; Duncan and Edwards 1994; Folbre 1991, 111; Laws 1996, 64–65; Millar 1992, 156; and Safa 1995, 166). The fact is, however, that in most societies welfare payments are so limited that they are hardly likely to provide an incentive for the formation of women-headed households. Having said this, it is conceivable that greater tolerance on the part of the state to lone motherhood (through varying combinations of female-friendly social programs, gender-aware legislation, and backing for women's organizations) may help to create a more sympathetic environment for the existence of women-headed households and thereby help to diminish some of the social opprobrium that constrains their emergence in so many countries (see Chant 1997a, chaps. 3–5, for fuller discussions of the wide range of economic, social, cultural, and other factors affecting female headship in different parts of the world).

15. Low levels of paternal maintenance are also apparent in other countries. For example, Helen Safa's study of female industrial workers in Puerto Rico revealed that virtually none of the household heads among them received support from the fathers of their children, and for the few who did, this was only in the immediate aftermath of conjugal breakdown (Safa 1995, 84). Data on employed black single mothers in Baltimore showed that only 37 percent received financial help from ex-partners, and then often on an irregular basis (McAdoo 1986, 158). In the United Kingdom, Bradshaw and Millar (1991) also found that only 29 percent of lone mothers received maintenance.

16. In Costa Rica, the passing of the Law Promoting Social Equality for Women in 1990 was followed by the introduction of a new clause in Article 572 of the Civil Code referring to legitimate heirs. This specified rights to goods and property by partners in consensual unions lasting three or more years, where both partners had remained unmarried to anyone else during this time and where the union had been known to

others, stable, and monogamous (see Vincenzi 1991, 86). Even if inheritance rights remained limited only to goods or property acquired during the duration of the relationship, this was an important step toward acknowledging common-law marriage. Moreover, in August 1995, a new series of articles was incorporated within the Family Code to strengthen the bases for legal recognition of consensual unions and to bring their rights more in line with those of married couples. This included reforms to Articles 84, 85, and 89, which established recognition of children born outside marriage (see Badilla and Blanco 1996, 160–61; CMF 1996, 22; and Colaboración Área Legal 1997). As for Mexico, Article 1635 of the Civil Code referring to the inheritance rights of cohabiting couples ("De la sucesión de los concubinos") states that these will be respected where unmarried couples have lived together as husband and wife for five years or have produced children, again with the proviso that both partners were technically free to marry throughout the duration of the relationship (Editorial Porrua 1992, 301).

17. This would appear to be borne out by studies of the North, such Bradshaw and Millar's survey of the United Kingdom, which revealed variations in patterns of financial support according to marital status: only 13 percent of single mothers received support, compared with 32 percent of separated women and 40 percent of divorcées (see Millar 1992, 15; also see Hardey and Glover 1991, 94).

18. An emphasis on how refuge in extrafamilial masculinities acts to compensate men for their failure to live up to normative expectations of family provider in situations of poverty has long featured in the literature on *machismo* and the family in Latin America (see, for example, Arizmendi 1980, Bridges 1980, and Pescatello 1976). For more recent studies of men, work, family, and the construction of masculine identities, see Escobar Latapí 1998, Fuller 2000, Gutmann 1996 and 2003, Kaztman 1992, and Lancaster 1992.

19. While the pilot research I conducted with eighty low-income men in Guanacaste in 1997 cannot in itself determine the relationship between male spending and behavior patterns and their labor market status, it appeared that many men valued the idea of being economic providers but found this hard to fulfill given the difficulties of getting work in the province. Several men also expressed concern about their "breadwinning role" being undermined by women's increased labor force activity (see Chant 2000 and 2002).

20. This said, Wartenburg's study of Colombia found that whereas in male-headed households there were 101 men for every 100 women, there were only 54 men for every 100 women in female-headed households (Wartenburg 1999, 89). By the same token, in Costa Rica it appears that the significance of coresident male adults in determining levels of poverty in female-headed households is less than that of the existence of young women aged 12–18 years who can help out in the home or take on other household obligations (see Marenco et al. 1998, 10).

21. Searches for new partners are more common in the Costa Rican study centers than in Mexico possibly because women in Guanacasteco towns have traditionally had only limited access to employment. Another plausible factor is the low incidence of formal marriage (which arguably makes a subsequent union easier), and greater social acceptance of serial partnerships in the Guanacaste region (see Chant 1997a, chaps. 6 and 7).

REFERENCES

Acosta-Belén, Edna, and Christine Bose. 1995. "Colonialism, Structural Subordination and Empowerment: Women in the Development Process in Latin America and the Caribbean." In *Women in the Latin American Development Process*, ed. Christine Bose and Edna Acosta-Belén, 15–36. Philadelphia: Temple University Press.

Appleton, Simon. 1991. "Gender Dimensions of Structural Adjustment: The Role of Economic Theory and Quantitative Analysis." *IDS Bulletin* 22, no. 1:17–22.

———. 1996. "Women-headed Households and Household Welfare: An Empirical Deconstruction for Uganda." *World Development* 24, no. 12:1811–27.

Arizmendi, Fernando. 1980. "Familia. Organización transicional. Estructura social. Relación objetal." In *Antropocultura*, ed. Carlos Corona, 68–87. Guadalajara: Universidad de Guadalajara.

Arriagada, Irma. 1998. "Latin American Families: Convergences and Divergences in Models and Policies." *CEPAL Review* 65:85–102.

Baden, Sally, with Kirsty Milward. 1995. *Gender and Poverty*. Bridge Report no. 30. Sussex: Institute of Development Studies.

Badia, Monica. 1999. *The Chilean "Social Integration" Approach to Poverty Alleviation: The Case of the Programme for Female Heads of Households*. Employment Studies Paper no. 25. Hertford: University of Hertfordshire Business School.

Badilla, Ana Elena, and Lara Blanco. 1996. *Código de la mujer*. San José: Editorial Porvenir S.A. / CECADE.

Baulch, Bob. 1996. "Editorial. The New Poverty Agenda: A Disputed Consensus." *IDS Bulletin* 27, no. 1:1–10.

Baylies, Carolyn. 1996. "Diversity in Patterns of Parenting and Household Formation." In *Good Enough Mothering? Feminist Perspectives on Lone Motherhood*, ed. Elizabeth Bortolaia Silva, 76–96. London: Routledge.

Benería, Lourdes, and Marta I. Roldán. 1987. *The Crossroads of Class and Gender: Industrial Homework, Subcontracting and Household Dynamics in Mexico City*. Chicago: University of Chicago Press.

Bibars, Iman. 2001. *Victims and Heroines: Women, Welfare and the Egyptian State*. London: Zed.

Blanc-Szanton, Cristina. 1990. "Gender and Inter-generational Resource Allocation Among Thai and Sino-Thai Households." In *Structures and Strategies: Women, Work and Family*, ed. Leela Dube and Rajni Palriwala, 79–102. New Delhi: Sage.

Blumberg, Rae Lesser. 1995. "Introduction: Engendering Wealth and Well-Being in an Era of Economic Transformation." In *EnGENDERing Wealth and Well-Being: Empowerment for Global Change*, ed. Rae Lesser Blumberg, Cathy A. Rakowski, Irene Tinker, and Michael Monteón, 1–14. Boulder, Colo.: Westview Press.

Bortolaia Silva, Elizabeth. 1996. Introduction to *Good Enough Mothering? Feminist Perspectives on Lone Motherhood*, ed. Bortolaia Silva, 1–9. London: Routledge.

Bradshaw, Jonathan, and Jane Millar. 1991. *Lone-parent Families in the UK*. London: HMSO.

Bradshaw, Sarah. 1995a. "Women's Access to Employment and the Formation of Women-headed Households in Rural and Urban Honduras." *Bulletin of Latin American Research* 14, no. 2:143–58.

———. 1995b. "Female-headed Households in Honduras: Perspectives on Rural-Urban Differences." In "Gender and Development." Special issue, *Third World Planning Review* 17, no. 2:117–31.

———. 1996a. "Female-headed Households in Honduras: A Study of their Formation and Survival Survival in Low-income Communities." Ph.D. diss., Department of Geography, London School of Economics.

———. 1996b. "Inequality Within Households: The Case of Honduras." Paper presented at the symposium "Vulnerable Groups in Latin American Cities," Annual Conference of the Society of Latin American Studies, University of Leeds, March 29–31.

Bridges, Julian. 1980. "The Mexican Family." In *The Family in Latin America*, ed. Man Singh Das and Clinton Jesser, 295–334. New Delhi: Vikas.

Bruce, Judith, and Cynthia Lloyd. 1992. *Finding the Ties That Bind: Beyond Headship and the Household.* New York and Washington, D.C.: Population Council / International Center for Research on Women.

Brydon, Lynne, and Karen Legge. 1996. *Adjusting Society: The IMF, the World Bank and Ghana.* London: I. B. Tauris.

Budowski, Monica. 2000. "'Yo Valgo.' The Significance of Daily Practice: The Case of Lone Mothers in Costa Rica." End of Award Report, Grant no. 82-04-27891. Berne: Swiss National Science Foundation.

Budowski, Monica, and Luis Rosero Bixby. 2003. "Fatherless Costa Rica? Child Acknowledgement and Support Among Lone Mothers." *Journal of Comparative Family Studies* 34, no. 2:229–54.

Bullock, Susan. 1994. *Women and Work.* London: Zed.

Buvinic, Mayra. 1990. "The Vulnerability of Women-headed Households: Policy Questions and Options for Latin America and the Caribbean." Paper presented at the meeting of the Economic Commission for Latin America and the Caribbean "Vulnerable Women," Vienna, November 26–30.

———. 1995. *Investing in Women.* Washington, D.C.: International Center for Research on Women, Policy Series.

Buvinic, Mayra, and Geeta Rao Gupta. 1993. "Responding to Insecurity in the 1990s: Targeting Woman-headed Households and Woman-maintained Families in Developing Countries." Paper presented at the International Workshop "Insecurity in the 1990s: Gender and Social Policy in an International Perspective," London School of Economics and European Association of Development Institutes, London, April 5–6.

———. 1997. "Female-headed Households and Female-Maintained Families: Are They Worth Targeting to Reduce Poverty in Developing Countries?" *Economic Development and Cultural Change* 45, no. 2:259–80.

Centro Legal para Derechos Reproductivos y Políticas Públicas (CRLP). 1997. *Mujeres del mundo: Leyes y políticas que afectan sus vidas reproductivas: América Latina.* New York: CRLP.

Centro Nacional para el Desarollo de la Mujer y la Familia (CMF). 1996. *Plan para la igualdad de oportunidades entre mujeres y hombres.* San José: CMF.

Chambers, Robert. 1983. *Rural Development: Putting the Last First.* Harlow: Longman.

———. 1988. "Poverty in India: Concepts, Research and Reality." IDS Discussion Paper no. 241. University of Sussex, Brighton.

———. 1989. "Vulnerability: How the Poor Cope." *IDS Bulletin* 20, no. 2:1–9.

———. 1995. "Poverty and Livelihoods: Whose Reality Counts?" *Environment and Urbanisation* 7, no. 1:173–204.

Chant, Sylvia. 1991a. *Women and Survival in Mexican Cities: Perspectives on Gender, Labour Markets and Low-income Households.* Manchester: Manchester University Press.

———. 1991b. "Gender, Households and Seasonal Migration in Guanacaste, Costa Rica." *European Review of Latin American and Caribbean Studies* 50:51–85.

———. 1996. *Gender, Urban Development, and Housing.* Vol. 2. United Nations Development Programme Publication Series for Habitat, no. 2.New York: United Nations Development Programme.

———. 1997a. *Women-headed Households: Diversity and Dynamics in the Developing World.* London: Macmillan.

———. 1997b. "Women-headed Households: Poorest of the Poor? Perspectives from Mexico, Costa Rica and the Philippines." *IDS Bulletin* 28, no. 3:26–48.

———. 1999. "Women-headed Households: Global Orthodoxies and Grassroots Realities." In *Women, Globalisation and Fragmentation in the Developing World,* ed. Haleh Afshar and Stephanie Barrientos, 91–130. Houndmills, Basingstoke: Macmillan.

———. 2000. "Men in Crisis? Reflections on Masculinities, Work and Family in North-West Costa Rica." *European Journal of Development Research* 12, no. 2:199–218.

———. 2002. "Whose Crisis? Public and Popular Reactions to Family Change in Costa Rica." In *Exclusion and Engagement: Social Policy in Latin America,* ed. Chris Abel and Colin Lewis, 340–77. London: Institute of Latin American Studies.

———. 2003. "Female Household Headship and the Feminization of Poverty: Facts, Fictions and Forward Strategies." New Working Paper Series, no. 9, London School of Economics, Gender Institute.

Chant, Sylvia, with Nikki Craske. 2003. *Gender in Latin America.* London: Latin America Bureau; New Brunswick: Rutgers University Press.

Chant, Sylvia, and Cathy McIlwaine. 1995. *Women of a Lesser Cost: Female Labour, Foreign Exchange and Philippine Development.* London: Pluto.

Collins, Stephen. 1991. "The Transition from Lone-Parent Family to Step-Family." In *Lone Parenthood: Coping with Constraints and Making Opportunities,* ed. Michael Hardey and Graham Crow, 156–75. Hemel Hempstead: Harvester Wheatsheaf.

Colaboración Area Legal. 1997. "Pulso legislativo: Nuevos proyectos de ley." *Otra Mirada* (CMF, San José) 1, no. 2:51.

Comisión Económica para América Latina (CEPAL). 2001. *Panorama social de América Latina, 2000–2001.* Santiago: CEPAL.

Dallos, Rudi. 1995. "Constructing Family Life: Family Belief Systems." In *Understanding the Family*, ed. John Muncie, Margaret Wetherell, Rudi Dallos, and Allan Cochrane, 125–70. London: Sage.

Department for International Development (DFID). 2000. *Poverty Elimination and the Empowerment of Women*. London: DFID.

Drèze, Jean. 1990. *Widows in Rural India*. Development Economics Research Programme No. 26. London: London School of Economics, Suntory-Toyota International Centre for Economics and Related Disciplines.

Duncan, Simon, and Rosalind Edwards. 1994. "Lone Mothers and Paid Work: State Policies, Social Discourses and Neighbourhood Processes." Mimeograph. Gender Institute, London School of Economics.

Dwyer, Daisy, and Judith Bruce, eds. 1988. *A Home Divided: Women and Income in the Third World*. Stanford: Stanford University Press.

Editorial Porrua. 1992. *Código civil para el Distrito Federal*. 60th edition. Mexico City: Editorial Porrua.

Edwards, Rosalind, and Simon Duncan. 1996. "Lone Mothers and Economic Activity." In *Social Policy: A Reader*, ed. Fiona Williams. Cambridge: Polity Press.

Engle, Patrice L. 1995. "Father's Money, Mother's Money, and Parental Commitment: Guatemala and Nicaragua." In *EnGENDERing Wealth and Well-Being: Empowerment for Global Change*, ed. Rae Lesser Blumberg, Cathy A. Rakowski, Irene Tinker, and Michael Monteón, 155–79. Boulder, Colo.: Westview Press.

Escobar Latapí, Agustín. 1998. "Los hombres y sus historias: Reestructuración y masculinidad en México." *La Ventana* (Universidad de Guadalajara) 8:122–73.

Fauné, María Angélica. 1997. "Costa Rica: Las inequidades de género en el marco de la apertura comercial y la reestructuración productiva: Análisis a nivel macro, meso, micro." In *Crecer con la mujer: Oportunidades para el desarrollo económico centroamericano*, ed. Diane Elson, María Angélica Fauné, Jasmine Gideon, Maribel Gutiérrez, Armida López de Mazier, and Eduardo Sacayón, 51–126. San José: Embajada Real de los Países Bajos.

Feijoó, María del Carmen. 1999. "De pobres mujeres a mujeres pobres." In *Divergencias del modelo tradicional: Hogares de jefatura femenina en América Latina*, ed. Mercedes González de la Rocha, 155–62. Mexico City Centro de Investigaciones y Estudios Superiores en Antropología Social.

Fernández-Kelly, María Patricia. 1983. "Mexican Border Industrialization, Female Labor Force Participation and Migration." In *Women, Men and the International Division of Labour*, ed. June Nash and María Patricia Fernández-Kelly, 205–23. Albany: State University of New York Press.

Folbre, Nancy. 1991. "Women on Their Own: Global Patterns of Female Headship." In *The Women and International Development Annual*, ed. Rita S. Gallin and Ann Ferguson, 2:69–126. Boulder, Colo.: Westview Press.

———. 1994. *Who Pays for the Kids? Gender and the Structures of Constraint*. London: Routledge.

Fonseca, Claudia. 1991. "Spouses, Siblings and Sex-linked Bonding: A Look at Kinship Organisation in a Brazilian Slum." In *Family, Household and Gender Relations in Latin America*, ed. Elizabeth Jelin, 133–60. London: Kegan Paul International; Paris: UNESCO.

Ford, Reuben. 1996. *Childcare in the Balance: How Lone Parents Make Decisions About Work*. London: Policy Studies Institute.

Fukuda-Parr, Sakiko. 1999. "What Does Feminisation of Poverty Mean? It Isn't Just Lack of Income." *Feminist Economics* 5, no. 2:99–103.

Fuller, Norma. 2000. "Work and Masculinity Among Peruvian Urban Men." *European Journal of Development Research* 12, no. 2:93–114.

Funkhouser, Edward. 1996. "The Urban Informal Sector in Central America: Household Survey Evidence." *World Development* 12, no. 11:1737–51.

Fuwa, Nobuhiko. 2000. "The Poverty and Heterogeneity Among Female-headed Households Revisited: The Case of Panama." *World Development* 28, no. 8:1515–42.

Gafar, John. 1998., "Growth, Inequality and Poverty in Selected Caribbean and Latin American Countries, with Emphasis on Guyana." *Journal of Latin American Studies* 30, no. 3:591–617.

Geldstein, Rosa. 1994. "Working Class Mothers as Economic Providers and Heads of Families in Buenos Aires." *Reproductive Health Matters* 4:55–64.

———. 1997. *Mujeres jefas de hogar: Familia, pobreza y género*. Buenos Aires: UNICEF-Argentina.

Gomáriz, Enrique. 1997. *Introducción a los estudios sobre la masculinidad*. San José: Centro Nacional para el Desarrollo de la Mujer y Familia.

González de la Rocha, Mercedes. 1988. "De por qué las mujeres aguantan golpes y cuernos: Un análisis de hogares sin varón en Guadalajara." In *Mujeres y sociedad: Salario, hogar y acción social en el occidente de México*, ed. Luisa Gabayet et al., 205–27. Guadalajara: El Colegio de Jalisco, CIESAS del Occidente.

———. 1994a. *The Resources of Poverty: Women and Survival in a Mexican City*. Oxford: Blackwell.

———. 1994b. "Household Headship and Occupational Position in Mexico." In *Poverty and Well-Being in the Household: Case Studies of the Developing World*, ed. Eileen Kennedy and Mercedes González de la Rocha, 1–24. San Diego: Center for Iberian and Latin American Studies, University of California at San Diego.

———. 1999. "A manera de introducción: Cambio social, transformación de la familia y divergencias del modelo tradicional." In *Divergencias del modelo tradicional: Hogares de jefatura femenina en América Latina*, ed. Mercedes González de la Rocha, 19–36. Mexico City: Centro de Investigaciones y Estudios Superiores en Antropología Social, Plaza y Valdés Editores.

———. 2001. "From the Resources of Poverty to the Poverty of Resources? The Erosion of a Survival Model." *Latin American Perspectives* 28, no. 4:72–100.

González de la Rocha, Mercedes, and Alejandro Grinspun. 2001. "Private Adjustments: Households, Crisis and Work." In *Choices for the Poor: Lessons from National Poverty Strategies*, ed. Alejandro Grinspun, 55–87. New York: UNDP.

Graham, Hilary. 1987. "Being Poor: Perceptions and Coping Strategies of Lone Mothers." In *Give and Take in Families: Studies in Resource Distribution*, ed. Julia Brannen and Gail Wilson, 56–74. London: Allen and Unwin.

Grosh, Margaret. 1994. *Administering Targeted Social Programs in Latin America: From Platitudes to Practice*. Washington, D.C.: World Bank.

Gutmann, Matthew. 1996. *The Meanings of Macho: Being a Man in Mexico City.* Berkeley and Los Angeles: University of California Press.

———. 1999. "A manera de conclusión: Solteras y hombres. Cambio e historia." In *Divergencias del modelo tradicional: Hogares de jefatura femenina en América Latina,* ed. Mercedes González de la Rocha, 163–72. Mexico City: Centro de Investigaciones y Estudios Superiores en Antropología Social.

———, ed. 2003. *Changing Men and Masculinities in Latin America.* Durham: Duke University Press.

Hackenberg, Robert, Arthur Murphy, and Henry Selby. 1981. "The Household in the Secondary Cities of the Third World." Paper prepared for the Wenner-Gren Foundation Symposium "Households: Changing Form and Function," New York, October 8–15.

Hardey, Michael, and Judith Glover. 1991. "Income, Employment, Daycare and Lone Parenthood." In *Lone Parenthood: Coping with Constraints and Making Opportunities,* ed. Michael Hardey and Graham Crow, 88–109. Hemel Hempstead: Harvester Wheatsheaf.

Harris, Olivia. 1981. "Households as Natural Units." In *Of Marriage and the Market,* ed. Kate Young, Carol Wolkowitz, and Roslyn McCullogh, 48–67. London: CSE Books.

Hewitt, Patricia, and Penelope Leach. 1993. *Social Justice, Children and Families.* London: Institute for Public Policy Research.

Hobson, Barbara. 1994. "Solo Mothers, Social Policy Regimes and the Logics of Gender." In *Gendering Welfare States,* ed. Diane Sainsbury, 170–88. London: Sage.

Hoddinott, John, and Lawrence Haddad. 1991. *Household Expenditures, Child Anthropomorphic Status and the Intra-Household Division of Income: Evidence from the Côte d'Ivoire.* Oxford: University of Oxford, Unit for the Study of African Economics.

Instituto Latinoamericano de las Naciones Unidas para la Prevención de Delito y Tratamiento del Delincuente (ILANUD). 1996. *Construcción de la identidad masculina.* San José: Programa Mujer, Justicia y Género, ILANUD.

Instituto Mixto de Ayuda Social (IMAS). 2001. *Area atención integral para el desarrollo de las mujeres. Programas: Creciendo juntas, construyendo oportunidades.* San José: IMAS.

Instituto Nacional de Estadísticas y Censos (INEC). 2001. *IX censo nacional de población y v de vivienda del 2000: Resultados generales.* San José: INEC.

Instituto Nacional de la Mujeres (INAMU). 2001. *Responsible Paternity Law.* San José: INAMU.

Jackson, Cecile. 1996. "Rescuing Gender from the Poverty Trap." *World Development* 24, no. 3:489–504.

———. 1997. "Post Poverty, Gender and Development." *IDS Bulletin* 28, no. 3:145–55.

Kabeer, Naila. 1994. *Reversed Realities: Gender Hierarchies in Development Thought.* London: Verso.

———. 1996. "Agency, Well-being and Inequality: Reflections on the Gender Dimensions of Poverty." *IDS Bulletin* 27, no. 1:11–21.

———. 1997. "Editorial. Tactics and Trade-offs: Revisiting the Links Between Gender and Poverty." *IDS Bulletin* 28, no. 3:1–25.

———. 1999. "Resources, Agency, Achievements: Reflections on the Measurement of Women's Empowerment." *Development and Change* 30, no. 3:435–64.

———. 2003. *Gender Mainstreaming in Poverty Eradication and the Millennium Development Goals: A Handbook for Policy-makers and Other Stakeholders.* London: Commonwealth Secretariat.

Kaztman, Rubén. 1992. "¿Por qué los hombres son tan irresponsables?" *Revista de la CEPAL* 46:1–9.

Kennedy, Eileen. 1994. "Development Policy, Gender of Head of Household, and Nutrition." In *Poverty and Well-Being in the Household: Case Studies of the Developing World,* ed. Eileen Kennedy and Mercedes González de la Rocha, 25–42. San Diego: Center for Iberian and Latin American Studies, University of California at San Diego.

Kumari, Ranjana. 1989. *Women-headed Households in Rural India.* New Delhi: Radiant Publishers.

Lancaster, Roger. 1992. *Life Is Hard: Machismo, Danger and the Intimacy of Power in Nicaragua.* Berkeley and Los Angeles: University of California Press.

Lara, Silvia, with Tom Barry and Peter Simonson. 1995. *Inside Costa Rica.* Albuquerque: Resource Center Press.

Laws, Sophie. 1996. "The Single Mothers Debate: A Children's Rights Perspective." In *Sex, Sensibility and the Gendered Body,* ed. Janet Holland and Lisa Adkins, 60–77. Houndmills, Basingstoke: Macmillan.

Lewis, David. 1993. "Going It Alone: Female-Headed Households, Rights and Resources in Rural Bangladesh." *European Journal of Development Research* 5, no. 2:23–42.

Lewis, Jane. 1989. "Lone Parent Families: Politics and Economics." *Journal of Social Policy* 18, no. 4:595–600.

Lind, Amy. 1997. "Gender, Development and Urban Social Change: Women's Community Action in Global Cities." *World Development* 25, no. 8:1187–203.

Lloyd, Cynthia, and Anastasia Gage-Brandon. 1993. "Women's Role in Maintaining Households: Family Welfare and Sexual Inequality in Ghana." *Population Studies* 47:115–31.

López de Mazier, Armida. 1997. "La mujer, principal sostén del modelo económico de Honduras: Un análisis de género de la economía Hondureña." In *Crecer con la mujer: Oportunidades para el desarrollo ecónomico centroamericano,* ed. Diane Elson, María Angélica Fauné, Jasmine Gideon, Maribel Gutiérrez, Armida López de Mazier, and Eduardo Sacayón, 215–52. San José: Embajada Real de los Países Bajos.

Mägde, E., and C. Neusüss. 1994. "Lone Mothers on Welfare in West Berlin: Disadvantaged Citizens or Women Avoiding Patriarchy?" *Environment and Planning* 26, 1419–33.

Marcoux, Alain. 1997. *The Feminization of Poverty: Facts, Hypotheses and the Art of Advocacy.* Rome: Food and Agriculture Organization, Population Programme Service, Women and Population Division.

Marenco, Leda, Ana María Trejos, Juan Diego Trejos, and Marienela Vargas. 1998. *Del silencio a la palabra: Un modelo de trabajo con las mujeres jefas del hogar.* San José: Segunda Vicepresidencia.

May, Julian. 2001. "An Elusive Consensus: Definitions, Measurement and the Analysis of Poverty." In *Choices for the Poor: Lessons from National Poverty Strategies,* ed. Alejandro Grinspun, 23–54. New York: UNDP.

McAdoo, Hariette Pipes. 1986. "Strategies Used by Single Black Mothers Against Stress." In *Slipping Through the Cracks: The Status of Black Women,* ed. Margaret C. Simms and Julianne Malvaux, 153–66. New Brunswick, N.J.: Transaction Books.

McIlwaine, Cathy. 1997. "Vulnerable or Poor? A Study of Ethnic and Gender Disadvantage Among Afro-Caribbeans in Limón, Costa Rica." *European Journal of Development Research* 9, no. 2:35–61.

———. 2002. "Perspectives on Poverty, Vulnerability and Exclusion." In *Challenges and Change in Middle America: Perspectives on Mexico, Central America and the Caribbean,* ed. Cathy McIlwaine and Katie Willis. Harlow: Pearson Education.

Mencher, Joan. 1989. "Women Agricultural Labourers and Landowners in Kerala and Tamil Nadu: Some Questions about Gender and Autonomy in the Household." In *Gender and the Household Domain: Social and Cultural Dimensions,* ed. Maithreyi Khrishnaraj and Karuna Chanana, 117–41. New Delhi: Sage.

Menjívar, Rafael, and Juan Diego Trejos. 1992. *La pobreza en América Central.* 2nd edition. San José: FLACSO.

Millar, Jane. 1992. "Lone Mothers and Poverty." In *Women and Poverty in Britain in the 1990s,* ed. Caroline Glendinning and Jane Millar, 149–61. Hemel Hempstead: Harvester Wheatsheaf.

———. 1996. "Mothers, Workers, Wives: Comparing Policy Approaches to Supporting Lone Mothers." In *Good Enough Mothering? Feminist Perspectives on Lone Motherhood,* ed. Elizabeth Bortolaia Silva, 97–113. London: Routledge.

Moghadam, Valentine. 1997. *The Feminization of Poverty: Notes on a Concept and Trend.* Women's Studies Occasional Paper no. 2. Normal: Illinois State University Press.

Molyneux, Maxine. 2001. *Women's Movements in International Perspective: Latin America and Beyond.* Houndmills, Basingstoke: Palgrave.

Monk, Sue. 1993. *From the Margins to the Mainstream: An Employment Strategy for Lone Parents.* London: National Council for One-Parent Families.

Moore, Henrietta. 1994. *Is There a Crisis in the Family?* Occasional Paper no. 3. Geneva: World Summit for Social Development.

———. 1996. "Mothering and Social Responsibilities in a Cross-cultural Perspective." In *Good Enough Mothering? Feminist Perspectives on Lone Motherhood,* ed. Elizabeth Bortolaia Silva, 58–75. London: Routledge.

Moser, Caroline. 1996. *Confronting Crisis: A Comparative Study of Household Responses to Poverty in Four Poor Urban Communities.* World Bank Environmentally Sustainable Development Studies and Monographs Series no. 8. Washington, D.C.: World Bank.

Moser, Caroline, Michael Gatehouse, and Helen Garcia. 1996a. "Urban Poverty Research Sourcebook, Module I: Sub-city Level Household Survey." Working

Paper Series 5, UNDP/UNCHS/World Bank—Urban Management Program, Washington, D.C.

————. 1996b. "Urban Poverty Research Sourcebook, Module II: Indicators of Urban Poverty." Working Paper Series 5, UNDP/UNCHS/World Bank—Urban Management Program, Washington, D.C.

Moser, Caroline, and Cathy McIlwaine. 1997. *Household Responses to Poverty and Vulnerability.* Vol. 3, *Confronting Crisis in Commonwealth, Metro Manila, Philippines.* Washington, D.C.: World Bank, Urban Management Programme.

Muthwa, Sibongile. 1993. "Household Survival, Urban Poverty and Female Household Headship in Soweto: Some Key Issues for Further Policy Research." Paper presented at the seminar "The Societies of Southern Africa in the 19th and 20th Centuries: Women, Colonialism and Commonwealth," Institute of Commonwealth Studies, University of London, November 19.

Panda, Pradeep Kumar. 1997. "Female Headship, Poverty and Child Welfare: A Study of Rural Orissa." *Economic and Political Weekly,* October 25, 73–82.

Paolisso, Michael, and Sarah Gammage. 1996. *Women's Responses to Environmental Degradation: Case Studies from Latin America.* Washington, D.C.: International Center for Research on Women.

Pescatello, Ann. 1976. *Power and Pawn: The Female in Iberian Families, Cultures and Societies.* Westport, Conn.: Greenwood.

Phoenix, Ann. 1996. "Social Constructions of Lone Motherhood: A Case of Competing Discourses." In *Good Enough Mothering? Feminist Perspectives on Lone Motherhood,* ed. Elizabeth Bortolaia Silva, 175–90. London: Routledge.

Presidencia de la República. 1996. *Consejo del sector social.* San José: Instituto Mixto de Ayuda Social.

Quisumbing, Agnes, Lawrence Haddad, and Christine Peña. 1995. "Gender and Poverty: New Evidence from Ten Developing Countries." Discussion Paper no. 9. International Food Policy Research Institute, Food Consumption and Nutrition Division, Washington, D.C.

Razavi, Shahra. 1999. "Gendered Poverty and Well-Being: Introduction." *Development and Change* 30, no. 3:409–33.

Rico de Alonso, Ana, and Nadia López Téllez. 1998. "Informalidad, jefatura femenina y supervivencia." *Revista Javeriana,* September, 193–97.

Roseneil, Sasha, and Kirk Mann. 1996. "Unpalatable Choices and Inadequate Families: Lone Mothers and the Underclass Debate." In *Good Enough Mothering? Feminist Perspectives on Lone Motherhood,* ed. Elizabeth Bortolaia Silva, 191–210. London: Routledge.

Safa, Helen. 1990. "Women and Industrialisation in the Caribbean." In *Women, Employment and the Family in the International Division of Labour,* ed. Sharon Stichter and Jane Parpart, 72–97. Basingstoke: Macmillan.

————. 1995. *The Myth of the Male Breadwinner: Women and Industrialization in the Caribbean.* Boulder, Colo.: Westview Press.

Safa, Helen, and Peggy Antrobus. 1992. "Women and the Economic Crisis in the Caribbean." In *Unequal Burden: Economic Crises, Persistent Poverty and Women's Work,* ed. Lourdes Benería and Shelley Feldman, 49–82. Boulder, Colo.: Westview Press.

Sancho Montero, Silvia María. 1995. *El programa hogares comunitarios en Costa Rica, sus primeros pasos: Primera parte*. San José: Institute Mixto de Ayuda Social, Dirección Hogares Comunitarios.

Scott, Alison MacEwen. 1994. *Divisions and Solidarities: Gender, Class and Employment in Latin America*. London: Routledge.

Secretaría de Gobernación. 1996. *Alianza par la igualdad: Programa nacional de la mujer, 1995–2000*. Mexico City: Secretaría de Gobernación.

Selby, Henry, Arthur Murphy, and Stephen Lorenzen. 1990. *The Mexican Urban Household: Organizing for Self-Defense*. Austin: University of Texas Press.

Sen, Amartya K. 1981. *Poverty and Famines*. Oxford: Clarendon Press.

———. 1985. *Commodities and Capabilities*. Helsinki: United Nations University, World Institute for Development Economics Research.

———. 1987a. *Hunger and Entitlements*. Amsterdam: North Holland Press.

———. 1987b. "Gender and Cooperative Conflicts." Working Paper 18, World Institute for Development Economics Research, Helsinki.

———. 1990. "Gender and Cooperative Conflicts." In *Persistent Inequalities: Women and World Development*, ed. Irene Tinker, 123–49. New York: Oxford University Press.

Shanthi, K. 1994. "Growing Incidence of Female Household Headship: Causes and Cure." *Social Action* (New Delhi) 44:17–33.

Stacey, Judith. 1997. "The Neo-Family-Values Campaign." In *The Gender/Sexuality Reader*, ed. Roger Lancaster and Michaela di Leonardo, 432–70. New York: Routledge.

Tasies Castro, Esperanza. 1996. "Mujer, pobreza y conflicto social." *Ciencias Sociales* (FLACSO, San José) 71:39–32.

Thomas, J. J. 1995. *Surviving in the City: The Urban Informal Sector in Latin America*. London: Pluto.

Tinker, Irene. 1990. "A Context for the Field and for the Book." In *Persistent Inequalities: Women and World Development*, ed. Irene Tinker, 3–13. Oxford: Oxford University Press.

Tokman, Victor. 1989. "Policies for a Heterogeneous Informal Sector in Latin America." *World Development* 17, no. 7:1067–76.

Townsend, Janet, Emma Zapata, Jo Rowlands, Pilar Alberti, and Marta Mercado. 1999. *Women and Power: Fighting Patriarchies and Poverty*. London: Zed.

Trejos, Juan Diego, and Nancy Montiel. 1999. *El capital de los pobres en Costa Rica: Acceso, utilización y rendimiento*. Washington, D.C.: IADB.

United Nations. 2000. *The World's Women 2000: Trends and Statistics*. New York: United Nations.

United Nations Division for the Advancement of Women (UNDAW). 1991. "Women and Households in a Changing World." In *Women, Households and Change*, ed. Eleanora Barbieri Masini and Susan Stratigos, 30–52. Tokyo: United Nations University Press.

Varley, Ann. 1996. "Women-headed Households: Some More Equal Than Others?" *World Development* 24, no. 3:505–20.

Vincenzi, Atilio. 1991. *Código civil y código de la familia*. San José: Lehmann Editores.

Waldfogel, Jane. 1996. "What Do We Expect Lone Mothers to Do? Competing Agendas for Welfare Reform in the United States." Discussion Paper no. 124. London School of Economics, Suntory and Toyota International Centre for Economics and Related Disciplines, Welfare State Programme, London.

Wartenburg, Lucy. 1999. "Vulnerabilidad y jefatura en los hogares urbanos Colombianos." In *Divergencias del modelo tradicional: Hogares de jefatura femenina en América Latina*, ed. Mercedes González de la Rocha, 77–96. Mexico City: Centro de Investigaciones y Estudios Superiores en Antropología Social / Plaza y Valdés Editores.

Weekes-Vagliani, Winifred. 1992. "Structural Adjustment and Gender in the Côte d'Ivoire." In *Women and Adjustment Policies in the Third World*, ed. Haleh Afshar and Carolyne Dennis, 117–49. Basingstoke: Macmillan.

Westwood, Sallie. "'Feckless Fathers': Masculinities and the British State." In *Understanding Masculinities: Social Relations and Cultural Arenas*, ed. Maírtín Mac An Ghaill, 21–34. Buckingham: Open University Press.

Willis, Katie. 1993. "Women's Work and Social Network Use in Oaxaca City, Mexico." *Bulletin of Latin American Research* 12, no. 1:65–82.

———. 2000. "No es fácil, pero es posible: The Maintenance of Middle-Class Women-headed Households in Mexico." *European Review of Latin American and Caribbean Studies* 69:29–45.

Winchester, Hilary. 1990. "Women and Children Last: The Poverty and Marginalisation of One-parent Families." *Transactions, Institute of British Geographers*, n.s., 15, no. 1:70–86.

World Bank. 2000. *World Development Report 2000/2001: Attacking Poverty*. New York: Oxford University Press.

Wratten, Ellen. 1995. "Conceptualising Urban Poverty." *Environment and Urbanisation* 7, no. 1:11–36.

Young, Kate. 1992. "Household Resource Management." In *Gender and Development: A Practical Guide*, ed. Lise Østergaard, 135–64. London: Routledge.

SIX

Protest in Contemporary Argentina: A Contentious Repertoire in the Making

Javier Auyero

We shall know that a new era has begun not when a new elite hold power or a new constitution appears, but when ordinary people begin contending for their interests in new ways.
—Charles Tilly, *The Contentious French*

During the 1990s, new and unconventional forms of popular contention transformed Argentina into a veritable storm of protest. As the events of December 2001 dramatically illustrate—people looting grocery stores and supermarkets, blockading roads and bridges throughout the country, banging pots and pans in the main plaza of Buenos Aires, and provoking the resignation of two presidents in less than a month—this storm is still under way. Over the past decade, sieges of (and attacks on) public buildings (government houses, legislatures, courthouses), barricades on national and provincial roads, and camps in central plazas occurred all over the country.

Current research on Argentina highlights the devastating effects of neoliberal adjustment policies: skyrocketing poverty levels reaching 27 percent and unemployment rates as high as 20 percent (Stillwaggon 1998; Villarreal 1997; O'Donnell 1998; Beccaria and López 1996; Barbeito and Lo Vuolo 1992; Minujin and Kessler 1995; Lloyd-Sherlock 1997). The staggering statistics have been followed by the rapid increase of both conventional forms of contention (strikes, marches, and street demonstrations) and more novel ones (road, highway, and bridge blockades) (Farinetti 1998, 2000; Scribano 1999; Laufer and Spiguel 1999; Entel 1997). This chapter scrutinizes the structural roots, forms, and meanings of the most recent waves of protest. It

* This research was funded by a fellowship from the John Simon Guggenheim Memorial Foundation and by the American Sociological Association's Fund for the Advancement of the Discipline Award supported by the American Sociological Association and the National Science Foundation.

draws on Charles Tilly's concept of *repertoire of collective action* to argue that during the past decade three macroprocesses linked to neoliberal economic reforms (the retrenchment of the semi-welfare state, the explosion of unemployment and underemployment, and the decentralization of state services) affected protesters' common grievances and interests, organizational forms, collective self-understandings, and opportunities to act, thus altering the frequency and types of popular contention. Three case studies serve as the empirical backbone for this inquiry. I pay particular attention to the effects of learning in the adoption of new forms of struggle, the continuities between protest and routine politics, and elite factionalism as an opportunity for mobilization.

Tilly in Argentina

Charles Tilly's "repertoire of collective action" theory and his examination of the large-scale causes of contentious politics offer potent tools for investigating changes in the methods and meanings of popular struggle in contemporary Argentina. An application of his framework, essentially a critical transposition of his insights into the last three centuries of popular struggle in Great Britain and France to the last two decades in Argentina, can help us to overcome persistent analytical shortcomings.[1] Understood as the set of routines by which people gather to act on behalf of shared interests, Tilly's notion of repertoire invites us to examine patterns of collective claim-making and regularities in the ways people band together to make their demands heard across time and space.

First, Tilly offers a model that brings together different levels of analysis, ranging from large-scale changes such as the development of capitalism (with the subsequent proletarianization of labor) and the process of state-making (with the parallel growth of the state's bulk and complexity, and the penetration of its coercive and extractive power), to patterns of citizen-state interaction. This model invites us to hold together *macrostructures* and *microprocesses* by looking closely at how large changes indirectly shape collective action, affecting the interests, opportunities, organizations, and identities of ordinary people. Furthermore, this framework makes clear the need for a simultaneous analysis of diachronic and synchronic analysis with its emphasis on both the forms of protest and their transformation.

Second, the notion of repertoire is eminently *political* in that contentious routines emerge from ongoing struggles against the state, bear a close relationship with daily life, and are constrained by patterns of state repression.[2] In this way, Tilly warns against views that see increases in protest solely as a result of grievances. Grievances, according to Tilly, and Sidney Tarrow (1998) later, are not enough to trigger collective action; they operate within a matrix of political relationships, prior collective struggles, and state responses to those struggles. Hence, contention tends everywhere to "flow out of a population's central political processes, instead of expressing diffuse strains and discontents within the population" (Tilly 1997b, 120).

Third, the notion of repertoire is *cultural* in that it focuses on people's habits of contention and on the form that collective action takes as a result of shared expectations and learned improvisations. The repertoire is then an array of *meanings* that arise relationally, in struggle—meanings that, as Clifford Geertz (2001, 76) puts it, are "hammered out in the flow of events." *Learning through struggle* is thus at the core of the theatrical metaphor used by Tilly: "Repertoires are learned cultural creations, but they do not descend from abstract philosophy or take shape as a result of political propaganda; they emerge from struggle" (Tilly 1995, 26). What do protesters learn? Tilly explains: "People learn to break windows in protest, attack pilloried prisoners, tear down dishonored houses, stage public marches, petition, hold formal meetings, organize special-interest associations. At any particular point in history, however, they learn only a rather small number of alternative ways to act together." How does this learning process affect subsequent ways of acting? "The existing repertoire constrains collective action; far from the image we sometimes hold of mindless crowds, people tend to act within known limits, to innovate at the margins of existing forms, and to miss many opportunities available to them in principle. That constraint results in part from the advantages of familiarity, partly from the investment of second and third parties in the established forms of collective action" (Tilly 1986, 390–91). Thus, the concept allows us to combine two interests that too often have been divorced, namely the impact of structural change on collective action and the transformation of the culture of popular protest (Tarrow 1996).[3]

Taking Tilly into the Argentine landscape of protest suggests that we should pay simultaneous attention to

1 Regularities in the forms of contentious collective action. The first part of this chapter thus looks at the last decade of protest in Argentina and unearths, from a wide variety of contentious actions, an increasingly normative modality of struggle, that is, the replacement of factory-level strikes with the manning of roadblocks on national and provincial roads.

2 Structural changes at the root of those regularities. The second part of this chapter examines deproletarianization, state-retrenchment, and decentralization of federal services (health and education) as three large-scale transformations affecting the dynamics of contention during the last decade.

3 Interplay between interests, organizations, opportunities, and identities that act as a translating machine of the pressure created by those large changes. The third part of the chapter shifts the level of analysis from macrostructures and processes to microlevel interactions (and from archival research to ethnographically informed historical fieldwork). I focus on the increasingly dominant identity claims of protesters (looking at the collective self-understanding that dichotomizes "the people" and "the political class"), their interests (describing how the protection of jobs and the acquisition or defense of an unemployment subsidy become the basis for contention), their organizations (examining the multiplication of grassroots associations of unemployed people), and their opportunities to act (observing mainly elite factionalism as a central aspect in the genesis of protest).

4 Continuities between protest and routine politics. The fourth and final section scrutinizes the relationship that popular contention has with one increasingly prevalent form of everyday politics in Argentina: clientelism. Particular attention is paid to the workings of clientelist networks, first as providers of crucial resources to spark mobilization, then as key factors in determining the form that protest takes, and finally, as outlets through which the material gains obtained by protesters, as a result of their collective claim-making, are distributed after an episode—leaving important contentious actors out of the distribution and thus sparking a second round of protest.

In the conclusion, I address several aspects of the notion of repertoire still in need of further research, namely, the process of collective learning through which the means and meanings of contention are apprehended and later exercised, the form that state repression took during the last decade and that constrained the modalities of protest, and the role played by governmental concessions in the adoption of the roadblock as a particular means of protest throughout the country.

This article is based on a large body of documentary and ethnographic data that includes content analysis of three major national newspapers (*La Nación, Clarín,* and *Página12*) covering major contentious gatherings from

1990 to 2000, content analysis of several regional newspapers covering specific protests (*La Mañana del Sur, Río Negro, El Litoral, El Liberal, Diario Norte,* and *El Tribuno*), and ethnographic fieldwork in the towns of Santiago del Estero, Cutral-co, and Plaza Huincul during the months of June and July 1999, July and August 2000, and January through March 2001, where I interviewed dozens of protesters, journalists, union leaders, priests and nuns, policemen, university professors, high school teachers, judges, and other local authorities (council members and former mayors). Fieldwork also comprised the procurement and analysis of leaflets, press communiqués, protesters' personal diaries, police records, and court case files to the extent that they were available. In addition, I watched many locally produced videos on different uprisings as well as footage from local TV channels.

From Strikes to Roadblocks

Three nationally known episodes (the *santiagazo,* the *pueblada,* and the *correntinazo*) best exemplify the novelty of popular protest; taken together they encapsulate much of the character of the insurgent collective action in contemporary Argentina.

One day in the northwest: On December 16, 1993, the northwestern city of Santiago del Estero witnessed what the *New York Times* (December 18, 1993, p. 3) called "the worst social upheaval in years." Thousands of public servants and city residents, demanding their unpaid salaries and pensions (three months in arrears) invaded, looted, and burned three public buildings (the government house, the courthouse, and the legislature) and nearly a dozen local officials' and politicians' private residences. Described by the main Argentine newspapers as "hungry and angry people," these disgruntled citizens voiced their discontent about widespread governmental corruption. This episode, known as *el santiagazo,* was the most violent protest in contemporary democratic Argentina and a very unusual event in modern Latin America—it was an uprising that converged on the residences of wrongdoers *and* the symbols of public power, without human fatalities and during which (almost) no store was looted.

One week in the south: Between June 20 and June 26, 1996, thousands of residents of Cutral-co and Plaza Huincul, two oil towns in the southern province of Neuquén, blocked all access roads to the area, effectively halting the movement of people and goods for seven days and six nights. *Los piqueteros,* as the protesters in the barricades named themselves, demanded "genuine sources of employment," rejected the intervention of their elected representatives and other local politicians (accusing them of dishonesty and of conducting "obscure dealings"), and demanded that the governor meet with them to discuss their claims. The sheer number of protesters, twenty thousand according to most sources, intimidated the troops of the Gendarmería Nacional, which had been sent by the federal government to clear the national road. On June 26, the day after the troops left town, Governor Felipe Sapag acceded to most of the protesters' demands in a written agreement he signed with a representative of the newly formed picketers' commission. *La pueblada,* as this episode came to be known, was another extraordinary event in contemporary democratic Argentina: it is unusual these days to see troops retreating in defeat and authorities conceding to popular demands.

Six months in the northeast: Between June 7 and December 17, 1999, hundreds of tents dotted the main square in the northeast city of Corrientes. *Los placeros,* as the teachers, lawyers, public servants, and courthouse employees camping in the plaza called themselves, demanded unpaid wages (two to five months in arrears), complained of recent layoffs in the public sector, and protested the generalized custom of public nepotism. Demonstrators ate and slept in the square, while organizing dozens of marches, demonstrations, and street and bridge blockades that, by mid-December, isolated the city of Corrientes from the rest of the country. By the end of the year, virtually no school classes had been held, most public employees and the police were on strike, and regular provision of social services was suspended. These six contentious months came to be known as *el correntinazo;* no other protest in contemporary democratic Argentina lasted as long.

El santiagazo, la pueblada, and *el correntinazo* were indeed unique episodes, but they were hardly isolated. Two other contentious cycles during the last decade serve to summarize recent modalities of popular protest. Between April and June of 1997, protesters organized roadblocks on national roads and attacked public buildings throughout the country. In April, town residents blocked access to the towns of Cutral-co and Plaza Huincul, demanding the fulfillment of the promises made by the governor in an effort to end the 1996 *pueblada.* Three months later, in Cutral-co, several hundred protesters besieged the government building and held provincial and municipal authorities hostage, appealing for a increase in unemployment subsidies. In May, twenty-one roadblocks, organized by municipal workers and the unemployed, isolated the province of Jujuy for twelve days. Governor Ferraro's entire cabinet was forced to resign as a result of this massive protest. Cutral-co and Jujuy became headline news in the three major national newspapers but they were hardly the only incidents. Between April and June, protesters barricaded national road 3 in Trelew (Province of Chubut); residents and unemployed people, organized by an umbrella organization called Multisectorial, blocked traffic on national road 38 in Cruz del Eje (Province of Córdoba); municipal workers interrupted traffic on national road 11 in Capitán Bermúdez (Province of Santa Fe). During these three months, roadblocks on national and provincial roads took place in Catriel (Province of Rio Negro), Banda del Rio Salí (Province of Tucumán), and in the city of Neuquén (Province of Neuquén), while teachers, coming from the provinces and the capital, converged in the Plaza de los dos congresos and erected a huge tent (since then known as the *carpa blanca*) to protest their meager wages and poor working conditions. The governor of Salta, not exactly an ally of protesters, best summarized what happened during this contentious cycle. In reference to the prolonged barricades organized by residents of oil-towns Tartagal and General Mosconi on route 34 he asserted that "the roadblock is a political practice that is spreading throughout the country."

Less than three years later, in November 2000, this form of protest had been learned and adopted throughout the country. Roadblocks cropped up in Isidro Casanova, Esteban Echeverría, and Glew (Province of Buenos Aires); Plottier (Province of Neuquén); Salvador Mazza, Tartagal, General Mosconi, Cuña Muerta, and Zanja Honda (Province of Salta); Libertador General San Martín (Province of Jujuy); Resistencia (Province of Chaco); and Belén (Province of Catamarca).

The two cycles illustrate new forms of protest in Argentina. Among numerous observers (see, for example, Schuster 1999 and Scribano 1999), it is probably Marina Farinetti (1998, 2000) who best diagnoses the transformations in the means of popular contention in that country. The 1990s were characterized, according to this author, by a shift in the locus of labor conflict from the industrial to the public sector; a decrease in the demands for wage increases and an increase in the demands for arrears and job security; a diminution in the number of strikes and an increase in the number of hunger strikes, *ollas populares*, and roadblocks (according to one count[4] roadblocks swelled from 51 in 1998, to 252 in 1999, to 514 in 2000, and to 1383 in 2001); the intensification of protest in the provinces (i.e., outside the metropolitan region of Buenos Aires); and the increased centrality of provincial and municipal unions as main contentious actors.

Despite their wide variety—barricades that isolate entire towns or that interrupt traffic, encampments in central plazas, shaming authorities, and burning down public buildings and private residences—the forms of contention in the

Argentina during the 1990s fall into a small number of well-defined types. These forms do not change dramatically from one round of action to the next when similar sets of actors (public employees or unemployed) are involved. Furthermore, protesters seem to be aware of the recurrence because they refer to theirs and others' actions of the same kind with similar terms, using, for example, the word *estallido* (explosion) to announce an impending protest. In addition, they deploy the same tactics—manning barricades or putting up tents—and use similar expressions to refer to themselves, with *piqueteros* being the most common one. What we have then are indications that mark the emergence of a bounded array of ways to assemble to act on joint interests. The emergence of a repertoire of collective action illustrates a well-known fact: political mobilization is not simply a reaction to present grievances but the effect of accumulated history. In the next section I examine the structural factors at the root of changes in modes of contention.

Deproletarianization, State-retrenchment, and Decentralization

Three processes characterize the structural context at the root of conflict. Although they can be separated analytically, these processes operate simultaneously and mutually reinforce one another: deproletarianization, state-retrenchment, and decentralization of educational and health services.

Argentina is a particularly relevant case for the analysis of effects brought about by structural adjustment policies, since its rulers have been star students of World Bank policies, especially since the "Convertibility Plan" was adopted by the Carlos Menem administration (1989–99).[5] In September 1998, the Ministry of Justice and Security of the Province of Buenos Aires announced that 3,700 new prisoners would be temporarily placed in the storage spaces of once-active industrial plants. "There's no room elsewhere to put the new prisoners; the jails are full, and so are the precincts," the ministry admitted.

Indeed, it should be no problem housing the prison population in former factories. From 1988 to 1998, the industrial heartland of Argentina (known as the Conurbano Bonaerense) lost 5,508 industrial plants, and industrial jobs decreased from 1,381,805 in 1985 to 1,082,600 in 1994 (a 22 percent loss in manufacturing jobs over nine years). As in the United States (Wilson 1997), the disappearance of work hit the poor, unskilled, and uneducated the hardest (Murmis and Feldman 1996; Beccaria and López 1996; Kessler 1996). Today, the harmful consequences of the privatization drive and export-oriented economic strategies applauded by the World Bank can be seen in Argentina's record-high 17 percent unemployment rate; since 1991, there has been a 300 percent increase in unemployment (INDEC 2000).

Rising poverty and inequality logically result from this veritable hyper-unemployment (Iñiguez and Sanchez 1996). In the last two decades, income disparity has dramatically increased. In 1974, the richest 10 percent held 28.2 percent of national wealth (savings, real estate, etc.), while today they hold 37.3 percent. The holdings of the poorest 30 percent dropped from 11.3 percent to 8.1 percent. Poverty rates also skyrocketed. In 1980, 11.5 percent of house-holds lived below the poverty line in Greater Buenos Aires. In 1995, one out of four households were below the same line (25.8 percent). As economist Ricardo Aronskind (2001, 18) summarizes: "21.5% of the population was poor in 1991, 27% at the end of 2000. Indigents were 3% of the population in 1991 and 7% in 2000. At the beginnings of the 1990s there were 1.6 million unemployed, at the end of the year 2000 there are 4 million unemployed."

The privatization of public companies (in the sectors of telecommunica-tions, transportation, utilities, postal delivery, and aircraft manufacturing) comprised a central dimension of the process of state retrenchment and has dramatically affected employment levels. Between 1989 and 1999, close to 150,000 workers lost their jobs as a direct consequence of the privatization process. The case of the oil company YPF (Yacimientos Petrolíferos Fiscales) is of central importance because it illustrates how many of these massive layoffs take place in communities whose very survival depends, to a great extent, on the activity of one company.

Located in the Argentine Patagonia, both Plaza Huincul and Cutral-co were born of and developed through oil activity. Since their founding in 1918 and 1933 respectively both towns grew apace with (and became highly depen-dent on) the state oil company, YPF (the first government company, founded in 1922). The rapid population growth of both towns parallels the expansion of YPF's activities. From 1947 to 1990, their total population increased from 6,452 to 44,711, an impressive demographic growth by all accounts (Favaro and Bucciarelli 1994). The cradle-to-grave welfare of YPF benefited its workers with higher than average salaries, modern housing serviced by company personnel, access to a very good hospital and health plan, and paid vacations. YPF's welfare even extended beyond the confines of the company. Its presence boosted social and economic life in the region. YPF built entire neighbor-hoods, provided others with sewers and lighting, erected a local high-quality hospital, a movie theater, and a sports center and provided school buses for most of the population. In other words, YPF "was everything for both towns: work, health, education, sports, and leisure" (Costallat 1999, 6).

In less than two years an economic system and a form of life that had lasted more than four decades was shattered. On September 24, 1992, the National Congress passed into law the privatization of YPF, and soon enough the region felt the devastating effects. YPF not only cut back its personnel from 4,200 employees to 600 in less than a year (Favaro, Bucciarelli, and Luomo 1997); it also ceased to be the welfare enterprise around which the life of both towns revolved (the company even moved its headquarters out of Plaza Huincul) and became an enclave industry functioning under strict capitalist guidelines. Today, in Cutral-co, 30 percent of the economically active population is unemployed. More than half of the population of both towns lives below the official poverty line. "If things keep going like this. . . . We are going to vanish," I was repeatedly told by local residents.

Far away, in the northern part of the country, a resident of General Mosconi (Province of Salta) described her town in painfully similar terms: "Ten years ago, Mosconi became a ghost town. The privatization of YPF marked the end of a golden epoch. . . . Now the people go out and block the road just to receive some charity."

The decentralization of health and education services is also crucial to understand two central features of the new contentious repertoire in Argentina, namely the increasing appearance of the provincial and municipal unions as key actors in the upsurge of protest, and the relocation of contention to the provinces of the Argentine interior. Starting in 1989, administrative responsibilities and financial obligations for education (mainly high schools) and health services (mainly public hospitals) were transferred from the federal to state and municipal levels. As Rothen (1999, 86) asserts for the case of secondary school services, "The share of total education spending by the provinces has increased from 65.9% to 75.5% between 1991 and 1997. Over the same time, the share of spending by the federal government has decreased from 31.8% to 22.7%." As of 1987, 53 percent of high school teachers were federal employees, ten years later only 3 percent of them remained at the federal level. Close to 47 percent of them were provincial employees in 1987. Ten years later 98 percent of them were working for the provincial governments. How does this transference of administrative and financial responsibilities from the federal to the state level affect protest? A teacher from the northern province of Santiago del Estero recalls the year that preceded el santiagazo, offering a perspective on the relevance of the decentralization process in the escalation of protest that would ultimately result in the events of December 16:

We could draw a picture of the year of 1993. It was very important to us as the teachers' union, which was one of the most combative organizations at the time. It is not a coincidence. In 1993 the transference of national schools to the province was taking place. . . . Our union grouped together precisely the schools that were going to be transferred completely. Obviously we started to get organized in order to resist that transference. Because we understood that it was a way of the national state to abandon or get rid of its role in education and of its obligation to support it—an obligation that cannot be delegated. And we could then see how its first operation was to throw the bundle to the provinces. We could also foresee that after that, the provinces were going to throw the bundle to the municipalities and, finally, the system was going to end up privatized and killed. Then we started to get organized. In January 1993 we were only seven or eight people in the streets with a megaphone and a poster [laughter]. Then that group of about ten people started to go out in the streets, and we started growing.

Decentralization of education and of health services has deepened the crisis because already deficient provincial administrations confront the new financial burden with meager funds. Provincial governments, incapable of providing resources, maintaining buildings, and paying their personnel, have become targets for the claims of the now "provincialized," state employees. The massive protests by teachers and health workers all over the country during the 1990s (the so-called *jeringazos* in public hospitals and the innumerable teachers strikes) can hardly be explained without noting that, as a result of the decentralization process, protesters now direct their claims at provincial states. We can witness a change in the locus of collective action: from being a national affair, protest has become a provincial issue.

Organizations and Interests

While decentralization transforms provincial administrations into main objects of claims, deproletarianization and state retrenchment place new actors (the unemployed) and new demands (jobs) at center stage *together with* workers, most of them from the public sector, attempting to procure their unpaid wages. During the 1990s with the upsurge of protest, grassroots organizations multiplied, especially those grouping the unemployed. Among the most active were Federación de Tierras y Vivienda, Movimiento de Trabajadores Desocupados, Corriente Clasista y Combativa, Movimiento Independiente de Jubilados y Pensionados, Movimiento Territorial de Liberación, Polo Obrero, Coordinadora Anibal Veron, Movimiento de Trabajadores Teresa Rodríguez, and the Frente de Trabajadores Combativos. Dozens of other organizations mushroomed during the roadblocks at the beginning of 2000: Red de Barrios (in Buenos Aires), Comisión de Desocupados (Salta), Frente Barrial Solidario (Jujuy).

Interrelation of interests, networks, opportunities, and insurgent identities: The case of Cutral-co and Plaza Huincul 1996. Early on June 20, 1996, one of the main radio stations of Cutral-co, Radio Victoria, aired the bad news: The provincial government called off a deal with Agrium, a Canadian company, to build a fertilizer plant in the region. The radio station then "open[ed] its microphones to listen to the people's reaction. . . . A neighbor called saying that the people should show their discontent . . . [another one] said that we should get together in the road, " Mario Fernández, director and owner of the radio station, recalls. All my interviewees mention those radio messages as central in their recollections, not only in terms of the ways in which the radio called on people but also in terms of the way in which the local radio *framed* the cancellation of the fertilizer plant project.[6] On Radio Victoria, the former mayor Adolfo Grittini and his political ally, the radio station owner and director Raul Fernández, depicted the cancellation of the deal with Agrium as a "final blow to both communities," as the "last hope gone," and as an "utterly arbitrary decision of the provincial government." Daniel remembers that "there was a lot of anger . . . the radio said that we should go out and demonstrate, they were saying that it was the time to be courageous." "I learned about the blockade on the radio . . . they were talking about the social situation," Zulma says. Daniel, Zulma, and the rest of my interview subjects point toward both the same framing articulator and its similar functions: the radio both made sense of the "social situation" and persuaded people to go to the road.

As the radio broadcast "the ire that we felt" (as Daniel described the process to me) and called people to the Torre Uno (the site that memorializes the discovery of oil in the region) on Route 22, cabs brought people there free of charge. Was this a sudden eruption of indignation? Were radio reporters and taxi drivers merely the first to spontaneously react? Hardly so. The factionalism within the governing party, the MPN, and particularly, the actions of the former mayor Grittini, who had been waging his own personal fight against Mayor Martinasso and Governor Sapag,[7] are at the root of both the "injustice framing"[8] and the mobilization of resources.[9] In an interview that he asked me not to tape ("because the truth cannot be told to a tape recorder") Daniel Martinasso offered the following explanation, "Grittini backed the protest during the first couple of days. How? Well, in the first place buying a couple of local radio stations so that they call people to the route." When I asked whether it was difficult to buy a radio station, he replied, "I personally paid Radio Victoria to broadcast nice things about my administration. The radio's reception area was built with the money I paid to the owner . . . that's how politics work in Cutral-co." Grittini and his associates' efforts (Radio Victoria's owner Fernández being a key figure at this stage) did not end there. Although there is no conclusive evidence, many sources (journalists, politicians, and picketers) indicate that he also regularly sent the trucks that brought hundreds of tires to the different pickets and some of the bulldozers to block the traffic. He has also been behind the free distribution of food, gasoline, firewood, and cigarettes in the barricades. Some even say that Grittini paid $50 per night to hundreds of young picketers and that his associates provide them with alcoholic beverages and drugs.

Thus, while the radio aired its angry messages (telling people that "something has to be done" and calling on them to go to the Torre Uno), cabs drove people there and to the other barricades for free, tires were brought to the pickets, food, cigarettes, and other essentials were distributed free of charge ("We even got diapers for the babies!" many women protesters recalled). This *mobilization of resources* and this *framing process* do not, however, operate in a vacuum but, first, under conditions that were ripe for a large-scale protest and, second, via well-established political networks

"*Che, esto no es joda*, this is no joke. There are very well dressed people in the crowd," an old policeman commented as the approximately two hundred gendarmes approached the twenty thousand residents who were blockading the access to the two towns on June 25, 1996. Without knowing it, the gendarme had made a very important sociological observation about the composition of the crowd. The twenty thousand protesters included "well-dressed people" (i.e., middle-class residents) *as well as* the poor and unemployed. The available evidence proves the gendarme right. More than half of both towns' populations awaited the soldiers sent by the federal government on that cold morning, among them poor people from the infamous 500 Viviendas and well-to-do residents from the city center.

How did protesters define themselves? As many a crowd before this one, this crowd described itself as *united* (saying "The *whole pueblo* is here"), *numerous* (asserting, "We are thirty thousand, not five thousand"), *committed* to reach a goal (claiming "We want jobs. We want Governor Sapag to come here and give us a solution"), *worthy* (insisting, "We provide the gasoline, the oil"), and *lacking leaders* (shouting, "There are no politicians here"). Both in the ways they named themselves and in the crowd's social composition—that is, in its discourse and in its social relations—the protesters put forward a participatory identity that revolved around the notion of "pueblo" or The People.

What does *pueblo* mean? What are the roots of this collective self-understanding? On the one hand, *el pueblo* refers to location, indicating that entire towns are present on the road. In residents' minds, theirs is a very special *pueblo* because it provides energy (natural gas and petroleum) to the rest of the country. Among residents, there is a widespread belief (rooted in an entrenched nationalist rhetoric) that the region's mineral resources belong to them. As a young picketer remarked just a couple of feet away from the gendarmes (a statement repeated many times during those days on the road), "We provide gasoline, oil, electricity, to the rest of the country and . . . is this the pay we get?" In other words, the collective self-understanding that was forged during those days has its origins (its material bases, I would say) not only in the current plight of Cutral-co and Plaza Huincul as towns at risk of collapse but also in the memories of the "golden times" of YPF and in the deeply held conviction concerning the ownership of natural resources. In this way, residents' collective recollection of welfare provisions gave them a powerful sense of solidarity that provided an impetus to fight for what they saw as their cities' interests.

There is, however, another crucial connotation of the term *pueblo* implicit in the roar of the crowd. Protesters constructed their identity and their demands in democratic terms against what they saw as politicians' obscure dealings and constant attempts to "use the people." From the picketers' point of view, who the protesters were and what they were shouting about had as much to do with the devastation provoked by state-retrenchment expressed in the privatization of the state-run oil company as with the ruin brought about by politicians' self-interested actions (a striking, if paradoxical, identity-focused development, given that this protest, as many others, began as part of an *interna política* or intraparty fight).

Picketers identified themselves against one main actor: the political class. It is, without the usual representatives (or better, in spite of them), that residents were able to broadcast their discontent about the towns' rapid decay to the whole country. "For once," Laura and many picketers told me, "politicians couldn't use us."

Elite factionalism and opportunities to mobilize: the case of the correntinazo. If the *pueblada* illustrates the way in which elite factionalism is linked with the mobilization of resources to spark initial protest, the case of the *correntinazo* shows the way in which elite infighting opens up the opportunity for mobilization. During the *correntinazo* protesters demanded unpaid wages (in arrears of five months), protested against layoffs in the public sector, and called for "punishment of those responsible for the situation"—that is, they protested against widespread public nepotism.

Since March, protests had been escalating in frequency and in numbers of people involved. Much like in Santiago del Estero, as school classes were scheduled to begin, teachers were the first to take to the streets demanding their unpaid December (1998) salary bonus. The teachers' union also led massive rallies during April demanding unpaid wages; on May 11, they joined other public employees (administrative, courthouse, etc.) and blockaded the General Belgrano Bridge (the bridge that connects Corrientes with the neighboring city of Resistencia, in the province of Chaco, across the Paraná river) for the first time that year. Following this, there was a generalization of protest with large marches and demonstrations, and strikes by public employees, teachers, and police.

Amid increasing factionalism among ruling elites, demonstrators redoubled their intensity, and the scale of demonstrations expanded to include more and more public employees, unemployed, and students. Following the month of April, two governors were deposed in rapid succession, and the mayor (and local strongman) of Corrientes removed and arrested under charges of embezzlement of payroll funds. A coalition of opposition parties (Peronist, Radicals, Autonomistas Liberales)[10] ousted the two governors and the mayor (the three of them from the PANU-Partido Nuevo), based on their charge that Governor Pedro Braillard Poccard mismanaged government funds and acted incompetently. A few weeks later, the local chamber of deputies decided to intervene in the municipality of Corrientes to remove Mayor "Tato" Romero Feris (Corrientes's foremost *caudillo* and former governor from 1993 to 1997) on charges of corruption.

The new government confronted an extremely difficult situation. The skyrocketing provincial debt contracted by the previous government had bankrupted the local administration. With the provincial government bankrupt and amid the escalation of violence and protest, the national government began to consider federal intervention. In order to avoid being ousted by trustees from the national government and to receive fresh funds to pay protesting public employees, the new government was forced to implement a "harsh adjustment."

In order to receive a credit that would allow him to calm protesters, the new governor (for whom the national government did not hide their distaste, since he had ousted one of their allies) was required to carry out an extensive program of cuts and privatization, including the sale of the provincial bank and the provincial energy company. Adjustment should, according to the national mandate, concentrate on the municipality of Corrientes's surplus of public employees (approximately five thousand employees according to national sources). Explicitly acknowledging the link between patronage and public employment, the new governor stated, "The municipality of Corrientes (former dominion of local caudillo "Tato" Romero Feris) has 7,000 employees when it has never had more than 2,000. . . . This is an aberration. We have to reduce the number of party members . . . hired with public funds."

The prediction that an "explosion" was to come did not merely derive from the benefit of hindsight. Since early June, approximately two hundred tents dotted the square in front of the Congress building. Teachers erected the first tents (modeling their protest on the *carpa blanca* [white tent] erected in Buenos Aires by teachers two years before); a week later workers from the interior of the province occupied the remaining space in the plaza. Lawyers, school transport workers, municipal workers, kindergarten teachers, courthouse employees, health workers, even relatives of police agents, and many others had their own tents, not all of them represented by their unions (dissident factions of large unions joined the protest as "autoconvocados" [self-convened]). The square became the spatial representation of the brokerage efforts of different unions and factions.

It was in the square where dozens of marches, demonstrations, and the street and bridge blockades were planned. On June 7, right before moving into the plaza 25 de Mayo and renaming it Plaza del aguante, nearly 25,000 people manned a roadblock at the General Belgrano Bridge. Less than a week later, the *placeros* (as those camping in the plaza came to be known) tried to break into the legislature when they learned that an ally of Mayor "Tato" Romero Feris, the main target of their critic and claims, might become the new governor.

During the month of June, public sector workers blockaded traffic in the main arteries of Corrientes several times. Prison guards, teachers, and public transport workers went on strike as professional workers from the private sector took to the streets for the first time that year. Workers were demanding not only their wages but also a dialogue with the authorities, "defending our right to be heard," as a leaflet distributed in the square read. On July 4 a teacher said, "They haven't paid us for three months. We don't have anything for our basic needs. We organized marches, asked for meetings, but no one attended to us." They were also asking for "justice," that is, the prosecution of the "corrupt and thieves" as another leaflet read. The best summary I was able to find about these demands came from the title of one of the pamphlets distributed in the square, *Aguanta. Hoja del Pueblo Correntino Autoconvocado.* The title reads: "Salaries or Justice?" At the bottom of the page it says: "Salaries *and* Justice." Demands changed in the course of the protest. After the PANU officials were deposed, and probably strengthened by their victory, the leaders of the plaza began to call for "the real and effective democratization of all the offices of the state, popular administration of public resources, provincial control of public services . . . and no layoffs in the public administration."

By mid-December the city of Corrientes was "practically isolated" because of the road and bridge blockades. Thousands of protesters had repeated clashes with the Gendarmería during the six days of the last bridge blockade. Shopkeepers closed their doors in fear of riots and because their shelves were bare. There had been almost no school classes throughout the year; most public employees and the police were on strike (the police force was also deeply divided in different factions: those loyal to "Tato" and those close to the new government); and regular provision of social services (such as soup kitchens) was suspended. In other words, everyday life was in complete disarray, given the fact that this was a city that "lives with the rhythm of public administration" (commercial sales decreased "approximately 80% in few months").

Mobilization networks and everyday forms of clientelism. One particular form of routine politics, that is, clientelism, is deeply embedded in the *genesis, course,* and *outcome* of popular contention. The case of Cutral-co and Plaza Huincul illustrates the relationship between patron-client networks and the origins of conflict. In this last section, I briefly examine two different episodes to show how the operation of clientelist networks also alters the shape of protest, as in Santiago del Estero in 1993, as well as the effects of protest, as in Salta from 1997 to 2000. Needless to say, further research is badly needed to understand the intricate and usually hidden links between clientelist and contentious politics.

On December 16, 1993, high school and university students, housewives, retired elderly, informal sector workers, and unemployed youth joined municipal and provincial government workers in a rally in front of the Government House of Santiago del Estero. Angry protesters threw bricks, sticks, bottles, and paving stones at the Government House while trying to enter the building. The police fired tear gas and rubber bullets at the crowd, who retreated toward the middle of the square. Soon, the police seemed to have run out of ammunition and abandoned the scene. In less than ten minutes, thousands of protesters became "the owners of the battlefield"; they were now "in charge of the situation," as the main local newspaper reported. By noon, the front part of the House was completely on fire, and the chief of police convinced Governor Fernando Lobo, who was still inside, to leave, "Governor . . . there might be a massacre here, leave the building with the cabinet members, and we will escort you." By 4:30 p.m., after almost a day of unrest, a crowd of 250 attacked the residence of former governor Gustavo Adolfo Mujica, burning both his house and car. Protesters took furniture and appliances out of his house while neighbors applauded and celebrated. Even later hundreds of demonstrators broke into the homes of former legislators Miguel Gauna and Angel Granda. Also invaded and burned were the homes of a member of the Supreme Court, the leader of the largest teachers' union, the former undersecretary of media and institutional relations, and legislator Nilda Riachi. Finally, at 9:30 p.m. one of the buildings of the Ministry of Social Welfare was assaulted. An hour later, the National Senate authorized federal intervention in Santiago del Estero. The national government sent in hundreds of troops from the Gendarmería Nacional and suspended the powers of the executive, judicial, and legislative branches, imposing its own officials as trustees. The next day, after a few more attacks in the neighboring city of La Banda, the protest was over.

The offices and private homes of the "political class" that protesters attacked on December 16 had been defined as "targets" in the previous months, to such an extent that moving from one "target" to another during the riot seemed "natural." Here's how a protester described what he calls "the procession" through downtown on the day of the "explosion": "When we were in the Government House, the public employees were applauding at the fire. It seemed *natural* to move on to the Congress." This explains the "precision" with which the crowd moved from one home to another, and that some observers used as "evidence" of the work of "subversive agitators."

How did protesters distinguish between those politicians who, as many a protester recalled, "deserved" to be burned out and those who did not? On the one hand, the targets had been implicitly defined in the previous months by the proliferation of reports of corruption scandals in the main newspapers. Media reports had unintentionally constructed a blueprint for protesters. "The targets were perfectly visible. This is a small town, everybody knows each other, and the media always remark who is who. . . . It was as if everyone understood that we had to go there," Mariano, a participant in the events, explained six years later. Rogelio, a policeman, told me, "At the time, many media were commenting on the amount of money officials made." On the other hand, the tacit itinerary involved the homes of the political bosses, the best-known political patrons; homes that many protesters used to visit quite frequently. As Carlos tells me, encapsulating in one single comment what deserves in-depth attention:

> Here, in Santiago, there are gangs that serve many, many purposes. These gangs are formed by marginal youngsters. The Radical party or the Peronist party invite these youths for a barbecue, taking them for party rallies in exchange for food or money. . . . Those youngsters know every single mechanism to get what they want from politicians, ministers, or members of the parliament. They are not Peronists or Radicals, they just go with everybody. They know the politicos' houses. They've been there, because the corrupt politicians invite them to their residences, and they begin to figure out how politics work. These are the youngsters who attacked the politicos' houses on December 16. They knew perfectly where they lived.

Much like Cutral-co and Plaza Huincul, the towns of General Mosconi, Aguaray, Salvador Mazza, Campamento Vespucio, and Tartagal in the province of Salta have been particularly affected by the privatization of YPF. With rates of unemployment ranging from 30 percent to 40 percent these small towns are, like their counterparts in the Patagonia, on the verge of becoming ghost towns. Campamento Vespucio, for example, lost its hospital, school, post office, and police precinct since the 1992 privatization of YPF. The area registers high levels of popular contention, with roadblocks lasting for weeks and recurring with greater intensity since 1997. On November 10, 2000, in an attempt to clear national road 34 of protesters, the local police killed picketer Anibal Verón. The following day, protesters attacked and burned down Tartagal's municipal building, the local branch of the National Bank, the office of a Peronist member of the parliament, the office of the local energy company, the offices of Atahualpa (the transportation company where Verón used to work), the offices of a provincial newspaper, and a few local shops. Protesters' actions and words squarely point toward the devastation wrought by the privatization of the state oil company and the rampant joblessness, but also speak to the corruption of local politicians and officials. As one picketer put it, "They steal every single coin they can get their hands on."

What do local officials do with the hoarded subsidies? Six months before, in the same area, picketers were demanding jobs and the removal of the local mayor and council-members because they "distribute the employment subsidies [which the picketers had obtained as a result of their prolonged protests months before] among their *punteros* (party brokers). And we don't have anything to feed our families." There is a lesson to be learned from Salta: material resources that protesters demand and get are sometimes distributed through party machines and clientelist networks; a form of allocation that usually excludes many protesters, making not only the next round of protest possible, but also adding a new object of claims (the local politicos) and a new demand (transparency) to the new wave of contention.

Conclusions

In this chapter I examined the structural factors at the root of changing forms of popular contention in Argentina and looked closely at how these factors impact protest by affecting actors' grievances, interests, organizations, and identities. I also inspected the continuities between political networks and mobilizing structures and the role elite in-fighting plays as an opportunity for contention. Needless to say, much more work needs to be done on these and several other dimensions of the current wave of Argentine contention. To conclude, I highlight some of the issues that deserve close attention.

When asked about the reasons for a particular roadblock, protesters throughout Argentina responded with a similar phrase, "This is the only way to attract their attention." And a pretty successful one, I should add. In fact, one could venture the hypothesis that the flourishing of that militant expression during the 1990s and 2000s was intricately related to its success in terms of fulfilling demands. Two examples should suffice to illustrate the sort of contagion that follows a victorious protest. On May 16, 2000, a few days after national officials had negotiated a solution to a long-term protest in the northern province of Salta, a group of women manned a roadblock on road 22 in Cutral-co. Women in Cutral-co claimed the very same work subsidies ("planes trabajar") that their counterparts in the North had, saying that "those who block roads are the only ones who obtain some help." On November of that same year, after government officials signed an agreement with the leaders of the *piqueteros* in La Matanza (Buenos Aires) conceding all of their demands, four new protests, with similar demands, surfaced in Buenos Aires (La Plata, Bosques, San Francisco Solano, and Sarandí) and in Salta. This contagion or "domino effect" should be studied in more detail. Future research should also pay sustained attention to the workings of particular actors who "do the teaching"—mainly members of the Catholic Church, some union leaders, and neighborhood activists—about the practicalities of protest.

On November 7, 2000, an article in a major Argentine newspaper described the roadblock as a form of protest that was, "born in the Patagonia . . . and is now at the doors of the Federal Capital." At present, roadblocks, along with camps in central plazas, and attacks on public buildings and residences of politicos and officials, are at the doors of the Federal Capital, making analysts and journalists pay attention. They are also at the core of the nation's psyche, guiding the ways in which ordinary Argentines collectively contend for their interests.

NOTES

1. Local and foreign analysts and journalists have pointed to immiseration, hyper-unemployment, and government neglect as the main causes behind the recent upsurge of contention. The so-called *estallidos*, the roadblocks, and the *puebladas* are thus responses to economic stimuli and official disregard. Pozzi's recent analysis of the upheavals known as *azos* (for *correntinazo*, *cutralcazo*, or *santiagazo*) is probably the best example of this perspective: "The azos of the 1990s . . . were clearly the product of neoconservative market economic policies and limited democracy. Hunger, unemployment, marginality, the impossibility of obtaining redress from elected representatives, and the lack of viable justice system are the most immediate causes" (Pozzi 2000, 68). Journalists recurrently point at the very same factors to "explain" the recent rise in contention (see various articles in *Clarín*, *Página12*, and *La Nación* during December 2001 and January 2002). Although they stress the "structural" roots of conflict, they also point toward spontaneity as the triggering factor in specific instances of protest while ignoring the decade-long history of contention. The director of the Argentine edition of *Le Monde Diplomatique*, Carlos Gabetta (2002), best represents this viewpoint. Referring to the events of December 19 and 20, he asserts, "Yet until 19 December, when tens of thousands spontaneously took to the streets, they seemed spellbound, powerless to express their discontent. Remembering the violent military dictatorship of 1976–83, the debacle of the Falklands war in 1982, and the traumatic hyperinflation of 1989, they bowed to political blackmail, threats of authoritarian rule and economic disaster." Even a superficial look at the hundreds of roadblocks, rallies, public sector strikes, and so on, casts doubt about this presumed "spell." I mention these two authors, obviously sympathetic to collective struggles, to highlight the fact that a disregard for history and for political processes at the root of contention is generalized even among "progressive" analysts, not only among those who (still) talk about the "mad crowd" when referring to the recent "riots." True, unemployment and poverty were the bases of contention during the 1990s, the grounds over which people collectively struggle, but protest has its roots in (and is shaped by) political processes and prior forms of contention (for a detailed analyses of these and other shortcomings, see Auyero 2002).

2. As Tilly (2001, 9) recently put it, "The spatial organization of repressive activities and their evasion significantly affects viability for different forms of contentious politics."

3. In its emphasis on the structured and structuring capacities of the repertoire, on the mutual imbrication of structural conditions, history, experiences, and practices, and on the centrality of habituation and of improvisation within established (but flexible) limits, Tilly's notion resembles Bourdieu's notion of *habitus* (see Bourdieu 1977). Indeed, one could speak of the repertoire of collective action as a sort of *contentious joint habitus.* Much like Bourdieu's *habitus,* the repertoire lives a double life: in the objectivity of prior contentious interactions between citizens and states, and in the subjectivity of protesters' (and officials') accumulated experience. And like *habitus,* the repertoire is a conditioned and conditioning set of means and meanings of acting together; a product and a producer of contentious history that, at the same time, leaves room for innovation within boundaries, "[Be]cause participants in a given struggle remembered what had happened before and planned their actions accordingly, and because the outcome of any particular struggle altered the positions of the participants, including third parties. Concessions the government made to a specific type of action by a certain actor . . . made it easier for other actors to press claims by means of that same type of action. True success of one petition drive opened the way to new petition drives . . . " (Tilly 1992, 15). It is probably the recurrent images that Tilly and Bourdieu draw upon to illustrate the workings of the repertoire and the *habitus* (images that come from the world of sports and music; jazz improvisation being the preferred one for both) that better encapsulate the character that, for both, practices share. From artistic endeavors and intellectual pursuits to the acts of banding together to make claims heard, practices are *interactively learned and then taken-for-granted, constrained, and improvised.* A character, I should add, that the voluntaristic and cerebral notion of "frame" does not capture.

4. Centro de Estudios para la Nueva Mayoría (www.nuevamayoria.com).

5. In March 1991, the finance minister of the Menem's administration, Doming Cavallo, announced the "convertibility plan," in which the exchange rate between the U.S. dollar and the Argentine peso was fixed at parity. Since then, any monetary creation had to be financially backed by an equivalent increase in foreign-exchange reserves at the National Central Bank.

6. On framing (and its critics) as a central element in the emergence and course of mobilization, see Snow and Benford 1988 and 1992; Benford and Snow 2000; Steinberg 1999; and Poletta 1998a.

7. Months before, in the party primaries current governor Sosbich allied with former Cutral-co mayor Grittini against then governor Sapag. Sapag won the primaries and Mayor Martinasso, who had initially sided with Sosbisch and Grittini, switched factions and joined Sapag's group.

8. An "injustice frame" is a mode of interpretation—prefatory to protest—produced and adopted by those who classify the actions of an authority as unjust. See Gamson 1992a and 1992b.

9. For classic statement on resource mobilization theory, see McCarthy and Zald 1973 and 1977 and Jenkins 1983.

10. Having lost against the governing PANU, this new coalition was an electoral minority but gathered enough votes in the local Chamber of Deputies to remove

Governor Braillard Poccard and later Vice-Governor Maidana, imposing one of their own, Peronist Julio Perié.

REFERENCES

Aguilar, Maria Angela, and Estela Vazquez. 2000. "De YPF a la ruta: Un acercamiento a Tartagal." In *Trabajo y población en el noroeste argentino*, ed. Marta Panaia, Susana Aparicio, and Carlos Zurita, 327–45. Buenos Aires: Editorial La Colmena.

Alvarez, Sonia, Evelina Dagnino, and Arturo Escobar, eds. 1998. *Cultures of Politics, Politics of Culture: Re-visioning Latin American Social Movements*. Boulder, Colo.: Westview Press.

Amin, Shahid. 1995. *Event, Metaphor, Memory: Chauri-Chaura, 1922–92*. Berkeley and Los Angeles: University of California Press.

Appadurai, Arjun. 1996. *Modernity at Large*. Minneapolis: Minnesota University Press.

Aronskind, Ricardo. 2001. *¿Más cerca o más lejos del desarrollo? Transformaciones económica en los '90s*. Buenos Aires: Libros del Rojas-Universidad de Buenos Aires.

Auyero, Javier. 1999. "Re-Membering Peronism: An Ethnographic Account of the Relational Character of Political Memory." *Qualitative Sociology* 22, no. 4:331–53.

———. 2000. "Los estallidos en provincia: Globalización y conflictos sociales." *Punto de Vista* 67:41–48.

———. 2001. "Glocal Riots." *International Sociology* 161, no. 1:33–55.

Barbeito, Alberto, and Ruben LoVuolo. 1992. *La modernización excluyente*. Buenos Aires: Losada.

Beccaria, Luis, and Nestor López. 1996. "Notas sobre el comportamiento del mercado de trabajo urbano." In *Sin trabajo. Las características del desempleo y sus efectos en la sociedad argentina*, ed. Luis Beccaria and Nestor López, 17–46. Buenos Aires: Losada.

Benford, Robert, and David Snow. 2000. "Framing Processes and Social Movements: An Overview and Assessment." *Annual Review of Sociology* 26:611–39.

Bourdieu, Pierre. 1977. *Outline of a Theory of Practice*. Cambridge: Cambridge University Press.

———. 1996. "Understanding." *Theory, Culture and Society* 13, no. 2:17–37.

———. 1999. "Hanging by a Threat." In *The Weight of the World*, ed. Pierre Bourdieu et al., 370–80. Stanford: Stanford University Press.

Bourdieu, Pierre, et al., eds. 1999. *The Weight of the World*. Stanford: Stanford University Press.

Brass, Paul. 1996a. "Introduction: Discourse of Ethnicity, Communalism, and Violence." In *Riots and Pogroms*, ed. Paul Brass, 1–55. New York: New York University Press.

———, ed. 1996b. *Riots and Pogroms*. New York: New York University Press.

Brubaker, Roger, and Frederick Cooper. 2000. "Beyond 'Identity.'" *Theory and Society* 29:1–47.

Burawoy, Michael, et al. 1991. *Ethnography Unbound: Power and Resistance in the Modern Metropolis*. Berkeley and Los Angeles: University of California Press.

Burawoy, Michael, et al. 2000. *Global Ethnography. Forces, Connections, and Imaginations in a Postmodern World.* Berkeley and Los Angeles: University of California Press.

Calhoun, Craig. 1994. *Neither Gods nor Emperors: Students and the Struggle for Democracy in China.* Berkeley and Los Angeles: University of California Press.

Camarasa, Jorge. 2002. *Días de furia. Historia oculta de la Argentina desde la caída de De la Rúa hasta la asunción de Duhalde.* Buenos Aires: Sudamericana.

Carreras, Julio. 1994. "Reconstruir, desde las cenizas de una conflictuada cultura." *El Estallido Social en Santiago,* 71–75.

Cerulo, Karen. 1997. "Identity Construction: New Issues, New Directions." *Annual Review of Sociology* 23:385–409.

Coronil, Fernando, and Julie Skurski. 1991. "Dismembering and Remembering the Nation: The Semantics of Political Violence in Venezuela." *Comparative Studies in Society and History* 33, no. 2:255–87.

Costallat, Karina. 1999. "Efectos de las privatizaciones y la relación estado-sociedad en la instancia provincial y local: El caso Cutral Co–Plaza Huincul." Buenos Aires, Instituto Nacional de Administración Pública (INAP). Manuscript.

Curiotto, Jose, and Julio Rodríguez. 1994. *Arde Santiago! La verdadera historia del estallido social de Santiago del Estero que asombro al país y al mundo.* Tucumán: Ediciones El Graduado.

Dargoltz, Raúl. 1994. *El santiaguenazo. Gestación y crónica de una pueblada argentina.* Buenos Aires: El Despertador Ediciones.

Darnton, Robert. 1991. "The Great Cat Massacre of the Rue Saint-Severin." In *Rethinking Popular Culture: Contemporary Perspective in Cultural Studies,* ed. Chandra Mukerji and Michael Schudson, 97–120. Berkeley and Los Angeles: University of California Press.

Davis, Diane. 1999. "The Power of Distance: Re-Theorizing Social Movements in Latin America." *Theory and Society* 28:585–638.

"Democracia Argentina." 1999. *Trabajo y sociedad* 1 (July-September). http: //habitantes .elsitio.com/proit/zmarina.htm/.

Edelman, Marc. 2001. "Social Movements: Changing Paradigms and Forms of Politics." *Annual Review of Anthropology* 30:285–317.

Emerson, Robert. 1983. *Contemporary Field Research: A Collection of Readings.* Boston: Little, Brown.

Entel, Alicia. 1997. *La ciudad bajo sospecha. Comunicación y protesta urbana.* Buenos Aires: Paidos.

Escobar, Arturo, and Sonia Álvarez, eds. 1992. *The Making of Social Movements in Latin America: Identity, Strategy, and Democracy.* Boulder, Colo.: Westview Press.

Farinetti, Marina. 1998. "Cuando los clientes se rebelan." *Apuntes,* no. 2/3:84–103.

———. 2000. "El estallido: La forma de la protesta." Manuscript. Buenos Aires.

———. "¿Que queda del 'Movimiento Obrero'? Las formas del reclamo laboral en la nueva democracia argentina." *Trabajo y Sociedad* 1 (July-September).

Favaro, Orietta, and Mario Bucciarelli. 1994. "Efectos de la privatización de YPF: ¿La desagregación territorial del espacio Neuquino?" *Realidad Económica* 127:88–99.

————. 1995. "El nuevo escenario político. Elecciones y crisis en un espacio provincial. El MPN: ¿Ruptura o continuidad de una forma de hacer política?" *Realidad Económica* 135:103–17.

Favaro, Orietta, Mario Bucciarelli, and Graciela Luomo. 1997. "La conflictividad social en Neuquen. El movimiento cutralquense y los nuevos sujetos sociales." *Realidad Económica* 148:13–27.

Favaro, Orietta, Mario Bucciarelli, and María Scuri. 1993. "El Neuquen: Limites estructurales de una estrategia de distribución (1958–1980)." *Realidad Económica* 118:123–38.

Gabetta, Carlos. 2002. "Argentina: IMF Show State Revolts." http://mondedipla.com/2002/01/12.

Gamson, William A. 1988. "Political Discourse and Collective Action." In *From Structure to Action: Comparing Social Movement Research*, ed. Bert Klandermans, Hanspeter Kriesi, and Sidney Tarrow, 219–44. Vol. 1 of *International Social Movement Research*. Greenwich, Conn.: JAI Press.

————. 1992a. "The Social Psychology of Collective Action." In *Frontiers in Social Movement Theory*, ed. Aldon Morris and Carol McClurg Mueller. New Haven: Yale University Press.

————. 1992b. *Talking Politics*. Cambridge: Cambridge University Press.

————. 1998. "Discourse, Nuclear Power, and Collective Action." In *The New American Cultural Sociology*, ed. Philip Smith. Cambridge: Cambridge University Press.

Geertz, Clifford. 1973. *The Interpretation of Cultures*. New York: Basic Books.

————. 2001. *Available Light: Anthropological Reflections on Philosophical Topics*. Princeton: Princeton University Press.

Ginsburg, Faye. 1989. *Contested Lives: The Abortion Debate in an American Community*. Berkeley and Los Angeles: University of California Press.

Goodwin, Jeff. 2001. *No Other Way Out*. Cambridge: Cambridge University Press.

Gould, Roger. 1995. *Insurgent Identities: Class, Community, and Protest in Paris from 1848 to the Commune*. Chicago: University of Chicago Press.

Gusfield, Joseph. 1994. "The Reflexivity of Social Movements: Collective Behavior and Mass Society Theory Revisited." In *New Social Movements. From Ideology to Identity*, ed. Hank Johnston, Joseph Gusfield, and Enrique Laraña, 58–78. Philadelphia: Temple University Press.

Helvacioglu, Banu. 2000. "Globalization in the Neighborhood. From the Nation-State to the Bilkent Center." *International Sociology* 15, no. 2:329–45.

Íñigo Carrera, Nicolás. 1999. "Fisonomía de las huelgas generales de la década de 1990." *PIMSA 1999*, 155–73.

Iñiguez, A., and A. Sanchez. 1996. "El conurbano bonaerense y al provincial de Buenos Aires: Condensación de la tragedia nacional de la desocupación." *Cuadernos del IBAP* (Buenos Aires) 7.

Instituto Nacional de Estadísticas y Censos (INDEC). 2000. "Encuesta permanente de hogares." October. Buenos Aires.

Jasper, James. 1997. *The Art of Moral Protest*. Chicago: University of Chicago Press.

Jenkins, Craig. 1983. "Resource Mobilization Theory." *Annual Review of Sociology* 9:213.

Kakar, Sudhir. 1996. *The Colors of Violence: Cultural Identities, Religion, and Conflict.* Chicago: University of Chicago Press.

Kessler, Gabriel. 1996. "Algunas implicancias de la experiencia de la desocupación para el individuo y su familia." In *Sin trabajo. Las características del desempleo y sus efectos en la sociedad argentina,* ed. Luis Beccaria and Nestor Lopez. Buenos Aires: Losada.

Klachko, Paula. 1999. "Cutral Co y Plaza Huincul. El primer corte de ruta." PIMSA 1999, 121–54.

Korzeniewicz, Roberto Patricio, and William C. Smith. 2000. "Poverty, Inequality and Growth in Latin America: Searching for the High Road." *Latin America Research Review* 35:7–54.

Laufer, Ruben, and Claudio Spiguel. 1999. "Las 'puebladas' argentinas a partir del 'santiagueñazo' de 1993. Tradición histórica y nuevas formas de lucha." In *Lucha popular, democracia, neoliberalismo: Protesta popular en América Latina en los años del ajuste,* ed. Margarita López Maya, 15–44. Caracas: Nueva Sociedad.

Laurell, Asa Cristina. 2000. "Structural Adjustment and the Globalization of Social Policy in Latin America." *International Sociology* 15, no. 2:309–28.

Lee, Ching Kwan. 2000. "The 'Revenge of History.' Collective Memories and Labor Protests in North-Eastern China." *Ethnography* 1, no. 2:217–37.

Lloyd-Sherlock, Peter. 1997. "Policy, Distribution, and Poverty in Argentina Since Redemocratization." *Latin American Perspectives* 24, no. 97:22–55.

Lodola, Germán. 2002. "Social Protests Under Industrial Reorganization Process. Argentina in the Nineties." Manuscript. Department of Political Science, University of Pittsburgh.

López Maya, Margarita, ed. 1999. *Lucha popular, democracia, neoliberalismo: Protesta popular en América Latina en los años del ajuste.* Caracas: Nueva Sociedad.

López Maya, Margarita, David Smilde, and Keta Stephany. 2000. "Identidades sociopolíticas en construcción." Paper presented at the Latin American Studies Association Twenty-first International Congress, Miami, March 16–18.

McAdam, Doug. 1982. *Political Process and the Development of Black Insurgency, 1930–1970.* Chicago: University of Chicago Press, 1982.

———. 1988. *Freedom Summer.* New York: Oxford University Press.

McAdam, Doug, Sidney Tarrow, and Charles Tilly. 2001. *Dynamics of Contention.* Cambridge: Cambridge University Press.

McCarthy, John, and Mayer Zald. 1973. *The Trend of Social Movements in America.* Morristown, N.J: General Learning Press.

———. 1977. "Resource Mobilization and Social Movements." *American Journal of Sociology* 82:1212–41.

Meyer, David, and Nancy Whittier. 1994. "Social Movement Spillover." *Social Problems* 41, no. 2:277–98.

Miller, Byron, and Deborah Martin. 1998. "Missing Geography: Social Movements on the Head of a Pin?" Paper presented at the Association of American Geographers, Boston, March 26.

Minujin, Alberto, and Gabriel Kessler. 1995. *La nueva pobreza en la Argentina.* Buenos Aires: Planeta.

Murmis, Miguel, and Silvio Feldman. 1996. "De sequir ai." In *Sin trabajo. Las características del desempleo y sus efectos en la sociedad argentina,* ed. Luis Beccaria and Nestor Lopez. Buenos Aires: Losada.

Oxhorn, Philip. 1998. "The Social Foundations of Latin America's Recurrent Populism: Problems of Popular Sector Class Formation and Collective Action." *Journal of Historical Sociology* 11, no. 2:212–46.

O'Donnell, Guillermo. 1998. *Contrapuntos.* Buenos Aires: Paidos.

Pile, Steve, and Michael Keith Pile, eds. 1997. *Geographies of Resistance.* London: Routledge.

Polletta, Francesca. 1998a. "Contending Stories: Narrative in Social Movements." *Qualitative Sociology* 21, no. 4:419–46.

———. 1998b. "'It Was Like a Fever . . .' Narrative and Identity in Social Protest." *Social Problems* 45, no. 2:137–59.

Pozzi, Pablo. 2000. "Popular Upheaval and Capitalist Transformation in Argentina." *Latin American Perspectives* 27, no. 114:63–87.

Putnam, Robert. 1993. *Making Democracy Work: Civic Traditions in Modern Italy.* Princeton: Princeton University Press.

Ragin, Charles, and Howard Becker. 1992. *What Is a Case?* Chicago: University of Chicago Press.

Ray, Raka. 1999. *Fields of Protest.* Minneapolis: University of Minnesota Press.

Robertson, Roland. 1995. "Glocalization: Time-Space and Homogeneity and Heterogeneity." In *Global Modernities,* ed. M. Featherstone et al. London: Sage.

Rofman, Alejandro. 2000. "Destrucción de las economías provinciales." *Le Monde Diplomatique,* August 6–7.

Rothen, D. 1999. "Global-Local Conditions of Possibility: The Case of Education Decentralization in Argentina." Ph.D. diss., Department of Education, Stanford University.

Routledge, Paul. 1997. *A Spatiality of Resistance: Theory and Practice in Nepal's Revolution of 1990.* In *Geographies of Resistance,* ed. Steve Pile and Michael Keith Pile, 68–86. London: Routledge.

Roy, Beth. 1994. *Some Trouble with Cows.* Berkeley and Los Angeles: University of California Press.

Rubins, Roxana, and Horacio Cao. 2000. "Las satrapías de siempre." *Le Monde Diplomatique,* August, 8–9.

Sawers, Larry. 1996. *The Other Argentina.* Boulder, Colo.: Westview Press.

Schuster, Federico. 1999. "La protesta social en la Argentina democrática: Balance y perspectivas de una forma de acción política." Manuscript. Buenos Aires.

Scribano, Adrian. 1999. "Argentina 'Cortada': Cortes de ruta y visibilidad social en el contexto del ajuste." In *Lucha popular, democracia, neoliberalismo: Protesta popular en América Latina en los años del ajuste,* ed. Margarita López Maya, 45–72. Caracas: Nueva Sociedad.

Snow, David E. and Robert Benford. 1988. "Ideology, Frame Resonance, and Participant Mobilization." In *From Structure to Action: Comparing Social Movement Research,* ed. Bert Klandermans, Hanspeter Kriesi, and Sidney Tarrow, 197–217. Vol. 1 of *International Social Movement Research.* Greenwich, Conn.: JAI Press.

―――. 1992. "Master Frames and Cycles of Protest." In *Frontiers in Social Movement Theory*, ed. Aldon Morris and Carol McClurg, 133–55. New Haven: Yale University Press.

Snow, David, Daniel M. Cress, Liam Downey, and Andrew W. Jones. 1998. "Disrupting the 'Quotidian': Reconceptualizing the Relationship Between Breakdown and the Emergence of Collective Action." *Mobilization* 3, no. 1:1–22.

Somers, Margaret. 1995. "What's Political or Cultural About Political Culture and the Public Sphere?" *Sociological Theory* 13, no. 2:113–44.

Somers, Margaret, and Gloria Gibson. 1994. "Reclaiming the Epistemological 'Other': Narrative and the Social Constitution of Identity, II." In *Social Theory and the Politics of Identity*, ed. Craig Calhoun, 37–99. Oxford: Blackwell.

Steinberg, Marc. "The Roar of the Crowd." In *Repertoires and Cycles of Collective Action*, ed. Mark Traugott, 57–88. Durham: Duke University Press, 1995.

―――. 1999. *Fighting Words: Working-Class Formation, Collective Action, and Discourse in Early Nineteenth-Century England*. Ithaca: Cornell University Press.

―――. 2000. "The Talk and Back Talk of Collective Action: A Dialogic Analysis of Repertoires of Discourse Among Nineteenth-Century English Cotton Spinners." *American Journal of Sociology* 105, no. 3:736–80.

Stillwaggon, Eileen. 1998. *Stunted Lives, Stagnant Economies: Poverty, Disease, and Underdevelopment*. New Brunswick: Rutgers University Press.

Swyngedouw, Eric. 1997. "Neither Global nor Local: 'Glocalization' and the Politics of Scale." In *Spaces of Globalization: Reasserting the Power of the Local*, ed. Kevin Cox, 137–66. New York: Guilford Press.

Tarrow, Sidney. 1992. "Mentalities, Political Cultures and Collective Action Frames: Constructing Meaning Through Action." In *Frontiers in Social Movement Research*, ed. Aldon Morris and Carol McClurg, 174–202. New Haven: Yale University Press.

―――. 1996. "The People's Two Rhythms: Charles Tilly and the Study of Contentious Politics." *Comparative Studies in Society and History*, 586–600.

―――. 1998. *Power in Movement: Social Movements and Contentious Politics*. New York: Cambridge University Press.

Tenti, Emilio. 2000. "Exclusión Social y Acción Colectiva en la Argentina de Hoy." *Punto de Vista* 67:22–28.

Tilly, Charles. 1978. *From Mobilization to Revolution*. Reading, Mass.: Addison Wesley.

―――. 1986. *The Contentious French*. Cambridge: Harvard University Press.

―――. 1991. "Domination, Resistance, Compliance . . . Discourse." *Sociological Forum* 6, no. 3:593–602.

―――. 1992. "How to Detect, Describe, and Explain Repertoires of Contention." Working Paper Series, no. 150, New School for Social Research, Center for the Study of Social Change.

―――. 1995. "Contentious Repertoires in Great Britain." In *Repertoires and Cycles of Collective Action*, ed. Mark Traugott, 63–87. Durham: Duke University Press.

―――. 1996. "Conclusion: Contention and the Urban Poor in Eighteenth- and Nineteenth-Century Latin America." In *Riots in the Cities*, ed. Silvia Arrom and Servando Ortoll, 225–42. Wilmington, Del.: Scholarly Resources.

―――. 1997a. "Parliamentarization of Popular Contention in Great Britain, 1758–1834." *Theory and Society* 26:245–73.

————. 1997b. *Roads from Past to Future.* Lanham, Mass.: Rowman and Littlefield.

————. 1998. "The Trouble with Stories." In *Teaching for the 21st Century: The Handbook for Understanding and Rebuilding the Social World of Higher Education,* ed. Ronal Aminzade and Bernice Pescosolido. Thousand Oaks, Calif.: Pine Forge Press.

————. 2001. "Stories, Identities, and Political Change." Manuscript. Department of Sociology, Columbia University.

————. Forthcoming. "Large-Scale Violence as Contentious Politics." In *Handbook of Research on Violence,* ed. Wilhelm Heitmeyer and John Hagan. Boulder, Colo.: Westview Press.

Tilly, Charles, Louise Tilly, and Richard Tilly. 1975. *The Rebellious Century, 1830–1930.* Cambridge: Harvard University Press.

Useem, Bert. 1998. "Breakdown Theories of Collective Action." *Annual Review of Sociology* 24:215–38.

Wacquant, Loïc. 1995a. "The Pugilistic Point of View: How Boxers Think and Feel About Their Trade." *Theory and Society* 24:489–535.

Walton, John. 1989. "Debt, Protest, and the State in Latin America." In *Power and Popular Protest: Latin American Social Movements,* ed. Susan Eckstein, 299–328. Berkeley and Los Angeles: University of California Press.

————. 1998. "Urban Conflict and Social Movements in Poor Countries: Theory and Evidence of Collective Action." *International Journal of Urban and Regional Research* 22, no. 3:460–81.

Walton, John, and David Seddon, eds. 1994. *Free Markets and Food Riots: The Politics of Global Adjustment.* Oxford: Blackwell.

Walton, John, and Jon Shefner. 1994. "Latin America: Popular Protest and the State. " In *Free Markets and Food Riots: The Politics of Global Adjustment,* ed. John Walton, and David Seddon, 97–134. Oxford: Blackwell.

Wilson, William Julius. 1997. *When Work Disappears: The World of the New Urban Poor.* New York: Vintage Books.

Wood, Elisabeth. 2001. "Pride in Rebellion: Insurrectionary Collective Action in El Salvador." Manuscript. Department of Politics, New York University.

Zald, Mayer. 1992. "Looking Backward to Look Forward: Reflections on the Past and the Future of the Resource Mobilization Research Program." In *Frontiers in Social Movement Theory,* ed. Aldon Morris and Carol McClurg Mueller. New Haven: Yale University Press.

Zemon Davis, Natalie. 1973. "The Rites of Violence: Religious Riot in Sixteenth-Century France." *Past and Present* 59 (May): 51–91.

Zhao, Dingxin. 1998. "Ecologies of Social Movements: Student Mobilization During the Prodemocracy Movement in Beijing." *American Journal of Sociology* 103, no. 6:1493–1529.

Zurita, Carlos. 1999a. "Estratificación social y trabajo: Imágenes y magnitudes en Santiago del Estero." *Trabajo y Sociedad* 1 (July-September): 1–22.

————. 1999b. "Estructura del empleo y formas de trabajo en una ciudad tradicional de la Argentina." Manuscript. Sociology Department, Universidad de Santiago del Estero, Argentina.

————. 1999c. *El Trabajo en una sociedad tradicional: Estudios sobre Santiago del Estero.* Santiago del Estero, Argentina: CICYT-UNSE.

SEVEN

The Even More Difficult Transition from Clientelism to Citizenship: Lessons from Brazil

Robert Gay

Recent political events in Latin America suggest a transformation in state-society relations. Across the region, there are indications that voter compliance and, as a result, elections can no longer be secured by the time-honored practice of exchanging votes for favors, otherwise known as *clientelism*. Indeed, the recent difficulties experienced by the Institutional Revolutionary Party (PRI) in Mexico and the continued success of the Workers' Party (PT) in Brazil have been interpreted as evidence that traditional mechanisms of political control are breaking down. If clientelism is not what it once was, however, democracy is by no means what it is supposed to be. It is more than clear that regularly held and free elections are necessary but insufficient conditions for the consolidation of democracy and, in particular, the establishment of citizens' rights.

This chapter marks an attempt to explore the conceptual spaces between clientelism and citizenship that were first suggested by Jonathan Fox in his research on Mexico. I argue that Fox's thesis introduces new and important ways of thinking about the transformational role of social movements in the process of democratization. Nevertheless, Fox ignores the largely informal and symbolic nature of state-society relations. While the specific form that clientelism takes may have changed, the function that it performs remains much the same. My comments in this chapter are based on a fifteen-year ethnographic research project on neighborhood organization and political change in two *favela*, or slum, neighborhoods in the city of Rio de Janeiro, Brazil.

Clientelisms

In the spring of 1994, Jonathan Fox published a critically acclaimed essay in the journal *World Politics* on the transition from clientelism to citizenship in Mexico (Fox 1994, 151–84). Fox argues that clientelism and citizenship represent analytical categories that are at opposite extremes of what is a continuum of state-society relations. Fox defines clientelism as a relationship "based on political subordination in exchange for material rewards" (153). In other words, clientelism operates where the least privileged members of a society vote for candidates for political office in exchange for access to resources that are controlled by the state.[1] Fox defines citizenship, on the other hand, as a status that is attained when the least privileged gain access to state resources without forfeiting their right to "articulate their interests autonomously" (153). In other words, what is alternatively referred to as universalism exists when state resources are distributed not as favors to be begged or bartered for, but rights.

Fox recognizes that the transition from clientelism to citizenship is a difficult one, marked by "cycles of social mobilization from below, openings from above, conflict and backlash within both state and society" (Fox 1994, 159), and that, as a consequence, it is difficult, if not impossible, to determine when a society passes from one situation or—in this case—stage to another. Indeed, Fox suggests that it is precisely the "multiplicity of political relationships in between that challenges analysts to develop categories appropriate to systems in transition" (157).

Fox's solution is to suggest the intermediate category of semi-clientelism. According to Fox, semi-clientelism can be distinguished from what he refers to as authoritarian clientelism in that semi-clientelism is based not on the threat or use of force but on exchanges between candidates for political office and groups in civil society that he characterizes as "unenforceable deals." Roughly translated, this means that instead of threatening "vote for me or you'll be punished," candidates for political office are reduced to saying "vote for me and you'll get this or that." I say *reduced* in this context because, at least for Fox, the transition from authoritarian clientelism to semi-clientelism is accomplished by cycles of popular organization and protest.

Fox's thesis made an immediate impact on the field for two reasons. First, it challenged what had become—and for the most part still are—frozen and reified images of state-society relations.[2] Standard definitions of clientelism in Latin America present it as an unequal exchange of excludable or what are referred to as individual or club goods for votes. In other words, clientelism involves paying off or rewarding dependents, accomplices, and known supporters. Fox's concept of semi-clientelism suggests not only that it involves public and, therefore, nonexcludable goods but, perhaps more significant, that the exchange relationship upon which clientelism is based can no longer be secured or guaranteed.[3] Second, Fox's thesis suggests new ways of integrating what are considered very different fields of inquiry. Explanations of democracy in Latin America identify clientelism as the instrument par excellence of political demobilization and control and blame it for everything from the survival of traditional elites and the weakness of political parties to the failure of popular movements and the Left.[4] Fox's thesis suggests not only that clientelism is flexible and assumes different forms but that changes in the nature of clientelist relations are part and parcel of the ongoing process of democratization.

Research from other contexts in Latin America confirms that textbook definitions of clientelism tend to be simplistic and flawed. The most sustained research on clientelism as an electoral phenomenon in Brazil has been conducted by Geert Banck, who warned us—a long time ago—that clientelism is a largely untested and static concept that "neither slips away nor is it immutable until some insurmountable contradictions destroy it" (Banck 1999, 520–22). Outside Brazil, research on semi-clientelist transactions has been carried out by Gerrit Burgwal in squatter settlements in Quito, Ecuador. It was Burgwal who suggested the phrase "collective clientelism" to describe how communities organize and learn to negotiate. Finally, it was Burgwal and more recently Jon Shefner in his work on Guadalajara, Mexico, who questioned the often-used but less than clear distinction between clientelist and so-called ideological or programmatic politics (Burgwal 1995; Shefner 2001).

Notes from the Field

In my own work on popular politics in two *favela* neighborhoods in Rio de Janeiro, Brazil, I have focused on the relationship between clientelism and the recent democratic transition. My research suggests that the liberalization of the Brazilian regime over the past three decades has transformed but by no means eliminated so-called traditional state-society relations. And, much like Fox, I have argued that openings from above and pressures from below have produced a series of hybrid political relations that question if not defy standard categories of classification and analysis.

In one of the *favelas* I have studied for the past fifteen years, the form and dynamic of clientelism have changed dramatically.[5] During the most recent period of military rule, the leaders of the neighborhood association in Vila Brasil routinely threw their support behind candidates for political office in the hope—rather than the expectation—that, as the representatives of the *favela*, they would receive something in return.[6] Few attempts were made to negotiate on behalf of the neighborhood, however, and little of any collective value materialized. Then, in 1979, a group of disgruntled residents were encouraged by local activists from the Catholic Church to take legal action against the leaders of what was clearly a disorganized and ineffective neighborhood association.

It was the activists' intent to bring to an end the practice of clientelism in the *favela*. The president who was subsequently elected to the neighborhood association made it his business, however, not to end the *favela's* relationship with politicians but to use it to his and his constituents' advantage. Instead of encouraging residents to vote in the hope of rewards, he let it be known that the *favela's* support would go—regardless of party affiliation or background—to the individual who bid and delivered the most prior to each election. This invitation provided the basis for what soon became a dense network of relationships between the president of Vila Brasil and politicians, the friends of politicians, and politicians-to-be in a wide range of parties and organizations of both the governmental and nongovernmental kind.

The president of the neighborhood association achieved such success over the years that it was often difficult to determine which party to the clientelist transaction enjoyed the upper hand. Indeed, in this particular *favela*, the exchange relationship became so routine and practiced that the president entertained as many as four candidates for political office at the same time. He would tell each one of them how much the neighborhood's votes would cost and play one contender off against another. The president of Vila Brasil was not always victorious in his endeavors. Whenever he was, however, the materials or money for the resources negotiated would be handed over before the elections took place. By all accounts, the president's greatest achievement was the paving of Vila Brasil on the eve of elections held in November 1982. Weeks before the voting, the president was approached by Jorge Leite, a candidate for a seat in the federal Chamber of Deputies for the incumbent Partido do Movimento Democrático Brasileiro (PMDB).[7] The neighborhood association's president vowed support if Leite arranged to have the *favela* paved. Eight days before the ballot boxes opened, municipal government trucks pulled into Vila Brasil and cemented not only the principal thoroughfare, but the footpaths and alleyways as well.[8]

Four years later, elections were on the horizon again. The president told me that his strategy was to persuade someone to pay for the construction of a second story atop the association's headquarters. He predicted that with twenty-eight political parties competing for only a handful of posts, the neighborhood association would be besieged by offers of financial assistance. By August, the president was receiving at least one phone call a day from candidates who were looking to buy votes. And by mid-August the president had received what he considered firm offers from five candidates from different political parties.[9]

Of those five, Noé Martins, an evangelical pastor who was running for state deputy on the PASART ticket, appeared the most interested. On August 20, Martins and a team of advisers knocked on the door of the neighborhood association and offered to finance the project. As part of the bargain, the president was to compile the names and addresses of dues-paying association members to create a mailing list for the candidate's publicity. The president refused to hand over the list or to begin campaigning on Martin's behalf, however, until the money for the project was safely in his hands. Within a week, it became obvious that no money was forthcoming, and Martins was not seen in the neighborhood again.

By mid-September the president had given up hope of persuading a candidate to pay for the construction of a second level in the neighborhood association building. It appeared that the asking price was perhaps too high for the number of votes promised. The president had, however, received offers from two other PMDB candidates for the office of state deputy. Carlos Alberto Rodrigues had already given the president the customary set of soccer shirts and promised a second set if he would help promote his campaign. The other, Henrique Oswaldo, offered to pay for the construction of two bathrooms in the recreational area that was used as a preschool at the back of the association's building. Not surprisingly, the president devoted most of his time and energy to Henrique Oswaldo.

For six weeks after the initial agreement was made the president of the neighborhood association and Henrique Oswaldo engaged in a process of intense negotiation. Oswaldo asked the president to estimate how much building the two bathrooms would cost. When the president obliged, the candidate claimed that that the price was too high, thus delaying the process. At that time the president was ready to distribute Henrique Oswaldo's campaign posters around the *favela* but he was unprepared to canvass from door to door until he had the necessary cash in hand. Deadlines for the transfer of funds were agreed upon and then broken. At more than one juncture it appeared that the entire deal would fall through.

Then, just ten days before the election, Henrique Oswaldo handed over a check for the agreed amount. He was then accompanied door to door around the *favela* and presented as the candidate favored by president of the neighborhood association.[10] No meetings to discuss the relative merits of other contenders or parties were held. There was never any question whether the president's choice was a good one. The selection of the candidate that the community was to support that year was left entirely to the association's president. The rationale for voting for Henrique Oswaldo was, pure and simple, that he had been willing to invest money in the neighborhood prior to the voting.

In this instance, it was less a case of a politician saying, "Vote for me and you'll get this or that," than of him stating, "If I do this or that, will you vote for me—please?" I am not suggesting that this is a process of negotiation between equals or that the many hierarchies and inequalities upon which clientelism is based have been eliminated. Nonetheless, the reconfiguration of the clientelist relationship entails, to some extent, a leveling of the political playing field. Community leaders understand the advantages derived from that shift, as illustrated by the favorite saying of the president of Vila Brasil: "Politicians are all thieves, but I'm a much a better thief than any of them!"

The president of Vila Brasil was greatly assisted in his exploits by the progressive liberalization of the Brazilian regime (Power 2000, 17–35). Brazil is one of few countries in the world where voting is compulsory. In 1985, after the withdrawal of the military, voting rights were extended to illiterates. Then, in 1988, the voting age itself was lowered to sixteen.[11] As a result, the Brazilian electorate has grown by almost thirty million in the past twenty years. Voting procedures are also extremely liberal. Elections for the federal Chamber of Deputies and the individual state assemblies are conducted according to an open-list, proportional-representation system that is almost unique to Brazil. Furthermore, for most of the period under discussion, there were no national electoral thresholds for parties, and extremely liberal rules governing multiparty alliances prevailed. The outcome was a competitive and inclusive system that generated multiple and unstable parties, high levels of party infidelity, and feverish inter- and intraparty competitions for votes.[12]

For our purposes, the question is the extent to which the relationships maintained by the president of Vila Brasil can be characterized as clientelist. First, they are clientelist because access to resources—in this case of both the public and private variety—is conditional on subordination or compliance. In other words, roads were paved and bathrooms constructed because, and only because, the residents of Vila Brasil "offered up" their votes. These transactions are also clientelist in that they involve informal deals, promises, and reciprocal exchanges. The candidates for office who make resources available, and the residents of Vila Brasil who pursue them, perceive the relationship as an explicit if somewhat unpredictable swap. The president of Vila Brasil's success was owed almost entirely to his ability to transform the relationship between the neighborhood association and candidates for political office from one based on dependence and long-term expectations to one based on an immediate and mercenary transaction.

Of course, the president of the neighborhood association's aptitude in deal making was based on his reputation as a local leader and broker who delivered. Candidates for public office approached him because they had been told that investments in Vila Brasil were worthwhile. In other words, they could be reasonably confident, based on past experience, that disbursements in the *favela* would translate into votes. Furthermore, once an election was over, candidates could obtain detailed maps—district by district—of the distribution of their votes. And while it was impossible to determine which individuals had voted for them, they were able to assess at a collective level whether the residents of a particular neighborhood had come through. It was in the president of Vila Brasil's interest, therefore, to keep his part of the bargain, because his standing as a broker and the prospect of future deals depended on it. Finally, it was in the president's interest to continue making deals because his power base at the local level also depended on it. Therefore, although, strictly speaking, the deals that the president negotiated were unenforceable, they were governed by a compelling logic and practical rationale.

As far as the residents of the *favela* of Vila Brasil were concerned, there was nothing to stop them from taking the collective goods that the president of the neighborhood association procured while retaining their right to political autonomy by voting for someone else. After all, as long as many, if not all, of their friends and neighbors voted for the president's candidate, there was little to lose. In other words, it was conceivable for someone to "vote their conscience" and still benefit from the newly paved roads and alleyways financed through the mediation of the president's favorite candidate. On the other hand, the success achieved by Vila Brasil's president suggests two things: first, that many of the most pressing problems facing the *favela* were of a collective nature, and second, that the conception of clientelism as an exchange of votes for individual favors is of limited explanatory value.

From Clientelism to Citizenship

Far more interesting and problematic than the distinction between authoritarian clientelism and semi-clientelism is the demarcation Fox makes between semi-clientelism and citizenship. To recapitulate, Fox argues that citizenship is a status attained when access to resources is no longer conditioned on political subordination or compliance. In other words, roads are paved and bathrooms constructed without reference to past or future elections or votes. According to Fox, this situation arises when civic activism broadens and deepens to the point where mechanisms for enforcing voter loyalty are ineffective and more and more citizens "vote their conscience."[13] As a consequence, state actors are no longer able to rely on the use or threat of force or, more important, on material inducements to generate support: they have to do more. Indeed, it is precisely because resources that once ensured compliance are emptied of their political content that state actors are no longer able — or even attempt — to violate the right to political autonomy (Fox 1994, 158).

Fox suggests that over time the least privileged will learn to appreciate that things they sat patiently awaiting, or begged and bartered for, are theirs by right of membership in the larger society. They will also become more adept at procuring resources through nonclientelist means and cast their votes in appreciation, not of particular or localized gains, but of policies and programs of a more universalistic nature.[14] Finally, Fox is also intimating that, under conditions of citizenship, political parties will not only fail in their attempts to exchange votes for what they represent as favors but that they will be publicly denounced when they attempt to do so. In other words, it becomes less a case of "vote for me and you'll get this or that," or even, "if I do this or that for you, will you vote for me, please?" than of "you'd better do this for me because it's your obligation and my right, and don't even think about asking for my vote, and, by the way, if you fail to fulfill what I consider to be your obligation, you have no hope of receiving my vote at all!"[15]

The progression Fox lays out is a familiar one. Throughout Latin America, recent transitions from authoritarian rule have been accompanied by waves of civic unrest and the emergence of so-called *new social movements* (Fox 1994, 105–16). In almost all cases, new social movements have been acclaimed as agents of democratization that will transform state-society relations. Early observers of new social movements in Brazil, for example, predicted that the combined forces of "authentic" labor unions, neighborhood associations, ecclesiastical base communities, and liberal professional organizations would destroy the legitimacy of the authoritarian state, undermine support for

clientelist parties, and sweep the Left—particularly the Partido dos Trabalhadores (PT)—to power.[16] Subsequent disappointments have given rise to a
gradualist but still optimistic perspective, of new social movements' effect on
the postauthoritarian regime. There is a consensus building that new social
movements—in their various guises—challenge dominant practices. In doing
so they create opportunities for more accountable, transparent, and universalistic forms of governance.[17]

In one of their best-known pieces, Sonia Alvarez and Evelina Dagnino go
so far as to claim that *social movement webs* have "rewoven or reconfigured . . .
the fabric of collective action in Brazil." They also maintain that social movement webs have fashioned new constituencies formed by "communities of
equals" that are confrontational, oftentimes disloyal, and committed to the
ideal of rights. These new popular movements, argue Álvarez and Dagnino, are
not to be confused with those that endured clientelist ties with the "populist-
corporatist and authoritarian political establishments" of the recent and not
so recent past (Alvarez and Dagnino 1995).

Not everyone is convinced, however. There are those who insist that civil
society remains a largely abstract concept and that there is an ever-widening gap
between democratic rhetoric and everyday practices. Elisa Reis, for example,
asserts that the impact of new collective actors in Brazil has been greatly
exaggerated and that the vast majority of the population has neither the means
nor the incentive to participate in public life (Reis 1995, 35–48; Bethell 2000,
1–27). Others point out that the least privileged continue to throw their
support behind what are widely considered elitist and traditional politicians
from equally elitist and traditional political parties and that, as a consequence,
executive power in Brazil remains firmly in the hands of the old elite.
Finally, there are those who argue that in spite of innovations in local governance, public resources continue to be allocated on the basis of political
favoritism—not social need—and that "universalism" and "citizenship" exist
in name only. In other words, the transition from clientelism to citizenship is
largely, to quote a well-known Brazilian expression, "para inglês ver."[18]

Government programs that have attracted attention most recently focus
on emergency assistance or social funds that target specific communities or
groups of communities. These initiatives have expanded in scope over the
past decades as governments in Brazil have sought to mitigate the effects of
global restructuring and neoliberal economic reform. Some analysts have
maintained that these more limited efforts—in contrast to structural and,
therefore, universal programs—afford government actors and agencies a wide
degree of discretion in terms of who benefits. Thus, Maria Castro and Vilmar

Faria argue that while the transition to democracy in Brazil has raised new questions about democratic participation and the concept of citizenship, programs for the poor have developed within the context of an exclusive and patrimonial state. They have thus recreated and expanded networks of clientelism and corruption (Castro and Faria 1989; Noreira de Carvalho and Laniado 1989).

Similar criticisms have been advanced of government programs in other Latin American countries. Judith Tendler believes that, despite their image, emergency assistance or social fund programs are well suited to political purposes and that the large number of small projects that they involve "provide political wherewithal to reward loyal constituents, to court those who are on the fence, or to withhold from the opposition" (Tendler 1999, 125).

Kenneth Roberts, in turn, thinks that targeted programs in Peru are both "direct and highly visible, allowing government leaders to claim political credit for material rewards," as a consequence creating stronger ties than the more obscure and truly universal benefits like price subsidies and exchange controls (Roberts 1995). Indeed, much of Fox's discussion of the transition from clientelism to citizenship in Mexico is conducted in light of the broader controversy over the character and effects of PRONASOL, former president Carlos Salinas de Gotari's national poverty alleviation program.

In *Transforming State-Society Relations in Mexico: The National Solidarity Strategy*, a volume dedicated entirely to an evaluation of PRONASOL, former president Salinas de Gortari is quoted as saying that that the program was designed to "eliminate all vestiges of paternalism, populism, clientelism, or political conditionality in the improvement of the welfare of the impoverished population" (Cornelius, Craig, and Fox 1994, 7). Nevertheless, Denise Dresser maintains that instead of building respect for community initiatives and full and effective participation, PRONASOL became a "tool for political survival" designed to "construct new patronage networks with low-income groups across the country, particularly those with electoral weight" (Dresser 1994, 147). Juan Horcasitas and Jeffrey Weldon agree with Dresser that "electoral considerations weigh in the mind of decision makers" and that "PRONASOL clearly deals mostly with the exchange of public goods, shared by a community for electoral support." They are unsure, however, whether or not PRONASOL should be classified as clientelist. After all, they point out, "When similar patterns of political exchange are identified in democratic regimes we do not call them clientelist. We call them 'pork-barrel politics'" (Horcasitas and Weldon 1994, 139–40).

Interestingly, Fox himself seems uncertain of what it is we are talking about, since in his own assessment of PRONASOL he states that "the geographical targeting of spending . . . does not necessarily mean that access to the program's benefits was systematically conditioned on . . . subordination" (1994, 166). He goes on to say, however, that while "much of the debate surrounding Solidarity's political character has been based more on ideological polemic than on empirical evidence . . . the most plausible hypothesis is that, on balance, most of the electoral targeted spending was probably delivered through semi-clientelist means" (166–67). In other words, Fox suspects that PRONASOL was a vehicle for Salinas de Gortari to broker a series of unenforceable deals.

The uncertainty over the nature of PRONASOL, and other such government programs in Latin America, speaks to the heart of the issue at hand. There is, without doubt, evidence that gains have been made in terms of the pressure that civil society has brought to bear on the state in the wake of recent transitions away from authoritarian rule. The suspicion remains, however, that the political system functions in old and familiar ways. In other words, the doubt is whether—much like before—government intervention is motivated not by a desire to empower and include, but by a desire to cultivate and hold in place a captive and politically passive clientele.

More Notes from the Field

Until 1977, the residents of the *favela* Vidigal gained little from their occasional participation in the political process. Like their counterparts in Vila Brasil, contacts with politicians were restricted almost exclusively to the period immediately prior to elections. In 1977, however, they were told to remove their possessions from the hillside they had occupied illegally for almost forty years. In desperation they turned to Paulo Duque, a local PMDB politician who, over the years, had insisted he was their patron and benefactor. That Paulo Duque refused—or was unable—to do anything about the situation convinced the *favela*'s leadership that clientelism as a mechanism of interest representation was of little or no use. As a consequence, the *favela* leaders turned their collective backs on so-called traditional politicians and the traditional political process to join forces with church groups and nongovernmental organizations that came to their aid. Unlike in Vila Brasil, however, the transformation of the neighborhood association in Vidigal effectively eliminated the practice of clientelism in the *favela*.[19]

By the mid-1980s the neighborhood association in Vidigal was firmly established as a well-organized, combative, and autonomous institution at the center of *favela* life. The leaders of the neighborhood association voiced their concerns and presented their demands not—as they had in the past—to politicians acting as gatekeepers or intermediaries between the *favela*'s population and local government, but to state secretaries and program directors in their offices downtown. More significant, public resources that were channeled toward the neighborhood association were accepted on the condition that they not be used to generate votes. It was the leadership's intent to convince people that public works projects were not favors to be rewarded at the ballot box. As one director of the neighborhood association put it: "You don't have to vote for a politician [to obtain such benefits]. The question of voting for one or another party is not a matter of public works, it's a broader question. You don't have to vote only because the government put in water, put in lighting, or resolved the problem of sewage ditches, and isn't prepared to resolve the problem of wages, to resolve the problem of education, and to really bring about change" (personal interview, 1986).

A collective recognition that government intervention had been used as an effective co-optation tool underpinned the attempts to separate public works from votes. Prior to 1977 the threat of removal was enough in and of itself to ensure compliance. Now, candidates who ran for parties that worked on public works projects with the neighborhood association were prohibited from campaigning on that basis. Instead, they were invited to attend weekly neighborhood association meetings to present their platforms and more general ideas to the public. Of course, there was nothing to stop candidates from appealing directly to individual voters in the *favela*. There was nothing the neighborhood association could do about that. The leadership was determined, however, that the neighborhood association would play no part in this process. And, more important, the reputation of the neighborhood association was such that no one dared suggest the type of deal that was regularly entertained by the president of Vila Brasil.

At the time, state and municipal governments in Rio were administered by the Partido Democrático Trabalhista (PDT). The PDT soon introduced a public works program, partly funded by international aid agencies, to improve the sewage, drainage, and water infrastructure of a large number of the city's then five hundred or so *favelas*, including Vidigal. Unlike prior state interventions, the program targeted *favelas* whether they were known PDT strongholds or not. Ostensibly, therefore, the program was implemented not on the basis of political favoritism but, instead, with regard to social need.[20] This aspect of the PDT's public works program was significant in light of the generalized hostility toward the clientelist practices employed by state agencies in the past. Indeed, the PDT's victory in 1982 was widely interpreted as evidence that clientelism—much like the military government—was a thing of the past.[21]

Not everyone was convinced. Opponents, primarily from the Left, charged that the PDT was planning on doing "just enough" in as many communities as possible to maximize the party's returns. In other words, the PDT's public works program was a fairly traditional vote-getting strategy dressed up in a modern, universalistic disguise. There were also those who claimed that public works projects were purposefully located in the most visible and accessible parts of each *favela* and that, therefore, they had more to do with campaign advertising than with addressing social needs. Others criticized the gradual implementation of public works projects, which unfolded into several stages, some occurring before an election and others taking place after the PDT was returned to office. Finally, there were those who maintained that public works projects were designed not just to generate votes, but to undermine the authority and autonomy of what was at the time an increasingly well-organized and combative *favela* movement.

The PDT appeared to say and do all the right things. It sponsored and organized conferences on the problems facing low-income communities that brought together leaders from across the state. It reserved places on party lists of candidates for the election of presidents of neighborhood associations and leaders of the *favela* movement. In addition it employed a good many neighborhood association presidents and directors in its administrative offices downtown. Nonetheless, the effect was to make criticism of the PDT and its programs more difficult and, significantly, to blur the distinction between the *favela* movement and the party. The president of a neighborhood association in Zona Oeste and an eventual state deputy for the PT, told me of the day his community inaugurated a public works project that was started prior to the emergence of the PDT as a regional political force in the early 1980s. On the morning of the inauguration, a bus load of PDT militants descended on the *favela* and distributed leaflets claiming that the project was not the product of the persistence and hard work of leaders of the neighborhood association but the generosity and largesse of the PDT. Clearly, the objective was to undermine the autonomy of the neighborhood association.

PDT representatives were, of course, incensed by criticisms of their programs and went out of their way to convince both the beneficiaries of state intervention and their opponents that the public works projects were what the population of the *favelas* expected and, more to the point, deserved. At one meeting that brought together the presidents and directors of a large and organized contingent of *favela* neighborhood associations, the state secretary for public works rose to his feet and told the audience that the PDT "wanted nothing in return; these are your rights," he insisted. As an outsider, I was convinced by the state secretary's speech and thought it was great! Nevertheless, I clearly did not understand the full meaning of his words. The person sitting next to me—himself the president of a *favela* neighborhood association—told me that what the state secretary was doing was asking for their votes.

As it turned out, the PDT lost the subsequent (1986) election for governor to a conservative alliance of parties that supported and was supported by the federal government. The PDT, however, did extremely well in poorer areas of the city and particularly in the *favelas*. The PDT also did extremely well in Vidigal, where despite the best efforts of the neighborhood association, the party-administered public works programs generated tremendous support (Gay 1994). How should we interpret or explain the PDT's success? On the one hand, it would be extremely difficult—given current definitions—to label the PDT's practices as clientelist. Access to resources was not conditioned on subordination or compliance. On the contrary, the leaders of the neighborhood association were never threatened, nor were they invited to make a deal. On the other hand, what happened in Vidigal was not all that different from what happened in Vila Brasil. In both cases, small-scale improvements to what are truly miserable and subhuman conditions were rewarded handsomely at the ballot box.

These situations reveal the limitations of our classificatory schemes. As I have stated before, the idea of semi-clientelism is important in that it accommodates and takes stock of recent changes in the fabric of civil society. Voters are no longer cultural dupes, imprisoned by ignorance and false consciousness. Instead, they are knowledgeable and rational actors whose insight and cunning enable them to make the best of what are undoubtedly very bad situations. Theoretically, the problem is that, in the process of restoring agency, we might reduce state-society relations in general, and clientelism in particular, to the level of calculation and conscious strategy. In other words, as civic activism "broadens and deepens," participation in or withdrawal from semi-clientelist arrangements becomes simply a matter of choice.

The idea that clientelism involves a series of negotiated deals guided much of my early field research. For a while, I was convinced that the practices that the president of Vila Brasil revealed to me were standard. After all, I had attended meetings where the presidents of neighborhood associations boasted openly about what they had managed to squeeze out of this or that candidate for office. As a consequence, I spent much of my time pursuing friendships with program administrators, field technicians, and heads of neighborhood associations in the hope that they would own up to the behind-the-scenes handshakes upon which their relationship with the state was surely based. Ultimately I came to realize that I was missing the point: clientelism was not only about the explicit and brokered relations between politicians and the president of the neighborhood association in Vila Brasil— what I have referred to elsewhere as "thick" clientelism. It was also the implicit and disguised relations between Vidigal residents and the PDT—what I label elsewhere as "thin" clientelism (Gay 1997, 65–92).

Exchanges, Gifts, and Rights

In *Poor People's Politics: Peronist Survival Networks and the Legacy of Evita* Javier Auyero examines how local-level activists build and maintain party support among the urban poor. Auyero's research focuses on the activities of Peronist brokers who distribute goods and make services available in exchange for attendance at rallies and support for party candidates at elections in a shantytown on Buenos Aires's periphery. Auyero notes that what is, objectively speaking, an exchange relationship is rarely if ever perceived or represented as such. In other words, both the brokers who make food, medicine, and other resources available and the clients who receive them make no mention of a price to be paid or of any future obligation. Auyero describes how— much like in the case of the state secretary of public works—an important part of the Peronist brokers' performance is to explicitly and emphatically "deny the political content of their actions" (Auyero 2001, 117).

Drawing extensively on the work of Pierre Bourdieu, Auyero asserts that the distribution of resources as "disinterested acts" or "gifts" in contexts of extreme hardship and material scarcity associated with neoliberal policy enables brokers to "possess the members of their inner circles" (Auyero 2001, 179). According to Bourdieu, a disinterested act or gift constitutes "an attack on the freedom of the one who receives it. It is threatening: it [creates] people obliged to recip-rocate" (Bourdieu 1998, 94). This "domination effect" is produced by what Bourdieu refers to as "symbolic capital." Symbolic capital—as opposed to material capital—is a form of recognition or "legitimate accumulation, through which the dominant secure a capital of 'credit' which seems to owe nothing to the logic of exploitation" (Bourdieu 1977, 197). In other words, unlike an exchange, the gift and the counter-gift that surely follows are not part of some preconceived or calculated scheme, but a "collective self-deception" or "misrecognition inscribed in objective and mental structures, excluding the possibility of thinking or acting otherwise" (Bourdieu 1998, 95). Symbolic capital is, therefore, "denied capital," which masks power and interest as legitimate and quite natural demands for subordination and compliance.

Auyero's research is significant for two reasons. First, it suggests that *how* something is given and, for that matter, received is critical to an understanding of state-society relations. The "cluster of beliefs, assumptions, styles, skills, and habits encompassing the exchanges—explaining and clarifying them, justifying and legitimizing them—is as important as the actual exchanges themselves" (Auyero 1999a, 461–93). In other words, the act of exchange is a performance. Second, Auyero's research reveals that clientelism often leads a "double life." On the one hand, there is the *objective* reality of an exchange of votes or political support for favors. On the other hand, there is the *subjective,* lived reality of a relationship that is experienced not as a transaction but as part of a universe of "habitual practical logic" that goes without saying (Auyero 1999b, 297–334).

Auyero states that the dynamic he describes refers only to the strong, interpersonal and affective ties that inhabit the brokers' "inner circles of doxic experience" (Auyero 2001, 180), and that, as a consequence, this form of denied exchange "can hardly account for the conquest of the vote and the building of electoral consensus that is usually attributed to clientelism" (180). I disagree and argue that Auyero's insights into the habitual and nonconscious nature of exchange have implications for state-society relations beyond the phenomenon of *assistencialismo,* which he describes.[22] I further argue that Auyero's insights are key to an understanding of the relationship between voters in Vidigal and the PDT.

There is little doubt that the leaders of the neighborhood association in Vidigal were successful in their efforts to procure resources through nonclientelist means. By attending meetings and dispatching delegations to occupy the time and offices of state secretaries and program directors downtown, they managed to get their hands on a consistent flow of goods and services. Throughout the 1980s and early 1990s, Vidigal's name appeared on most lists of *favelas* to benefit from government action. This was important, because it meant that neighborhood association leaders no longer had to beg or barter for goods. It also meant that access to benefits could no longer be conditioned on subordination or compliance. Resources were passed the neighborhood association's way without mention of past or future elections, or votes. The neighborhood association further ensured this by forbidding the types of deals that were solicited by the president of Vila Brasil and by making it clear that public works in Vidigal were not for sale. In fact, the state secretary for public works was told in no uncertain terms that he would not be allowed to campaign on the basis of the work that he and the PDT had undertaken in the *favela*. Candidates for political office who offered money were told that the neighborhood association would do nothing to either encourage or guarantee political support.[23]

Ultimately, however, the leaders of the neighborhood association failed in their attempts to "empty public works of their political content." Much to their dismay, public works were never received routinely or as a matter of fact but as generous gifts and special favors that were attributed to and synonymous with the PDT.[24] It mattered not that representatives of the PDT publicly insisted otherwise or that Vidigal was one of a large number of *favela* communities that profited from government action. It mattered not that representatives of the neighborhood association in Vidigal insisted with good reason that resources would be forthcoming regardless of which alliance, party, or faction occupied the municipal, state, or federal government offices downtown. Practical logic suggested otherwise. Apparently, it was too much to ask people to believe that anything could be accomplished in the absence of some sort of a personalized relationship. And it was certainly too much to ask that abstract systems of distribution and justice should be trusted (da Matta 1987, 307–35).

The outcome was that silently, as if by command or prior agreement, the population of Vidigal voted overwhelmingly for the PDT, to thank the party for its generosity and, more important, to reaffirm the special relationship that, they believed, existed between them and their benefactors. Nothing was added because nothing needed to be added. In the words of Bourdieu (1998, 103), "It went without saying, that there was nothing else to do."

At the time, I desperately wanted to believe that the neighborhood association in Vidigal had indeed eliminated clientelism and that support for the PDT was based on factors other than the setting in concrete of open sewage ditches. After all, the PDT was a relatively progressive party that consistently defended the interests of the poor and opposed the neoliberal policies of the federal government. To my dismay, however, I watched over the years as parties of the Right and Center courted and then seduced the population of the *favela* with their own versions of what is referred to on the ground as *obrismo*.[25] In other words, while there were no deals to be struck in Vidigal, people did their duty. They returned the favor. And it was only recently that a former president lamented that the neighborhood association's role had been reduced to doing the (political) work of whichever alliance, party, or faction was in power.

Conclusion

In his essay "Illusions About Consolidation," in the *Journal of Democracy*, Guillermo O'Donnell calls for students of democratization to free themselves of a "fixation" on formal organizations and procedures that "prevents us from seeing an extremely influential, informal, and sometimes concealed institution: clientelism and, more generally, particularism" (O'Donnell 1996, 40). O'Donnell argues that while democracy may well be the only game in town, "formal rules about how political institutions are supposed to work are often poor guides to what actually happens." Moreover, O'Donnell insists that in many countries of Latin America it is the "widely shared and deeply rooted" informal rules, and not the formal rules, that are "highly institutionalized" (40).

At face value, Brazil is a solid and robust democracy. Since the mid-1980s regular and competitive elections have brought the vast majority of Brazilians to the ballot box. However, the right to vote and have that vote count is arguably the only right that has been established in Brazil. As a consequence, it is a right that has been used, primarily, to catch the eye of an otherwise negligent and disinterested state. By inviting competition and insisting on payment up front, the president of Vila Brasil perfected the art of playing politicians at their own game and, in doing so, transformed the relationship between the neighborhood association and the powers that be from a lopsided and abusive friendship to a strategic and more evenly matched game. The outcome was the democratization of clientelism.

The leaders of the neighborhood association in Vidigal went a step further, attempting to eliminate the practice of clientelism altogether. From their perspective, elections were unique opportunities not to barter or give thanks for local spoils but to sit in judgment of different representations of power. The leaders of the neighborhood association were successful in changing the discourse of political engagement in Vidigal. They were less than successful, however, in their attempts to change the content of politics. They failed to convince people that the scraps that are occasionally thrown their way are unworthy of the vote. The outcome was a series of disguised or denied exchanges and, I would argue, the clientelization of democracy.

Postscript

At a little after ten o'clock on a cold September morning, local government representatives and dignitaries from the Inter-American Development Bank descended on Vidigal to celebrate the completion of public works projects associated with the program *Favela-Bairro*. The program was designed to transform *favelas* into regular neighborhoods in an effort to stem the rising tide of drug-related violence and what many describe as a process of social disaggregation. In Vidigal, the program involved the construction of a public square and daycare center and the renovation of a health clinic, among other things.

The visitors were greeted at the foot of the hill by the president of the neighborhood association, who invited them to watch a display of Brazilian music, dance, and martial arts performed by a group of local children. They were then driven to the top of the *favela* where they inspected and marveled at the "Olympic Village" that provides local youth with much needed sports and leisure facilities. They were not told, however, that the leader of a drug gang started the "Olympic Village" and that it was "discovered" by a police helicopter. They were not told either that two years prior, representatives from the drug gang marched, fully armed, into the neighborhood association's offices and demanded the resignation of the last democratically elected president of the *favela*. Finally, they were not told that the body parts of one of the presidents of the neighborhood association appointed by the drug gang washed up on the beach near where the visitors were staying in Ipanema.

NOTES

1. Not all clientelist relations involve the state. State-society relations have been the focus of most recent discussions of this issue, however, because of the widespread use of public funds to generate votes and, in part, the high costs associated with election campaigns.

2. For the role of ideas as "metonymic prisons," see Appadurai 1988.

3. The underlying assumption, of course, is that voters used to do what they were told or what was expected of them. This remains an assumption. Geert Banck points out that, at least in Brazil, politicians have always reminisced about a past when voter loyalty could be trusted. And Victor Nunes Leal observes that there were reports of employees betraying their landlords in Brazil as far back as the elections in 1945 (Banck 1999; Leal 1975, 12).

4. See, for example, Hagopian 1996.

5. For an overview, see Gay 1999.

6. This is not strictly authoritarian clientelism in Fox's sense of the term. Nonetheless, it could be argued that the neighborhood association's decision to support candidates for political office was motivated, in essence, by desperation and fear. Richard Graham argues that these are in fact two sides of the same coin (Graham 1990, 24).

7. The Movimento Democrático Brasileiro (MDB), which became the PMDB, was the party of opposition throughout the period of restricted democracy during military rule. The MDB in Rio differed from the national party organization, however, in that its leaders cultivated explicitly clientelistic ties with the population at large and enjoyed an amicable relationship with the military. See, for example, Diniz 1982, 58–60.

8. The PMDB ended up losing the election for governor to Leonel Brizola and the Partido Democrático Trabalhista (PDT). Jorge Leite himself was successful in his bid for the federal house of representatives. Indeed, he amassed more than 170,000 votes, making him the fifth-most-voted-for federal deputy in all of Rio and by far the most-voted-for PMDB candidate for federal deputy.

9. These parties were the Partido da Frente Liberal (PFL), the PDT, the Partido Democrático Cristão (PDC), the Partido Socialista Agrário e Renovadora Trabalhista (PASART), and the PMDB.

10. It is important to note that, unlike Jorge Leite, Henrique Oswaldo was not an incumbent.

11. Voting is not compulsory for illiterates, sixteen and seventeen year olds, and persons over the age of seventy.

12. Institutionalists attribute the pervasiveness of clientelism in Brazil to the properties of the system. The pervasiveness of clientelism in Latin America in such a wide variety of social and institutional contexts has yet to be explained, however. See Hagopian 1996, 78.

13. Fox (1994, 150) argues that in the Mexican case, this led the government to rely increasingly on fraud.

14. Jon Shefner (2001) notes in his work on Mexico the idea that alternative forms of interest representation have to "deliver" to be successful.

15. A similar progression is suggested by Thomas Guterbock in his work on the evolution of state-society relations in Chicago. See Guterbock 1980.

16. The literature on new social movements is vast. Among the earlier, more influential pieces, are Cohen 1985, Escobar and Álvarez 1992, Evers 1985, and Durham 1984. For a more recent perspective, see Doimo 1995.

17. The most celebrated of the new government practices has been the participatory budgeting process adopted by the PT. For a discussion of this administrative innovation, see Abers 1996 and Santos 1998.

18. Literally "for the English to see," meaning any change has been superficial and strictly for "show."

19. Ironically, the neighborhood associations in Vidigal and Vila Brasil were products of the same political movement. In Vidigal, however, the leaders of the neighborhood association decided to take their mentors' advice to refuse to "deal" with politicians. For an elaboration of the differences between the two favelas, see Gay 1994.

20. Of course, there is a tendency for every administration to represent itself as being the first to do things in a nonpartisan manner. And if the PDT's program was innovative in certain respects, it was by no means the first. For a discussion of previous programs in Rio, see Bronstein 1982 and Santos 1981.

21. See, for example, the comments made by PMDB candidates following their defeat at the hands of the PDT. *Jornal do Brasil*, November 19, 1982, 4.

22. *Assistencialismo* is a term used in Brazil to describe the practice of offering services free of charge to the poor and needy in a politician's constituency. In December 1999, the *Jornal do Brasil* reported that forty out of seventy state deputies in Rio provided such services and that together they attended to an estimated ten thousand persons each day. *Jornal do Brasil* (Cidade), December 20, 1999.

23. The neighborhood association's stance discouraged almost everyone. On the eve of the election, the brother of the opposition party's candidate for governor called the leaders of the neighborhood association and offered to pay for the renovation of the neighborhood association building. When told that the neighborhood association would do nothing to promote his brother's candidacy, however, the offer was withdrawn.

24. For similar perspectives on the implied nature of exchanges in low-income neighborhoods in Rio, see Alvito 2001 and Kurschnir 2000.

25. The term describes vote-getting strategies that are based on public works (*obras*).

REFERENCES

Abers, Rebecca. 1996. "From Ideas to Practice: The Partido dos Trabalhadores and Participatory Governance in Brazil." *Latin American Perspectives* 23:35–53.
Alvarez, Sonia E., and Evelina Dagnino. 1995. *Para além da "democracia realmente existente": Movimentos sociais, a nova cidadania e a configuração de espaços públicos alternativos*. Rio de Janeiro: ANPOCS.
Alvito, Marcos. 2001. *As Cores de Acari: Uma favela carioca*. Rio de Janeiro: Fundação Getulio Vargas.
Appadurai, Arjun. 1988. "Putting Hierarchy in Its Place." *Cultural Anthropology* 3, no. 1:36–49.
Auyero, Javier. 1999a. "From the Client's Point(s) of View: How Poor People Perceive and Evaluate Political Clientelism." *Theory and Society* 28:297–334.
———. 1999b. "Performing Evita: A Tale of Two Peronist Women." *Journal of Contemporary Ethnography* 27, no. 4:461–93.
———. 2001. *Poor People's Politics: Peronist Survival Networks and the Legacy of Evita*. Durham: Duke University Press.
Banck, Geert A. 1999. "Clientelism and the Brazilian Political Process: Production and Consumption of a Problematic Concept." In *Modernization, Leadership, and Participation: Theoretical Issues in Development Sociology*, ed. Peter J.M. Nas and Patricio Silva. Leiden: Leiden University Press.
Bethell, Leslie. 2000. "Politics in Brazil: From Elections Without Democracy to Democracy Without Citizenship." *Daedalus* 129, no. 2:1–27.
Bourdieu, Pierre. 1977. *Outline of a Theory of Practice*. Cambridge: Cambridge University Press.
———. 1998. *Practical Reason: On the Theory of Action*. Stanford: Stanford University Press.
Bronstein, Olga. 1982. "De Cima para Baixo ou de baixo para Cima? Considerações em torno da oferta de um serviço público nas favelas do Rio de Janeiro." Paper

presented at the Associação Nacional de Pós Graduação e Pesquisa em Ciências Sociais meetings (ANPOCS), Friburgo, Brazil, April 14.

Burgwal, Gerrit. 1995. *Struggle of the Poor: Neighborhood Organization and Clientelist Practice in a Quito Squatter Settlement*. Amsterdam: CEDLA.

Castro, Maria Helena Guimarães, and Vilmar E. Faria. 1989. "Política social e consolidação democrática no Brasil." In *O estado e as políticas públicas na transição democrática*, ed. Alexandrina Sobreira de Moura, 194–215. São Paulo: Vertice.

Cohen, Jean. 1985. "Strategy or Identity: New Theoretical Paradigms and Contemporary Social Movements." *Social Research* 52, no. 4:663–716.

Cornelius, Wayne, Ann L. Craig, and Jonathan Fox, eds. 1994. *Transforming State-Society Relations in Mexico: The National Solidarity Strategy*. San Diego: Center for U.S.-Mexican Studies.

da Matta, Roberto. "The Quest for Citizenship in a Relational Universe." In *State & Society in Brazil*, ed. John D. Wirth, E. de Oliveira Nunes, and T. E. Bogenschild. Boulder, Colo.: Westview Press.

Diniz, Eli. 1982. *Voto e máquina política: Patronagem e clientelismo no Rio de Janeiro*. Rio de Janeiro: Paz e Terra.

Doimo, Ana Maria. 1995. *A vez e a voz do Popular: Movimentos sociais e participação política no Brasil pós-70*. Rio de Janeiro: ANPOCS.

Dresser, Denise. 1994. "Bringing the Poor Back In: National Solidarity as a Strategy of Regime Legitimation." In *Transforming State-Society Relations in Mexico: The National Solidarity Strategy*, ed. Wayne Cornelius, Ann L. Craig, and Jonathan Fox. San Diego: Center for U.S.-Mexican Studies.

Durham, Eunice. 1984. "Movimentos sociais e a construção de cidadania." *Novos Estudos* 10:24–30.

Escobar, Arturo, and Sonia Alvarez, eds. 1992. *The Making of Social Movements in Latin America*. Boulder, Colo.: Westview Press.

Evers, Tilman. 1985. "'Identity': The Hidden Side of New Social Movements in Latin America." In *New Social Movements and the State in Latin America*, ed. David Slater. Amsterdam: CEDLA.

Fox, Jonathan. 1994. "The Difficult Transition from Clientelism to Citizenship: Lessons from Mexico." *World Politics* 46, no. 2:151–84.

Gay, Robert. 1994. *Popular Organization and Democracy in Rio de Janeiro: A Tale of Two Favelas*. Philadelphia: Temple University Press.

———. 1997. "Entre el clientelismo y el universalismo: Reflexiones sobre la política popular en el Brasil urbano." In *¿Favores por votos? Estudios sobre clientelismo político contemporáneo*, ed. Javier Auyero, 65–92. Buenos Aires: Losada.

———. 1999. "The Broker and the Thief: A Parable (Reflections on Popular Politics in Brazil)." *Luso-Brazilian Review* 36, no. 1:49–70.

Graham, Richard. 1990. *Patronage and Politics in Nineteenth-Century Brazil*. Stanford: Stanford University Press.

Guterbock, Thomas M. 1980. *Machine Politics in Transition: Party and Community in Chicago*. Chicago: University of Chicago Press.

Hagopian, Frances. 1996. "Traditional Power Structures and Democratic Governance in Latin America." In *Constructing Democracy Governance: Latin America and the Caribbean in the 1990s—Themes and Issues*, ed. Jorge I. Domínguez and Abraham F. Lowenthal, 64–86. Baltimore: Johns Hopkins University Press.

Horcasitas, Juan Molinar, and Jeffrey A. Weldon. 1994. "Electoral Determinants and Consequences of National Solidarity." In *Transforming State-Society Relations in Mexico: The National Solidarity Strategy*, ed. Wayne Cornelius, Ann L. Craig, and Jonathan Fox. San Diego: Center for U.S.-Mexican Studies.

Jornal do Brasil. November 19, 1982, 4.

Jornal do Brasil (Cidade). December 20, 1999.

Kinzo, Maria D'Alva Gil. 1988. *Oposição e autoritarismo: Gênese e trajetória do MDB, 1966–1979.* São Paulo: Vértice.

Kurschnir, Karina. 2000. *O cotidiano da política.* Rio de Janeiro: Zahar.

Leal, Victor Nunes. 1975. *Coronelismo, enxada e voto: O município e o regime representativo no Brasil.* São Paulo: Alfa-Omega.

Noreira de Carvalho, Inaiá Maria, and Ruthy Nádia Laniado. 1989. "Transição democrática, políticas públicas e movimentos sociais." In *O estado e as políticas públicas na transição democrática*, ed. Alexandrina Sobreira de Moura. São Paulo: Vertice.

O'Donnell, Guillermo. 1996. "Illusions About Consolidation." *Journal of Democracy* 7, no. 2:40–58.

Power, Timothy J. 2000. *The Political Right in Postauthoritarian Brazil: Elites, Institutions, and Democratization.* University Park: Pennsylvania State University Press.

Reis, Elisa P. 1995. "Desigualdade e solidariedade: Uma releitura do 'familismo amoral' de Banfield." *Revista Brasileira de Ciencias Sociais* 10, no. 29:35–48.

Roberts, Kenneth. 1995. "Neoliberalism and the Transformation of Populism in Latin America: The Peruvian Case." *World Politics* 48, no. 1:82–126.

Santos, Boaventura de Sousa. 1998. "Participatory Budgeting in Porto Alegre: Toward a Redistributive Democracy." *Politics & Society* 26, no. 4:461–510.

Santos, Carlos Nelson Ferreira dos. 1981. *Movimentos urbanos no Rio de Janeiro.* Rio de Janeiro: Zahar.

Shefner, Jon. 2001. "Coalitions and Clientelism in Mexico." *Theory and Society* 30, no. 5:593–628.

Tendler, Judith. "The Rise of Social Funds: What Are They a Model of?" Report to the MIT/UNDP Decentralization Project Management Development and Governance Division (January), 125.

EIGHT

INFORMAL POLITICS IN THE MEXICAN DEMOCRATIC TRANSITION:
THE CASE OF THE PEOPLE'S URBAN MOVEMENT

Juan Manuel Ramírez Sáiz

What are the factors accounting for the ascent, transformation, and decline of grassroots movements? How is that evolution related to democratic expansion or contraction? In this chapter I investigate those two questions by tracing the rise and eventual waning of Mexico's Movimiento Urbano Popular (MUP), whose remarkable activities between 1977 and 2002 coincided with nationwide efforts to install democratic forms of political participation.

My study is the result of nearly two decades of archival, journalistic, and academic research. I have conducted participant observation and interviewed scores of public officials, activists, union representatives, and academics.[1] More than a localized case of limited value, the Movimiento Urbano Popular presents quasi-experimental conditions that allow for a better understanding of the interplay between state representatives aiming to expand public welfare while maintaining social order and grassroots organizations making claims to advance their own class interests.

Recent works on social movements highlight their potential to advance democracy (see, for example, Touraine 1997 and Melucci 1989) and also the extent to which democratization improves material living conditions (Lipset 1981 and Przeworski 1998). Seymour Lipset and Adam Przeworski, for example, maintain that the flowering of democracy depends on whether or not a country can first reach satisfactory levels of economic and social development. In that perspective, increased political participation depends on the reduction of social inequalities and the diffusion of better standards of living. Others take the opposite view—they see democracy as a precondition for economic advancement (Huntington 1991). What neither of the two outlooks sufficiently clarifies is the *type* of connection needed for democratic participation and prosperity to work in concert. In other words, beyond formal analyses of the interaction between democracy and improved material conditions lies the need to understand the *qualitative* or *substantive* dimensions of the phenomenon. This pursuit lies at the core of my investigation.

An inquiry into the substantive links between politics and economics requires that we consider the relative autonomy of the two realms. According to system-based models, political behavior (including democratic transition) is governed by its own rules, which are not necessarily the same as the ones guiding economic action. Something similar may be said about the economy with respect to politics. In other words, many aspects of social life (economic, legal, scientific, educational, and political) develop their own rationality, thereby forming "subsystems" that are relatively bounded and self-enclosed. Niklas Luhman, among others, states that these subsystems operate according to distinct functional codes and, therefore, assimilate external "messages" only to the extent that they can be translated into the subsystem's internal logic. In that view, there is no single focus organizing collective action—each subsystem is comparatively autarchic and politics is but one of several spheres unable to wholly influence the rest (Luhman 1987).

By contrast to system-based models, my research shows that political action has a powerful influence beyond its own bounds. Politics, the economy, law, and even science are interdependent fields. As a result of recent processes of globalization, crossing the boundaries between them has become a common occurrence. Similarly, the relationship between economy and polity is fluid and overlapping; subsystems interlock or separate depending on the stock of material, symbolic, and human resources available to competing groups.

As an illustration, I investigate the changing relationship between democratic transition and socioeconomic improvements in Mexico during the period of expansion and decline of the Movimiento Urbano Popular (Bultmann 1995; Alonso 1986; Ramírez Sáiz 1986; Moctezuma 1984). I ask, at what point did democratic opening reinforce socioeconomic advances? How and why was that relationship broken? This is tantamount to asking under what conditions do social, economic, and political subsystems interpenetrate or deviate from each other.

In the first section, I analyze the MUP's ability for social vindication across changing governments and within a constraining political economy. I examine how grassroots leaders fought for adequate housing and urban services, and identify some of the conditions that enabled the movement to take advantage of government-proposed solutions. Next I describe how economic adjustment programs imposed by the governing party—Partido Revolucionario Institucional

(PRI)—led to a breakdown in low-income housing policy. In the third section, I assess the political costs paid by the MUP for participating in electoral battles. Finally, since it represents a key factor in the country's political evolution, I examine whether the recent turnover of power—to the Partido Acción Nacional (PAN) and the Partido de la Revolución Democrática (PRD)—is creating new opportunities for the movement.

The MUP in Economic and Political Context

Throughout the twentieth century the relationship between the Mexican state and informal workers was characterized by mutual dependence. Sometimes unwilling but mostly unable to provide services and shelter to the popular classes for lack of human and material resources, government tolerated the expansion of squatter settlements in the periphery and interior of Mexico's larger cities. *Arrabales* and *ciudades perdidas*, augmented by the steady arrival of rural-urban migrants, became the paradoxical mark of modernization through imperfect industrialization. Typically, residents in those proletarian neighborhoods assembled ramshackle homes out of cardboard, scrap metal, or plywood, and gradually added rooms and stories built out of more solid materials. By subsidizing their own shelter, informal workers spared government the responsibility of providing housing and other related services. By tolerating illegal settlements, often at the expense of private landowners, the state contained unrest among the popular classes. Once neighborhoods were thus constituted, government further sanctioned this symbiotic relationship by paving streets and providing water and electricity in exchange for political support.

In other words, while in advanced industrial countries access to home ownership is mainly an economic transaction—workers buy houses through direct investment of part of their salaries—in developing countries like Mexico, home ownership among the working classes has always depended on political mobilization. Formal workers relied on government programs like those instituted by the Instituto del Fondo Nacional de la Vivienda para los Trabajdores (INFONAVIT), or the Fondo de la Vivienda para los Trabajadores del Instituto de Seguridad y Servicios Sociales de los Trabajadores del Estado (FOVISSSTE), both funded by employer contributions. Low-income workers, most of them informal, depended on patron-client relationships with the state to build or purchase homes.

It is therefore not surprising that sociologists and political scientists, especially those in the United States, have focused so much attention on grassroots organizations linked to the Partido Revolucionario Institucional (PRI) (Cornelius, Craig, and Fox 1994; Eckstein 1988; Velez-Ibañez 1983; Davis 1994). Those groups are typically portrayed as corporatist units mired in patronage and led by individuals directly tied to the official party. A central finding in those studies is that renter and neighborhood organizations yield to the dominant political system, thus avoiding independent political positions and conflict.

Starting in the 1970s, however, an emerging Movimiento Urbano Popular upset the relationship between the Mexican state and informal workers by gradually defining adequate housing and urban services as entitlements of citizenship. Even earlier, in the late 1960s, independent community groups contested PRI dominance and asserted their autonomy with respect to the state and the official party. The MUP brought together those groups of disparate origins and levels of strength. Some had grown out of sudden mass invasions of *ejidal*, communal or private lands, while others were the result of gradual occupation; still others had emerged after land was legally acquired and deliberate urban planning was attempted.

In the pursuit of their goals MUP leaders confronted a complex political environment. Encroached systems of patronage perpetuated by PRI officials and new radical ideologies advanced by left-of-center activists presented equally daunting challenges. For example, local *ejido* committees, clandestine developers, and PRI leaders tolerated squatters on *ejido* holdings. Those lands, however, were often sold fraudulently as PRI militants promised the delivery of urban services in exchange for support from impoverished residents. At the same time, PRI opponents—including activists in the 1968 student movement and Catholic Base Communities—began to organize workers in the same neighborhoods.[2] As if the landscape were not murky enough, some MUP leaders were members of nascent parties and therefore aimed to attract popular backing for their own purposes. To a lesser extent, a few leftist agitators made their marks by identifying with MUP demands and joining the movement.[3] Finally, MUP campaigners themselves added to the complex landscape by attempting to erode authoritarian structures through their incorporation of grassroots members in decision-making processes.

Democratic Transition: Emergence and Evolution

The Movimiento Urbano Popular was the most dynamic social current in Mexican cities for over three decades.[4] Over that span it underwent five overlapping stages, each characterized by distinct spurts of activity and different leadership. The mobilization of low-income residents in urban fringes was especially vigorous between 1968 and 1987. Renters' movements grew strong between 1975 and 1985. New popular organizations flourished in the aftermath of the 1985 earthquake, which left thousands of people without homes. Independent groups demanding land and housing proliferated and deployed their most impressive demonstrations between 1987 and 1990. Finally, the last decade of the twentieth century witnessed an increasing paralysis on the part of MUP leadership. These different moments and expressions show that this was not a monolithic movement but a broad front for action on the part of low-income urban groups.

The MUP's trajectory reveals variations in dominant actors but also in degree of discipline, type of organization, and social and political goals. Independent neighborhood residents took to the streets in the 1960s and 1970s, disdainful of public and private property, and unwilling to abide by city ordinances. During the same period other, more disciplined groups appropriated undeveloped land and built their own houses in major metropolitan areas. They often participated in marches and public demonstrations to oppose actions taken by the authorities or to force them to acquiesce to their demands. Local governments often turned to violence and repression when their attempts to co-opt such groups failed (Ramírez Sáiz 2002).

In September 1985, a massive earthquake destroyed large numbers of rental and tenant-owned properties in downtown Mexico City. Homeless crowds showed a remarkable capacity to mobilize, propose policy, and negotiate with government officials who, at the time, faced budgetary strangleholds resulting from neoliberal policies. Groups demanding everything from land to the construction of government-subsidized housing sprang up everywhere. Under MUP aegis those groups achieved high levels of discipline and offered carefully drawn-up proposals. Some of those proposals received government support.

Variations were also evident throughout the country with respect to the goals and internal composition of MUP groups. In some cases organization was minimal and existed primarily to push for immediate concessions. In other instances, more durable groups with well-defined functions were formed. Intermediate bodies and permanent or temporary committees took care of administrative tasks. MUP leaders worked to decentralize leadership as part of a strategy to invalidate traditional forms of PRI patronage. Leaders were regularly rotated out and held accountable, although loyalties based on personalism were not completely expunged.

The MUP's local focus changed at the beginning of the 1980s with the creation of regional and national structures that augmented its scope of action.

Illustrative of this trend was the Confederación Nacional de Movimientos Urbanos Populares (CONAMUP), a broadly based network that remained active until 1990 and whose role was to coordinate MUP functions. By the mid-1980s, the CONAMUP had organized 100,000 families in 49 cities located in 25 states, and in all delegations in the Federal District, the country's capital. This feat can only be appreciated when noting that the total population of Mexico at that time was approximately 80 million. The MUP, therefore, was directly affecting almost 10 percent of the country's residents.

The MUP began by addressing only social needs like rent controls, land acquisition, access to housing credit, and the extension of services—schools, markets, and public transportation, among others. Eventually, however, it also tackled political questions. In the beginning, the movement's relationship with municipal authorities, governors, and the occasional cabinet member had not rested on claims over "rights." Adequate shelter, sewers, and paved streets were not explicitly acknowledged as entitlements. Instead, pleas were backed by raw pressure—the result of massive public demonstrations—and, to a lesser degree, negotiation. Consciousness-raising was narrowly aimed at direct social action. MUP success between 1970 and 1985 depended solely on its proven ability to organize and activate large numbers of urban residents.

Later on, however, the movement's strategy shifted, taking into account public policies and normative procedures. Increasingly, MUP activists relied on legal knowledge and administrative expertise provided by NGO consultants. NGOs also assisted MUP leaders in tasks such as applying for and obtaining credit earmarked for low-income housing, or abiding by zoning codes. In that favorable milieu, political demands became explicit. They included the right to organize independently, the right to free speech and public demonstration, and participation in decision-making processes affecting urban development. Toward the end of the 1980s, respect for a democratic and lawful electoral process became the main priority, at times displacing the MUP's original goals (see Shefner, this volume).

This ascent to prominence coincided with attempts to dismantle corporatist structures, the affirmation of society's autonomy before the state as a separate space for political engagement, and the creation of state-society relations based on independence and mutual complementarity (Linz and Stepan 1996). The fledgling transition toward democracy entailed the expansion of nonelectoral settings for decision making based on voting, majority rule, and respect for minorities (Bobbio et al. 1982). The MUP's main contribution to this process was to supply a relatively independent sphere rooted in civil society where government policy was contested.[5]

To summarize, between 1970 and 1990, the MUP was a fertile training camp for those seeking social and political change. As a durable contribution it changed the urban landscape, increased organizational capacity, and provided new ideological resources. The MUP gained influence as groups combined demands with proposals in community and habitat design, and participated in the planning and construction of low-income housing. The MUP also changed the balance of power and influence in Mexico by attaining a legitimate status in the political arena, creating links with other organizations, and allying with democratic movements throughout the country. Such extensive learning did not take place in all instances but the higher levels of awareness acquired through active participation transformed MUP members from passive subjects into social and political forces. The struggle for housing and adequate services became a means for political expression (Moctezuma 1999).

In the next section I examine how government response to MUP demands was mediated by a changing political economy.

Government, Housing, and Mexico's Popular Urban Movement

From Debt Crisis to Financial Disaster

Starting in 1981, Mexico underwent a series of devastating financial setbacks that eventually prevented government from paying the burgeoning interest on its national debt. Austerity policies and neoliberal economic adjustments were considered and then gradually implemented. By the early 1990s, during Carlos Salinas de Gortari's administration, free market ideology was dominant as illustrated by Mexico's strong support for the North American Free Trade Agreement (NAFTA).

Under constraints imposed by changing economic conditions, Mexico's government adjusted housing policies in response to MUP demands and tactics. Presidents Luis Echeverría, José López Portillo, and Miguel de la Madrid (1970–88), on the one hand, and Carlos Salinas de Gortari, Ernesto Zedillo, and Vicente Fox (1988–2002), on the other, took different tacks. The first two pursued populist solutions to housing demands. More interested in obtaining political dividends than in using technological and financial acumen, Echeverría and López Portillo returned to models first put in place in the 1930s by Lázaro Cárdenas (Perló 1979). Since then, housing policy had neglected the land acquisition and resource redistribution necessary to build low-income residential developments. The federal government addressed local needs by permitting homesteaders to seize land but delayed the introduction of basic services, favoring certain groups and places over others at its own discretion. Services became political currency.

The result was disordered urban growth throughout the nation. The few public housing institutions attending to the informal sector lacked new ideas or resources to harness the rapid expansion of low-income neighborhoods on city fringes. Negligible, for example, was the influence of the Instituto para el Desarrollo de la Comunidad (INDECO), a community development agency. The Comisión Regularizadora de la Tenencia de la Tierra (CORETT), whose putative objective was to rationalize land use, became instead the instigator of new illegal settlements, given its reduced capacity to resolve conflicts between squatters and landowners.

In that environment—and paradoxical as it may seem—MUP neighborhood organizations, many of which openly opposed government, began to endorse housing models designed by PRI representatives for their affiliate groups. The main low-income developments of the period built in Monterrey, Acapulco, Durango, and the Federal District are a leftist version with a Maoist spin of PRI-sponsored housing. Perhaps MUP leaders appropriated the official model in an attempt to receive equal treatment and a housing product similar to the one obtained by corporatist groups. Perhaps their gaining strength led them to compete for government resources. There was one key difference, however: MUP organizations relied on their own internally generated resources. Neither the state nor the MUP directly addressed issues of equality in housing rights.

The corporatist model implemented by the Mexican government between 1970 and 1988 depended on comparatively abundant financial assets. Presidents Echeverría, López Portillo, and De la Madrid tapped into funds derived from foreign credit, oil surpluses, and World Bank largesse. Post-1982 austerity policies limited domestic expenditures, but the disastrous aftermath of the 1985 earthquake temporarily loosened restrictions imposed by the International Monetary Fund—government assets were used to finance low-cost housing and public services.

In other words, the MUP succeeded when its ability to mobilize and exert pressure complemented openness in the political system and flexibility in the allocation of financial resources. Under those favorable conditions government officials showed a willingness and capacity to learn from experience. Attempts at co-optation and negotiation through calculated concessions and signed agreements gradually replaced repression and violence. Although many of those pacts were eventually forgotten, they expressed an intention to recognize MUP representatives as legitimate players. Selective force continued to be used, mostly against leaders operating outside the MUP's embrace.

At the end of his administration, López Portillo implemented an innovative policy aimed at giving informal workers the capacity to buy homes. The Centro Operacional de Vivienda y Poblamiento (COPEVI), a nongovernmental organization, offered consulting services to grassroots groups. López Portillo's government showed political vision as well when, in 1981, it created the Fondo Nacional de la Habitación Popular (FONHAPO). Its purpose was to set aside land and plan, finance, and improve the development of low-income subdivisions. It also offered the option of building through professional firms or through neighbor collaboration. FONHAPO's new model was created to handle housing demands in correspondence with MUP's collective character. It therefore provided one of the few institutional alternatives within reach of informal workers in need of homes.

At the beginning of his administration (1982–88), Miguel de la Madrid continued to apply López Portillo's urban policies to the extent that international credits (mainly from the World Bank) allowed. The remarkable mobilization of earthquake victims and their supporters in 1985, especially in the Federal District, convinced the president to both maintain existing programs and create new ones. De la Madrid's efforts relied on additional resources contributed by international agencies and charitable institutions.

During the first seven years of its existence, between 1981 and 1987, FONHAPO abandoned corporatist criteria, accepting and approving applications from independent groups, including those in the MUP. Several factors explain this sea change in urban policy. First, independent grassroots organizations had grown significantly, as had their capacity to protest and mobilize. Second, the PRI's federation of grassroots organizations, the Confederación Nacional de Organizaciones Populares (CNOP, later called UNE), whose charge had been to bring the urban poor into the system, lost clout and creativity during that period. Third, the old model of urban populism proved obsolete as low-income urban settlements grew rapidly. Finally, the growth of public resources made new and innovative policies feasible. In political terms, the new policies had a dual purpose: to respond more rationally and efficiently to MUP demands, and to regulate and control the movement's growing social and political influence.

Yet the felicitous correspondence between MUP advances and state support did not last indefinitely. State and municipal election losses in 1986 drove the PRI back into the lap of corporatist and patron-client practices meant to regain support from fickle constituencies. As a result, the federal government modified FONHAPO's procedures. It eliminated financial support for land acquisition, and gradually reintroduced corporatist criteria for extending credit—members of approved groups received preferential treatment. Not long afterward, in 1989, the program was canceled. Some of its functions were transferred to local authorities. The loss of an institutional venue to acquire housing through collective action dealt a severe blow to the popular urban movement.[6]

Free-market policies and structural adjustment measures endorsed by the Mexican government since the mid-1980s reduced employment stability and the direct and indirect wages accruing to urban workers. Unemployment and underemployment rose even as access to social benefits decreased. The informal economy grew as well—as did the prices of land and building materials—limiting the negotiating capacity of the MUP vis-à-vis government. These economic trends diminished public expenditures and gutted social programs (see González de la Rocha, this volume). Compensatory and adjustment procedures centered on so-called national solidarity funds managed by PRONASOL and the Programa de Educación, Salud y Alimentación (PROGRESA). Since 1988, the bulk of Mexican social policy has been channeled through those two programs. How have they reacted to the MUP's housing demands, and what has been the MUP's response to them? I broach that question next.

Targeting the Poor

The Programa Nacional de Solidaridad (PRONASOL), and the housing policies that it deployed, aimed at bolstering the legitimacy of Carlos Salinas de Gortari's administration, which came to power in 1988 through a widely impugned and likely fraudulent electoral process. PRONASOL was funded through assets acquired from the privatization and sale of public companies. The program relied on a two-pronged strategy: (a) the solicitation of proposals by groups applying for benefits, and (b) the use of targeted funds. Resources were earmarked for a wide variety of ends, including the expansion of basic services (water, sewers, electricity, schools, clinics, markets, and so on) for informal workers in low-income neighborhoods. The implementation of this program depended on collective action and, therefore, excluded individuals as potential beneficiaries.

At first blush, collective brokering seemed to be in agreement with the activist logic of the MUP. Nevertheless, PRONASOL favored recently formed ad hoc groups to the detriment of existing grassroots organizations, especially those connected to the PRI. PRONASOL practices thus favored a form of neo-corporatism. In fact, Carlos Salinas de Gortari saw PRONASOL as part of a plan to buttress a political force separate from the PRI's decaying CNOP. His administration fomented the dismantling of the CNOP to make room for PRONASOL groups in an attempt to rebuild the PRI's increasingly disaffected base (for more on PRONASOL, see Cornelius, Craig, and Fox 1994).

Government's offer of monetary support and the rise of ad hoc groups in search of benefits stirred intense debate and division within the MUP. Some groups wanted to use the new resources, arguing that they weren't PRI property but came from taxes or international credits backed by the country's economic capacity. Most members, however, were strongly against accepting official support for fear that it would turn them into government clients and decrease the movement's autonomy. A limited number of MUP groups applied for PRONASOL support, and only a few ever profited from it. Groups that received funding did so because their size, organizational strength, and high level of political consciousness turned them into forces that could not be ignored. Others were pushed aside. For the most part, the MUP was left with no institutional outlets for its housing demands.[7]

In other words, PRONASOL fulfilled three political purposes: (a) it arrested the progress of independent MUP groups or, when possible, co-opted them; (b) depending on circumstances, it revitalized some corporatist groups and excluded others; and (c) it incorporated into Salinas de Gortari's project large urban sectors not linked to the PRI or to the opposition parties.

Also altering the MUP's capacity for concerted action was PROGRESA, implemented during Ernesto Zedillo's administration (1994–2000). Unlike PRONASOL, it excluded organized groups and considered only individuals as applicants and beneficiaries. Furthermore, PROGRESA focused for the most part on rural needs, largely ignoring urban poverty. In explaining the shift away from groups and organizations, federal officials stated that collective involvement undermined public credibility—a problem that in their opinion, had negatively affected PRONASOL's capacity to implement policy. They also saw risks in collectivism to the extent that it could foment popular uprising and conflict (Yaschine 1999, 10).

Vicente Fox's PAN administration (2000–2006) has deployed two new policy instruments: CONTIGO ("with you") and OPORTUNIDADES ("opportunities"). Both partially correct the rural bias of PROGRESA by including explicit measures to address urban poverty, especially in mid-sized cities. Those new programs fund the refurbishing of roofs, floors, and sanitary facilities in preexisting homes, but because of their recent implementation, no data are available yet on the extent to which they have benefited MUP organizations.

The preceding account shows that housing policy fluctuated significantly in Mexico over the last twenty-five years, with varying effects on the capacity of the popular urban movement to realize goals. MUP's potential to act as an autonomous social movement has been partly arrested by recent programs requiring the creation of new social groups (PRONASOL) or supporting individuals rather than organizations (PROGRESA and OPORTUNIDADES). The last three administrations have tried not so much to repress as to manipulate, assimilate, or exclude MUP groups (Moctezuma 1999).

Although "social rights" allegedly constitute the rationale behind PRONASOL, PROGRESA, and OPORTUNIDADES, various obstacles have kept those rights from being fulfilled. Political manipulation and the temporary character of the three programs are main impediments. Simple administrative procedures can turn some individuals into beneficiaries while denying others access to resources. Moreover, those programs are not governed by universal or egalitarian principles, but by administrative rules and short-term goals. Emilio Duhau argues with respect to PRONASOL a point equally relevant to PROGRESA and OPORTUNIDADES: "The citizen and his or her rights are replaced by the poor person and his or her unmet needs. . . . Access [to government benefits] is not a right but a *possible bestowal* that depends on [local criteria]. These are programs . . . subject, to decisions made in the administrative sphere" (Duhau 1997, 3, 9, 11 and 12).

Thus, a main consequence of economic and policy change in Mexico since the 1990s has been the diminished capacity of grassroots organizations to effectively mobilize and obtain satisfaction for popular needs, especially housing. This case suggests that when living conditions deteriorate, social claims do not necessarily increase proportionally—on the contrary, they can diminish because impoverished urban residents spend more time chasing scarce resources to survive and have less of it to invest in political action. This is all the more obvious among unemployed and informal workers. In fact, job security is literally becoming a matter of life and death for the few employed workers that participate in the MUP. The consequence of economic and political change has been to transform the discussions of social rights into an empty rhetorical device.[8]

To recapitulate, from 1970 to 1988, housing policies implemented by the Mexican state did not invoke social rights. Between 1988 and 2002, rights were recognized but not fulfilled. The political and electoral reforms carried out during the same period did not address social welfare. The transition to democracy did not produce sensible improvements in the living conditions of low-income city residents. Indeed, the MUP's participation in the democratic transition had a perverse effect on political mobilization, a subject to which I turn in the next section.

Political Action and the Costs of Participation

In its early stages the MUP was not a partisan movement. Yet its capacity to coordinate massive demonstrations in the 1970s, the national influence it achieved through CONAMUP in the 1980s, and its support of the 1985 earthquake victims in their mobilizing efforts transformed it into a strong political force. In addition, the MUP pushed an alternative· political culture. In low-income neighborhoods on city fringes and in downtown areas MUP constituents openly attacked and neutralized PRI influence. This made a contribution to democratization by weakening presidential hegemony, party dominance, and corporatism. Such practices still exist today, but they are being eroded partly as a result of the movement's efforts.

In response to the noxious mixture of patronage, corporatism, and repression, the MUP created alliances and established agreements with compatible organizations. It sought support and solidarity against common enemies and to counteract government measures that negatively affected grassroots organizations. It also sharpened class consciousness by promoting joint interests and supporting common demands with other groups. The MUP thus sought to alter the balance of power between civil society and the state (Shefner 2001). Especially significant in that respect were the MUP's alliances with teachers' unions and independent *campesino* leagues. Strengthened by mutual support, those coalitions enjoyed some protection when facing police repression during public marches and demonstrations.[9] Those partnerships, as well, led to MUP involvement in nationwide strikes in 1983 and 1984, and to an active opposition of neoliberal economic policies. In those years, the MUP regularly joined actions in defense of wage increases, and against austerity measures and food shortages (Carr 1986).

Success in the 1980s, when many of the MUP's social demands were realized, brought the movement to the attention of left-wing parties. The Partido de la Revolución Democrática (PRD) and the Partido del Trabajo (PT) sponsored MUP candidates willing to run for public office. This represented a shift away from social struggle and toward partisan politics—the MUP became an electoral

player, the role it had refused to take prior to 1988. Previously, MUP constituents, especially those linked to the Organization of the Revolutionary
Left, had consistently spoken out against electoral participation, calling it a
farce. The new developments split the movement. One bloc initially linked
up with the National Cardenista Front (FNC, which later became the PRD).
Others attached themselves to the Revolutionary Workers' Party (PRT).[10]

The MUP's partnership with political machines in federal and local elections
had mixed outcomes. It had beneficial effects to the extent that it heightened
the movement's visibility. In the 1988 federal election that brought Salinas de
Gortari to power, most organizational leaders believed that fraud was rampant.
The MUP worked arduously to get the vote out and organized numerous
actions to denounce violations. Such activities taught MUP groups a great
deal about national campaigns and the extent to which the state was willing
to go to protect its prerogatives. Other developments were not as constructive.
The MUP's collaboration with the PRD and the PRT led to the election of
MUP leaders, but despite the movement's rhetoric about building "people
power," those recently appointed officials were unable to define and implement measures to address the needs of their constituents. The MUP did not
have the social clout to propose or negotiate innovative social policies for the
new left-wing governments to enact.

The partisan turn had other negative effects. For example, the opera-
tional link-up with parties caused confusion over social and political goals
(Bultman 1995, 186 and 188).[11] Even more distressing was the movement's
loss of autonomy vis-à-vis political machines. By turning electoral participation
into the main channel to achieve policy change, the MUP was forced to assume
a factional mindset, that is, to act more like a party than a social movement.
As a result MUP organizations ended up working against their own interests.
The advantages they had enjoyed as outsiders diminished even as their capacity
to satisfy popular demands as insiders declined (Bultman 1995). An indicator
of shrinking influence was the MUP's pervasive silence with respect to the
passage of the North American Free Trade Agreement (NAFTA), the corner-
stone of Salinas de Gortari's economic project. Not only was the movement
unable to influence public opinion, but some MUP organizations went so far
as to publicly support the treaty. That was in stark contradiction to the MUP's
earlier participation in public demonstrations against austerity measures and
neoliberal policies.

Such developments led to the MUP's sharp diminution of influence (Moctezuma 1999). Since the 1990s, MUP organizations have mostly participated

in projects promoted by other groups like the Movimiento Zapatista de Liberación Nacional (MZLN). No popular actions similar to those that took place in the mid-1980s are in evidence at present. In 1989 the CONAMUP, the movement's national consortium of popular urban associations, suffered an internal split. The new coordinating entity, Asamblea Nacional del Movimiento Urbano Popular (ANAMUP), held its last national meeting in 1990 and vanished gradually in subsequent years.

Although the MUP has lost most of its power at the national and regional levels, some local organizations in places like Durango and the Federal District are still fighting for isolated causes. Other local MUP units have been decimated and torn apart—it is doubtful that they will be able to participate in future elections. Consensus is growing that the MUP's incursion into electoral politics was a devastating strategic error.

As if all this were not enough, the ghost of corporatism is eerily rising in the MUP ruins. Ties between the movement and left-wing parties are disturbingly similar to those that existed between urban grassroots organizations and the PRI. Every group expects its members and leaders to be awarded political appointments and jobs in exchange for support. As an organization, the MUP has not derived benefits from specific victories because organizations within the movement have established independent links with partisan groups in accordance with an older patron-client format. In short, no political innovations have resulted from the relationship between left-wing parties and urban movements. Despite its influence on Mexico's fleeting transition to democracy, the MUP could not maintain its position as an impartial advocate of working-class interests.

The Partido Acción Nacional (PAN), the party currently in power, appears even less likely to grant concessions to the MUP. Ever since he became president in 2000, Vicente Fox has implemented few social policies at the municipal, state, or federal levels. There has never been a direct dialogue between the MUP and the PAN because of the movement's emphasis on collective action and the party's misgivings about group mobilization. No specific strategies have been designed to address the needs of low-income urban groups. The PAN gives priority to individual participation and distrusts marches and demonstrations. Claims on material and political benefits as *rights* have been abandoned, at least for the time being. On the bright side, the PAN is gradually defining procedures to erode corporatist support for the PRI and to create its own base among street vendors', taxi drivers', and neighborhood organizations (Ramírez Sáiz 2002). Although the party still lacks an urban grassroots base, it is starting to gain a foothold through its influence in the election of "neighborhood committees" whose members are recognized by the authorities for representation at the municipal level.[12]

In brief, throughout the 1980s, the MUP's focus on popular mobilization and avoidance of partisan politics brought about sizable improvements in the living conditions of its members. By contrast, recent political and electoral involvement has not raised standards of living for MUP constituents. Nor is the democratic transition bringing about new social welfare policies. In other words, political turnover has not met the needs and interests of low-income sectors, including those represented by the MUP.

Conclusion

The Movimiento Urbano Popular achieved meaningful political and social victories as a result of its coordination of groups and organizations at the local, regional, and national levels. It blossomed into a broad-based movement in the 1980s and grew as a social force not beholden to the state or political machines. Subsequently, its ties with left-wing parties and its incursion into electoral politics unhinged the MUP's coordinating capacity and did nothing to improve living conditions, particularly with respect to housing. Paradoxically, the MUP's political entanglements did not improve its political strength

Housing policies implemented by the Mexican state between 1970 and 1988 included no explicit recognition of housing and other services as social rights. From 1988 to 2002 those social rights were acknowledged but not realized. More recent developments under the first PAN administration suggest that even the rhetoric surrounding "rights" may be dwindling. Neither democratic transition nor political turnover is bringing about improvements in standards of living for the urban poor.

Two central questions arise in light of these trends. Why did the MUP's influence at the grassroots level decrease as it expanded its participation in the electoral and political arenas? Why aren't political turnover and democratic transition leading to policies benefiting low-income urban groups like those once so effectively represented by the movement?

One possible answer to the first question is that party bureaucracies have a limited capacity to mobilize popular groups (Michels 1973) because their structure is geared toward self-perpetuation, not the fulfillment of needs at the grassroots level. In this case, however, it is not so much that Mexico's left-wing parties depended on bureaucratic structures but that the MUP shifted to become more like a political party. In other words, it was independence from the political apparatus that originally conferred upon the movement legitimacy and a capacity for action. A system-based model would have predicted that the MUP would gain strength as a result of its incorporation into party politics. Yet that was not the case—it was when its influence was wielded from the outside that the movement was most effective. A *party mindset* subordinated the MUP to factional interests, including the constant search of resources necessary to participate in the electoral process.

An answer to the second question—Why isn't political opening improving living conditions in Mexico?—forces us to reconsider common assumptions about the relationship between democratization and economic development. A commonly held belief is that the transition to democracy is achieved through pacts between national elites and social and political agents (O'Donnell, Schmitter, and Whitehead 1986). In Mexico, however, there were no such dealings. Democratic rule did not replace a military dictatorship, as was the case in Brazil, Argentina, Chile, Spain, and Portugal. Nor was it the result of a massive collapse of the political apparatus as illustrated by the dismantling of the Soviet Union. Finally, democratic governance was not achieved in Mexico by means of social activism, as with Poland's Solidarity movement.

In Mexico a hegemonic party regime gradually opened up through electoral means. As has been stated before, "the Mexican transition wasn't agreed on, it was voted in" (Becerra, Salazar, and Woldenberg 1999). That process began with the political reforms of 1977 and continued up to 1996 with other electoral amendments. In other words, it took a staggering twenty-two years to make elections credible throughout the country. Over that period legislative action was used to gradually incorporate opposition parties into municipal, state, and federal governments and to make it possible for party representatives to serve in legislative chambers. Contested electoral processes culminated in 2000 when Vicente Fox, the PAN's nominee for president, broke the PRI's long grip on power.

In advanced nations, welfare states were built in tandem with widening political rights and electoral involvement. In Mexico, by contrast, a doubly contradictory evolution took place. On the one hand, for over forty years (1940–82), advances in the implementation of welfare programs paralleled the suppression of political rights. The cost of expanding social benefits was the curbing of citizenship. Currently, social well-being has been "downsized" while political rights are being expanded. There is, therefore, a lack of correspondence between growing political participation and a halting social policy to address the needs of low-income citizens. To put it yet another way, the deepening of poverty and inequality strangely coincides with the expansion of opportunities for democratic expression and participation.

The reasons underlying such a contradiction must be found in the changing economic conditions that paralleled the rise and decline of the MUP. The capacity of the Mexican state to respond to the demands of the movement was severely curtailed when neoliberal policies were applied in the late 1980s and then extended through the passage of the North American Free Trade Agreement in the 1990s. The curtailment of social expenditures made it nearly impossible to link political opening to improvements in the living conditions of the poor, most of whom are informal workers. It was when the MUP operated as an outsider and the Mexican state possessed the necessary financial resources that complementarity between democratization and economic advances was possible. That relationship was altered by the extension of neoliberal policies.

Thus, although claims for social change were articulated as part of the new political vision, the Mexican transition to democracy is in large measure disconnected from material improvements for the working class. Similarly, the Mexican transition did not fuse democratization with the recognition of basic rights. In the late 1980s adequate housing almost became recognized as a citizen-entitlement thanks largely to the MUP's efforts. At present market atomization prevails—only those with means can acquire shelter. Finally, neither democratic transition nor the turnover of power has managed to create new institutions for establishing a viable relationship between independent social movements and the state. The demise of the Movimiento Urbano Popular is a sobering reminder of that fact.

NOTES

1. For other studies on this subject, see Shefner, this volume.

2. Among those political organizations were the Organization of the Revolutionary Left—Line of Masses (OIR-LM), Critical Point Revolutionary Organization (ORPC), People's Revolutionary Movement (MRP), Revolutionary National Civil Association (ACNR), Union for Revolutionary Struggle (ULR), and Socialist Current (CS).

3. The parties in question were the Communist Party (later, the Unified Socialist Party of Mexico), the Mexican Work Party (PMT), the Socialist Workers' Party (PST), the Revolutionary Work Party (PRT), and the Democratic Revolution Party (PRD).

4. Other movements active in this period included the *campesino* movement, through the National Coordinating Body of the Ayala Plan (CNPA), and the teachers' movement, through the National Coordinating Body for Educational Workers (CENTE).

5. Main political reforms were carried out in 1977, 1982, 1986, 1989, 1993, 1994, and 1996.

6. Administrative decentralization brought about the transfer of functions previously handled by federal offices to local offices but financial resources were not equally reallocated. As a result, local offices and urban housing programs suffered severe constraints

7. Of the MUP groups benefited by PRONASOL, one of the most significant was the People's Defense Committee (CDP), in Durango, which managed to enter a cooperation agreement, signed by President Salinas de Gortari in 1989. As a result of that agreement, homes were built and infrastructure and urban services introduced in several low-income neighborhoods in the city of Durango, where the group was influential. This was the only pact signed by a president and an independent low-income organization

8. Since 1995 the time invested by low-income workers in obtaining material resources has increased, and more family members are involved. Poor neighborhoods are practically deserted during the day and have become "bedroom communities." In a number of low-income neighborhoods in Guadalajara, I found that MUP members have moved to the United States looking for jobs as undocumented aliens.

9. From 1981 to 1984, the most important links were established between the CONAMUP and other coordinating bodies like the National Coordinating Body for Educational Workers (CENTE), the National Union Coordinating Body (COSINA), the National Coordinating Body of the Ayala Plan (CNPA), the National Front against Repression (FNCR), and the People's Solidarity and Reconstruction Committee (COPOSOR).

10. In the elections of 1988, 1991, 1992, 1994, and 1995, several MUP groups nominated their own candidates. They contended for posts as municipal council members, presidents and vice presidents, state and federal representatives, and in Mexico's capital, members of the Representative Assembly and heads of one of the city delegations.

11. There are still today a number of urban low-income organizations that act as party factions and are involved in the selection of leaders and candidates (Farrera 1997, 167).

12. NGOs have changed their strategy and tactics. In Mexico City (where the largest number of NGOs and MUP groups are concentrated) NGOs have become lobbyists trying to influence public policy.

REFERENCES

Alonso, Jorge, ed. 1986. *Los movimientos sociales en el valle de Mexico.* Mexico City: Siglo XXI.

Alonso, Jorge, and Alberto Azíz. 2002. "Del viejo orden a los gobiernos de alternancia." In *México al inicio del siglo XXI. Democracia, ciudadanía y desarrollo.* Guadalajara: CIESAS.

Becerra, Ricardo, Pedro Salazar, and José Woldenberg. 1999. *La mecánica del cambio político en México. Elecciones, partidos y reformas.* Mexico City: Editorial Cal y Arena.

Bobbio, Norberto, et al. 1982. *Diccionario de política*. Mexico City: Siglo XXI.

Bultmann, Ingo. 1995. "Movimientos populares vecinales y transformaciones del sistema político en México, 1982–1992." In *¿Democracia sin movimiento social?* 131–200. Caracas: Nueva Sociedad.

Cansino, César. 2000. *La transición Mexicana*. Mexico City: Centro de Estudios de Política Comparada.

Carr, Barry. 1986. "The Mexican Left, the Popular Movements, and the Politics of Austerity, 1982–1985." In *The Mexican Left, the Popular Movements, and the Politics of Austerity*. Monograph Series, 18. San Diego: Center for U.S.-Mexican Studies, University of California.

Cornelius, Wayne A., Ann L. Craig, and Jonathan Fox, eds. 1994. *Transforming State-Society Relations in Mexico: The National Solidarity Strategy*. San Diego: University of California, San Diego, Center for U.S.-Mexican Studies.

Davis, Diane E. 1994. *Urban Leviathan: Mexico City in the Twentieth Century*. Philadelphia: Temple University Press.

Dresser, Dense. 1991. *Neopopulist Solutions to Neoliberal Problems: Mexico's National Solidarity Program*. San Diego: University of California, San Diego, Center for U.S.-Mexican Studies.

Duhau, Emilio. 1997. "Pobreza, ciudadanía y política." *Ciudades*, no. 36:3–13.

Eckstein, Susan. 1988. *The Poverty of Revolution—The State and the Urban Poor in Mexico*. Princeton: Princeton University Press.

Farrera, Javier. 1997. "El movimiento urbano popular, la organización de los pobladores y la transición política en México." In *La construcción de la democracia en México*. Mexico City: Siglo XXI.

González de la Rocha, Mercedes. 1994. *The Resources of Poverty: Women and Survival in a Mexican City*. Oxford: Blackwell.

Greene, Kenneth. L. 1997. "Complejidad, cohesión y longevidad de un movimiento urbano popular. asamblea de los barrios de la ciudad de México." In *Movimientos sociales e identidades colectivas*. Mexico City: Ediciones CIIH-UNAM.

Huntington, Samuel. 1991. *The Third Wave: Democratization in the Late Twentieth Century*. Norman: University of Oklahoma Press.

Linz, Juan. 2000. *Totalitarian and Authoritarian Regimes*. Boulder, Colo.: Lynne Rienner.

Linz, Juan, and Alfred Stepan. 1996. *Problems of Democratic Transition and Consolidation*. Baltimore: Johns Hopkins University Press.

Lipset, Seymor M. 1981. *Political Man The Social Bases of Politics*. Baltimore: Johns Hopkins University Press.

Luhman, Niklas. 1987. "The Representation of Society Within the Society. *Current Sociology* 35, no. 2.

Marván, Ignacio. 1987. "El movimiento de damnificados de Tlaltelolco." *Revista Mexicana de Sociología* 4.

Melucci, Alberto. 1989. *Nomads of the Present: Social Movements and Individual Needs in Contemporary Society*. Philadelphia: Temple University Press.

Michels, Robert. 1973. *Los partidos políticos*. Buenos Aires: Amorrurtu.

Moctezuma, Pedro. 1984. "El movimiento urbano popular mexicano." *Nueva Antropologia* 6, no. 24.

————. 1999. *Despertares: Comunidad y organización urbano popular en México, 1970–1994.* Mexico City: Universidad Ibero Americana, Universidad Nacional Autónoma de México.

O'Donnell, Guillermo, Philippe C. Schmitter, and Lawrence Whitehead. 1986. *Transition from Authoritarian Rule: Latin America.* Baltimore: Johns Hopkins University Press.

Perló, Manue. 1979. "Política y vivienda en México, 1910–1952." *Revista Mexicana de Sociología* (July-September).

Piven, Frances F., and Richard Cloward. 1979. *Poor People's Movements: Why They Succeed, How They Fail.* New York: Vintage Books.

Przeworski. Adam. 1998. *Democracia sustentable.* Mexico City: Paidos.

Ramírez Sáiz, Juan M. 1986. *El movimiento urbano popular en México.* Mexico City: Siglo XXI.

————. 1987. *Política urbana y lucha popular.* Mexico City: Universidad Autónoma Metropolitana.

————. 2000. "Pobreza y participación ciudadana. Los planteamientos programáticos de PRONASOL y PROGRESA." In *Los dilemas de la política social.* Mexico City: Universidad de Guadalajara, Universidad Iberoamericana, ITESO.

————. 2002. "Las organizaciones cívicas en la democratización de la sociedad y del sistema político." In *México al inicio del siglo XXI: Democracia, ciudadanía y desarrollo.* Guadalajara: CIESAS.

Schmitter, Philip C. 1974. "Still the Century of Corporativism?" *Review of Politics* 6, no. 1(January).

Shefner, Jon. 2001. "Coalitions and Clientelism in Mexico." *Theory and Society* 30, no. 5:593–628.

Schumpeter, Joseph. 1942. *Capitalism, Socialism, and Democracy.* New York: Harper and Brothers.

Przeworski, Adam, and Susan Stokes. 1999. *Democracy, Accountability and Representation.* New York: Cambridge University Press.

Touraine, Alain. 1997. *What Is Democracy?* Boulder, Colo.: Westview Press.

————. 2000. *Can We Live Together? Equality and Difference.* Stanford: Stanford University Press.

Vélez-Ibañez, Carlos. 1983. *Rituals of Marginality: Politics, Process, and Culture Change in Central Urban Mexico, 1969–1974.* Berkeley and Los Angeles: University of California Press.

Villa, Manuel. 1991. *La institución presidencial.* Mexico City: Porrúa.

Yaschine, Iliana. 1999. "The Changing Anti-Poverty Agenda: What Can the Mexican Case Tell Us?" Manuscript. London School of Economics and Politics.

Zermeño, Sergio. 1996. *La sociedad derrotada.* Mexico City: Siglo XXI.

NINE

"Do You Think Democracy Is a Magical Thing?" From Basic Needs to Democratization in Informal Politics

Jon Shefner

How have the changes in Mexico's electoral politics influenced political demand-making in poor urban neighborhoods? One answer comes from examining the trajectory of that nation's democratization movement. Research from a community in Guadalajara, Jalisco, reveals how the movement made strategic choices that shifted demands away from the provision of basic needs to electoral reform. That strategy proved successful, as the overturning of dominant party power demonstrates. My case study suggests, however, that the informal politics of the urban poor have changed in ways that the advocates of democratization did not expect.

Guadalajara provides a useful locale for the examination of poor people's politics amid electoral change. The birthplace of the PAN (Partido Acción Nacional), the party at long last able to topple the PRI (Partido Revolucionario Institucional), Jalisco became an opposition–governed state in 1995. In Jalisco, I argue, the organizations of the Urban Popular Movement (Movimiento Urbano Popular) supplied a great deal of the force that brought about electoral change. In doing so, the movement joined with a large network of supporters from nongovernmental organizations, working in ways that aided democratic change. Yet after opposition victories in Guadalajara and Jalisco, many NGO organizers turned away from the popular struggle, working instead to exploit the political openings created by the new governments. In so doing, NGO organizers left many of their colleagues from the *colonias* behind. As a partial

---

* I am grateful to Sherry Cable, and especially to Patricia Fernández-Kelly, for their comments on this chapter.

result, the earlier vibrant social movement declined, and some of the channels for demand-making were blocked.

This chapter proceeds as follows: after a brief discussion of methods and data sources, I review the changes in Mexican urban politics and the impact of neoliberal policies. Second, I examine the juxtaposition of two scenarios from different moments of urban political action to exemplify changes. Next, I describe the trajectory of a Guadalajara political organization and its relationship with other actors during and in the aftermath of Mexican electoral transformation. I conclude with a discussion of the limits of democratization as both rhetorical tool and organizational goal.

This chapter is based on research I conducted on urban politics in Mexico between 1993 and 2001. During that time, I conducted eighteen months of participant observation in organizations demanding urban services for residents in the periphery of Guadalajara, Mexico's second-largest city. Additional study focused on NGOs working for fair elections and to build the power and coherent voice of a nongovernmental opposition in Jalisco, Mexico. I observed organizational meetings, protests, workshops, gatherings with government officials, and electoral campaigns, among many other events. I conducted over one hundred interviews with movement leaders, members, and critics, and with government officials representing state and municipal offices. In addition, the organizations I studied opened their archives to me, and I examined documents generated by movement organizations, government entities, and other researchers.

Politics of the Urban Poor and the Neoliberal Shift

The participation of the urban poor in the democratization movement is best understood as part of a long tradition of research. Studies from the 1970s and earlier found that the urban poor in Mexico—including unregulated and marginal workers—engaged in political action largely through clientelist relationships with the PRI.[1] The informal politics of urbanization followed a consistent path. Exploding city size and growing real estate prices drove many to seek housing opportunities on the periphery of large cities. Squatter communities organized and seized land on city outskirts, often under the protection of PRI patrons. Families built their own homes, adding concrete block rooms to the shanties that originally stood on their lots. The squatters laid out their own streets and began to petition their PRI patrons for urban services, often beginning the installation of public facilities on their own. Communities worked through brokers whose leadership was based on their connections to powerful party leaders or government functionaries. In response to community petitioning, government stepped in and helped provide streets, sewers, and electricity, as well as regularize the land tenure of squatter neighborhoods. The provision of such services, not coincidentally, often accompanied local and national elections and was consistently supplied in exchange for political support. Through this basic pattern, neighborhoods on city outskirts emerged through self-help punctuated at predictable times by government and party investment. In this way, the PRI could count on the loyalty of the urban poor at relatively low cost to the party and government. Although the informal politics of the urban poor allowed the PRI to prioritize system maintenance over the satisfaction of community needs, the political procedure also worked for the urban poor because their communities' needs were satisfied over time.

Basic needs provision proved a viable political strategy while the national economy expanded. But the debt crisis and subsequent multinational demands on Mexico brought an end to economic growth. In the 1970s, the Mexican state's heavy borrowing on the world capital market increased significantly with the discovery of oil reserves that generated overly enthusiastic estimates. As interest rates rose over the decade, more foreign exchange was required to pay the burgeoning debt, and the primary source of foreign exchange was oil sales. Simultaneous with interest rate increases came a fall in oil prices, leaving Mexico in 1982 with a debt it could not pay. Government's debt obligations added to the technocratic views of Mexico's new leaders (Centeno 1994) ushered in a neoliberal shift in economic policy.

The neoliberal shift imposed deep hardships on most of Mexico's population. Austerity measures were negotiated to address the International Monetary Fund's demand that debt payment and open access for international capital be prioritized over the basic needs of Mexican citizens. Wages decreased drastically with annual drops ranging between 7.7 percent to 12.3 percent in an almost uninterrupted fall that lasted from 1982 through 1997 (Friedmann, Lustig, and Legovini 1995; Lustig 1998). The urban poor suffered greatly from shrinking wages. The number of households below the official poverty line increased from 34 percent in 1970 to 43 percent in 1996 (Lustig 1998). Growing numbers of industrial jobs brought little relief, as new factories paid wages 60 percent lower than their predecessors (González de la Rocha 2001). Real wages in 1998 were 57 percent of real wages in 1980; the minimum wage in 1998 was 29.5 percent of the minimum wage in 1980 (Dussel Peters 2000, 72).

Unemployment also increased, interrupted by a short period during the early 1990s (González de la Rocha and Escobar Latapí 1991; Friedmann, Lustig, and Legovini 1995; Lustig 1998). Income inequality polarized Mexican society, with "the richest 10 percent of the population earning 55 percent more in real terms in 1992 than in 1977 while the real income of other social groups declined" (González de la Rocha 2001, 82). The 1980s "lost decade" of faded development promises stretched into the 1990s, and recent reports on Mexico's economy confirm that the "lost decade" has yet to be found (Thompson 2002).

Neoliberal policy, with its attendant reduction in resources and national spending prerogatives, undercut the logic behind clientelist informal politics. In short, the pool used by the government for basic needs provision dried up, as the neoliberal mandate reduced all forms of social expenditure. The urban poor, confronted with economic policies under which their political worth was devalued, responded by rejecting clientelist politics.[2] Without even intermittent rewards, why remain clients? Instead, poor neighborhoods organized independently of party affiliation, became less deferential and more confrontational, based their demands on citizenship claims rather than partisan loyalty, and coalesced with other similar organizations around increasingly nonlocal demands.[3] The neoliberal shift has thus had a notable effect on the political practices of the urban poor: with less and less money available to the state and predominant parties for patronage, urban services, and social welfare provision, the poor discovered that old, risk-averse political behaviors no longer satisfied their needs, which led them to seek out new political opportunities.

The debt crisis and austerity polices have affected all sectors of Mexican society. Researchers suggested that austerity produced greater relative impoverishment among the urban non-business-owning middle class than among any other sector (Escobar Latapí and Roberts 1991). Many of the positions that disappeared as a result of state retrenchment were white-collar, middle-class positions. Additionally, interest rates increased substantially, making it difficult for both middle-class entrepreneurs and consumers to maintain living standards.

Economic change also precipitated political adaptation among the middle class. Long enjoying a position of relative privilege, the urban middle class had been a bulwark of PRI support. With the debt crisis, both opposition social movements and electoral organizing increased. The middle-class political actors that coalesced with the urban poor to form the democratization movement were found largely among civic nongovernmental organizations. Research on Mexican NGOs found that class standing characterizes human rights functionaries: 77 percent are *licenciados*, that is, they hold the equivalent

Table 1   Contrasts in political process among Mexico's urban poor

	Clientelist neighborhoods	Politically independent neighborhoods
Political grievances	Precipitated by local needs	Precipitated by both local needs and national issues
Community leaders	Obtain local benefits through ties to powerful extra-community actors	Reflect the characteristics of their constituencies
Political demands	Partially satisfied by extra-community actors in exchange for systemic support	Based in an ethos of citizenship and participation
Extralocal ties	Community isolated from potential allies. Isolation helps maintain the local focus of political action.	Increasingly characterized by links to other political actors and presence in multiple coalitions. Coalition work pushes organizations to make extralocal demands.
Extralocal control	State or party responses to local demands designed to channel dissent in ways that maintain hegemony	Popular organizations seek as much autonomy from the state and political parties as possible

of a bachelor's degree. Twenty percent of NGO participants self-define their background as academic, while 19 percent come from professional backgrounds (Aguayo Quezada and Parra Robles 1997, 13, 15).

As Table 1 shows, the informal politics of the urban poor underwent important changes in process. A key component of those shifts was the increasing coalition work that brought Mexican neighborhood groups together with NGOs in the democratization movement. The formerly isolated urban poor became partners of organizations increasingly devoted to reforming the formal operations of electoral politics. As Juan Manuel Ramírez Sáiz shows in his contribution to this book, many organizations in the Urban People's Movement (MUP) began to work toward electoral reform rather than to satisfy basic needs. Concurrent with the emergence of the democratization movement, the rhetoric of democratization became championed by advocates of neoliberal policies.

Current neoliberal views see advantages in political democratization because "democracy is a powerful stimulus to development . . . it provides a more conducive environment for market-led economic growth and . . . it carries the potential for more efficient and accountable government" (Luckham and White 1996, 284). The confidence that neoliberals have in markets has been extended to political structures. In this perspective democratization provides a market logic for political processes and offers open access to those who seek available information to resolve political problems such as corruption, inefficiency, and lack of legitimacy (Glade 2000). Truly free markets require democratic institutions; democracy, in turn, requires unfettered free markets (Diamond et al. 1999).

William Robinson (1996) supplies a crucial corrective to the uncritical linking of democratization and free markets. For Robinson, democratization provides a rhetoric with which "consensual domination" may be achieved. As coercive power declined as a useful tool of international social control, intellectuals and policymakers turned to democratic values to build consensus and maintain elite power over global politics and economics. Democratization provides inclusion into a social order, which in turn nurtures legitimacy. The extent of genuine democratic participation brought about by such incorporation, according to Robinson, is minimal.

Who are the actors that bring about democratization? Among both neo-liberals and their critics, civil society has recently gained high profile as a social actor significant to the democratization process (Garretón 1997; Jelin and Hershberg 1996; Petras and Morley 1992; Oxhorn 1995; Escobar and Álvarez 1992). Active and growing civil societies influence democratization by changing "the balance of power between state and society," by "playing a disciplinary role" over those used to acting with impunity, "by enforcing standards of public morality," by serving as a mediator between state and society, and by offering greater possibilities of popular representation (White 1996, 186). Civil society redefines the political rules of the game.

The question of who exactly composes "civil society," and what their political interests are, is not often asked. Largely, the relevant literature counterposes "civil society" to the state, and as such, many of its interests are in contrast to those of the state. How has "civil society" contested authoritarian politics in Mexico? Are the political interests of this sector as internally consistent as researchers have assumed? The following scenarios begin to answer these questions.

United for Democracy

On a hot, dusty afternoon in May 1994, a flatbed truck and a van pulled up to a street corner in the southern metropolitan area of Guadalajara called Cerro del 4. A group of men who had been standing around and talking walked over to help the new arrivals unload pieces of scaffolding and staging. The waiting men were neighborhood residents who worked with a local political organization known as the Unión de Colonos Independientes (the Union of Independent Settlers, or UCI). The UCI had fought for over five years for urban services, secure land tenure, and democratic change. The recent arrivals were members of a nongovernmental organization, the Movimiento Ciudadano Jaliscience (MCJ, or Jalisco Citizen Movement). A coalition of several city organizations, the MCJ defined itself as a pro-democracy movement. MCJ members organized political awareness campaigns to convince people to vote for the best democratic alternative in the impending presidential elections.

Both groups quickly erected a four-foot high stage and two scaffolds. With these preparations finished, the newcomers opened the van doors and began to remove a variety of electronic equipment. Van passengers started stringing wires, placing lights, and connecting a soundboard and speakers, while others gingerly unpacked an enormous television and sophisticated video equipment.

More vehicles brought actors who unpacked stilts and costumes. Passersby were startled and amused as one man donned a brilliant red devil's costume. Children clamored around the actors, demanding to try their stilts. Around five p.m., the drivers of the van announced that the march was about to begin. The *Foro Callejero*, or street forum, was under way.

Scores of women, men, and children followed the van. Three actors, costumed, heavily made-up, and walking on stilts that made them about ten feet tall, picked their way precariously among the rocks, potholes, and garbage of the unpaved street. While the driver of the van exhorted other residents to join the march, the devil pounded a drum and darted through the group, teasing the marchers. Many of the women held signs reading "We want democracy," and "We demand the collector," giving the devil fodder for his teasing. "Demand!? Who do you think you are? A rich person, that we should listen to?" After a short walk, the van turned around and led approximately 150 participants back to the stage area.

Yolanda Zamora, a radio talk show host, acted as moderator, welcoming the audience and introducing other participants. Yolanda emphasized that this was an event sponsored by the MCJ, a coalition of groups and individuals "working together so we can bring about a change." She introduced a brief video detailing the history of the coalition, showing footage of urban life, including protests, traffic, and sidewalk food stands. The speakers boomed out: "In 1993, the MCJ was born to rescue the rights of the citizenry, to manifest their need to be listened to, in an attempt to show that democracy is not just a legal issue, but a way of life. To this end, the MCJ engaged in a project of citizen education for democracy." The video continued to describe their strategy, which included bringing events such as the *Foro Callejero* to the *colonias*.

The next video began with shots of light traffic passing calmly through the well-kept and recently renovated boulevards central to Guadalajara's middle- and upper-class areas. Pictures of other just-completed public works in affluent areas followed, juxtaposed immediately with images more familiar to the *Cerro* residents. Insistent images of unpaved streets flashed across the screen, as the audience viewed scenes from their own *colonias*. Children chased each other, jumping across streams of sewage that made trenches in the pounded earth streets. Families walked by monstrous piles of garbage that choked wide avenues into narrow passageways. City buses dodged huge divots while maneuvering through the streets. The camera showed a brick sewer manhole leading to nothing, testimony to construction having begun and never finished. The video ended with upbeat images of small group meetings, community meals, and dances, as the voice-over intoned: "The settlement Cerro del 4 in the city of Guadalajara, Jalisco, is made up of thirteen *colonias*. In seven of these, sewer work began in 1990, and still is not in service. There is still no collector for sewer water. The organized settlers have requested a response from the appropriate authorities, because the discharge of sewage puts the health of the residents at risk. Even though the federal Social Development Secretariat says there is money for the works, the state government denies it."

The video over, the devil and the actors on stilts captured the crowd's attention. One actor represented the corrupt Mexican system, and was mustachioed, dressed in a long black frock coat, white shirt and tie, and a top hat. The two others were dressed up to represent Mexico's Everyman and Everywoman, in work clothes and hats that were reminiscent of rural backgrounds. They engaged in a comic scene, with the devil acting as the shill for the top-hatted system representative, as both of them heartlessly responded to the other actors' voicing of people's needs. The action got the audience involved in catcalls against the devil and his boss. The moderator then entered the crowd and elicited more comments. "Wait a minute, wait a minute, this is the moment where we the people get to express our opinions. You, Señora, what do you think? What does your *colonia* need?"

A woman with children hanging on her answered: "Well, we don't have the necessary services. First, we need water."

"And you, Señora?"

An older woman, very solid and dignified, commented: "What we need is paving of the streets, collection of the garbage, and the sewer." Further answers reiterate the need for services and secure land titles. One woman commented: "Another thing is that no one in the government is concerned for us. All of the work that gets done here is through our own will. Who put in the (unpaved) streets? We did! Who hooked up the electricity? We did!"

Yolanda returned to the stage, and introduced a new video. A green bubbling cauldron spewing smoke appeared on the screen. Soon the viewers saw candles, playing cards, strings of garlic, masks, and horseshoes. A heavily made-up witch appeared, dressed in a green shawl with numbers and odd symbols. She cackled continuously, punctuating her comments. Facing the camera, she asked,

> Do you think democracy is a magical thing? In Mexico, more is produced all the time. From 1980 to 1992, industrial production increased 20 percent. Yet, in Mexico, there is less work and fewer workers. From 1980 to 1992, those employed in industry decreased by 16 percent. Currently three million employable Mexicans are without work, and nine million are underemployed. Is it true that unemployment in our country is a thing of inexplicable magic? The numbers count—or no?

Here she pointed at the viewers, the cauldron bubbled again, and the statistics-quoting witch disappeared. The credits rolled with the motto, "We're all going to play a clean game," followed by the logo of the MCJ.

The event continued with a folksinger celebrating the uprising in Chiapas, an encore by the video witch, and a panel discussion by UCI and MCJ organizers, and other NGO activists. Many speakers continued to exhort citizens to participate in the elections. Others highlighted the contrast of material benefits supplied to the upper class, while long-suffering residents of Cerro del 4 received nothing. Local residents continued to point out their missing infrastructure and their worries about the legality of their land tenure. As the sun set, lingering spectators helped break down the stage, the van and truck sped away, and Cerro del 4 residents returned to their homes.

Seven years later, on a May Sunday in 2001, a group of nongovernmental organizations joined together to hold a rally in support of Guadalupe Morfin, the head of the Jalisco state Comisión Estatal de Derechos Humanos. They organized the rally in the Plaza Tapatía, a huge square in the center of Guadalajara's downtown. Morfin, an independent activist with strong support from leftist party members and human rights- and democratization-oriented NGOs, was up for reelection as president of the state commission. The governor, a recently elected member of the PAN, did not favor her candidacy, nor did many in the state congress. With the rally, the NGO organizers were trying to alert the public to their cause. At a small stage in the Plaza Tapatía, organizers set up sound equipment, while others busily blew up balloons with slogans in support of Guadalupe Morfin. They gave balloons away to Mexican families enjoying the shopping and sights near the Plaza, while other organizers circulated among the small crowd, asking people to sign a petition and take leaflets with political information.

The few people clamoring around the stage asking for balloons left when the flag lowering began. The ceremony is performed daily in the Plaza Tapatía by a different branch of the military. This day it was the Army's turn. A squad of twenty soldiers entered the plaza in closed ranks, led by an officer wearing a sword and barking out orders. The officer, accompanied by a bugler, walked up to the raised platform that held the flagpole. Slowly they lowered the huge flag, then folded it into a long strip. Finally four soldiers were left to carry the folded flag, which they deposited on a stretcher, careful not to let it touch the ground. The crowd, which must have reached three hundred by this time, shifted as gun-toting soldiers cleared the way for the squadron to march toward the Palacio de Gobierno. The soldiers passed into the open gate of the Palacio, and the crowd dispersed.

Despite the stage set up near the event and the music playing from the loud speakers, few families did more than pass by. The balloon blowers moved to the back of the demonstration area when a woman from the group supporting Morfin made a quick speech detailing the issues to an audience no larger than thirty. She introduced a guitar player who sang in favor of human rights. He played while the organizers put up a string bearing papers that described the efforts of Morfin's commission. After the guitar player finished, the mistress of ceremonies returned to the stage to introduce various speakers. Their testimonials detailed the important impact Morfin's commission had made both in individual cases and in creating a new political culture that would no longer stand for governmental impunity. The thinning crowd drifted away after a final plea to contact newspapers, radio stations, and congressional members.

These two vignettes represent a distinct contrast in the strategies of Mexico's democratization movement. The actors in the first scenario include members of the UCI, an organization advocating the needs of poor residents in Guadalajara's southern border, as well as organizers from various nongovernmental organizations pressing for electoral reform. The first scenario illustrates strategies pursued by the democratization movement from the mid-1980s through the mid-1990s—organizing in *colonias*, where members of Urban Popular Movement organizations lived and waged their struggles. Prior to the *foro*, MCJ organizers attended several UCI meetings to discuss how to create a large turnout for the event. In addition, UCI organizers accompanied MCJ filmmakers in a tour of their community, pointing to problems in streets and houses, and even organizing extra meetings so the filmmakers would have footage showing the lives of the Cerro del 4 residents.

NGO activists made the point that democracy's absence was responsible for the poor quality of urban services endured by Cerro del 4 residents. The solution, they said, was obvious—democratization would improve the satisfaction of material needs and the delivery of public services to an area that lacked basic infrastructure. Democratic government, they asserted, would create a more equitable division of social goods.

The MCJ's presentation resonated with the experience of Cerro del 4 dwellers. Early on, as the community was growing, urban service delivery had been accompanied by a patron-client alliance with the state party. UCI members' opposition to clientelism predisposed them to the argument that a more equitable satisfaction of material needs would require a democratic transition.

By 2001, the time of the second event, much had changed. The opposition party, PAN, had ruled Jalisco for seven years, and the nation enjoyed a newly elected government. Yet the influence of the UCI had shrunk, and the focus of their nongovernmental colleagues had changed. The second vignette reveals new strategies pursued by NGOs focused on democratization. Rather than going to the neighborhoods of the urban poor, NGOs expected the democratization struggle to elicit the participation of popular sectors. Nongovernmental organizations tried to exploit new opportunities that arose in the wake of government transition. The pursuit of new opportunities resulted in moving away from previous arenas of struggle.

Responding to Hardships: Democratization from Below

The Union de Colonos Independientes (Union of Independent Settlers, or UCI) emerged in response to long-standing material deprivation and the failure of clientelism. The organization's emergence and life was marked by extensive contacts with political entities whose concerns pushed UCI leaders to look much further than Cerro del 4.

Settlers began buying lots and moving to Cerro del 4 in the early 1970s. The lots were sold illegally by unscrupulous land sellers associated with the PRI and small leftist parties, leaving residents with a host of problems. In 1974, the municipal government acknowledged the existence of the first illegal settlement within its borders; by 1994, over 300,000 citizens lived in an area with few urban services and insecure legal status. In 2001 many of those problems remained despite years of political struggle.

Guadalajara's population explosion drove expansion into Cerro del 4. The city itself grew from its 1960 level of 736,000, reaching 2,952,325 by 1990 (González de la Rocha 1994). Similar growth occurred in surrounding neighborhoods, until the metropolitan area of Guadalajara extended over the contiguous municipalities of Tonalá, Zapopan, and Tlaquepaque. As the greater metropolitan population grew, the search for land on the city's periphery intensified.

Most of the growth in Cerro del 4 occurred during the debt crisis. The fiscal limits upon the state added to Guadalajara's rapid growth, resulting in denials or long delays of urban infrastructure installation in the humble *colonia*. In 1994, most streets in the area remained unpaved and were filled with craters, boulders, and streams of loose sewage. Although sewer pipes had been installed under a few blocks, they were unconnected to either runoff grates or networks to carry the waste away, leaving pipes useless. Power lines hung over neighborhoods, but few residents possessed legal electricity. Many households tapped into the lines overhead, tired of waiting for the Federal Electricity Institute to install home lines. Access to water was even sparser. Approximately 21 percent of the homes had water piped in, while another 11 percent had other forms of water access on their property. On many street corners, both PRI and independent neighborhood organizations installed shared *hidrantes*, communal faucets, which served whole city blocks. About 60 percent of the households on Cerro del 4 lived without *hidrantes* or piped water and relied on trucks with large tanks selling water of dubious quality. Other missing or inconsistent services included garbage collection and police patrols. Elections brought new promises for services, but rarely yielded change.

The history of Cerro del 4, from its first settlement on illegal lots sold by PRI patrons, to the ongoing deprivation of public services promised by the same patrons, served to delegitimize the government for many residents. In the 1980s, students and faculty members from a local Jesuit university formed CEBS (Comunidades Eclesiales de Base, or Christian base communities), organizing neighborhood groups for Bible study and protest. By the mid-1980s separate *colonia* groups spoke for the urban poor on much of Cerro del 4 and had won neighborhood goods such as communal laundry areas and greater availability of water and transportation. In 1984 and 1986, the neighborhood organizations gained strength by preventing the police and bulldozers from pushing residents off their long-held land. The willingness of neighborhood groups to aid each other to oppose these threats convinced organizers they could achieve more as a unified group. The opportunity to unite came in the late 1980s, with the active intervention of SEDOC.

In 1977, the Mexican Provincial Company of Jesus formed SEDOC (Educational Services of the West—Servicios Educativos de Occidente), an NGO devoted to promoting social change among Mexico's poor. SEDOC formed teams of Jesuit fathers and students and laypersons to work in local projects in order to "develop a critical consciousness and transform unjust structures" (SEDOC 1989, 5). In 1985, SEDOC helped unite several independent neighborhood groups in northern Guadalajara, and in 1989, SEDOC initiated such a project on Cerro del 4.

SEDOC considered itself an organ of political change for Mexico and tried to nurture neighborhood organizations into becoming larger movements. With UCI, SEDOC's efforts proved quite successful. At its peak, in 1991, the UCI consisted of approximately twenty-five small neighborhood groups containing approximately 1250 active members. During demonstrations and rallies on Cerro del 4, the UCI was able to mobilize well over two thousand people; protests at government offices downtown brought fewer but still significant numbers of participants.

Over time, SEDOC became increasingly open about opposing the state, as the following revised mission statement demonstrates: "To support the consolidation of the independent popular movement . . . and create closer relations between them and the support centers, in order to form a common front . . . to link ourselves with wide social movements, with whose planning and goals we are aligned" (SEDOC 1986, 14).

One of the strategies pursued by SEDOC and UCI in its alliance with the wider social movement was to participate in local elections. Although largely supported by UCI leaders, many rank and file members thought that electoral participation belied the group's independence and lessened the strategic terrain on which they could petition the PRI. The strong support by SEDOC organizers, however, who possessed the legitimacy of greater education, higher class backgrounds, and church affiliation won the day, and UCI ran candidates under the PRD banner in 1991 and 1992. The UCI-PRD candidates lost by large margins, and popular support declined in response to the electoral choice and the energy the campaigns took from other organizing priorities. In addition,

SEDOC was severely criticized by the Jesuit hierarchy for its electoral strategy and was forced to dissolve.[4]

By 1994, the UCI had shrunk to approximately ten neighborhood groups, but was still able to mobilize committed participants to events on and off the hill. In addition, the UCI in 1994 relied on the leadership of six activists and a paid staff person who had been part of the organization since its birth. Although SEDOC has not survived, the links between some groups that it helped to forge and the UCI persisted in the form of consultants from NGOs and Jesuit academies and universities. Many UCI members participated in neighborhood groups because of the community's material needs, but the contacts with other political actors led the UCI to participate in many extra-local campaigns pushing for democratization.

With the aid of Jesuit promoters and other NGOs, the UCI's political aims became wider than those of traditional clientelist *colonia* organizations. Although the UCI saw urban services as an integral element of their citizen-ship rights, *la vida digna* entailed much more than material change. As Tito, a long-time UCI organizer put it:

> Look, UCI definitely was born out of the need for social services. Then the people's visions were increased, that it was not only to have services, but the right to live with dignity . . . their visions increased, widened, that there were other issues beyond those of services. And this was the way the human rights role emerged. What UCI was looking for was after finishing with the services, we could move into other phases that could still affect life—the right to health, the right to culture, all of this. We're still working on the services, but the vision widened to these other issues. There are other aspects, like democracy.

The UCI worked toward Mexico's democratization in four distinct, yet related areas. First, it participated in calls to action with human rights networks. Second, it worked in multiple coalitions, pursuing both the UCI's urban services agenda and supporting the struggles of others. Third, it used multiple tactics to participate in local and national elections. Finally, its anticlientelist stance offered a local alternative to politics as usual. Such a position militated against the antidemocratic tradition of exchanging political support for goods.

Several human rights networks emerged in the late 1980s and the 1990s in response to government impunity, selective repression, and austerity policies.

The UCI participated in coalitions such as Red Derechos Humanos "Todos los Derechos para Todos," the Foro de Apoyo Mutuo, and other groups with national profiles. The UCI's work with these organizations included sending letters of protest in response to human rights violations, attending planning meetings, holding educational workshops on human rights, asking electoral candidates to endorse human rights, and forming their own human rights subgroup, which petitioned the government for redress of local violations

Other coalitions with which the UCI worked ranged widely. Some united groups similar to the UCI, with goals of urban service attainment. Other alliances formed to demand justice in response to local tragedies such as the explosions suffered by the city on April 22, 1992. Still others formed out of UCI's relations with various nongovernmental organizations in the effort to create a new politics. The UCI participated in still other partnerships that resisted repression against *chiapanecos* while advocating the civil society visions offered by the *Zapatistas* following their short-lived armed struggle.[5]

The UCI also expended a great deal of effort in work directly aimed at democratization of the electoral process. Tasks ranged from organizing democracy workshops to time-consuming citizen action at the polls. In addition to working with the MCJ as detailed above, UCI members worked as poll watchers for the Alianza Cívica during the 1994 elections. Many attended a daylong event to become observer trainers, then participated in a workshop to be certified. The poll watchers on Cerro del 4 were coordinated by UCI leaders, who kept moving around various locations all day, giving instruction and moral support, and carrying information regarding violations of electoral law to AC organizers. Leaders and members documented breaches. Then the poll observers had to follow up after the election, making charges and supplying evidence they had compiled.

Finally, the political stances taken by the UCI during its struggle for local change may be interpreted as a campaign for democratization. Cerro del 4 was defined from the beginning as a place dominated by the PRI through clientelist control. After years of such control, UCI members based their resistance on liberation theology, which defied the exchange ethos integral to clientelism. Negotiation was considered part of the political process but exchange of political support for citizenship rights was no longer allowed. Neither were attempts made by power holders to co-opt UCI leaders by enticing them with patronage goods. This very stance helped push democratization further by refusing to honor the foundation of Mexican authoritarianism.

The democratization movement would have been stillborn without organizations like the UCI supplying person-power for both dissent and constructive efforts such as electoral observation. In addition to a popular base, *colonia* organizations provided the mobilizing experience of neighborhood activists and multiple locales from which the movement could launch its struggle. Finally, although the changing political culture nurtured *colonia* groups, this relationship had a reciprocal impact. That is, even as the movement helped *colonia* groups withstand clientelism, the anticlientelist stances aided democratization by loosening the PRI's grip on local power.

In turn, the movement supplied a number of political benefits. It heightened the UCI's profile, defining it as increasingly important on both local and national stages. Ties to other groups also protected the UCI from repression and nurtured its efforts to move firmly away from clientelism, and the isolation on which clientelism feeds. The shared discussions regarding strategy and democratic values helped the UCI to define an emerging culture of citizenship, equal participation, and human rights. The program and ties created through democratization forged a base on which the UCI could rely for mostly nonmaterial aid, including a flow of information that aided its popular education campaign. Finally, the UCI benefited from the unity and solidarity accruing from a wider front.

In summary, the UCI's urban political action was defined by the creation of active coalitions. Links with NGOs nurtured participants on all sides at a time when the language of democratization was at its peak. In the next section I discuss what happened more recently to Cerro del 4, the UCI, and the host of NGOs it worked with.

Exploiting the Electoral Opportunity

Many of the nongovernmental staff that played leadership roles in the Jalisco branch of Mexico's democratization movement continued their feverish activity. Electoral change in 1995 encouraged NGOs to increased work through official channels. Government turnover led organizers to believe that innovative political strategies best suited the new political environment. Protest was largely dispensed with. Instead, leaders tried to generate support for policy reform through two mechanisms: (1) legislative initiatives, and (2) negotiating accords with electoral candidates through the state and national organization Poder Ciudadano (PC), an entity that emerged out of several NGO networks to pressure presidential candidates for the 2000 elections.

In the fall of 1999, nearly six hundred organizations from eighteen states met repeatedly to create Poder Ciudadano and propose an agenda for the next Mexican federal government. They asked candidates for federal, state, and municipal offices to commit themselves to supporting their call "for a new political economy to gain sustained and equitable growth to create jobs, remunerative salaries, the recovery of the countryside and an integral social development . . . long-term strategies that respond to and recover the productive capacity of the nation . . . recognize indigenous rights and culture . . . construct a new culture of peace . . . [and launch] a democratic reform of the state."

This formulation altered strategy. A good number of NGO organizers mentioned efforts to introduce an initiative against family violence as an example of the new direction in popular mobilization. Rigoberto Gallardo, an organizer and researcher with ITESO, Guadalajara's Jesuit university, described a recent endeavor in which groups joined together throughout the state to collect thousands of signatures supporting proposed legislation to turn family violence into a crime. Once the petition drive was over, organizers communicated the proposal to the state congress.

Although the legislation passed was not the one proposed, Rigoberto Gallardo found drafting a new law, convincing officials and the public, and gaining legislative power a useful experience—an indication of civil society's new potential to affect government. The exercise defined a new moment of access, showing "what happens when a group of citizens and their organizations dare to introduce an important theme to public opinion and carry it through legislative channels." Similar efforts were institutionalized within Poder Ciudadano.

According to Jose Bautista, Jalisco director of the organization, Poder Ciudadano won commitments from all of the presidential candidates except the PRI's. The next step was to replicate the process at the state level: "State agendas were put together by organizations around themes like the economy, citizens' participation, social politics, political policy, and what they tried to do was concentrate these proposals in three strategic axes. One of these had to do with ideas for public policy, another had to do with modification of the relationship between the government and civil society, and the third had to do with . . . budgets for the operations of these kinds of proposals for public policy."

PC's intention was to create genuine access for citizens to influence the democratizing of government. In José Bautista's words: "What we are trying to do is to be included in decision-making, allocating resources and elaborating programs and work projects so that the proposals and demands of social organizations be incorporated into the local and state government agendas. With this we want to promote the participation of citizens in public issues. . . . This is the aim . . . to make politics a citizen concern, that politics not remain exclusive to just a few, whether they are parties or professional politicians." In Rigoberto Gallardo's view, PC's work would "begin to establish a dialogue with [governments] regarding what organized citizens bring forth as an agenda of principal needs and demands that authorities and political parties should comply with." In other words, Poder Ciudadano allows nongovernmental organizations to propose public policy prior to elections. In Jalisco, PC monitored candidates' pledges at the state and municipal levels, affiliating with organizations to police newly elected functionaries, and pressuring them to fulfill their promises. According to José Bautista: "This is where the organizations are aiming now, to affect public policy, to affect the designation of public resources. It is a change that has come from . . . the country's advances in electoral democratization and advances at international levels in which the role and function of the state is being interrogated." Furthermore: "Electoral issues have taken up a great deal of attention among civil and social organizations and political parties because they require follow up. If there is no possibility of alternatives in power, we will not be able to advance. Without changes in the group in power, it would be very difficult to make progress in other ways. We think this is one of the main reasons that so many of organizations attend to this, and prioritize the electoral process."

Pushes for electoral reform also led the democratization movement to alter its priorities. Felipe Alatorre, a long-time organizer in partnership with NGOs, commented on the impact of government change on attitudes and action:

> Changes in government have brought about hopes and expectations of cleaner, less corrupt, and more efficient government, and even more so of changes at the federal level. Many are waiting to see what happens. And so they don't mobilize. . . . There are inklings but they are very limited—we see no *coordinadoras*, or reviving of the MUP.[6] . . . Our work is now to link ourselves with these groups to push, above all, initiatives at a high level, that can affect public policy. We still connect [with] small community programs but that is not the current priority. We link ourselves more to programs with greater reach.

Alatorre went on to say that many of the NGO links to community-based movement organizations have dissolved, in part because of the decline of popular organizations: "The economic situation is very difficult. And this forces people to work for survival. I don't think it is easy for people to organize . . . also . . . to the extent that there have been democratic openings, there has been a change in people's perspective. . . . The changes in Jalisco have brought about a mountain of expectations."

Many organizers agreed that NGOs that formerly nurtured popular movements' growth and activity have changed their focus. Tito, a long-time organizer with the UCI and other movements, found that in contrast to an earlier emphasis on material needs, many NGOs were now working through governmental channels for human rights and democratization. A partial effect, according to Tito, was that popular organizing had diminished; grassroots mobilization was in retreat. Tito thought the changed focus was caused by inadequate financing.

Sofía de la Peña, another organizer and researcher who had worked with the UCI, agreed with Tito's assessment. NGOs, in her view, have moved away from working with the base. She saw NGO workers expressing much greater interest in the opportunities opened by government reform. She concurred with Tito and others that little funding was being allocated for popular mobilization, but also asserted that many organizers believed it was not worth the trouble to work at the grassroots level. In Sofía's opinion, complaints about inadequate resources supplied a rationale for declines well beyond those that would have been caused by insufficient funding.

Carlos Peralta was another NGO organizer who had worked with the UCI in the 1990s bolstering its educational campaign toward social change and democratization. He too saw decreases in community-based organizing: "Yes, they [NGOs] have a much lesser presence. There are many factors. [One is that] their leadership has entered into political parties . . . and many of the people at the base have to work longer hours, sometimes holding two jobs, so their presence has diminished. Meanwhile the NGOs have had a certain stability."

Peralta felt that NGOs have shifted their focus away from groups that represent the poor because of legal changes and altered priorities in the new electoral landscape. His colleague Rigoberto Gallardo disagreed. In Gallardo's view, NGOs that used to work in popular areas had not changed. Instead, there had been a

diversification of work done by NGOs . . . their cadres have been professionalized, they can count on more resources for their actions, and they are able to work simultaneously in diverse environments. I don't think the accompaniment of popular processes has been abandoned. [NGOs] are offering the same services they have always offered, advice, pedagogy, organizational training, contacts with those in the press, etc. [At the same time] they have expanded in other areas . . . but I don't want to say that we are abandoning the others. We are working [on several fronts] simultaneously.

Cerro del 4 residents disputed Gallardo's view.

Shrinking Organization and Stagnant Services: Cerro del 4 Responds

By 2001, the UCI had shrunk to one single group led by longtime activist Javier Cruz López. According to Cruz López, "We have about fourteen who are working in a very committed way. As a whole we can count on approximately three hundred people. But it is the fourteen who are always struggling." He attributed the UCI's decline to three factors: (1) family survival needs, (2) the choice several leaders made to pursue partisan work, and (3) the diminution of external support.

According to Cruz López, groups that formerly belonged to the UCI want to continue organizing throughout the hill, but many of the group leaders are hindered by family responsibilities. Cerro del 4 residents are mostly poor and work in Guadalajara's low-paying service sector. Many households face great economic difficulties, which were exacerbated after the 1994 drop in the peso's value.[7] Meeting survival needs decreased the time available for political organizing. Other UCI members left because they were interested in working with political parties in the newly opened electoral landscape. The PRI's defeat created spaces to connect with political parties. In one instance a leader left to pursue party affiliation.[8]

Despite the UCI's decline, Javier Cruz López offered evidence of several recent actions demonstrating that the UCI still held some capacity to mobilize residents but lacked the aid that had been provided earlier by NGOs. A Jesuit social promotion group had facilitated UCI's very emergence as a union of neighborhood associations. That external assistance had dissipated in recent years. According to Cruz López:

> The UCI continues in the same struggle . . . but not with the same people. Now it is solely with people from the base. . . . The people in the UCI, we aren't intellectuals anymore. We are not the Jesuits, we are not the missionaries . . . we are nothing more than local people — housewives, workers like me. We know little, and we struggle a lot.

We don't have the advice of those that say, "look, let's follow this direction, not the other." Before in UCI meetings, we expressed a wider vision. Not now, now we are much more limited. . . . And so we are more vulnerable, easier to defeat. We still continue on but they beat us down every so often.

Javier Cruz López talked further about the dearth of funding from religious groups and NGOs. Both types of group had maintained a significant presence on Cerro del 4 for many years. Cruz López, a deeply spiritual man whose personal experiences led him to favor religious entities, spoke with disdain about those who had withdrawn their aid. Neither religious nor political organizations helped the UCI with counsel, connections, or money. The support made available was so meager as to be unrealistic, according to Javier. The Jesuits wanted him to push for people to start savings accounts, a goal that he sarcastically discounted saying few had enough to pay bills, let alone save. Many residents were like Javier, whose local bakery barely provided his family enough to eat: "Now we can't count on aid from the Missionaries, the Jesuits. . . . We have had no advice, nothing. We have been working on our own. They have left us alone. They haven't come to help us. . . . Now there are no promoters—we are all from the base." Furthermore, the groups with whom the UCI had worked in the democratization movement were conspicuously absent in 2001. The UCI's allies diminished as they pursued new avenues in the new electoral environment. Without their participation, the UCI suffered. The effect of its decline on leaders was notable. Javier Cruz López described his fatigue at great length: "The reality is that I am tired. Every day I feel more tired and with less support. I wonder how much longer can I go on because people are always going to have needs, and I would like to stay in the struggle because I benefit. . . . My dreams are that we go on, but I see many difficulties in that. At best, my children will carry on, who knows? They are real strugglers."

Fatigue and pessimism matched the physical surroundings of Cerro del 4. In 2001 I noticed few more paved streets for bus routes than in 1994. Trash was everywhere, and streams of sewage still ran into the roads. Several streets were dotted with drain covers but they remained disconnected from sewer networks. Water continued to be supplied by *hidrantes*, although it appeared that there were more water facilities installed in people's houses. A few more stores had opened; their walls were covered with gang-related graffiti, as were many houses. Huge boulders obstructed the streets. Little had changed; indeed it appeared that Cerro del 4 was a place frozen in time.

Conclusion: New Politics, Old Outcomes, and the Limits of Democratization

In this chapter I have discussed the activities of a popular organization, which added national democratization to its local agenda of urban service delivery. The participation of the Unión de Colonos Independientes in the democratization movement helped it heighten its profile, increasing the networks upon which it could rely. In turn, organizations like the UCI greatly benefited the democratization movement. Among other things, popular organizations supplied the movement with mass pressure above and beyond the efforts of political parties and offered a wide series of locales for contention.

Recent data from Mexico (González de la Rocha, this volume; Thompson 2002) reveal that the hardships imposed by neoliberalism define the lives of both the urban poor and the middle class. Why, after such significant electoral changes, have the constituencies of the democratization movement fared so poorly? This chapter answers that question by focusing on altered goals and popular struggle processes.

The experience of the UCI and its allies illustrates changes in the politics of the urban poor. In response to neoliberal economic policies that opened new paths for political action and brought potential allies, the UCI reconfigured its political agenda. It resisted the fragmentation, isolation, and local focus characteristic of clientelist neighborhood politics in Mexico. Its rejection of the exchange ethos of clientelism and its willingness to pursue confrontational tactics brought it into common struggle with other political actors in the democratization movement.

Yet once the poor were incorporated, and some measure of victory won, the democratization movement shifted from mass mobilization to incorporation into the electoral transition. NGOs now focus on pressuring newly elected governments and formulating public policy. Even as quality of life declined, NGOs drew their allies in Mexico's streets away from demands for basic needs and toward democratization as the goal of political demand making. Once electoral change was won, many of the external actors fled popular struggles to participate in the new democratic process. Under the auspices of neoliberal reform, political practices among the urban poor have changed; the outcome of marginalization has not.

Frances Fox Piven and Richard Cloward (1977), the chroniclers of poor people's movements in the United States, eloquently argued that the only means to secure social justice is through disruptive protest; that the only weapon poor people hold is the withholding of participation in the larger society. In that view, effort to enact changes through electoral channels is futile. Organizations embedded in routine electoral politics may quickly become tools of elite control, rather than expressions of mass dissent.[9] The Mexican experience to date confirms that view.

Democratization significantly changed the politics of the urban poor by giving it a focus beyond the immediate locale, contacts with other political actors, and a new language of political struggle. Yet the push for basic needs provision was displaced. That shift severely damaged the UCI. In ways reminiscent of clientelist politics, democratic inclusion channels opposition into approved modes, derailing the possibility of independent political action, and reducing substantial change. Wider electoral options are likely to prove empty in a political economy that continues to preclude genuine economic choice.

The experience of the UCI forces us, like Robinson (1996), to recognize that studies of democratization must look beyond a Schumpeterian circulation of elites and attend to how political power is distributed, whether subordinate claims can be made, and whether basic needs provision results from changes in political institutions. It forces us also to cast a less romantic view on civil society. Civil society places multiple demands on democratic institutions, not all of which can be addressed through formal participation in democratic governance. Many activists in the front lines of democratic struggle demand not just *human* rights but also *economic* rights, not just freedom from repression and political violence, but also access to urban services by virtue of citizenship. That is, civil society is as stratified as any other social institution. Different sectors have different political needs, and it is not enough to suggest that democratizing formal institutions and facilitating political contestation will provide equal benefits to all.

It is neoliberal policymaking that provides the greatest barrier to achieving democratization through genuine inclusion of the poor. Many have noted the contradictions between democratization and the neoliberal project. Lechner repeats Polanyi's warning that the market should not be a higher priority than other social institutions, finding tragedy and irony in a neoliberal project which "in pursuit of imposing in unrestrained fashion the rationality of the market . . . seeks to withdraw the economy from all processes of democratic decision-making" (1998, 29). Neoliberal policymakers suggest that greater political participation will increase material prosperity. In contrast, I argue that democratization cannot improve the material life of the poor because neoliberalism irreparably diminishes the resources with which states may satisfy popular demands. Rather than creating mechanisms by which states can satisfy their constituents' needs, neoliberal policymakers have created a strict model that decreases domestic policymaking prerogatives while limiting the political space of those most harmed by neoliberal policies. The economic resources of the poor are now stretched too thin. The political resources of the poor may be understood in similar ways. Democratic inclusion cannot increase in a neoliberal environment that holds the economic rights of powerful groups over the political rights of the most vulnerable.

NOTES

1. This summary draws on the research of, among others, Cornelius (1975), Eckstein (1977), Vélez-Ibañez (1983), Fagen and Tuohy (1972), Gilbert (1994), Rangel (1989), and Vasquez (1990).

2. This summary is based on research by Ramírez Sáiz (1986, 1990), Ramírez Sáiz and Nuncio Hermosillo (1994), Alonso (1986), Davis (1990), Carr and Montoya (1996), Moctezuma (1984), Regelado Santillan (1986), Tavera (1999), and Shefner (1999, 2000, 2001).

3. The contrast in urban political process is summarized in Table 1. Table 1 and the literature cited here do not suggest that there were no insurgent urban political efforts prior to the debt crisis, or that austerity dealt the final death blow to clientelism. These generalizations do not apply to every urban political relationship before or after the debt crisis

4. For more on SEDOC and UCI, see Shefner 1999.

5. For more on the UCI's coalition work, see Shefner 2001.

6. Movimiento urbano popular, or urban popular movement

7. See Mercedes González de la Rocha's chapter in this volume on the declining margin of survival of the urban poor.

8. According to several interviewees, those with greatest access to the PAN and the PRD were former leaders of PRI neighborhood groups who could bring clients with them.

9. Piven and Cloward, of course, analyzed an entirely different context. Yet moments of electoral change, according to Piven and Cloward, are exactly the time when disruptive action is threatening, and so may exact even more concessions. At these moments, organizational focus on working within the electoral system may be counter-productive, as this may tend to curb militancy just when elites are ready to deal.

REFERENCES

Aguayo Quezada, Sergio, and Luz Paula Parra Rosales. 1997. *Las organizaciones no gubernmentales de derechos humanos en México: Entre la democracia participativa y la electoral*. Mexico City: Academia Mexicana de Derechos Humanos.

Alonso, J., ed. 1986. *Los movimientos sociales en el valle de Mexico*. Mexico City: CIESAS.

Carr, Barry, and Ricardo Anzaldùa Montoya, eds. 1986. *The Mexican Left, the Popular Movements, and the Politics of Austerity.* Monograph Series, 18. San Diego: Center for U.S.-Mexican Studies, University of California.

Centeno, Miguel Angel. 1994. *Democracy Within Reason: Technocratic Revolution in Mexico.* University Park: Pennsylvania State University Press.

Cornelius, W. A. 1975. *Politics and the Migrant Poor in Mexico City.* Stanford: Stanford University Press.

Diamond, Larry, Jonathan Hartlyn, Juan Linz, and Seymour Martin Lipset, eds. 1999. *Democracy in Developing Countries: Latin America.* 2nd edition. Boulder, Colo.: Lynne Rienner Publishers.

Dussel Peters, Enrique. 2000. *Polarizing Mexico: The Impact of Liberalization Strategy.* Boulder, Colo.: Lynne Rienner Publishers.

Eckstein, Susan. 1988. *The Poverty of Revolution — The State and the Urban Poor in Mexico.* Princeton: Princeton University Press.

Escobar, A., and S. Álvarez, eds. 1992. *The Making of Social Movements in Latin America: Identity, Strategy, and Democracy.* Boulder, Colo.: Westview Press.

Fagen, Richard, and William S. Tuohy. 1972. *Politics and Privilege in a Mexican City.* Stanford: Stanford University Press.

Friedmann, Santiago, Nora Lustig, and Arianna Legovini. 1995. "Mexico: Social Spending and Food Subsidies During Adjustment in the 1980s." In *Coping With Austerity,* ed. Nora Lustig. Washington, D.C.: Brookings Institution.

Garretón, M. 1992. "The Political Evolution of the Chilean Military Regime and Problems in the Transition to Democracy." In *Elites and Democratic Consolidation in Latin American and Southern Europe,* ed. R. Gunther and J. Higley. Cambridge: Cambridge University Press.

————. 1997. "Social Movements and Democratization." In *Social Movements in Development,* ed. S. Lindberg and A. Sverrisson. New York: St. Martin's Press.

Gilbert, Alan. 1994. *The Latin American City.* London: Latin American Bureau.

Glade, William. 2000. "On Markets and Democracy." In *Pathways to Democracy: The Political Economy of Democratic Transitions,* ed. J. F. Hollifield and C. Jillson. New York: Routledge.

González de la Rocha, Mercedes. 1994. *The Resources of Poverty: Women and Survival in a Mexican City.* Oxford: Blackwell.

————. 2001. "From the Resources of Poverty to the Poverty of Resources? The Erosion of a Survival Model." *Latin American Perspectives* 28, no. 4:72–100.

González de la Rocha, Mercedes, and A. Escobar Latapí. 1991. *Social Responses to Mexico's Economic Crisis of the 1980's.* San Diego: Center for U.S.-Mexican Studies.

Jelin, E., and E. Hershberg, eds. 1996. *Constructing Democracy: Human Rights, Citizenship, and Society in Latin America.* Boulder, Colo.: Westview Press.

Lechner, N. 1998. "The Transformation of Politics." In *Fault Lines of Democracy in Post-Transition Latin America,* ed. F. Aguero and J. Stark. Miami: North-South Center Press.

Luckham, R., and G. White. 1996. "Democratizing the South." In *Democratization in the South: The Jagged Wave,* ed. Robin Luckham and Gordon White. Manchester: Manchester University Press.

Lustig, Nora. 1998. *Mexico: The Remaking of an Economy*. 2nd edition. Washington, D.C.: Brookings Institution.

Marshall, T. H. 1963. *Class, Citizenship and Social Development*. Westport, Conn.: Greenwood Press.

Moctezuma, Pedro. 1984. "El movimiento urbano popular mexicano." *Nueva Antropologia* 6, no. 24.

Oxhorn, Philip. 1995. *Organizing Civil Society: The Popular Sectors and the Struggle for Democracy in Chile*. University Park: Pennsylvania State University Press.

Otero, Gerardo, ed. 1996. *Neoliberalism Revisited: Economic Restructuring and Mexico's Political Future*. Boulder, Colo.: Westview Press.

Petras, J., and M. Morley. 1992. *Latin American in the Time of Cholera: Electoral Politics, Market Economics, and Permanent Crisis*. New York: Routledge.

Piven, Frances F., and Richard Cloward. 1979. *Poor People's Movements: Why They Succeed, How They Fail*. New York: Vintage Books.

Poder Ciudadano. 1999. "Síntesis de las propuestas de la agenda nacional." Photocopy.

Polanyi, K. [1944] 1957. *The Great Transformation: The Political and Economic Origins of Our Time*. Boston: Beacon Press.

Ramírez Sáiz, Juan Manuel. 1986. *El movimiento urban popular en Mexico*. Mexico City: Siglo XXI.

———. 1990. "Urban Struggles and Their Political Consequences." In *Popular Movements and Political Change in Mexico*, ed. Joe Foweraker and Ann L. Craig. Boulder, Colo.: Lynne Rienner Publishers.

Ramírez Sáiz, Juan Manuel, and Héctor Nuncio Hermosillo. 1994. *Entre la iglesia y la izquierda: El comite popular del sur*. Guadalajara: Universidad de Guadalajara.

Rangel, Rafael López. 1989. *Urbanización y vivienda en Guadalajara*. Guadalajara: Centro de Ecodesarollo.

Regelado Santillán, Jorge. 1986. "El movimiento popular independiente en Guadalajara." In *Perspectivas de los movimientos sociales en la región Centro-Occidente*, ed. J. Tamayo. Mexico City: Editorial Linea.

Robinson, William I. 1996. *Promoting Polyarchy: Globalization, U.S. Intervention, and Hegemony*. Cambridge: Cambridge University Press.

SEDOC. 1986. *Estatuos de servicios educativos de occidente, A.C*. Guadalajara, Jalisco.

———. 1989. *Planeación de servicios educativos de occidente, 1989–1993*. Guadalajara, Jalisco.

Shefner, Jon. 1999. "Sponsors and the Urban Poor: Resources or Restrictions?" *Social Problems* 46, no. 3.

———. 2000. "Austerity and Neighborhood Politics in Guadalajara, Mexico." *Sociological Inquiry* 70:3.

———. 2001. "Coalitions and Clientelism in Mexico." *Theory & Society* 30, no. 5:593–628.

Tavera, L. 1999. "Social Movements and Civil Society: The Mexico City 1985 Earthquake Victims Movement." Ph.D. diss., Department of Sociology, Yale University.

Thompson, Ginger. 2002. "Free-Market Upheaval Grinds Mexico's Middle Class." *New York Times*, September 4, 2002.

Vásquez, Daniel. 1990. *Guadalajara: Ensayos de interpretación*. Guadalajara: Colegio de Jalisco.

Vélez-Ibañez, Carlos. 1983. *Rituals of Marginality: Politics, Process, and Culture Change in Central Urban Mexico, 1969–1974.* Berkeley and Los Angeles: University of California Press.
White, G. 1996. "Civil Society, Democratization and Development." In *Democratization in the South: The Jagged Wave.* Manchester: Manchester University Press.

Contributors

Javier Auyero is an Associate Professor in the Department of Sociology at the State University of New York, Stony Brook. His research interests include political ethnography, contentious collective action, urban poverty and social inequality, and Latin American studies. His books include *Poor People's Politics: Peronist Survival Networks and the Legacy of Evita* (Duke University Press, 2001) and *Contentious Lives: Two Argentine Women, Two Protests, and the Quest for Recognition* (Duke University Press, 2003). He is the editor of the journal *Qualitative Sociology*.

Miguel Angel Centeno is Professor of Sociology and Director of the Institute for International and Regional Studies at Princeton University. His research areas include political sociology, Latin American society and politics, historical-comparative sociology, organizational theory, and public policy. He is the author of *Mexico in the 1990s* (Center for U.S.-Mexican Studies, 1991), *Democracy Within Reason: Technocratic Revolution in Mexico* (Penn State University Press, 1997), *and Blood and Debt: War and Statemaking in Latin America* (Penn State University Press, 2002). He is the editor or co-editor of *Toward a New Cuba* (Lynne Rienner Publishers, 1997), *The Politics of Expertise in Latin America* (Macmillan Press, 1997), and *The Other Mirror: Grand Theory and Latin America* (Princeton University Press, 2000).

Sylvia Chant is Professor in the Geography and Environment Department at the London School of Economics and Political Science. Her research interests include gender and development with particular interests in families and households, lone parenthood, men and masculinities, migration, employment, poverty, and household livelihoods. She is the author or co-author of *Women in the Third World: Gender Issues in Rural and Urban Areas* (Edward Elgar/Rutgers University Press, 1989; reprinted 1993), *Women and Survival in Mexican Cities: Perspectives on Gender, Labor Markets, and Low-Income Households* (Manchester University Press/St. Martin's Press, 1991), *Women of a Lesser Cost: Female Labor, Foreign Exchange, and Philippine Development* (with Cathy McIlwaine) (Pluto Press, 1995), *Gender, Urban Development, and Housing* (UNDP, 1996), *Women-headed Households: Diversity and Dynamics in the Developing World* (Macmillan, 1997), *Three Generations, Two Genders, One World* (Zed Press, 1998), *Mainstreaming Men into Gender and Development: Debates, Reflections, and Experiences* (Oxfam, 2000), and *Gender in Latin America* (Latin America Bureau/Rutgers University Press, 2003).

John Cross is Assistant Professor in the Department of Sociology at the University of Texas–Pan American. His research interests include political sociology, Latin America, informal economy, urban sociology, deviance and drug policy, and social stratification. His research in Mexico City dates back to 1991 and led to the publication of *Informal Politics: Street Vendors and the State in Mexico City* (Stanford University Press, 1998). He is currently continuing his research in Mexico City on "street pirates," who sell pirated music and movies, and is also studying the informal economy of the Mexican border region of the United States. He is co-editing a volume entitled *Street Sales: Commerce in a Globalizing World* (Routledge Press, forthcoming).

Patricia Fernández-Kelly is a Senior Lecturer at the Princeton University Department of Sociology and an associate of Princeton's Center for Migration and Development. Her research interests include international economic development, industrial restructuring, gender/class/ethnicity, migration/global economy, and women and ethnic minorities in the labor force. Fernández-Kelly is the author of *For We Are Sold, I and My People: Women and Industry in Mexico's Frontier* (State University of New York Press, 1983), *Hialeah Dreams: The Remaking of the Cuban American Working Class* (Rutgers University Press, forthcoming), and the editor of *The Political Economy of Gender* (Johns Hopkins University Press, forthcoming). She is also the co-producer of the Emmy award-winning documentary, *The Global Assembly Line*.

Robert Gay is Professor and Chair of Sociology and Director of the Toor-Cummings Center for International Studies and the Liberal Arts at Connecticut College. Gay's research focuses on clientelism, democracy, and civil society in Brazil and other countries of Latin America. His books include *Popular Organization and Democracy in Rio de Janeiro: A Tale of Two Favelas* (Temple University Press, 1994) and *Lucia: Testimonies of a Brazilian Drug Dealer's Woman* (Temple University Press, 2005).

Mercedes González de la Rocha is a social anthropologist at the Centro de Investigaciones y Estudios Superiores en Antropología Social–Occidente in Guadalajara, Jalisco, Mexico. Her research interests include gender, poverty, and household survival in the neoliberal era. She was the Simon Bolivar Chair in Latin American Studies at Cambridge University from 2004 to 2005. She is the author of *The Resources of Poverty: Women and Survival in a Mexican City* (Basil Blackwell, 1994) and co-editor of *Mujeres y Sociedad: Salario, hogar y acción social en el occidente de Mexico* (CIESAS, 1988) and *Social Responses to Mexico's Economic Crisis of the 1980s* (Center for U.S.-Mexican Studies, 1991).

Jose Itzigsohn is Associate Professor in the Department of Sociology at Brown University. His research interests include race and ethnic relations, Latino immigration, and development. He is the author of *Developing Poverty: The State, Labor Market Deregulation, and the Informal Economy in Costa Rica and the Dominican Republic* (Penn State University Press, 2000).

Sergio Peña is an Assistant Professor at the Institute for Policy and Economic Development at the University of Texas at El Paso. His research interests include urban and regional planning, public administration, and economics, and the relationship between institutions and policy outcomes. He is the co-editor of *Planeación Binacional y Cooperación Transfronteriza en La Frontera México–Estados Unidos* (El Colegio de la Frontera Norte & UACJ, 2005).

Alejandro Portes is Chair and Howard Harrison and Gabrielle Snyder Beck Professor of Sociology of the Sociology Department at Princeton University. He is also the Director of the Center for Migration and Development at Princeton University. His research specialties include national development, international migration, Latin American and Caribbean urbanization, and economic sociology. His recent books include *City on the Edge: The Transformation of Miami* (University of California, 1993), *Immigrant America: A Portrait* (University of California, 1996), and *Legacies: The Story of the Immigrant Second Generation and Ethnicities: Children of Immigrants in America* (University of California, 2001, co-authored with Rubén G. Rumbaut).

Juan Manuel Ramirez Sáiz is a Professor in Political Science at the Instituto Tecnológico y de Estudios Superiores de Occidente (ITESO) in Guadalajara, Jalisco, Mexico. His interests include social movement, urban development, urbanization, housing, and democratization. His books include *Entre la Iglesia y la Izquierda* (Universidad de Guadalajara, 1994), *¿Cómo gobiernan Guadalajara? Demandas ciudadanas y respuestas de los ayuntamientos* (Ed. M. A. Porrúa, 1998), *La vivienda popular y sus actores* (Ed. de la Red Nacional de Investigación Urbana, 1993), and *El movimiento urbano popular en México* (Siglo XXI, 1986).

Jon Shefner is an Associate Professor of Sociology and Director of Global Studies at the University of Tennessee. His research interests include the intersection of the global economy and local politics, democratization, social movements, and IMF austerity protests. He is currently working on a book on the experience of the democratization movement in Guadalajara, Jalisco, Mexico, and another book on changing immigration trends in Tennessee.

Index

Page numbers in *italics* indicate tables.

agency theory, 58
Alatorre, Felipe, 258
Alonso, William, 53–54
Altamirano, Teófilo, 110
Álvarez, Sonia, 203
Anderson, Annelise, 59
Argentina
    collective action approach in, 169–72
    cultural repertoires in, 13–14
    decentralization in, 174–75
    deproletarianization in, 172–73
    neoliberal economic policies in, 165–66
    organizations and interests in, 175–84
    state retrenchment in, 173–74
    unemployed population in, 43 n. 4
Aronskind, Ricardo, 173
arrabales, 221
Arriagada, Irma, 129
Assaad, Ragui, 58
assets, of families, 137
Auyero, Javier, 115, 209, 210

Balassa, Bela, 4
Banck, Geert, 197
Bautista, Jose, 257–58
Baylies, Carolyn, 141
Ben-Ner, Avner, 58
birth certificates, nonregistration of fathers'
    names on, 134
black market, 51
Blanc-Szanton, Cristina, 142
"bodyguard" class, 37
bounded solidarity, 8
Bourdieu, Pierre, 186 n. 3, 209
Braillard Poccard, Pedro, 179
Brazil
    favela neighborhoods in, 197–201, 205–9,
        210–11, 212–13
    Sinos Valley of, 86, 90, 91
    transition between clientelism and
        citizenship in, 14–15
    voting in, 200, 212
    Workers' Party in, 195
"browning of Latin America," 35
Burgwal, Gerrit, 197
Buvinic, Mayra, 129, 147

Campamento Vespucio, Argentina, 183
capital
    relationship between labor and, 2
    transaction costs and, 37
Capecchi, Vittorio, 5, 6, 89
Cárdenas, Lázaro, 225
Castells, Manuel, 26, 27, 59, 60
Castro, Maria, 203–4
Centro Operacional de Vivienda y
    Poblamiento, 227
Cerro del 4, Mexico, 246–51, 252–53, 255,
    260–61
Chambers, Robert, 137
Chile, 43 n. 5, 140
citizenship
    clientelism and, 14–15, 17, 202–5
    Fox on, 106
    housing and urban services as entitlements
        of, 222, 230–31
    meaning of, 8
    in Mexico, 235–36
civil society and democratization, 246, 263
clientelism
    in Argentina, 168
    deals and, 208–9
    democratic transition and, 197–201
    "double life" and, 210
    everyday forms of, 181–84
    innovative forms of, 19
    PRI and, 242–43
    transition between citizenship and, 14–15,
        17, 106, 202–5
    in Vidigal, Brazil, 205–8, 210–11
Cloward, Richard, 262–63
Coase theorem, 55
collective action approach
    decentralization and, 174–75
    deproletarianization and, 172–73
    effects of, 184–85
    episodes in Argentina of, 169–72
    organizations, interests, and, 175–84
    overview of, 58
    repertoire of, 166–69
    state retrenchment and, 173–74
Colombia, 130–31
coloniality of power, 83

Comisión Regularizadora de la Tenencia de
la Tierra, 226
communities, government programs for, 203–5
competition, 90–91
Comunidades Eclesiales de Base (CEBs),
252–53
concentrations, 63, 65
Confederación Nacional de Movimientos
Urbanos Populares (CONAMUP), 224
Confederación Nacional de Organizaciones
Populares, 227
CONTIGO, 229–30
contractual system, 36–37
cooperation
in informal economy, 85–89
neoliberalism and, 92–93
social bases and limits of, 89–92
el correntinazo, 170, 179–81
Corrientes, Argentina, 170, 179–81
Cortés, Fernando, 105
Costa Rica
dependency ratio in, 139
feminization of household headship in,
128–29
remittances and, 8
Sarchi, 85–86, 87, 88, 89–91
social welfare assistance in, 132–36, 147
costs of informality, 34–37
crack sales in New York City, 70–72, 74
Creciendo Juntas, 132, 133
Cross, J. C., 72
Cross, John, Informal Politics: A Study of
Street Venders in Mexico City, 7
Cuba, 147
cuidades perdidas, 221
cultural affinities, 90
cultural repertoires, 13–14
cumulative disadvantage, 109
Curtis, Ric, 71
Cutral-co, Argentina, 169–71, 173–74, 176–78,
181, 184

Dagnino, Evelina, 203
Dallos, Rudi, 142
debt crisis in Mexico, 105, 225–28, 244, 252
decentralization in Argentina, 174–75
de la Madrid, Miguel, 225, 226, 227
de la Peña, Sofía, 259
democratic participation
in Brazil, 212

patronage and, 16–17
urban poor and, 242–46
democratization in Mexico
from below, 251–56
economic development and, 235, 236,
241–42, 245–46
electoral reform and, 256–60
limits of, 262–64
stages of, 249–51
UCI and, 255–56
dependency ratio, 139
deproletarianization, 172–73
de Soto, Hernando
"extralegal" regulatory mechanism and, 52,
59
on informality, 36
on mercantilist states, 28–29
The Other Path, 2, 3, 25
on regulatory control, 74
on unregulated endeavors, 82
despotic state, 29–30
development
democratization in Mexico and, 235, 236,
241–42, 245–46
export-oriented models of, 109, 172–73
of informal economy, 83–85
"disinterested act," 209–10
domestic chores, 106, 107, 108
Dominican Republic, 8, 9, 87–88, 91
Dresser, Denise, 204
drug trafficking
crack sales in New York City, 70–72
mafia model and, 74
regulatory control and, 5–6
Duhau, Emilio, 230
Duque, Paulo, 205

earnings
feminization of poverty and, 130–31
intra-household resource distribution and,
140–42
sources of, 116–17
uses of, by gender, 12–13
earthquake in Mexico City, 223
Echeverría, Luis, 63, 225, 226
economic development. See development
economic exclusion, 110
economic fields, relationship between, 11–12, 12
economics and politics, 220. See also
neoliberal economic policies

economic sociology, 8, 53, 58, 75
Ecuador, 86, 90
education, decentralization of in Argentina,
    174–75
effective state, 29–30
ejidal, 222
electoral reform in Mexico, 256–60
elite factionalism, 179–81
El Salvador, 128
Embraer, 41
Emilia-Romagna, Italy, 5, 6
enclave formal economy, 28
Escobar Latapí, Agustín, 101, 111
Evans, Peter, 41
exchange relationships, 209
export-oriented models of development, 109,
    172–73
extralegal regulatory mechanism, 52, 53

Fagan, J. A., 71
family strategy, concept of, 100
Faria, Vilmar, 203–4
Farinetti, Marina, 171
female-headed households
    control over resources and, 108
    costs and benefits of, 144–45
    definition of, 149 n. 1
    delinking from discourse on feminization
        of poverty, 145–49
    policy attention and, 146–49
feminization
    of labor force, 12, 110, 111–12
    of poverty, 126–27, 145
feminization of household headship. *See also*
    female-headed households
    composition of household and stage in life
        course, 139–40
    employment, earnings, and, 138–39
    intra-household resource distribution and,
        140–42
    overview of, 125–26
    perceptions of poverty and, 143
    "poorest of the poor" stereotype and, 136–38
    poverty and, 126–30
    rationales for poverty and, 130–36
Fernández, Mario, 176
Fernández, Raul, 176–77
Figueres, José María, 132
Figueroa, Adolfo, 110
financial support from external parties, 131–36

Folbre, Nancy, 142
Fondo Nacional de la Habitación Popular,
    227–28
Fonseca, Claudia, 139, 143–44
Fontes, Virginia, 110
Fox, Jonathan, 195, 196–97, 202, 204–5
Fox, Vicente, 225, 229–30, 233, 235
framing process, 177
Freeman, Carla, 8
"free riding," 58
frustrated state
    criticism of, 39
    description of, 28–29, 33
    market failure and, 52
    process of informalization under, 30
functions of informality, 32–34

Gabetta, Carlos, 185 n. 1
Gallardo, Rigoberto, 257, 258, 259–60
Geertz, Clifford, 167
gender. *See also* feminization; men; women
    economic conditions in Mexico, effects of
        on, 115–16
    emigration, unemployment, and, 113–14
    of household head, 108, 116
    of income earners, 106–7
    involvement in informal sector and, 130–31
    poverty and, 126–30
    uses of earnings by, 12–13
General Agreement on Tariffs and Trade, 105
"gifts," 209–10
global economy
    informality and, 85–86
    subcontracting networks and, 86–87
    teamwork and, 87–88
globalization, 7–8
Global Platform for Action, 127
González de la Rocha, Mercedes, 81, 84, 137,
    143
government model of regulatory control,
    54–57
government structures and informal actors,
    4–7, 8–9
Graham, Hilary, 140–41, 143
Granda, Angel, 182
grassroots market economies, 82–83, 85,
    92–93. *See also* informal economy
grassroots organizations. *See* Movimiento
    Urbano Popular (MUP)
Grest, Jeremy, 7

grievances, 167
Grinspun, Alejandro, 137
Grittini, Adolfo, 176–77
Grossman, Herschel, 59–60
grupos solidarios loan method, 87
Guadalajara, Mexico
    colonia in, 16–17
    description of, 98–99, 105
    NGOs in, 241–42
    population of, 252
Guana, Miguel, 182
Guanacaste, Costa Rica, 134
Guatemala, 86–87, 90, 128
Gupta, Geeta Rao, 129, 147

habitus, 186 n. 3
Haddad, Lawrence, 148
Hagedorn, J. M., 71
Hart, Keith, 1, 24–25
health services, decentralization of in
    Argentina, 174–75
Hirschman, Albert O., 35
home ownership, 221
Honduras, 131
Horcasitas, Juan, 204
household. *See also* poverty of resources;
    resources of poverty
    change and, 100–101
    composition of and stage in life course,
        139–40
    definition of, 149 n. 1
    earners in, 138–39
    feminization of headship of, 125–30
    head of, and poverty, 108, 116
    intra-household resource distribution, 140–42
    as political category, 9–13, 18
    poverty of female-headed, 130–36
    restructuring of, 104–8
    survival strategies of, 97–98, 99, 100–101
housing
    policies for in Mexico, 225–31
    squatter settlements, 221–22, 242–43
human rights networks, 254–55

illegal enterprise, 26, 51, 60–61
impersonal interaction, 49–50, 54–55
income, sources of, 116–17. *See also* earnings
independent neighborhood vendors, 63
informal economy
    benefits of, 73

definitions of, 25–26
development and, 42, 83–85
dimensions of, 60–61
neoliberalism and, 82–83, 85, 92–93
origins of concept of, 24–25
in shadow of state, 23–24
state in shadow of, 26–32
trust and cooperation in, 85–89
underground vs. illegal, 51
informality
    costs of, 34–37
    definition of, 1
    functions of, 32–34
    internal dynamics and effects of, 2–3
    modernization and, 18
    origins and persistence of, 2
    as political, 18
    spatial dimensions of, 3
informalization
    under frustrated states, 30
    under totalitarian state, 32
*Informal Politics: A Study of Street Venders in
    Mexico City* (Cross), 7
Inkeles, Alex, 4
Instituto para el Desarrollo de la Comunidad,
    226
internal dynamics and effects of informality, 2–3
internally oriented developmentalism, 83–84
International Labor Organization (ILO), 2
International Monetary Fund, 243
Itzigsohn, José, 40

Jagganathan, V. N., 53–54, 58
Jalisco, Mexico, 241–42
Joekes, Susan P., 115
Johnson, B. D., 72
Jujuy, Argentina, 170–71

Kabeer, Naila, 142
Kennedy, Eileen, 128

labor
    debt crisis and, 106–7
    feminization of labor force, 12, 110, 111–12
    households and, 10–11, 101–2
    poor and, 104–5, 108
    relationship between capital and, 2
    reorganization of in Mexico, 115
    self-provisioning and, 114
    unstable conditions of, 111

laissez-faire model of regulatory control,
    53–54, 57, 64–65, 73–74
Latin America. *See also specific countries*
    civil society in, 23–24, 35
    frustrated states in, 29, 30
    new social movements in, 202–3
    picture of, 37
    weak states in, 31, 34–36
Laws, Sophie, 145–46
Lechner, N., 263
Leite, Jorge, 198
Lewis, Arthur W., 83
liberal state, 30, 33–34, 38
Lipset, Seymour, 219
Lobo, Fernando, 182
Lomnitz, Larissa, 29, 102–3, 114
López, Javier Cruz, 260–61
López Portillo, José, 63, 225, 226, 227
"low state-integration," conditions of, 57
Luhman, Niklas, 220

MacDonald, Edwina, 34
mafia regulatory model
    crack sales and, 70–71, 74
    description of, 59–60
    street vending and, 67–69
mafia state, 5–7
Mann, Michael, 39
manufacturing in Mexico, 110
maquiladoras, 105, 110
Marenco, Leda, 139–40
market failure, 52–53, 55
market liberalization, 38–39
marketplace, formal/legal, 50–51
markets and neoliberalism, 82–83
Martinasso, Daniel, 177
Martins, Noé, 199
Marxist interpretations, 2–3
men
    extra-domestic expenditures of, 141
    as sons, 143–44
Menem, Carlos, administration of, 172
mercantilist state, 29
metro vendors, 64, 68
Mexican Provincial Company of Jesus, 253
Mexico. *See also* democratization in Mexico;
    Movimiento Urbano Popular (MUP); PRI
    (Partido Revolucionario Institucional)
    Cerro del 4, 246–51, 252–53, 255, 260–61
    colonia in, 16–17

debt crisis in, 105, 225–28, 244, 252
effects of economic conditions in, 115–16
electoral reform in, 256–60
Guadalajara, 16–17, 98–99, 105, 241–42, 252
household earners in, 138–39
housing policies in, 225–31
labor reorganization in, 115
manufacturing in, 110
oil activity in, 243
paternal support in, 133–36
poverty in, 12
radical exclusion in, 98
regulatory system in, 57
street vending in, 7, 61, 63–70
unemployment in, 111, 112–14
urban poor, neoliberal shift, and, 242–46
migration to United States, 113
mobilization networks, 181–84
mobilization of resources, 177
modernization, 4, 18
Moghadam, Valentine, 127, 128, 130, 148
Montias, J. M., 58
Moore, Henrietta, 146
Morfin, Guadalupe, 249–50
Moser, Caroline, 109, 129
Movimiento Ciudadano Jaliscience (MCJ),
    247–49, 251
Movimiento Urbano Popular (MUP)
    achievements of, 234
    between 1970 and 1990, 222–25
    debt crisis and, 225–28
    in economic and political context, 221–22
    electoral reform and, 245
    as grassroots organization, 219
    influence of, 234–36, 241
    overview of, 15
    political action and, 231–34
    PRONASOL and, 228–31
Mujica, Gustavo Adolfo, 182
Muthwa, Sibongile, 141

neo-informality, 84
neoliberal economic policies
    in Argentina, 13–14, 165–66
    democratization and, 263–64
    diffusion of in 1990s, 7–8
    effects of, 17–18, 81–82, 84, 109–10
    intention of, 38
    markets and, 82–83
    in Mexico, 16, 243–44, 245–46

neoliberal economic policies (*continued*)
    poverty of resources and, 10
    private and public spheres and, 18
    purpose of, 92–93
    resistance to, 40
    as wrong recipe, 38–41
Neuberger, Egon, 58
new social movements, 202–3
New York City, crack sales in, 70–72, 74
Nicaragua, 128
non-Marxist interpretations, 2–3
North American Free Trade Agreement
    (NAFTA), 225, 232

O'Donnell, Guillermo, 35, 212
oil activity
    in Argentina, 173–74
    in Mexico, 243
OPORTUNIDADES, 229–30
organization of cooperative institutions, 88–89
Oswaldo, Henrique, 199–200
Otavalo, Ecuador, 86, 90
The Other Path (de Soto), 2, 3, 25

Panama, 128
Partido Acción Nacional (PAN)
    Jalisco and, 241
    MUP and, 221, 233–34, 235
    policy instruments of, 229–30
Partido de la Revolución Democrática (PRD),
    65, 221, 231–32, 253–54
Partido del Trabajo (PT), 231–32
Partido Democrático Trabalhista (PDT),
    206–8, 210–11
Partido Revolucionario Institucional (PRI)
    clientelism and, 195, 242–43
    housing policy and, 220–21, 226
    middle class and, 244–45
    squatter settlements and, 222
    street vending and, 61, 63, 65
paternal support for family, 133–36
Peña, Christine, 148
Peralta, Carlos, 259
Pérez Sáinz, Juan Pablo
    on informal economy, 85, 86, 87, 90–91
    on neo-informality, 84
    on socioterritoriality, 89
Petrobras, 41
Phoenix, Ann, 145
los piqueteros, 169–70

Piven, Frances Fox, 262–63
los placeros, 170
Plaza Huincul, Argentina, 169–70, 173–74,
    176–78, 181
Plaza Tapatía, Mexico, 249–50
Poder Ciudadano (PC), 256–58
Polanyi, Karl, 92, 263
political, informal economy as, 1, 18
politics
    contentious, causes of, 166–69
    economics and, 220
    of middle class in Mexico, 244–45
    of urban poor, and neoliberal shift, 242–46,
        262–64
polyarchy, 17
popular movements, stages of, 15
Portes, Alejandro, 26, 27, 59, 60
poverty
    delinking association of female-headed
        households with, 145–46
    female household headship and, 125–36
    feminization of, 126–27, 145
    gender and, 126
    holistic conceptualization of, 136–37
    perceptions of, and power, 142–44
poverty of resources
    grassroots economies and, 93
    neoliberalism and, 81
    overview of, 10
    survival strategies and, 108–12
    sustained crisis and, 112–15
    transition from resources of poverty to, 98
Pozzi, Pablo, 185 n. 1
privatization
    in Argentina, 172–74, 183
    neoliberalism and, 38–39
Programa de Educación, Salud y
    Alimentación, 228
PROGRESA, 229
Programa Nacional de Solidaridad (PRONASOL),
    204–5, 228–31
property rights approach, 58
protectionism, 39–40
Przeworski, Adam, 219
PT (Partido del Trabajo), 231–32
public market/plaza vendors, 64, 66–67, 68
public mobilization, 13–18
public welfare legislation, 11
la pueblada, 170
el pueblo, 178

Quijano, Anibal, 83
Quisumbing, Agnes, 148

radical exclusion in Mexico, 98
Radio Victoria, 176–77
Ramírez Sáis, Juan Manuel, 245
reciprocal exchange, 107
Regional Program for Education in Latin
    America and the Caribbean (PREALC), 2
regulatory control
    of crack sales in New York City, 70–72
    dominant, 50–51
    government model of, 54–57
    grassroots economies and, 92
    of illegal versus informal sectors, 51–52
    of impersonal interactions, 49–52
    informality, illegality, and, 60–61
    laissez-faire model of, 53–54, 57, 64–65, 73–74
    mafia model of, 59–60, 67–71, 74
    models of, 52–53
    risk factors and, 72–75
    situating, 4–9
    social-institutional model of, 57–59, 65–66,
        71–72
    state, of street vending, 66–67, 68
    types of, 61, 62
Reis, Elisa, 203
remittances, 8, 9, 88–89, 140
rent, 53
repertoire of collective action theory, 166–69
resources of poverty
    creation of, 84
    implications of model of, 103–4
    income sources and, 116–17
    overview of, 10, 101–3
    strain on, 91–92
    transition to poverty of resources from, 98
Riachi, Nilda, 182
risk management, 49–50, 55–56
roadblocks, 170–71, 176–78, 184–85
Roberts, Kenneth, 204
Robinson, William, 17, 246, 263
Rodrigues, Carlos Alberto, 199
Rodríguez, Miguel Angel, 132
Rojas, Georgina, 99, 109, 111, 112, 116
Romero Feris, "Tato," 179, 180
Rothen, D., 174

Salinas de Gotari, Carlos
    fraud and, 232

NAFTA and, 225
    PRONASOL and, 204, 228, 229
San José, Costa Rica, 87, 89–90, 91
San Pedro Sacatepequez, Guatemala, 86–87,
    90
el santiagazo, 169
Santiago del Estero, Argentina, 169, 181–83
Santo Domingo, Dominican Republic,
    87–88, 91
Sapag, Felipe, 167, 176–77
Sarchi in Costa Rica, 85–86, 90–91
Schmitz, Hubert, 86, 91
Scott, Alison MacEwen, 137
SEDOC, 253–54
self-employment, 107, 114
self-provisioning, 114
semi-clientelism, 108, 196, 202
Sen, Amartya, 136, 137
Shefner, Jon, 197
Sinos Valley, Brazil, 86, 90, 91
Smith, David, 4
Smith, E. M., 57–58
social development, theories of, 55
social inequalities, 37
social-institutional model of regulatory
    control
    crack sales and, 71–72
    overview of, 57–59
    street vending and, 65–66, 66
social integration, 85
social isolation, 114
social movement webs, 203
social networks, 102–3, 114–15
socioterritoriality, 89
Solis, Camacho, 66–67
"son substitution," 143–44
spatial dimensions of economic informality, 3
squatter settlements, 221–22, 242–43
state
    antithesis between informality and, 27–32
    by regulatory capacity and intent, 28
    roles of, 26–27
state retrenchment in Argentina, 173–74
state-society relations. See also clientelism
    continuum of, 196–97
    MUP and, 224
    understanding of, 210
    strains on resources of poor, 91–92
street vending
    government regulation and, 57

street vending (*continued*)
  laissez-faire model and, 64–65
  mafia model and, 67–69
  in Mexico, 7, 61, 63–70
  regulatory control of, 69–70
  rent and, 53–54
  social-institutional model of regulatory
    control and, 59, 65–66, 66
  state regulation of, 66–67, 68
  types of, 63–64
subcontracting networks, 86–87
subsistence sector of informal economy, 89–90
Sulmont, Denis, 110
"symbolic capital," 209–10

Tendler, Judith, 204
territorial proximity, 89–90
Thailand, 142
tianguis, 63–64, 65
Tilly, Charles, 13, 26, 166–69
toreros, 64, 69
totalitarian state, 31–32, 32
transaction costs, 36–37, 55, 58
transaction risk, 55–56
transnational activities, 85, 88–89
transnational communities, 7–8
transnational economic strategies, 9
trust
  in informal economy, 85–89
  neoliberalism and, 92–93
  social bases and limits of, 89–92

"underemployment," 25
underground transactions, 3, 51
unemployment in Mexico, 111, 112–14
Unión de Colonos Independientes (UCI)
  description of, 247, 250
  political action of, 253–56, 260–61, 262, 263
United Nations Economic Commission for
  Latin America and the Caribbean
  (ECLAC), 83
United States
  migration to, 113

options to formal sector in, 73
regulatory system in, 57
"untamed market," 24
Uruchurtu, Ernest P., 66
usufruct rights, 58

Verón, Anibal, 183
Vidigal, Brazil, 205–9, 210–11, 212–13
Vila Brasil, Brazil, 198–201

Wartenburg, Lucy, 144
"Washington consensus," 38, 42. *See also*
  neoliberal economic policies
weak state
  description of, 28–29
  in Latin America, 31, 34–36
Weber, 55
"Weberian" state bureaucracy, 41
Weldon, Jeffrey, 204
welfare state
  description of, 30–31
  as model, 41, 42
Wendel, Travis, 71
Williamson, O. E., 58
Willis, Katie, 129
Wolf, Diane Lauren, 100–101
Wolf, Eric, 19
women
  debt crisis and, 106, 108
  divorce, separation, and, 116
  exercise of agency by, 136
  financial support from external parties for,
    131–36
  perceptions of poverty by, 143
Women, Fourth World Conference on, 127
"working poor," 104

Yenal, Hatice Deniz, 8
YPF oil company, 173–74, 183

Zamora, Yolanda, 247
Zedillo, Ernesto, 225, 229